MATTERING

Mattering

Feminism, Science, and Materialism

Edited by Victoria Pitts-Taylor

NEW YORK UNIVERSITY PRESS

New York and London

NEW YORK UNIVERSITY PRESS
New York and London
www.nyupress.org

References to Internet websites (URLs) were accurate at the time of writing. Neither the author nor New York University Press is responsible for URLs that may have expired or changed since the manuscript was prepared.

Library of Congress Cataloging-in-Publication Data
Names: Pitts-Taylor, Victoria, editor.
Title: Mattering : feminism, science, and materialism / edited by Victoria Pitts-Taylor.
Description: New York : New York University Press, [2016] | Series: Biopolitics: medicine, technoscience, and health in the twenty-first century | Includes bibliographical references and index.
Identifiers: LCCN 2016010311| ISBN 9781479833498 (cl : alk. paper) | ISBN 9781479845439 (pb : alk. paper)
Subjects: LCSH: Feminist theory. | Feminism and science. | Materialism. | Human body.
Classification: LCC HQ1190 .M3778 2016 | DDC 305.4201—dc23
LC record available at https://lccn.loc.gov/2016010311

New York University Press books are printed on acid-free paper, and their binding materials are chosen for strength and durability. We strive to use environmentally responsible suppliers and materials to the greatest extent possible in publishing our books.

Manufactured in the United States of America

10 9 8 7 6 5 4 3 2 1

Also available as an ebook

CONTENTS

ACKNOWLEDGMENTS

The idea for this volume was born with the *Mattering: Feminism, Science and Materialism* conference held in February 2013 at the Graduate Center, City University of New York. I thank Sahar Sadjadi for co-organizing the conference with me. I thank the Committee on Interdisciplinary Science Studies (and its director Jesse Prinz), the Advanced Research Collaborative (and director Don Robotham), and the Center for the Study of Women and Society for funding it. I thank Karen Barad for giving the keynote address at the conference; the influence of her work on authors collected here is palpable. Only a fraction of the papers presented at the conference could be developed for publication here (while additional authors were included), but all of them stimulated our thinking about contemporary feminist engagements with matter. I thank NYU Press, editor Ilene Kalish, and several anonymous reviewers for their help in bringing this volume to fruition.

Mattering

Feminism, Science, and Corporeal Politics

VICTORIA PITTS-TAYLOR

Attention to matter, and matter*ing*—matter's ongoing processes of self-generation—is transforming feminist thought. The urgency of attending to matter and mattering springs from multiple fronts, three of which I will address here. First, it is stimulated by transformations in the sciences, and importantly, the concomitant naturalization of other fields, where dualisms between the social and the biological are being supplanted by the more monist notion of the "biocultural." Second, attention to mattering is made crucial by recognition of contemporary modes of power, including those rendering biological data, matter, and processes into capital, resulting in the production of new kinds of populations and forms of life. Finally, it arises from internal debates in feminist scholarship, where the sustained theorization of the body has come up against the limits of representational paradigms, and where the onto-epistemological questions posed by feminist scientists and in feminist science studies now appear more relevant than ever. In the following discussion, I briefly situate feminist work on matter and mattering in its larger intellectual and biopolitical context, and also highlight some of the endogenous concerns feminists bring to the consideration of matter. My primary aim is not to persuade feminist scholars to take a more material or ontological approach to the body, subject, and power. This case has been made elsewhere, sometimes at the expense of recognizing the multiple ways feminists have, in fact, been concerned with materiality. I am more pressed to highlight the utility of feminist (and queer, anti-racist, postcolonial) approaches that take matter seriously in light of broader investments in matter, nature, and bioculture. Many disciplines and fields have newly embraced materialism and ontology, but a sustained focus of feminist inquiry is power. Feminist orientations demand we ask certain questions of matter/ing and its interlocution. In what ways is matter involved in, or shot through with, sex/gender, class, race, nation, citizenship, and other stratifications? How are these power relations involved in the understanding and management of biology or "life itself," and how do they materialize in bodies, corporeal processes, and environments? What sorts of theoretical and methodological innovations are required to address matter as thusly situating and situated?

Nature's Becoming

Feminist concerns with matter take place in the context of a much broader intellectual shift that has emerged in the wake of humanism, structuralism, and poststructuralism. This transdisciplinary movement, being described as new or "neo-"materialism, simultaneously naturalizes social thought and redresses modernist ideas about nature. Reacting to the linguistic emphases of much twentieth-century thought, the movement rejects wholly or primarily representationalist accounts of the self and social world, and disallows the strict demarcation of the "social" from the biological. Social theory long defined itself through its investments in the human subject, in symbolic culture, and in representation or discourse. The notions of the mind as intellectualist or abstract, of the subject as built by representational processes, of culture as purely symbolic, and of the body as inscribed through social institutions or power/knowledge give agency to language and culture over nature. These investments may be necessary, *in the face of a fixed understanding of the physical world*, to account for human historicity and diversity, allow for novelty and unpredictability, address inequality and power relations, and envision possibilities for change. Yet, they can also result in an elusory grasp of humans' fleshly and embodied character, ecological and evolutionary situatedness, biological capacities and non-human entanglements. Representational paradigms, if they exclude matter or render it passive, also preserve the binaries of nature and culture, body and mind, and animality and humanness—dualisms which, it must be noted, feminists, postcolonial scholars, and others have long linked to harms against women and people of color.

If there is a crisis around representation in feminist thought, it emerges specifically out of the project of articulating sex and gender. Even the briefest sketch of this would have to cite *The Second Sex*, where Simone de Beauvoir (1953) details "woman" as a creature who shares physical commonalities—indeed, physical burdens—with other female mammals. However, as she famously insists, biology is not destiny; woman's character and situation are social products. For de Beauvoir, the specifically human capacity to transcend the (fixed, biological) demands of the species both renders her alienated and also allows her *becoming*. Gayle Rubin (1975) describes a "sex/gender system" that confers social meanings onto biological sex, and later argues the biological body does not establish for sexuality "its content, its experiences, or its institutional forms" (Rubin 1984, 10). Beyond merely transcending the body, Rubin gives culture the capacity to make and remake embodied experience. Poststructuralist feminism offered the more radical claim that the material body, rather than a pre-discursive ground for culture, is in fact produced within and through it. In Judith Butler's theory of performativity (1990, 1993), biological sex is enacted and stylized through its cultural intelligibility, via the continually repeating performance of gender. Butler re-conceptualizes the material (sexed) body from a fixed entity to an ongoing process animated by signification. This move opens up the problem of how the body itself matters—if, indeed, there *is* a body "itself," which Butler's (early) work seems to throw into question.

In his 1996 essay "Mattering," which inspires this volume's title, Pheng Cheah responds by asking whether the body has any endogenous quality of dynamism, or if it is only culture that holds the capacity to instantiate its materialization. He contrasts Butler's view with Elizabeth Grosz's (1994) account of biology as a source of action, movement, and potential. For Grosz, "Biology cannot be understood as a form whose contents are historically provided, nor as a base on which cultural constructs are founded, nor indeed as a container for a mixture of culturally or individually specific ingredients." Rather, it is "an open materiality," but one "whose developments will necessarily hinder or induce other developments and other trajectories." Like Donna Haraway (1991), who insists on the inseparability or intra-action of these realms, Cheah questions the stability between the oppositions of nature and culture. He demands we "unlearn the distinctions between form and matter, history and nature, the active and the passive that come to us by reflex" (136–37). Echoing Haraway's notion of the "material-semiotic" and anticipating the work of Karen Barad (2007), Cheah looks to an "as yet unexplored causal relation between intelligibility and matter in general." Two decades on, this has become a key problematic of feminist thought.

Most broadly, new materialism aims to rethink the terms of social theory, such that the *social* is seen as a part of, rather than distinct from, the natural, an undertaking that requires a rethinking of the natural too. New materialists are interested in exposing the movement, vitality, morphogenesis, and *becoming* of the material world, its dynamic processes, as opposed to discovery of immutable truths. New materialism sees a physical and biological world operating not according to fixed laws and blueprints, but rather one teeming with dynamism, flexibility, and novelty. Such a world is not determined; rather, it is constantly in the processes of its making. The paradigm draws from process philosophy, pragmatism, phenomenology, and other schools, and from figures such as Henri Bergson, William James, Alfred North Whitehead, and Gilles Deleuze, who "resist a simple functionalist reading of evolution" and "oppose strong theories of genetic determination" (Connolly 2011, 792). Although evolution is commonly invoked to defend universal principles of fitness or to justify the status quo, it can be understood as an open, dynamic process. Rather than deterministic, linear, or unidirectional, natural selection can be said to demonstrate the value of mutation, diversity, and deviation in a constantly changing environment. For example, in Grosz's reading of Darwin, "Beings are impelled forward to a future that is unknowable and relatively uncontained by the past; they are directed into a future for which they cannot prepare and where their bodies and capacities will be open to recontextualization and reevaluation. It is only retrospection that can determine what direction the paths of development, of evolution or transformation, have taken" (2008, 42). As Janet Wirth-Cauchon examines in this volume, Grosz's adherence to binary sexual difference and her emphasis on sexual selection limits her account of evolution's *becoming*. Nonetheless, Grosz's insistence on the dynamism of evolution means organisms are historicized, not simply in abstract, symbolic, or discursive ways, but in their physical, material, biological existence in space and time. It also points to the intra-being of humans, non-human animals, and things, their co-becoming within ecological contexts.

The term "new materialism," as Stephanie Clare notes here, is not adopted by many of the authors whose work is central to articulating matter as such. In the feminist context, the term might even obscure longstanding feminist efforts to theorize materiality, such as work on embodied knowledge and perception, the malleability of biology in response to experience, and the modification of bodies and biological processes in technoscience and global biocapitalism. (Among the authors in this volume, Sigrid Vertommen, Julian Gill-Peterson, and Lisa Weasel emphasize the limits of feminism's engagement with matter, while Meißner and Clare underscore the continuities between "old" and "new" materialisms.) The new is best understood to signal not a wholly novel moment for feminism or social theory, but rather a fresh vision of the physical and biological world, engendered through engagement with contemporary scientific fields such as quantum physics, epigenetics, and neuroscience. In quantum physics, for example, elementary entities do not have fixed properties. They can behave as either particles or waves, and they actively take part in their materialization, through their intra-action with (specifically, measurement of) other entities, gaining their characteristics in this process. Thus, "there are no inherently bounded and propertied things that precede their intra-action with particular apparatuses" (Barad in Kleinman, 80). For Karen Barad (2007, 2010), quantum insights inform an onto-epistemology in which the measurement of a thing is inseparable from its ontology—where, in other words, meaning *literally* matters. Barad's agential realist perspective, discussed below, informs and provokes many of the authors of this volume. (Most of the chapters here began as papers presented at an international conference on the new materialisms, for which Barad offered the keynote address.)[1]

New materialism is also animated by research programs in epigenetics and neural plasticity, which stress organisms' experiences in the present as much as the genetic past. Epigenetics, the study of how gene expression is modulated by interaction with the internal and external environment, is conceived as a bridge between nature and nurture, a medium through which social and environmental experiences materialize at the molecular level. Lisa Weasel argues in her chapter here that epigenetics might be understood in intersectional terms—linked to race, class, and gender—and claims that its study can help to ground feminist theories of intersectionality. Neural plasticity also suggests biological malleability in response to environmental changes. While the human brain's development was once considered complete in childhood, according to the contemporary view, experience changes the wiring of neuronal circuits as well as the strength of neuronal connection. Collections of neural pathways in specific brain areas can switch tasks. Grey matter in particular areas of the brain can increase in thickness or density in response to learning and repetitive action. Studies of experience-dependent plasticity are interpreted to suggest "the continuous formation and reconstruction of the brain via subjective experience" (Fuchs 2002, 262). This view supplants neuroreductionism and biological determinism with a sense of "the continual, dynamic, dialectical interpenetration of organisms and their environment" (Cromby 2007, 166).

The depiction of brain matter as constantly self-organizing and transformed by experience has been tremendously influential across the disciplines. For example, in analytic philosophy, mind and consciousness are being described as both inescapably neurobiological and radically embodied. Some proponents of "neurophilosophy" are reductionist, defining mind wholly in terms of neurons and neural networks, but others describe the mind as non-reductively physical, comprised of embrained, bodily experience and modified by its environment (Damasio 1996; Fuchs 2002; Prinz 2005, 2008; Clark 2007; Solomon 2007). In cultural studies, theories of synaptic plasticity, via Deleuze, underpin the study of affect, thought not merely as emotion but as the capacity to affect and be affected before and below consciousness, and theorized also as a material force extending beyond the human, circulating between the human, non-human animals, things, and capital (Connolly 2002, 2011; Massumi 2002; Protevi 2009, 2013; Clough 2010). In feminist thought, as Anelis Kaiser's chapter in this volume demonstrates, the brain's plasticity is explicitly positioned to contest theories of innate sex difference and to address the interface of the body, culture, and psyche (Wilson 2004, 2010; Malabou 2008, 2012; Jordan-Young 2010; Fine et al., 2013). This considerably varied literature shares a conception of neurobiological matter as dynamically situated in and entangled with the world.

Contemporary scholarship on matter and mattering enacts multiple shifts in philosophy and social theory. The materialization of social thought—in the context of a vitalized and dynamic nature—potentially allows the thinking of the social in fleshly, biological and ecological terms, and allows the human (and non-human animal) to be considered in her physical, embodied, and experiential realities. Conversely, it makes possible the consideration of nature and biology as processes of intra-action and relationality, which can take on the unpredictability, novelty, and contingencies once reserved for culture. It reframes the relationship between corporeality and experience. New materialist thought decenters the intellectualist and discursive subject, linking the mind to the experiential, affective, phenomenological, and neurophysiological body. It rethinks the boundary of the human/non-human, and proposes the agentic potential of things, objects, and physical processes. It demands the theorization of Haraway's *natureculture*, where neither part of the term retains its modernist singularity. Ultimately, it also casts doubt on some of the strategies of critical social thought. For instance, social constructionist theories arguably fail to fully address the stakes of contemporary biopolitics and necropolitics, where bodies and biological processes are materially transformed through the capital and state production of populations. So might poststructural approaches, if they limit the analysis of power to questions of intelligibility or the production of the subject (Barad 2007; Bennett 2010; Clough 2012; Puar 2012). However, as Clare explicates, the turn to matter/ing raises a host of new questions for feminists and others concerned with politics, or power, inequality, and suffering.

Mediated Bodies and Onto-Epistemology

While scientific data are sometimes treated as a more or less neutral resource for theorists, for feminists, attention to matter must reckon with its scientific mediation. Critics complain that enthusiasm for the "new sciences" ignores their contradictions and incompatibilities. For instance, in an exchange with William Connolly in *Critical Inquiry*, Ruth Leys protests that affect theorists draw liberally from neuroscience without confronting its reductionist assumptions. In one of her examples, she notes that Connolly, working with Antonio Damasio's neurobiological account of emotions, understands laughter as a "complex, social-cognitive phenomenon" (Leys 2011, 460). Yet for Damasio, laughter is an "automatic [biological] response to stimuli without regard to the meaning those stimuli might have for us" (ibid.).[2] I make a similar case regarding neuro-scientific accounts of mirror neurons, which are widely touted as evidence of the inherent sociality of the brain (Pitts-Taylor 2013). Even while it opens up neural processes to intercorporeality, the strong view of mirroring favored in the neuroscientific literature is reductionist and essentialist, attributing complex phenomena such as empathy to mirror neurons (or mirror systems) alone, and fixing the functions they are thought to support. With respect to genetics, Susan Oyama argues in this volume, "despite much critique, even dismissal, of nature-nurture dualisms, despite increasingly nuanced scientific reports and ever-greater public sophistication about genes, the old queries about the relative importance of biological or cultural causes abound." Meanwhile, feminists are combating overt displays of heteronormative bias in brain studies, where "sex difference" researchers newly armed with neuroimaging technologies are delimiting masculine and feminine traits (understood in binary terms) as the effects of prenatal brain organization (Fine 2010; Jordan-Young 2011; Fine et al. 2013).[3] Despite all the talk of neural plasticity, it appears to some neurocognitive scientists that biology is destiny after all.

Feminists have insisted that these incompatibilities and paradoxes be confronted, but even more fundamentally, have cast doubt on ontological claims about biology. While second-wave theorists warned, "we never encounter the body unmediated by the meanings that cultures give to it" (Rubin 1984, 10), feminists working in and observing the lab since the 1980s demystified science as a set of culturally contextualized practices. Feminist accounts of scientific practice underscore the heteronormative and racial biases of researchers, demonstrate the embeddedness of scientific practices in histories of gender and racial oppression, and articulate alternatives to scientific empiricism (e.g., Sayers 1982; Harding 1986; Fausto-Sterling 1992; Birke 1999; Asberg and Birke 2001; Roy 2004; Fujimura 2006; Stengers 2010; Longino 2010). In response to scientific aims of neutrality and objectivity, some feminists, many trained in the sciences, have proposed a more critical empiricism that would include self-reflexivity and accountability to the subjects of research. Feminist empiricism "deeply undercuts assumptions of traditional empiricism," while still maintaining that some kind of truth about the world can be discerned using the scientific method (Harding 1986,

183). Others more thoroughly question the "pre-existence of specific objects before they have been delimited by science in precisely the way they are delimited by science" (Knorr-Cetina 1992, 557). This constructivism does not strictly disallow a material view of the world, but often effectively places ontology outside the reach of critical thought (Latour 2004; Kirby 2008; Wilson 2010).

I will not rehearse the limitations of social constructionism here, except to say that contemporary biopolitics crosses "the epistemic threshold" (Vatter 2009, n.p.); it involves not just the representation but also the government and management of biological life (Foucault 2009). In biopower, matter is meaningful, and meanings are materialized in matter. Not merely inscribed, bodies, organic parts, and biological processes reconfigure themselves in intra-action with institutional forces, such as biocapitalism and securitization. The contributions collected here explore how such forces are racialized, classed, and gendered. They are, for example, entangled with the global structuring of bodies as biocapitalist resources, and with institutional forms of governmentality and control, such as national border policing or the techno prison industrial complex. These forces do not overwrite biological bodies, but they intra-act with them in ways that both reflect and generate power and privilege.

How to reconcile the insights of constructionism with the need to take up the "real," fleshly body, nature, and ontology? This requires modes of seeing the relation between knowledge *of* matter and matter itself. Barad, like Haraway before her, refuses to demarcate epistemology and ontology. She shows that matter all the way down to the subatomic intra-acts in agentic ways, taking measure and affecting simultaneously. For Barad, reality is the material configuration of *phenomena*. A phenomenon includes not only the object or entity of interest, but also the observer, the measuring apparatuses and the "conceptual-discursive normativity" that shapes the looking. All practices do not equally participate in material configurations, and all accounts do not equally capture a phenomenon. This isn't a slippery slope to relativism. Instead her realism is "reformulated in terms of the goal of providing accurate descriptions of that reality of which we are a part and with which we intra-act, rather than some imagined and idealized human-independent reality" (Barad 2007, 207). Reality for Barad, as Donna Haraway observes, is "not a matter of opinion but of the material consequences of constructing particular apparatuses of bodily production" (1997, 116). Agentic realism accepts the reality of biological facts without presuming that those facts are simply transparent reflections of the world; on the contrary, facts are certain materialization of matter, against other possibilities or potential facts, and they carry ethical and practical implications (Rouse 2004).

Mattering Now

The problematic of mattering may still need elucidation, but it is by now a powerful thematic of contemporary feminist scholarship. At the close of the first decade of this century, feminist interest in materialism coalesced in the publication of two groundbreaking anthologies (Alaimo and Hekman 2008; Coole and Frost 2010). These volumes engender a critique of dematerialized treatments of the body in feminist thought, on the one hand, and propose alternative models of feminist engagement with biology, corporeality, science, and matter, on the other. The editors make the case for a "renewed" materialist feminism (Coole and Frost) or a "material" feminism (Alaimo and Hekman), distinct from histori-cal materialism, that takes up materiality not simply in social-structural but also in physical, biological, and natural terms. The collected authors variously reflect on the "exhaustion and limits of the linguistic turn" (Colebrook 2008, 52) and identify what is at risk of being obscured or ignored in the focus on representation. In conversation with social constructionist critiques of science (Wilson 2008), and with feminist poststructuralism (Barad 2008), they articulate the need for new ori-entations toward nature, biology, evolution (Grosz 2008), and physical processes. Some writers also explore the entanglements of power, iden-tity, and the self with the material body, the physical environment, and the ecological world, especially in relation to physical suffering and vul-nerability, pain, or loss (Bost 2008; Mortimer-Sandilands 2008; Siebers 2008). The gaps between what are experienced as bodily realities and representations of them in both feminism and science beg for a rap-prochement between physical and cultural accounts of the body.

If those volumes aimed to define and justify a new intellectual move-ment, the task has already matured to some degree. Materialism is pervad-ing many realms, and the question now is not whether feminists should take it up in some way, but how they are doing so, and with what implications. While the case for an ontological turn, an embrace of matter, a material grasp of the body, and a post-humanist orientation have each been vigorously championed, the implications of these for feminist knowledge, theory, and praxis—and engagements with science—are not yet fully realized. How relevant are hard-fought critical frameworks and conceptual resources—the emancipatory aims of historical materialism, the theory of situated knowledge, or the feminist conception of intersectionality, for example—in the study of matter? Does the turn toward molecules and atoms, non-human animals and objects, and away from the human subject, render them less tenable? What kinds of politics are enabled (or disabled) in posthumanist thought? What sorts of methodological challenges are raised by attention to *phenomena*, rather than objects, and by human and non-human assemblages such as multi-species entanglements?

One line of inquiry, explored here in part I, *Probing New Theories of Matter*, furthers the discussion begun in the aforementioned volumes of the intellectual stakes of the new materialist turn. To begin, Roy and Subramaniam question the novelty of materialism in feminist thought. Far from ignoring or dismissing biology, they argue that feminists in science studies have long invested in the "bios," even as they have questioned the "logos." They also interrogate what sort of matter is reclaimed in new materialist thought—is it abstract, generic, and universalizing, or particular and situated? Drawing from postcolonial theory as well as science studies, they argue for seeing materiality as utterly inextricable from power and privilege, and as specifically enacted in actual and differentiating conditions and contexts. They write: "if there is no generic 'universal' woman, then there can also be no universal or generic 'body' or 'matter.'" The other chapters in this section also critically assess the materialist turn and look to expand its foundational literatures. Stephanie Clare's chapter, discussed below, compares the works of Barad and Jane Bennett, and Wirth-Cauchon's chapter asks how much is achieved by Grosz's reworkings of evolutionary theory. Finding the latter's reading of Darwin to be both enormously fruitful and stubbornly heteronormative, Wirth-Cauchon turns to Luciana Parisi, who places evolutionary thought in the context of technological transformations, including those that destabilize binary sex difference and reproduction (see also Clough 2012).

The shift toward matter and ontology allows a decentering of the human subject and her epistemic capacities, in favor of recognizing the material agency of things, non-human animals, systems, networks, molecules, and atoms. What happens to conceptions of power and agency in this shift? Hanna Meißner explores the relation between "old" and "new" materialisms, and asks after the emancipatory ideals of the former in light of the post-humanism of the latter. She notes with reference to Marx that "to question something is not to fundamentally do away with it," and envisions the lessons of new materialism as expanding rather than restricting emancipatory aims. In her chapter found in part III of this volume, Sigrid Vertommen applies such a cross-materialist approach to examining female tissue donations in the stem cell industry. The new materialist approach would cite not only the female body of the donor but also the researcher, the embryo, the laboratory tools, and other non-human actants as co-producers of stem cell lines, whereas the Marxist feminist approach would look to the gendered, classed, and racialized stratifications of biocapitalism to address the production of new forms of biovalue. Vertommen offers a sustained comparison of the two paradigms and comes to a proposal similar to Meißner's, "to productively and diffractively use the permanent tension between these two ostensibly contradictory feminist materialist paradigms." Clare also addresses the stakes of post-humanism, specifically its treatment of things and non-human animals as agentic actors. She proposes that some versions of post-humanism are more hospitable than others to a political framing. Clare favors a view of politics as distinctly human, but suggests that new materialism forces a rethinking of what the human is, and her autonomy from the non-human. In various ways, the chapters in this section engage in diffractive readings of theory in order to confront the political implications of materialism.

A second line of inquiry explores the relevance of feminist theories to the scientific study of biological bodies and vice-versa. Do contemporary modes of scientific inquiry, such as evolutionary biology, genetics, epigenetics, and neuroscience, really foster nuanced understandings of matter/ing as multiple, dynamic, and open? Further, are they compatible with feminist models of gender/race/class and other stratifications, and if so, how are these revealed at the level of biological systems, genes, or molecules? If not, what innovations are needed in both scientific practice and feminism to think power and ontology together? Part II, *Nature/Culture in the Twenty-First Century Sciences*, engages with specific research programs in the sciences, beginning with Susan Oyama's discussion of genetics. Somewhat ironically, Oyama describes how the treatment of biological processes as information in the biological sciences enacts their de-materialization. In contrast to a view of development as driven by information, she champions its contextual, emergent materiality, a view better afforded by developmental systems theory. Lisa Weasel highlights epigenetics as a field amenable to material feminist theorization, and more specifically, proposes reading epigenetics through an intersectional feminist lens. The modifiability of gene action in response to experience suggests embodied intersectionality—"the ways in which multiple, simultaneous social constructions feed off of and into material networks and be-comings, collaboratively back and forth again." However, she argues that we have yet to see many practical, materially grounded explorations of intersectionality, and asks whether epigenetics can "enact an intersectional sociomaterial politics consistent with feminist goals and experience."

The other two chapters in this section take up neuroscience, particularly with respect to the problems and promises of neural plasticity. Anelis Kaiser examines neuroimaging research as a contested site for the exploration of sex/gender in material terms. In challenging empirical accounts of dichotomous sex in the brain, Kaiser finds in Butler and Barad resources for considering brain matter "in its active-agential and performative doing"—that is, in its sex/gendered becoming. Neural plasticity, she argues, can be seen as a neuroscientific equivalent of performativity, a continual enactment of becoming that depends upon repetition for its appearance of stability. Kaiser questions Barad's agential realism for its refusal to distinguish between living and non-living matter. Does the theory work equally well for neuro-matter as for subatomic particles? Is it problematic to give independent agency to "subcortical matter itself"? Despite her misgivings, Kaiser draws from Barad's ethical onto-epistemology to address the making of gender as a biomaterial reality in the neuroscience lab. In contrast to Kaiser's treatment of neural plasticity as a resource for queer theorizing of the brain, for Schmitz, plasticity is a double-edged sword. On the one hand, it enables a view of the body as biologically malleable and historicized in response to experience; this is the plasticity embraced by feminists. On the other, it fosters the cerebral subject, understood as driven by and reducible to brain processes, and underpins neuro-governmentality; this is what Schmitz understands as "modern neurobiological determinism." The paradox of plasticity—the malleable cerebral subject reduced to the brain—plays out in the brain/body's intra-action with technical apparatuses, examined here with reference to Brain-Computer-Interfaces (BCI). Schmitz identifies the multiple agencies at work in the realization of neurally transformed "brainbodies" through BCI. "Who decides," she asks, "on intelligible codes, on form, content and processes of these communications? Who has the power to define which information processing is more favorable than others?"

Schmitz's chapter segues the volume into part III, *Biopolitics and Necropolitics*. The chapters in this section examine the material stakes of scientific and technological practices, their complex entanglements, and their differential and differentiating effects on the lives and prospects of living beings. Josef Barla looks at the use of biometrical identification technologies for transnational border policing and identity control in the UK Border Agency's Human Provenance Pilot Project. This ill-fated national security project, begun in 2009, attempted to find markers in DNA and isotopes from mouth swabs, hair, and nail samples to verify the ethnicity and nationality of asylum seekers. Rather than viewing the biotechnologies as either neutral resources or singular instruments of control, Barla sees them as intra-acting with biological processes and sociopolitical forces that work to racialize and nationalize bodies. Together, these constitute what Haraway (1991) and Barad (2007) call apparatuses of bodily production, within which, he argues, bodies behave as "potentially unruly actors" that are not passively inscribed, but rather take part in their own materialization. Just as Barla is interested in the "differently configured bodies" emerging out of such intra-actions, Teena Gabrielson argues for the plurality of bodies in the history and practices of toxicology. She traces a shift from investigation into the nature of substances (as poisons) to effects of toxins (as degrees of harm), and ultimately to assemblages of people, workplaces (factories and farms), animals, chemicals, machinery, legislation, and public health. The apparatuses of the contemporary toxic body, she argues, work to mask the uneven distribution of toxic exposure and harm to the detriment of poor communities most affected.

The next two chapters extend Schmitz's discussion of neuro-governmentality with attention to psychopharmaceuticals. These insinuate the molecular both into "technologies of human development" via the treatment of childhood ADHD and into technocorrections via the drugging of prisoners. The "mass medication" of children for ADHD, Julian Gill-Peterson argues, opens bodies up to constant augmentation and bio-mining for "infinitely extractable future value through overlapping fields of modulation." Gill-Peterson links the neurobiological modulation of attention both to neoliberal norms of performance and to "sexed and racialized standards of plasticity, eugenically eligible for improvement." Rather than reject brain-based or material accounts of cognition and attention, as some critics of medicalization do, he argues for a neurofeminist, eco-pharmacological approach that can trace the differential distribution of neurobiological capacities and affects. In their discussion of psychotropic use in prisons, Anthony Hatch and Kym Bradley demonstrate the close proximity of bio- and necropolitics. The administering of psychotropics as chemical restraints signals "new relations of biopower that have turned against life." The practices, they argue, call into question not only the political rationale of mental health treatment in correctional institutions, but also the "ontological space that separates waking life from certain death." These and other chapters in this section demonstrate the urgency of a specifically feminist, antiracist materialism.

In the final section, *New Materialism and Research Practices*, three chapters address the methodological challenges raised by attention to matter/ing; they echo and extend methodological innovations in feminist science studies that distribute agency across the human and nonhuman. Mary Kosut and Lisa Jean Moore's api-ethnography, for example, recalls Evelyn Fox Keller's account of Barbara McClintock's "feeling for the organism." Kosut and Moore conduct a study of urban beekeeping, a trend that has emerged as a response to the crisis of widespread colony collapse created by industrial agriculture, monocropping, genetic modification, pollution, and global trade. Recognizing their existing entanglements, Kosut and Moore use ethnography to grasp the embodied, material transformations created in api-human contact. They attempt to know and feel, without anthropomorphizing, the non-human, highlighting the ways "hive-minds" challenge human-centered, individualist ideas of agency. The final two chapters address methods, following Haraway and Barad, as material-discursive practices that are part of the phenomenon they appear to merely observe. Natasha Mauthner shows how the feminist method of narrative analysis does not merely represent but rather enacts the realities under investigation. Mauthner undertakes a "diffractive geneaology" of the method to imagine its posthumanist performative possibilities. Marsha Rosengarten utilizes the apparatus of bodily production to explain how body-subjects of research actively participate in their own materialization. Rosengarten addresses randomized control trials of HIV prophylactic drugs. In these experimental studies of vulnerable populations, "failures" are attributed to recalcitrant subjects who refuse to adhere to trial protocols. Rosengarten argues instead that research practices utilizing biomedical interventions co-produce their own experimental subjects who "kick back."

While feminism's turn to matter has necessarily generated a state of reflexive retrospection about its theories of sex/gender, the biological body, and the mediations of science, the aim is not really more nuanced, abstract theoretical perspectives, the overcoming of epistemic impediments to grasping nature, nor even the ontology of matter per se. Rather, it is the concrete, particular, and situated lives of beings as they are caught up in the workings of power/knowledge/ontology. The authors here expose mattering's differential distributions and its conflations within bio- and necropolitical forces. The complex relations of technoscientific research and global capitalism, biosecurity, technocorrections, governmentality, pharmacology, toxicology, global health and environmental crises, and racialized, sex/gendered relations of power comprise just some of the situations in which matter becomes itself, while also playing roles as actants that co-produce it. As opposed to a universalized or generic mattering, feminists can help to elucidate its specificity and particularity, and to reveal the stakes of doing so.

NOTES

1 The *Mattering: Feminism, Science and Materialism Conference* was held at the Graduate Center of the City University of New York, February 14–15, 2013. This conference, organized jointly by the Center for the Study of Women and Society, the Committee on Interdisciplinary Science Studies, and the Advanced Research

Collaborative at the Graduate Center, addressed feminist perspectives on the onto-epistemological questions raised by the materialist turn.

2 In response, Connolly advocates positive engagement with neuroscientists whose work is generally amenable to cultural theorizing.

3 The absorption of gender into the brain does not, in this instance, suggest its material performativity (Dussauge and Kaiser 2012; Kaiser this volume; Pitts-Taylor 2016), but rather reverts to a modernist idea of sex/gender as fixed in nature.

REFERENCES

Ahmed, Sarah. 2008. "Open Forum Imaginary Prohibitions: Some Preliminary Remarks on the Founding Gestures of the 'New Materialism.'" *European Journal of Women's Studies* 15, no. 1: 23–39.

Alaimo, Stacey and Susan Hekman. 2008. "Introduction: Emerging Models of Materiality in Feminist Theory," pp. 1–22 in *Material Feminisms*, ed. Alaimo and Hekman. Bloomington: Indiana University Press.

Asberg, Cecilia and Lynda Birke. 2010. "Biology Is a Feminist Issue: Interview with Lynda Birke." *European Journal of Women's Studies* 17, no. 4: 413–23.

Bao, Ai-Min and Dick F. Swaab. 2011. "Sexual Differentiation of the Human Brain: Relation to Gender Identity, Sexual Orientation and Neuropsychiatric Disorders." *Frontiers in Neuroendocrinology* 32: 214–26.

Barad, Karen. 2007. *Meeting the Universe Halfway: Quantum Physics and the Entanglement of Matter and Meaning*. Durham, NC: Duke University Press.

Barad, Karen. 2010. "Quantum Entanglements and Hauntological Relations of Inheritance: Dis/continuities, Spacetime Enfoldings, and Justice-to-Come." *Derrida Today* 3, no. 2: 240–68.

Bennett, Jane. 2010. *Vibrant Matter: A Political Ecology of Things*. Durham, NC: Duke University Press.

Birke, Lynda. 1999. *Feminism and the Biological Body*. Edinburgh: Edinburgh University Press.

Bost, Suzanne. 2008. "From Race/Sex/Etc. to Glucose, Feeding Tubes, and Mourning: the Shifting Matter of Chicana Feminism," pp. 340–372 in *Material Feminisms*, ed. Alaimo and Hekman.

Butler, Judith. 1990. "Performative Acts and Gender Constitution: An Essay in Phenomenology and Feminist Theory," pp. 270–282 in *Performing Feminisms: Feminist Critical Theory and Theatre*, ed. Sue-Ellen Case. Baltimore, MD: Johns Hopkins University Press.

Butler, Judith. 1993. *Bodies that Matter: On the Discursive Limits of 'Sex'*. New York: Routledge.

Cheah, Pheng. 1996. "Mattering." *Diacritics* 26.1: 108–39.

Clark, Andy. 2007. "Re-Inventing Ourselves: The Plasticity of Embodiment, Sensing, and Mind." *Journal of Medicine and Philosophy* 32, no. 3: 263–82.

Clough, Patricia. 2010. "The Affective Turn: Political Economy, Biomedia, and Bodies," pp. 206–228 in *The Affect Theory Reader*, ed. Melissa Gregg and Gregory Seigworth. Durham, NC: Duke University Press.

Clough, Patricia. 2012. "Feminist Theory: Bodies, Science and Technology," pp. 94–105 in *Routledge Handbook of Body Studies*, ed. Bryan S. Turner. New York: Routledge.

Colebrook, Claire. 2008. "On Not Becoming Man: The Materialist Politics of Unactualized Potential," pp. 52–84 in *Material Feminisms*, ed. Alaimo and Hekman. Bloomington: Indiana University Press.

Connolly, William. 2002. *Neuropolitics: Thinking, Culture, Speed*. Minneapolis: University of Minnesota Press.

Connolly, William. 2011. "The Complexity of Intention." *Critical Inquiry* 37, no. 4: 791–98.

Coole, Diana and Samantha Frost. 2010. "Introducing the New Materialisms," pp. 1–46 in *New Materialisms: Ontology, Agency and Politics*, ed. Frost and Coole. Durham, NC: Duke University Press.

Cromby, John. 2007. "Integrating Social Science with Neuroscience: Potentials and Problems." *BioSocieties* 2: 149–69.

Damasio, Antonio. 1996. "The Somatic Marker Hypothesis and the Possible Functions of the Prefrontal Cortex." *Philosophical Transactions of the Royal Society* 351: 1413–20.

De Beauvoir, Simone. 1953. *The Second Sex*. New York: Vintage.

Dussauge, Isabelle and Analeis Kaiser. 2012. "Re-Queering the Brain," pp. 121–44 in *Neurofeminism: Issues at the Intersection of Feminist Theory and Cognitive Science*, ed. Robyn Bluhm, Anne Jaap Jacobson, and Heidi Lene Maibom. New York: Palgrave Macmillan.

Fausto-Sterling, Anne. 1992. "Building Two-Way Streets: The Case of Feminism and Science." *NWSA Journal* 4, no. 3: 336–49.

Fine, Cordelia. 2010. "From Scanner to Sound Bite: Issues in Interpreting and Reporting Sex Differences in the Brain." *Current Directions in Psychological Science* 19: 280–83.

Fine, Cordelia, Rebecca Jordan-Young, Anelis Kaiser, and Gina Rippon. 2013. "Plasticity, Plasticity, Plasticity . . . and the Rigid Problem of Sex." *Trends in Cognitive Science* 17, no. 11: 550–51.

Foucault, Michel. 2009. *Security, Territory, Population: Lectures at the College de France 1977–78*. Trans. Graham Burchell. New York: Picador.

Fuchs, Thomas. 2002. "Mind, Meaning, and the Brain." *Philosophy, Psychiatry and Psychology* 9, no. 3: 261–64.

Fujimura, Joan. 2006. "Sex Genes: A Critical Sociomaterial Approach to the Politics and Molecular Genetics of Sex Determination." *Signs* 32, no. 1: 49–82.

Grosz, Elizabeth. 1994. *Volatile Bodies: Towards a Corporeal Feminism*. Bloomington: Indiana University Press.

Grosz, Elizabeth. 2008. "Darwin and Feminism: Preliminary Investigations for a Possible Alliance," pp. 23–51 in *Material Feminisms*, ed. Alaimo and Hekman.

Grosz, Elizabeth. 2010. "The Untimeliness of Feminist Theory." *NORA- Nordic Journal of Feminist and Gender Research* 18, no. 1: 48–51.

Haraway, Donna. 1989. "The Biopolitics of Postmodern Bodies: Determinations of Self in Immune System Discourse." *differences: a Journal of Feminist Cultural Studies* 1, no. 1: 3–43.

Haraway, Donna. 1991. *Simians, Cyborgs, and Women: The Reinvention of Nature.* New York: Routledge.

Haraway, Donna. 1997. *Modest_Witness@Second_Millennium.FemaleMan_Meets_OncoMouse: Feminism and Technoscience.* New York: Routledge.

Harding, Sandra. 1986. *The Science Question in Feminism.* Ithaca, NY: Cornell University Press.

Jordan-Young, Rebecca. 2011. *Brainstorm: Flaws in the Science of Sex Difference.* Cambridge, MA: Harvard University Press.

Jordan-Young, Rebecca and Rafaela Rumiati. 2012. "Hardwired for Sexism? Approaches to Sex/Gender in Neuroscience," pp. 105–120 in *Neurofeminism: Issues at the Intersection of Feminist Theory and Cognitive Science,* ed. Bluhm, Jacobson, and Maibom.

Kirby, Vicki. 2008. "Subject to Natural Law: A Meditation on the 'Two Cultures' Problem." *Australian Feminist Studies* 23, no. 55: 5–17.

Kleinman, Adam. 2012. "Intra-actions" (interview with Karen Barad). *Mousse* 34: 76–81.

Knorr-Cetina, Karin. 1981. *The Manufacture of Knowledge: An Essay on the Constructivist and Contextual Nature of Science.* Oxford: Pergamon.

Knorr-Cetina, Karin. 1992. "The Couch, the Cathedral and the Lab: On the Relationship between Experiment and Laboratory Science," pp. 113–38 in *Science as Practice and Culture,* ed. A. Pickering. Chicago: Chicago University Press.

Latour, Bruno. 2004. "Why Has Critique Run out of Steam?" *Critical Inquiry* 30, no. 2: 225–48.

Leys, Ruth. 2011. "The Turn to Affect: A Critique." *Critical Inquiry* 37, no. 3: 434–72.

Longino, Helen. 2010. "Feminist Epistemology at Hypatia's 25th Anniversary." *Hypatia* 25, no. 4: 733–41.

Malabou, Catherine. 2008. *What Should We Do with Our Brain?* New York: Fordham University Press.

Malabou, Catherine. 2012. *The New Wounded: From Neurosis to Brain Damage.* New York: Fordham University Press.

Massumi, Brian. 2002. *Parables of the Virtual: Movement, Affect, Sensation.* Durham, NC: Duke University Press.

Mortimer-Sandilands, Catriona. 2008. "Landscape, Memory and Forgetting: Thinking Through (My Mother's) Body and Place," pp. 265–90 in *Material Feminisms,* ed. Alaimo and Hekman.

Pitts-Taylor, Victoria. 2013. "I Feel Your Pain: Embodied Knowledges and Situated Neurons." *Hypatia* 28, no. 4: 852–69.

Pitts-Taylor, Victoria. 2016. *The Brain's Body: Neuroscience and Corporeal Politics.* Durham, NC: Duke University Press.

Prinz, Jesse. 2005. "Passionate Thoughts: The Emotional Embodiment of Moral Consciousness," pp. 93–114 in *Grounding Cognition: The Role of Perception and Action in Memory, Language and Thinking*, ed. Diane Pecher and Rolf A. Zwaan. Cambridge: Cambidge University Press.

Prinz, Jesse 2008. "Is Consciousness Embodied?" pp. 419–36 in *Cambridge Handbook of Situated Cognition*, ed. Phillip Robbins and. Murat Aydede. Cambridge: Cambridge University Press.

Protevi, John. 2009. *Political Affect: Connecting the Social and the Somatic*. Minneapolis: University of Minnesota Press.

Protevi, John. 2013. *Life, War, Earth: Delueze and the Sciences*. Minneapolis: University of Minnesota Press.

Puar, Jasbir. 2012. "I'd Rather Be a Cyborg than a Goddess: Becoming-Intersectional in Assemblage Theory." *PhilSOPHIA* 2, no. 1: 49–66.

Restivo, Sal and Jennifer Croissant. 2007. "Social Constructionism Science and Technology Studies," pp. 213–29 in *Handbook of Constructionist Research*, ed. James A. Holstein and Jaber F. Gubriumd. New York: Guilford Press.

Roberts, Cecelia. 2008. "Relating Simply? Feminist Encounters with Technoscience in the Early Twenty-First Century." *Australian Feminist Studies* 23, no. 55: 75–86.

Rouse, Joseph. 2004. "Barad's Feminist Naturalism." *Hypatia* 19, no. 1: 142–61.

Roy, Deboleena. 2004. "Feminist Theory in Science: Working Toward a Practical Transformation." *Hypatia* 19, no. 1: 255–79.

Rubin, Gayle. 1975. "The Traffic in Women: Notes on the Political Economy of Sex," pp. 157–209 in *Toward an Anthropology of Women*, ed. Rayna Reiter. New York: Monthly Review Press.

Rubin, Gayle. 1984. "Thinking Sex: Notes for a Radical Theory of the Politics of Sexuality," pp. 143–178 in *Pleasure and Danger: Exploring Female Sexuality*, ed. Carole Vance. Boston: Routledge.

Sayers, Janet. 1982. *Biological Politics: Feminist and Anti-Feminist Perspectives*. London: Tavistock.

Siebers, Tobin. 2008. "Disability Experience on Trial," pp. 291–307 in *Material Feminisms*, ed. Alaimo and Hekman.

Solomon, Miriam. 2007. "Situated Cognition," pp. 413–28 in *Philosophy of Psychology and Cognitive Science*, ed. Paul Thagard. New York: Elesvier.

Stengers, Isabelle. 2010. *Cosmopolitics I*. Minneapolis: University of Minnesota Press.

Vatter, Miguel. 2009. "Biopolitics: from Surplus Value to Surplus Life." *Theory & Event* 12, no. 2. Accessed online doi: 10.1353/tae.0.0062.

Wilson, Elizabeth. 2004. *Psychosomatic: Feminism and the Neurological Body*. Durham, NC: Duke University Press.

Wilson, Elizabeth. 2010. "Underbelly." *differences* 21, no. 1: 194–208.

PART I

Probing New Theories of Matter

1

Matter in the Shadows

Feminist New Materialism and the Practices of Colonialism

DEBOLEENA ROY AND BANU SUBRAMANIAM

In a culture seemingly ruled by technologies of hypervisibility, we are led to believe not only that everything can be seen,
but also that everything is available and accessible for our
consumption. In a culture seemingly ruled by technologies
of hypervisibility, we are led to believe that neither repres-
sion nor the return of the repressed, in the form of either
improperly buried bodies or countervailing system of value
or difference, occurs with any meaningful result.
—Avery Gordon, *Ghostly Matters*, 1997: 16

This work focuses on the "body" and its materiality. What is it? How
should we study it? Who should study it? The answers to these questions produce an unsurprisingly complicated and contentious narrative.
We are interested in the debates within the feminist studies of science
around the materiality of the body, in particular biological bodies, and
the "body" of recent work that has emerged as "new materialism." What,
we wish to ask, is feminist about this developing field and how is it new?
We argue that while feminist new materialism draws on a specific reading of poststructuralism's influence on feminist theory and feminist
theory's consequent "flight from nature" (Alaimo 2000), it has perhaps
improperly and too quickly buried many of feminism's old "bodies" and
exhumed a new "body" that is not entirely feminist or even particularly new. We are interested in examining the matter that lurks in the
deep, dark shadows of the "old" feminist critiques of science of earlier
feminisms, the silhouettes of matter being brought forward in the feminist new materialisms, and the glints of attention to matter that have

recently surfaced in postcolonial science studies, to argue that while each encounter is valuable, none are sufficient on their own for the project of feminist science studies.

Early feminist scholars of science were centrally focused on biology, primarily on human bodies, and in particular women's bodies.[1] They explored and documented the scientific emergence of "difference" in material bodies and their biological conceptions. These scholars systematically analyzed how the scientific enterprise through experiments, and anatomical, physiological, and behavioral studies came to understand "difference" as being located and originating in the material body. Central to their claims is that scientific institutions have translated *political and cultural* privilege into *biological* privilege. In several cases, this emphasis on the political and cultural was also accompanied by efforts to redefine feminism's relationships to the study of biology and health (Our Bodies Our Selves 1973; Rose 1983; Birke 2000; Murphy 2012). Furthermore, work from this era persuasively shows that hierarchical understandings of bodies were central not only to the colonial project but also to the evolution of science, scientific inquiry, and technologies themselves (Stepan 1986; Schiebinger 1989; Philip 2004; Hammonds and Herzig 2009; Harding 2011). Scientific racism may have served as a building block for the formation and even birth of certain disciplines such as anatomy, physiology, neuroscience, and behavioral sciences. Power, these scholars have argued, is central to the project of science. Given the history of science, we cannot talk about the biological body without science or science without the biological body, and the circulation of power is deeply implicated in both.

Early feminist work on the "biological" body is therefore largely read as a political intervention. By using the disciplinary tools of biology, philosophy, history, literature, anthropology, and sociology, feminist scholars attempted to *trace* and make partially visible the ontological, epistemological, and methodological assumptions and frameworks that were operating in the production of bodies and our understandings of difference. They explored and documented the scientific emergence of multiple and different bodies shaped by the politics of race, nation, gender, class, sexualities, abilities, etc. This early work in women's studies is often read as a "critique" of the sciences or the feminist critiques of science. For many reasons (that we won't go into here), the (inter)discipline of women's studies has largely remained within the realms of humanities and social science departments, and the vast majority of scholars come from these fields. Therefore, while the critiques revealed the deeply political nature of science's construction of the "body," the project of imagining an account of the "body" using feminist biological insights has been underdeveloped (Wilson 1998; Barad 2003; Roy 2007). Biological inquiry and the natural and hard sciences in general, conceived as hegemonic and oppressive forces, have remained marginal to the field of women's studies through most of its history. The "body" however, especially the female body and the materiality of reproduction, have served as central points of inquiry in feminist studies. We want to suggest, however, that this body, which has been a critical point of departure, when addressed in biological terms, was treated as an object of analysis in very particular ways. For example, the early invention of the term "gender" separated the idea of a biological body or "sex" from the social body or "gender." Although this separation would now likely be read as indicative of feminist theory's incapability of directly accessing nature or matter, it has been deeply influential. We propose that the separation between sex and gender has been productive in its own right, generating enormous growth in the understanding of a "socially constructed body," through its objectification and commodification, and by examining the ways in which bodies and matter are implicated and imbricated in complex social and political networks of representation, commerce, labor, reproduction, sexual violence, and medicalization. In the meantime, feminist scholars of science continued to build an engaged and robust critique (often done by feminist biologists with intimate knowledge of their disciplines) of the accounts of the body produced by the biological sciences, particularly aimed at countering the pervasive claims of biological determinism in fields such as genetics, neuroscience, and endocrinology. This body of work has provided a complementary narrative to the canonical narrative of the social constructions of the female and male bodies.

Over the last two decades, however, some scholars have noted several common approaches or tendencies in feminist engagements with biology and science and have in turn launched a critique of the feminist critiques of science through the new feminist materialism, material feminisms, neo-materialism, or the new sciences. Three main issues animate this critique. First, that feminist scholars have entirely marginalized, even excluded, the sciences from a central focus of the field of feminist studies and from the development of feminist theory. Their claim is that if the sciences exist within the field of feminist studies, they are largely treated as a body of oppressive and hegemonic work to be critiqued. Second, some new materialists claim that feminists influenced by poststructuralist theory have transformed the material body into a "text" that is only to be read, seen, and studied in the abstract, thus creating a lack of critical engagement with the actual "matter" of the body. When the material body did emerge in feminist scholarship, it was most often treated as a "primordial" body—that is pre-language and pre-social—on which society and culture went to work to "socially construct" gendered humans. What therefore emerges centrally within feminist scholarship is a systematic analysis of the social world only, and more specifically, analyses of the ways in which this social world constructs and exploits the female body. Third, scholars of new materialisms note that feminists have extended the sex/gender, male/female binaries in unproductive ways to create new binaries—nature/culture, science/feminism, and matter/text. They argue that the latter are not binaries—nature and culture are not separate, feminism need not be opposed to science, and matter is not the binary opposite of text. They argue that feminists have created fundamentally flawed theoretical tools and methods that reinforce these binaries in unhelpful, unproductive, and intellectually regressive ways.

Scholars working in the tradition of new feminist materialisms are fundamentally interested in producing different kinds of engagements with science, biology, and matter. These scholars have called for and begun an exciting area of work that seeks to redress the fundamental critiques they raised. First, the work engages centrally with science and scientific knowledge. For example, in her book *Meeting the Universe Halfway* (2007), Karen Barad establishes the new ontological, epistemological, and ethical framework of agential realism for thinking through our involvement and relationship to matter by drawing on her expertise in quantum physics. By deploying her theoretical contributions of intra-actions, and new understandings of entanglements and phenomena, Barad's work has enlivened our engagements with matter. In another example, Elizabeth Wilson in her book *Psychosomatic* (2004) argues that the soma and the psyche are not different "realities" of the body, but rather that psychic and somatic forces are co-constituted and co-produced. Her new work on "gut feminism" is precisely blurring the boundaries between nature/culture and emphasizing how a feminist understanding of the material body is important, indeed central, for feminist and critical theory. Second, by refusing to relegate the material body to science and the social to feminism, new materialisms attempt to build accounts that do not privilege one over the other. Finally, new materialists have created new ontological frameworks to engage with the sciences and build a body of work that refuses the binaries of sex/gender, nature/culture, and science/feminism.

From our vantage point as feminist postcolonial STS scholars, both trained as biologists, we view the development of new materialisms and critiques of feminist critiques of science with interest and irony because the preceding, now canonical reading of the historical development of feminist thought, also reveals to us the blind spots of disciplinary thought. We wonder, as in the opening quote from Avery Gordon, what can be seen and recognized in this new genealogy that is relevant to feminist science and technology studies? Some of the theoretical gestures of new feminist materialisms have us simultaneously looking back to see what bodies of work have and have not been included in these conversations, and also looking forward to see whether this call to engage with materiality is being followed up with an influx of feminists entering into labs to practice the science they are describing, getting their hands dirty with the matter they wish to know, and participating in scientific knowledge production themselves. An uncritical embrace of modern science that ignores science's imbrication in systems of power that early feminists raised seems hardly worth celebrating. However, we want to approach the different and previous generations of feminist entanglements with materiality with an openness or what Cecilia Åsberg suggests as being the posthumanist ethic of learning "to re-vision, meet up with and *inhabit well* the continuums of naturecultures" and "how we organize ourselves scholarly" (2013, 6). These claims of "new" and "feminist" in new feminist materialisms have forced us to reflect on the ways in which disciplines construct their disciplinary objects and analyses, and especially on how the critiques also take particular forms. Therefore, in this piece, we wish to take up two main questions that for us are hovering closely in the shadows, namely (i) how we understand and theorize biology and specific biological bodies; and (ii) how we understand and theorize the materiality of sex, gender, race, sexuality, disability, class, and more. Indeed, each of the three bodies of work—feminist critiques of science, feminist new materialisms, and postcolonial science studies—is rich and has much to offer us. But each given its own historical blind spots and disciplinary development has failed to offer an account that takes science, biology, matter, power, politics, gender, feminism, and history seriously. The project we are interested in pursuing is one that can benefit from making connections between the earlier feminist critiques of science, new materialisms, and postcolonial STS.

Three sets of arguments inform our intervention. First, a different body of work within feminist thought is important here. Feminists of color, third world feminists, lesbian feminists, and working-class feminists among other groups, have, over the last three decades, called into question the notion of the "universal woman" that animates and dominates much of feminist thought. They conclude that the generic woman is usually a western, white, upper-class, heterosexual, and able-bodied woman. By extension, we would like to argue here that if there is no generic "universal woman," then there can also be no universal or generic "biological body" or "matter." It is interesting to us that much of the work of new materialisms (although by no means all) recovers an abstract and generic material body, one that is often nonhuman, microbial, molecular, or atomic. As biologists, we recognize the importance of this posthuman turn, yet the hidden and shadowy matters of feminist thought reemerge in these critiques. To us, there can be no decontextualized generic body or matter, be it human or nonhuman, organic or inorganic. Second, colonial and postcolonial studies remind us about the very material bodies of colonialism, in all their contradictory and violent histories. Postcolonial studies of science particularly illustrate how western scientific knowledge was not just a tool, mechanism, or logic, but developed alongside and was thus co-constituted with colonialism, and deeply invested and imbricated in colonial governance and expansion. For example, Evelynn Hammonds, in writing about the origins of gynecology, reminds us how black women's bodies were deemed similar enough to white women's bodies and therefore worthy of experimentation, yet different enough that they did not need anesthesia during surgery because black women's bodies were different and did not feel pain (Hammonds 1999). The history of racial colonial science and medicine forcefully reminds us that we must not "decontextualize" matter from natural and cultural contexts because it is the "context" that is central to the shaping of "science" as well as to the shaping of the material "body" (Prakash 1999; Hammonds and Herzig 2009; Seth 2009). Context and histories must be central to building new feminist materialisms. To simply incorporate popular scientific theories, paradigms, and data into feminist theory is not a sign of progress, but rather can be read as a convenient sidestep away from the very difficult work of contextualizing the process and techniques of scientific inquiry—work that has been attempted and addressed by several previous feminist scientists, feminist empiricists, and feminist philosophers of science. Colonialism also involved disciplining and controlling the colonized "body," and the field has emphasized "the corporeality of the quotidian practices of colonialism" (Seth 2009). Indeed, these histories suggest that we should understand the history of almost all modern science as "science in a colonial context" (ibid.). It would seem then that the question of "matter" is very much up in the air. Paralleling the development of new materialisms in feminist scholarship, there has been a similar call to pay attention to materiality in postcolonial studies (Anderson 2009; Seth 2009). Finally, we follow Nivedita Menon's call to take seriously non-individualist modes of identity formation (Menon 2015). She argues that in many non-western contexts such as India, national identities have long been constructed not around individual citizenship but through those of communities, be they caste, religious, or ethnic groups. She reminds us that women's movements in the global South have always located the identity of women both in the nation and in communities. Such a mode of analysis refuses not only a notion of a universal "woman," but even the possibility of an unproblematic individual "woman." Exploring such alternate modes of scale and identity is critical for any project interested in theorizing the material body in its global complexities. We see our work as a fruitful and productive conversation between feminist and postcolonial studies of science, and in our contribution to understanding the materiality of bodies, it is a contextual and situated materialism that we wish to develop.

'Bios,' 'logy,' and the Improperly Buried Bodies of Biology

And yet, there is a politics to how we distribute our attention.
—Sara Ahmed (2008, 30)

In her article "Imaginary Prohibitions: Some Preliminary Remarks on the Founding Gestures of the 'New Materialism'" (2008), Sara Ahmed suggests that *some* (not all) of the impetus of new materialisms is based on a logic that previous feminist engagements with biology, including those enacted by early feminist biologists, have not only placed too much value on the social and constructed the material body simply into a text, but, quoting Wilson, that they "retain, and encourage, the fierce antibiologism that marked the emergence of second wave feminism" (Wilson 2004, cited in Ahmed 2008, 24). Ahmed claims that the genealogy traced by these gestures is curious as they actively attempt to draw the disciplinary boundaries of feminist science studies, pointing out that what is also at stake here is what has been included as "theory" in feminist scholarship. Ahmed states,

> What is clear then is that the gesture of pointing to feminist anti-biologism either excludes feminist work on the biological from what counts as theory; forgets feminist work on the biological by arguing that we have forgotten the biological; or recalls that work by reading it as a symptom of anti-biologism. (2008, 31)

New materialist Iris van der Tuin (2008) has responded to Ahmed's piece suggesting that by drawing so heavily on the work of a limited number of early feminist biologists and feminist critiques of biology, Ahmed herself is drawing boundaries around what counts as feminist science studies. She claims that Ahmed's analysis of feminist science studies places it in the position of becoming a "neo-discipline" (ibid., 412). Van der Tuin however agrees with Ahmed regarding the positioning of previous feminist engagements with biology. She states,

> I could not agree more with the politics of feminist generation laid out here. The effect of ascribing an anti-biological stance to second-wave feminists is analogous with readings of second-wave feminism as simply

essentialist or universalist. A stance Ahmed explains as anti-biological de-terministic instead. However, if one goes back to second-wave sources, you will find their arguments to be much more complex. The post-feminist move to discard second-wave feminisms may be described as a narcissistic move (i.e. a celebration of the—post-feminist—present). In my work on new materialism, I argue against narcissism and nostalgia. (412)

Indeed, van der Tuin suggests that in her articulation, she views new materialisms "as the inheritor of feminist standpoint theory, and as such, as an epistemic strand that engages with historical materialism but not solely so" (414).

In a similar vein, a voice has emerged from within postcolonial STS that shares the same desire and drive as new materialism for a turn to materiality and to the natural and hard sciences, and is also accompanied by a castigation of previous modes of engagements with the sciences. While describing the collection of essays published in *Postcolonial Studies* as a special issue on "Postcolonial Science Studies," Suman Seth describes the set of papers in the issue as a:

(Modest) attempt at an answer for a question Anderson had posed in earlier programmatic statements concerning postcolonial technoscience, namely: what an infusion of materialist science studies might do for post-colonial theory. (2009, 381)

In reference to dealing with materiality and in a reflective moment that could very well have originated from some feminist theorists of new materialism, Warwick Anderson states,

[M]ost postcolonial theorists, perhaps displaying lingering effects of a British imperial education in which humanities students are taught to loathe science, have flocked instead to the analysis of literary texts. (2009, 390)

Many feminist and/or postcolonial STS scholars who have attempted to train and work in the natural sciences and pure sciences, or engage in the materiality of the biological body either as social scientists or cultural theorists, will no doubt be puzzled by these indictments of "antibiologism" and "loathing." However, it takes little time to realize that it is the stance against essentialism within biology or "against a specific model of biology" (Ahmed 2008, 28) that has been brought to us over the last four decades by feminist critiques of science, that is regrettably being misinterpreted either as an unwillingness to consider the role of biology, or as a stance against the scientific discipline of biology itself. In a recent article aimed at developing a queer feminist materialist approach in science studies and advancing a theory of "biopossibility," Angela Wiley also attends to the debates (Ahmed 2008; Davis 2009) surrounding the founding gestures of new materialism. Wiley carefully delineates the confusion and slippages on both sides of the debate between "biology as the study of the body—or the body produced within the context of scientific inquiry—and biology as 'the body itself'" (Wiley 2016). The feminist critiques of science have not been of the stem word "bios," but of the suffix "logy." Issue has been taken with the "study of" or "knowledge of" bios, and with processes related to the meaning of the Greek verb "legein" from which the suffix "logy" is derived, such as to gather, to select, to speak, and to say (Greek Word Study Tool). To be critical of these processes does not mean that one rejects matter, bios, the body, or repudiates a field entirely.

We think it is prudent here to consider more carefully the terms biologism and antibiologism, and to do so, we return to an earlier piece written by Elizabeth Grosz. In her essay "Conclusion: A Note on Essentialism and Difference" written in 1990, she develops an argument about the role of "essentialism and its cognates" in feminist work. She states,

> Feminists have developed a range of terms and criteria of intellectual assessment over the last twenty years or so years which aim to affirm, consolidate, and explain the political goals and ambitions of feminist struggles. These terms have tended to act as unquestioned values and as intellectual guidelines in assessing both male-dominated and feminist-oriented theories. Among the most frequent and powerful of these terms are those centred around the question of the nature of women (and men)—essentialism, biologism, naturalism, and universalism. While these terms are closely related to each other, sharing a common concern for the fixity and limits definitionally imposed on women, it is important

to be aware of the sometimes subtle differences between them in order to appreciate the ways in which they have been used by and against feminists. (1990, 333)

More specifically, she defines the term "biologism" in the following way:

Biologism is a particular form of essentialism in which women's essence is defined in terms of their biological capacities. Biologism is usually based on some form of reductionism: social and cultural factors are regarded as the effects of biologically given causes. In particular, biologism usually ties women closely to the functions of reproduction and nurturance, although it may also limit women's social possibilities through the use of evidence from neurology, neurophysiology, and endocrinology. Biologism is thus an attempt to limit women's social and psychological capacities according to biologically established limits: it asserts, for example, that women are weaker in physical strength than men, that women are, by their biological natures, more emotional than men, and so on. In so far as biology is assumed to constitute an unalterable bedrock of identity, the attribution of biologistic characteristics amounts to a permanent form of social containment for women. (334)

Keeping in mind Åsberg's posthumanist ethics and van der Tuin's attention to the politics of feminist generation, we can see why feminist engagements with the "logy" of bios have involved challenging concepts of fixity, the overreliance on reductionism, and claims to limited capacities. It is, however, also fair to say that these struggles have taken a great deal of energy and time away from the work of reimagining *how* we as feminists can think about biology differently, and *what* that biology could teach us. We want to emphasize that many different generations of feminist and postcolonial thought have made it possible for us at this moment to try to think differently about bodies, biology, and matter. For instance, moving from Haraway's use of the term "material-semiotic" (1988) to her conceptualization of "naturecultures" (2003) alone, we can see that feminist work spanning over several decades has prepared us to consider new ontological, epistemological, and ethical frameworks to think with and about the organisms and elements of which we are a part. These reorientations to nature/nurture, sex/gender, and biology/culture divides are indicative, we hope, of a new "logy" for "bios" and of a future where we gather, select, and speak differently to redefine ourselves.

As feminist biologists we are therefore indeed interested in seeing for instance the outcomes of this renewed call for a "return" to biology. If, as a result, new materialism opens up previously unattended avenues of engagement with biology, this will be of great benefit. To our knowledge, however, the biological referents of new materialist projects have thus far been too limited. In many of these works, organisms such as bacteria are treated as abstract models of biological curiosity rather than with a recognition that "we are in a knot of species coshaping one another in layers of reciprocating complexities all the way down. Response and respect are possible only in those knots, with actual animals and people looking back at each other, sticky with all their muddled histories" (Haraway 2008, 42). Two curious points of interest come to mind here. First of all, despite running the risk of being called out on harboring anti-biologistic tendencies ourselves, we are indeed interested in asking the question, why pay attention to this particular knowledge and why return to this particular body of scientific scholarship now? It is important to look for any openings or radical potentials in scientific research, but it is almost as if under the aegis of new materialism, one now has the license to return to dominant and sometimes highly problematic scientific theories, research, and data and appreciate the science for "what it is." Second, while we are not arguing for the centrality of the human in new materialism, we are curious about the choices of particular referents. We are made aware of how the scholarly attention in new materialism is being distributed. What is interesting in the choice of these referents is that the curiously disembodied nature of this work is coming to light. While we support the idea that learning more about bacteria (Hird 2004, 2009; Kirby 2008) for instance is important for feminists, we must also realize that these analytic practices make it much more possible (though also problematic) to think about birds, lizards, and bacteria in evolutionary and aesthetic terms without having to refer to the embodied materialities effected through their contact with political systems of power such as gender, class, race, or colonialism. The posthumanist slant under which this work is proceeding is quite interesting, but we wonder—does this also signal an inability to deal with the biologies and embodied materialities *in* their political and historical contexts?

Situated Materialities of Sex, Gender, and Sexuality

We must ask who speaks for nature, why and what political
economic networks they are caught up in.
—Kavita Philip (2004, 194)

We join recent scholars in the nature versus nurture debates that all
binary formulations of nature/nurture or nature/culture—whether it is
nature *and* nurture, nature *through* nurture, nature *via* nurture etc.—
are all insufficient (Ridley 2003; Keller 2010; Longino 2013). It is not
as though there is a primordial material body that exists *before* nature
on which nurture acts to produce the material body. Rather, we need
to reject the nature/nurture and nature/culture binaries to develop an
account of materiality that is simultaneously an account of power and
privilege—as a co-constituted co-production. If there is no nature without nurture and no nurture without nature, how then do we account for
the "body"?

To address our concern of decontextualization as mentioned earlier,
we wish to draw the attention of feminist science studies scholars who
are interested in theories of new materialism to several critical modes of
analysis posited within postcolonial STS, including the recognition of
situatedness, the articulation of local points of interest within larger networks, the detection of contact zones of empire, and the destablization
of the central to become another local. We believe that an exploration
of the relation between the two fields is rich and can help us to develop
a situated, molecular, material account of the body *and* of power. Such
an analysis helps us to better theorize the body. While this is too brief a
chapter to elaborate, we have elsewhere explored how these frameworks
help us to analyze the overlapping genealogies of such cases as the chemical devastation of methyl isocyanate in Bhopal and the recent technologies of surrogacy in India (Roy and Subramaniam 2013). We have aimed
to share more than just scientific and decontextualized knowledge about
the molecular "properties" of methyl isocyanate. We have attempted to
create knowledge about the materiality and molecular properties of a
"phenomena" (as Barad might say), brought to us by many agents including a malfunctioning valve, a southeasterly wind, 40 tons of methyl
isocyanate gas, and an unfortunate number of organic substrates in the

form of mucous membranes and ovarian tissues belonging to the victims of the Bhopal Gas Tragedy. The emphasis on situatedness and engagement with local points of interest is most useful for us in the context of exploring the materiality of chemical damage or the consequences of a peculiarly medicalized pregnancy on the bodies of surrogate mothers, particularly in the Indian context where the legacies of colonialism still linger in the form of gender and class structures in contemporary Indian societies. This is evident when we see that certain classes and castes of women have been differentially affected by the chemical devastation of the Bhopal gas plant leak. We also see that compensation for surrogate mothers, or women's access to compensation, and medical treatment after the gas leak are also severely stratified. Similarly, legacies of colonialism still shape which women are being recruited to become surrogate mothers, and how the material and indeed molecular conditions of their pregnancy are imagined, and structured.

So what might this analysis of materiality look like, one that combines cells, molecules, gases, chemical plants, sex, gender, sexuality, class, race, and more? What kinds of questions would a contextualized and situated materiality allow us to pursue? Our research involves the materiality of a specific group of women in India, but in foregrounding this particular figuration, our intention is not to look or speak for the suppressed voices of Indian surrogate mothers, thereby painting an idealized or essentialized voice of this other. Nor is it to recuperate and romanticize a method of "indigenous scientific knowledge" of women's bodies in India. But rather, in the spirit of engaging with new materialism in what we consider to be a more contextualized way, we are interested in examining some of the technologies that are shaping the bodies of certain women in India, in a specific time, and in a specific place. If however we are to engage with this new materialism and also try to combine it with the tools of contextualization derived from postcolonial studies of science and technology, we may then have to argue that we are not merely interested in the material bodies of Indian surrogate mothers. We must look at the "situatedness," "local effects," and the "contact zones of empire" expressed in the material bodies not only of certain Indian surrogate mothers, but also in the compound methyl isocyanate upon its encounter with water, in insects exposed to carbamate pesticides such as Sevin, in the Union Carbide plant and its workers in Bhopal, in plants and animals surrounding the immediate area of the chemical disaster, in the use of new reproductive and genetic technologies in IVF clinics, in the export of highly coveted Dutch sperm to India, and much more. As a joint analytic framework, we can begin to inquire into the global inequalities mounted by global circuits of capital, or practices of reproductive tourism, and examine the local articulations of these practices that become manifested in the materiality of sex, gender, sexuality, and the body. With the analytic tools of postcolonial STS, we can learn that in attempting to analyze the devastation of the gas leak on women's bodies or the materiality of surrogate mothers in India, it is not just the contemporary body and their biology that we must think about, but also the historical constructions and disciplining of Indian bodies as gendered and raced bodies.

We end here by bringing to your attention a growing number of clinical studies in epidemiology, social neuroscience, and epigenetics that are providing evidence for the physiological effects of cumulative oppressions such as sexism and racism over one's life. These studies show us that politics, both local and global, are inscribed into our bodies—bodies that in some way already exist, circulate, and express themselves in transnational bioeconomies. A recent surge of interest in epigenetics is demonstrating the ways in which material conditions can fundamentally reshape bodies in subsequent generations. The field of environmental epigenetics attempts to get at these intersections (Guthman 2012). These findings remind us that the nature versus nurture paradigm is too simplistic a formulation and that we need to attend to questions of power and social justice as central frames in order to understand the matter of the body (Guthman 2014). Some findings emerging from research in social neuroendocrinology for example have also revealed both short-term and long-term effects of sexism on the levels of stress hormones in women's bodies. "Race," as a social category, and racial classifications that follow, could be "responsible for generating important biological differences" (Kaplan 2010, 288) and may be contributing causes of health disparities observed for example between white and black Americans. Many of these studies have been chronicled in an excellent PBS documentary series called "Unnatural Causes: Is Inequality Making Us Sick" (Adelman and Smith 2008). We suggest that these studies provide an exciting possibility for designing new scientific inquiries into the body and materiality. In our specific case, they help us to frame questions regarding the chemical devastation of women's bodies and surrogacy in India that have been shaped by a joint analytic of new materialism, feminist science studies, and postcolonial techno-science studies. For instance, can we start designing ways to measure the physiological effects not only of methyl isocyanate gas, but also of the political economies of capitalism that are running through the flesh of surrogate mothers? Can we begin to analyze the immune response in surrogate mothers that is elicited by methyl isocyanate as well as the mutual reorganization of global and local economies of eggs, sperm, and wombs? Can we begin to know the hormonal fluxes in bodily fluids that serve as substrates for not only methyl isocyanate but also the transnational trafficking of people and technologies? The questions we learn how to ask will bear different epistemological weights. Which questions we ask will make a difference in our pursuit of social justice and situated understandings of materiality.

Therefore, as we begin to devote our energy and time to reimagining how we can "do" biology differently, we must keep in mind that the tasks for a new materialist and feminist postcolonial STS approach to the world are: (i) to develop an approach where we recognize the natural and cultural worlds, science and society and politics as being inextricably interconnected—co-constituted and co-produced. We want to develop a feminist practice that does not approach matter through the binaries of natures and cultures, but also proceeds with a recognition of the "uneven epistemological weight" of certain ways of knowing; (ii) to recognize how colonialism and patriarchy (and categories of sex, gender, race, class, sexuality, ability, nation) are imbricated in the development of dominant western sciences and thus in its theories, methods, and institutions; (iii) to resist the urge for any easy translation between privileged western knowledge practices and those deemed unscientific, incoherent, or incommensurable. This is not to say these are all equivalent or equally important knowledges—only that we need to pay close attention to them; (iv) to take seriously theories, ideas, concepts from the non-west as legitimate, valuable, and relevant resources for understanding western and global contexts (Menon 2015); (v) to trace the transnational circuits of power that attempt to extract knowledge and resources into increasingly global hegemonic institutions and systems; and (vi) to develop a situated materialist account of the world, one that is cognizant of matter across scales. Since one of us is a molecular biologist and the other an organismal biologist, we want to keep different kinds and levels of matter always in view—from the molecules, molecular bonds, and interstitial cellularity to its embodied global and local political, economic, cultural, and social contexts in which matter resides, enacts, and evolves.

Materiality should be understood as a "process" rather than a product—matter makes, is made, and remade. We need to foster greater interdisciplinarity across fields and generations to draw on the insights and wisdom that multiple fields have to offer. Drawing on analyses from multiple locations sheds light on the shadows within our disciplines, rendering more perceptible the complexity of how matter and biologies come to be. We urgently need to develop models of a situated materiality and by doing so, turn to improperly buried bodies that perhaps still matter.

NOTES

> The authors would like to thank Victoria Pitts-Taylor for organizing the conference "Mattering: Feminism, Science, and Materialism" at the CUNY Graduate School in 2013 and for giving us the opportunity to collaborate on this project. We would also like to thank Sharyn Clough for providing comments on an earlier draft of this chapter.

1　Here we are thinking of scholars such as Ruth Bleier (1984), Brighton Women and Science Group (1980), Anne Fausto Sterling (1985), Evelynn Hammonds (1994), Donna Haraway (1990), Sandra Harding (1991), Ruth Hubbard (1990), Evelyn Fox Keller (1985), Helen Longino (1989, 1993), Emily Martin (1992) Carolyn Merchant (1980), Hilary Rose (1994), Sue Rosser (1992), Londa Schiebinger (1989), and Nancy Tuana (1989, 1993) (listed in alphabetical order).

REFERENCES

Adelman, Larry and Llew Smith. 2008. "Unnatural Causes: Is Inequality Making Us Sick?" San Francisco, California Newsreel with Vital Pictures, Inc.

Ahmed, Sara. 2008. "Imaginary Prohibitions: Some Preliminary Remarks on the Founding Gesture of the 'New Materialism.'" *European Journal of Women's Studies* 15(1): 23–39.

Alaimo, Stacy. 2000. *Undomesticated Ground: Recasting Nature as Feminist Space.* Ithaca, NY: Cornell University Press.

Alaimo, S. and Hekman, S. 2008. "Introduction: Emerging Models of Materiality in Feminist Theory," in *Material Feminisms*, ed. S. Alaimo and S. Hekman. Bloomington: Indiana University Press.

Anderson, Warwick. 2009. "From Subjugated Knowledge to Conjugated Subjects: Science and Globalization, or Postcolonial Studies of Science?" *Postcolonial Studies* 12(4): 389–400.

Åsberg, C. 2013. "The Timely Ethics of Posthumanist Gender Studies." *feministische studien* (1): 7–12.

Barad, Karen. 2003. "Posthumanist Performativity: Toward an Understanding of How Matter Comes to Matter." *Signs: Journal of Women in Culture and Society* 28(3): 801–31.

Barad, Karen. 2007. *Meeting the Universe Halfway: Quantum Physics and the Entanglement of Matter and Meaning.* Durham, NC: Duke University Press.

Birke, Lynda. 2000. *Feminism and the Biological Body.* New Brunswick, NJ: Rutgers University Press.

Bleier, Ruth. 1984. *Science and Gender: A Critique of Biology and Its Theories on Women.* New York: Teachers College Press.

Brighton Women and Science Group. 1980. *Alice Through the Microscope: The Power of Science Over Women's Lives.* London: Virago.

Davis, Noela. 2009. "New Materialism and Feminism's Anti-Biologism: A Response to Sara Ahmed." *European Journal of Women's Studies* 16(1): 67–80.

Fausto Sterling, Anne. 1985. *Myths of Gender: Biological Theories About Women and Men.* New York: Basic Books.

Gordon, Avery. 1997. *Ghostly Matters: Haunting and the Sociological Imagination.* Minneapolis: University of Minnesota Press.

Greek Word Study Tool. http://www.perseus.tufts.edu/hopper/morph?l=legein&la=greek. Accessed June 11, 2013.

Grosz, Elizabeth. 1999. "Conclusion: A Note on Essentialism and Difference," in *Feminist Knowledge: Critique and construct,* ed. Sneja Gunew. New York: Routledge.

Guthman, Julie. 2012. "The Implications of Environmental Epigenetics: A New Direction for Geography Inquiry on Health, Space, and Nature-Society Relations." *Progress in Human Geography,* November 26.

Guthman, Julie. 2014. "Doing Justice to Bodies? Reflections on Food Justice, Race, and Biology." *Antipode* 46(6): 1153–71.

Hammonds, Evelynn. 1994. "Black (W)holes and the Geometry of Black Female Sexuality" (More Gender Trouble: Feminism Meets Queer Theory). *differences: A Journal of Feminist Cultural Studies* 6:2–3 (summer-fall): 126–46.

Hammonds, Evelynn. 1999. "The Logic of Difference: A History of Race in Science and Medicine in the United States." Talk at the Women's Studies Program, UCLA.

Hammonds, Evelynn and Rebecca M. Herzig. 2009. *The Nature of Difference: Sciences of Race in the United States from Jefferson to Genomics.* Cambridge, MA: MIT Press.

Haraway, Donna. 1988. "Situated Knowledges: The Science Question in Feminism and the Privilege of Partial Perspective." *Feminist Studies* 14(3): 575–99.

Haraway, Donna. 1990. *Simians, Cyborgs, and Women: The Reinvention of Nature.* New York: Routledge.

Haraway, Donna. 2003. *Companion Species Manifesto: Dogs, People, and Significant Otherness*. Chicago: Prickly Paradigm Press.

Haraway, Donna. 2008. *When Species Meet*. Minneapolis: University of Minnesota Press.

Harding, Sandra. 1991. *Whose Science? Whose Knowledge? Thinking from Women's Lives*. Bloomington: Indiana University Press.

Harding, Sandra. 2011. *The Postcolonial Science and Technology Studies Reader*. Durham, NC: Duke University Press.

Hird, Myra J. 2004. *Sex, Gender, and Science*. New York: Palgrave.

Hird, Myra J. 2009. *The Origins of Sociable Life: Evolution after Science Studies*. New York: Palgrave Macmillan.

Hubbard, Ruth. 1990. *The Politics of Women's Biology*. New Brunswick, NJ: Rutgers University Press.

Kaplan, Jonathan. 2010. "When Socially Determined Categories Make Biological Realities: Understanding Black/White Health Disparities in the U.S." *The Monist* 93(2): 281–97.

Keller, Evelyn Fox 1985. *Reflections on Gender and Science*. New Haven, CT: Yale University Press.

Keller, Evelyn Fox. 2010. *The Mirage of a Space between Nature and Nurture*. Durham, NC: Duke University Press.

Kirby, Vicky. 2008. "Natural Convers(at)ions: Or, what if culture was really nature all along?" in *Material Feminisms*, ed. S. Alaimo and S. Hekman. Bloomington: Indiana University Press.

Longino, Helen. 1990. *Science as Social Knowledge*. Princeton, NJ: Princeton University Press.

Longino, Helen. 2013. *Studying Human Behavior: How Scientists Investigate Aggression and Sexuality*. Chicago: University of Chicago Press.

Lorde, Audre. 1984. *Sister Outsider*. Berkeley, CA: Crossing Press.

Martin, Emily. 1992. *The Woman in the Body*. Boston: Beacon Press.

Menon, Nivedita. 2015. "Is Feminism about 'Women'? A Critical View on Intersectionality from India." *Economic and Political Weekly* Vol.—L, no. 17, April 25.

Merchant, Carolyn. 1980. *The Death of Nature: Women, Ecology, and the Scientific Revolution*. San Francisco: Harper & Row.

Murphy, Michelle. 2012. *Seizing the Means of Reproduction: Entanglements of Feminism, Health, and Technoscience*. Durham, NC: Duke University Press.

Our Bodies Our Selves. 1973. *Our Bodies Our Selves: A Book by and for Women*. New York: Simon & Schuster.

Philip, Kavita. 2004. *Civilizing Natures: Race, Resources, and Modernity in Colonial South India*. New Brunswick, NJ: Rutgers University Press.

Prakash, Gyan. 1999. *Another Reason: Science and the Imagination of Modern India*. Princeton, NJ: Princeton University Press.

Ridley, Matt. 2003. *The Red Queen: Sex and the Evolution of Human Nature*. New York: Harper Perennial.

Rose, Hilary. 1983. "Hand, Brain, and Heart: A Feminist Epistemology for the Natural Sciences." *Signs: Journal of Women in Culture and Society* 9(1): 73–90.

Rose, Hilary. 1994. *Love, Power, and Knowledge: Towards a Feminist Transformation of the Sciences.* Cambridge, UK: Polity Press.

Rosser, Sue. 1992. *Biology and Feminism: A Dynamic Interaction.* New York: Twayne.

Roy, Deboleena. 2007. "Somatic Matters: Becoming Molecular in Molecular Biology." *Rhizomes: Cultural Studies in Emerging Knowledge* 14: Summer Issue. Available from http://www.rhizomes.net/issue14/roy/roy.html

Roy, Deboleena and Banu Subramaniam. 2013. "Situated Molecular Materialism: Feminist New Materialism and the Practices of Colonialism," Mattering: Feminism, Science, and Materialism Conference, The Graduate Center, CUNY, February 14, 2013.

Schiebinger, Londa L. 1989. *The Mind Has No Sex? Women in the Origins of Modern Science.* Cambridge, MA: Harvard University Press; New York: Tavistock Publications.

Seth, Suman. 2009. "Putting Knowledge in Its Place: Science, Colonialism, and the Postcolonial." *Postcolonial Studies* 12(4): 373–88.

Stepan, Nancy. 1986. "Race and Gender: The Role of Analogy in Science." *Isis* 77(2): 261–77.

Tuana, Nancy. 1983. *Feminism and Science.* Bloomington: Indiana University Press.

Tuana, Nancy. 1993. *The Less Noble Sex: Scientific, Religious, and Philosophical Conceptions of Women's Nature.* Bloomington: Indiana University Press.

van der Tuin, I. 2008. "Deflationary Logic: Response to Sara Ahmed's Imaginary Prohibitions: Some Preliminary Remarks on the Founding Gestures of the 'New Materialism.'" *European Journal of Women's Studies* 15(4): 411–16.

Wiley, Angela. 2016. "Biopossibility: A Queer Feminist Materialist Science Studies Manifesto, with Special Reference to the Question of Monogamous Behavior." *Signs: Journal of Women in Culture and Society* 41(3).

Wilson, Elizabeth A. 1998. *Neural Geographies: Feminism and the Microstructure of Cognition.* New York: Routledge.

Wilson, Elizabeth A. 2004. *Psychosomatic: Feminism and the Neurological Body.* Durham, NC: Duke University Press.

2

New Material Feminisms and Historical Materialism

A Diffractive Reading of Two (Ostensibly) Unrelated Perspectives

HANNA MEIßNER

A specific interest in materiality is the focus of many recent debates in feminist theory. Glossed as "material turn" (Alaimo & Heckman 2008) or "new materialism" (Coole & Frost 2010), the founding move of these debates is a "turn" away from tendencies of social determinism seen as inherent to constructionist perspectives. The focus on social structures, discourse, culture, and human agency as explanatory factors for the specific formation of our historical reality is criticized for its lack of attentiveness to the agency and historicity of the material. As a sociologist with a background in feminist engagements with the historical materialism of Karl Marx, I am very interested in these debates on materiality. The attention to the agentive dynamism of matter, and the critical reflection that the becoming of the world is not exclusively an effect of cultural inscriptions or human activity, represent important challenges to the notion of emancipation as it is implied in the traditions of historical materialism.

I am intrigued, however, by the apparent lack of communication between the recent debates about *new material* feminism and the traditions of *materialist* (Marxist) feminism. Stacy Alaimo and Susan Hekman even state that it is important to distinguish "material feminism" from (Marxist) "materialist feminism" (Alaimo & Hekman 2008: 18). A discussion of the possible reasons and implications of such gestures of distinction would go beyond the scope of this chapter; my argument here focuses on the assumption that there is much to be learned from an engagement that tries to put these perspectives in touch with each other.[1] Framing this assumption in terms of considering two "perspectives" obviously implies problematic simplifications. First of all, there is no unitary perspective of feminist engagements with Marx (Hennessy & Ingraham 1997), and whether, or in which sense, different authors can be subsumed under the label of new materialism or new material feminism is still being negotiated and established (Hird 2009; van der Tuin 2011; Coole 3013). However, since my objective is to tease out some general questions I have when I find myself emphatically agreeing with important issues raised by historical materialism on the one hand and new feminist materialism on the other hand, it seems helpful to resort to a manageable simplification of confronting two perspectives. Specifically, I am interested in confronting new materialism's critique of the anthropocentric notion of agency as a human privilege and the social ontology of historical materialism that is committed to emancipatory human subjectivity.

Keeping Oppositions in Tension

Karen Barad's work offers an interesting approach to this confrontation by allowing me to stage it as a *diffractive* confrontation. The metaphor of diffraction, as it was proposed by Donna Haraway and elaborated by Barad, supplies an image for what could happen if we engage with these perspectives in a way that lets them "interrupt each other productively" (Haraway in Schneider 2005: 149). This implies a generosity in the reading of different perspectives; it is not a critique that dismisses one theory from the standpoint of another, it is not "a practice of negativity that [. . .] is about subtraction, distancing and othering"(Barad in Dolphijn & van der Tuin 2012: 49). It is a respectful engagement attempting to carefully read the questions being asked and the arguments being made while at the same time being attentive to their (necessary) presuppositions and limitations as well as to their possibly universalizing presumptions.

Theories, in this sense, are not perceived as representations of a somehow pre-existent reality (and may thus be judged as correct or incorrect, complete or incomplete), but as "sighting devices" (Haraway 2004: 64), as conceptual apparatuses that let us experience reality in a particular way. Theories are thus neither more or less innocent mappings of reality nor are they simply different, equally adequate, stories. In this sense, the point is not to expose the blind spots of a theory and to offer a more complete account. The point, rather, is to make a theory accountable for its specific visualizations by recognizing and responding to the fact that "bringing something into view depends on the active displacement and marginalization of other things to which they are connected" (Castree 1996: 49).

Barad, engaging with Niels Bohr's philosophy-physics, discusses the intricate epistem-onto-logical implications of such a perception of theory as sighting device. By restaging the notion of the referent as a phenomenon, Barad can claim that theories (or concepts) are neither purely cultural artifacts that impose meaning, nor simply reflections of an observer-independent reality. Phenomena, in Barad's understanding, are not constituted by relations of preexisting entities but are constitutive of particular entities in their relations. This concept of phenomena as "primary ontological units" (Barad 2007: 140) not only blurs the separability of referent and concept, it also implies that agency cannot be attributed to single entities or substances; the dynamics of the constitution of phenomena are not conceived in terms of an interaction of different agents, they are processes of intra-acting agencies (Barad 1995: 59). This ontological claim that the world is not made up of individual things underlies Barad's discussion of the principle of complementarity, which Bohr proposed in opposition to Werner Heisenberg's uncertainty principle. Heisenberg points out that it is impossible to simultaneously determine momentum and position of a particle, thus posing the question of the fidelity of measurements as an epistemological problem (we cannot know both position and momentum simultaneously). In Barad's interpretation, Bohr, on the other hand, argues that what is at stake is an ontological problem: particles do not have determinate properties like momentum and position. The position of a particle is a phenomenon that is constituted as such (as a property of a particle) in a specific measurement apparatus; the determination of a particular property (position) is an intra-active achievement, which, at the same time, implies the exclusion of the constitution of other properties (momentum). Barad underlines the element of contextuality and partiality implied in this thinking, stating that "[r]eaders familiar with contemporary feminist theories will recognize Bohr's 'phenomenon' as a sign of the impossibility of a fixed, acontextual, simplistic, or final resolution" (1995: 58). There are always other possible phenomena that can be achieved through other apparatuses.

This concept of complementarity puts an interesting spin on the strategy of a diffractive confrontation of different theories as well as on the notion of generosity involved in this confrontation. A generous engagement with theories does not imply magnanimous gestures of inclusion; rather, it is a gesture of humility, of responding to the fact that theories necessarily produce exclusions when visualizing particular realities and are thus to be made accountable for their effects of displacement and marginalization. Reading different theories diffractively can contribute to such accountability by disrupting any possible aspiration for comprehensiveness or universal generalizability. This reading, then, does not aim for comprehensive closure with different perspectives complementing each other like pieces of a puzzle. Instead, an interesting opening lies in the possibility that different, even contradictory, points of view can be considered as equally possible—or perhaps equally necessary in terms of a project of emancipation.

In the following, I explore the prospects of working with the two material/ist "perspectives" in terms of different (theoretical) apparatuses measuring different phenomena, visualizing different, even oppositional, realities. Whilst new material feminism focuses on the processes of becoming and the potentiality of their openness, historical materialism takes into account specific socially constituted limits that configure the possibilities of becoming. Rather than concluding that a confrontation of these oppositional perspectives calls for decisions, for resolution, I will argue that it is more promising to be attentive to the "points of heresy," to "paradoxical though it may sound, [. . .] hold two contradictory discourses simultaneously" (Balibar in Duvoux/Sévérac 2012: 2).

The Elusive Quality of Matter

Starting from the (cursory) observation that the term *materiality* refers to conditioned possibilities in historical materialism and to unconditioned potentiality in new materialism, I want to argue that this "structured opposition" (Balibar in Duvoux/Sévérac 2012: 2) points to a specific episteme, to a "common discursive space [. . .] formed as a result of generative conflicts" (ibid.: 3). Inhabiting such a common space, which is "founded on the unity of opposites" (2), both perspectives attempt to hold the tension of this unity (of opposites such as meaning and matter, form and content, active and passive, etc.), resisting the impulse to resolve it by choosing one of the two possibilities—and yet slipping in this attempt. This slippage, constituting the points of heresy, is probably unavoidable, due to a particular commitment of visualization; the question I want to raise in the following, however, is how to resist reaffirming a particular unity by contextualizing this commitment in a specific epistemic economy.

Historical materialism is rooted in the political commitment of making "visible" that human activity is a positive force in the constitution of reality. Marx's social theory is a project of critique that applies the "visualizing 'power' of theory" (Castree 1996: 48) in order to make conceivable that certain structures of our historical reality are effects of human practices and can thus be transformed by cooperative human agency. The specifically materialist momentum of Marx's social ontology lies in the fact that he locates the key to transformational human agency not in individual motives or capacities, but in the social conditions that produce and enable individual motives and capacities. This qualification of historical materialism as "*emancipatory critical knowledge*" (Hennessy & Ingraham 1997: 4) is the base of its general appeal for feminists who, in their commitment to a politics of social transformation, see a necessity for theorizing the intersections of social inequalities of gender (and race) with the structures of the mode of production. As Momin Rahman and Anne Witz point out, however, there is a certain slippage in the meaning of the term "material"; the qualification of a materialist analysis as one concerned with systemic structures and power relations begs the question, "[w]hat, precisely, is the 'materiality' of the material?" (Witz & Rahman 2003: 251). Witz and Rahman go on, not unreasonably, to wonder "whether, in such deployments, the material is simply being substituted for the social" (252).

New materialism, on the other hand, is explicitly critical of tendencies of social determinism. The focus on the formative dimension of the social is perceived as a *retreat from materiality*, as a lack of attentiveness to the agency and historicity of the material. Mira Hird draws a distinction between new material feminism and historical materialism on the basis of the latter's inattention to "affective physicality of human-nonhuman encounters and relations. What distinguishes emerging analyses of material feminism [. . .] is a keen interest in engagements with matter" (Hird 2009: 329f.). Again, however, echoing the question posed by Witz and Rahman, we have to ask what the term "matter" refers to in this context. And who engages with this matter? On whose terms? In Hird's text, as in many other contributions to these debates, there is an interesting slippage from a general proclamation of an engagement with *matter* to a specification of an engagement of feminist theory or of humanities/social sciences with *science and technology*. The material appears as metonymy for diverse objects of science and technology: genes, electrons, bodies, hurricanes, earthquakes, and technical artifacts.

These parallel slippages can be seen as symptomatic for debates situated within a particular textual economy, operating with fundamental binaries, like meaning/matter, form/content, and culture/nature. Both perspectives grapple with these dichotomies; both share the assumption that it is impossible to regard the two terms as separate ontological entities. Both, however, resolve the tension by focusing on one of the two terms. Historical materialism, in its insistence on material conditions as the formative powers of reality, is committed to visualizing these conditions as social relations constituting specific forms of human practices that trans*form* the material world. As can be shown in Marx's discussion of the commodity (as a specific historical form of human products), this form does not exist apart from its particular substance. Marx defines the commodity as a unity of two things—of use value and exchange value. Nevertheless, there is an attribution of activity (form/exchange-value) and passivity (substance/use-value); although the formative activity cannot go beyond the given possibilities of the substance, it *is* the form-giving power. New material feminism, in turn, contests the human exceptionalism implied in this focus on *social* relations and practices as trans*formative* power. This perspective is committed to a visualization of the agentive power of non-human materiality, of the openness in the processes of becoming, which cannot be attributed to the formative power of social forms. In its final consequence, this generalization of activity beyond the realm of the social/human, in turn, makes it difficult to distinguish any particular political commitment in terms of intentional interventions.

Interesting avenues for a diffractive confrontation of these perspectives can be found in Jacques Derrida's problematizing that the concept of matter is "too often reinvested with 'logocentric' values, values associated with those of a thing, reality, presence in general, sensible presence, for example, substantial plenitude, content, referent etc." (Derrida 1981: 64). As Pheng Cheah points out, Derrida makes an intriguing remark (in *Spectres of Marx*) about his "obstinate interest in a materialism without substance" (Derrida in Cheah 2010: 72). This notion of a materialism without substance points to a helpful distinction between a notion of the material in terms of specific materializations (material-semiotic phenomena) on the one hand and a concept of matter as a term that denotes the *inaccessible* on the other hand. Matter as radical alterity implies a specific non-phenomenality of matter. However, this non-phenomenality does not imply an absence: "It has happened that I have spoken of nonpresence, in effect, but by this I was designating less a negated presence, than 'something' (nothing, indeed, in the form of presence) that deviates from the opposition presence/absence (negated presence), with all that this opposition implies" (Derrida 1981: 95).

Derrida points to the specific textual economy within which the term "matter" does its work: the notion of matter as non-presence points to the excess of an opposition of presence/absence; matter is that which *exceeds* material-semiotic phenomena. Derrida acknowledges the term "materialist" as an adequate qualification of his own work "to the extent to which, *matter* in this general economy designates [. . .] radical alterity" (Derrida 1981: 64) and, significantly, he adds the specification that this radical alterity relates to philosophical oppositions: "if, and in the extent to which, *matter* in this general economy designates [. . .] radical alterity (*I will specify: in relation to philosophical oppositions*), then what I write can be considered 'materialist'" (ibid., emphasis added).

I think this specification is significant because it raises the question of the knowing subject in its historicity. It only makes sense to say that something is radically other, or *inaccessible*, in a particular way to or for a particular "someone": to the subject committed to deconstructing philosophical oppositions of a logocentric economy from within. The specific predicament of this subject lies in the dynamics of a textual economy in which opposition to the classical notion of objectivity seems to lead to an irrevocable self-referentiality of language and signification (Chow 2006). Both historical materialism and new material feminism address this predicament. Gayatri Spivak, for instance, proposes a discontinuist reading of Marx's notion of the twofold nature of the commodity, positing use-value as "both outside and inside the system of value-determination" (Spivak 1996: 118). This reading avoids resorting to a self-referentiality of the social form (exchange-value); use-value becomes a deconstructive lever, disrupting the closure of this form. In a similar vein, Barad points to the dynamics of such a "deconstructive lever," arguing that the notion of the constitutive outside should not be reduced to "an exteriority *within language*" (Barad 2003: 825), which would imply a self-referential concept of language "as an enclosure that contains the constitutive outside" (ibid.).

The constitutive outside, instead of referencing a presence, points to a radical heterogeneity. It is that which the social form, meaning, language can never fully grasp, confine, or determine—it is thus inaccessible to the subject operating within the epistemic economy of meaning, representing, and knowing. This subject plays an important—yet mostly not adequately acknowledged—role in historical materialism as well as in new material perspectives: it is the focus of hope that human-made problems can be solved by emancipatory action, and it is the focus of a critique of humanist presumptions that the world is shaped by human action. If it is reasonable to assume that both perspectives share the desire to make practical differences in order to "get more promising interference patterns on the recording films of our lives and bodies" (Haraway 1997: 16), this desire should be contextualized; the engagement with matter and material conditions should be seen as a specific desire of a specific historical subject.

The Knowing Subject

New materialism opposes a perceived social determinism with the claim of bringing the material "into the forefront of feminist theory and practice" (Alaimo & Hekman 2008: 1). This can be read as a deconstructive move of overcoming dichotomies of culture and nature or meaning and materiality that prioritize culture and meaning while relegating nature and materiality to passivity. However, this move is primarily one of re-valuation, of establishing that matter, too, has agency, and as such it is only one of two deconstructive steps. Stopping at this move, the attempt to overcome representationalism leads to a "better" representation, an affirmation of matter as an agential presence—a reinvestment of matter with logocentric values. The desire to bring the material "back in" should thus include the second deconstructive step of displacement, which locates matter as a constitutive condition in the heart of any meaning. This can account for the problem that, in our epistemic economy, any attempt to bring the material back in, or to acknowledge the agency of matter, *always is a representation*, an act of a specific subject with a specific political commitment.[2] At the same time this displacement decenters and unsettles the representation by acknowledging that it depends on inaccessible alterity, which it will never fully grasp.

The focus on the historical situatedness of the knowing or representing subject is crucial to Derrida's work: "the project of grammatology is obliged to develop *within* the discourse of presence. It is not just a critique of presence but an awareness of the itinerary of the discourse of presence in one's *own* critique, a vigilance precisely against too great a claim for transparency" (Spivak 1988: 293). This situatedness poses the question, or problem, of othering in its *historicity*: Derrida "articulates the *European* Subject's tendency to constitute the Other as marginal to ethnocentrism and locates *that* as the problem with all logocentric and therefore also all grammatological endeavors [. . .]. *Not* a general problem, but a *European* problem" (ibid.).

This highlights social dimensions of human subjectivity: historical conditions shaping encounters of knowing subjects and their (human and non-human) others. In the case of the current feminist commitment to an engagement with matter, constitutive conditions are formed by the historical heritage of occidental metaphysics, enlightenment, capitalism, and colonialism. These conditions have to be acknowledged and taken into account in order to avoid conflating the notion of *the human* with a specific historical form of subjectivity. If it is not clearly specified, for instance, who ('we'?) is engaging in a problematization of the dualism of human/non-human, this non-specification turns into a universalism that reestablishes the "West-centered humanism" (Schueller 2009: 237) it purports to overcome.[3]

Furthermore, the notion of "overcoming" does not seem adequate to capture what is at stake with the problematization of dichotomies such as human/non-human. In this respect, we learn from Marx's notion of materialism that to fundamentally question something (like foundational categories, dichotomies—or the commodity fetish) does not mean that we can simply do away with it. The (human) subject can be deconstructed, questioned, and posited as a contingent historical figure, but it cannot be dissolved or overcome by rational decision. "We," who discuss questions of mattering in the setting of late modern academia, are deeply mired in a form of subjectivity that is configured by a specific historical heritage—and as such we are provincial figures (Chakrabarty 2000), the contemporaries of other human subjectivities and non-human agents. As part of "our" heritage the notion of humanity—referencing an abstract sameness of all humans—is a powerful element of critique and emancipatory transformation. Nevertheless, it is a figure that is constituted by exclusions, drawing boundaries confining the definitions of a livable human life and thus constituting others—the non-human, the less developed, the pathological, but also the abject. These are problematic implications and effects; "certain versions of the subject are politically insidious" (Butler 1992: 13). The complicated, or even paradoxical, moment, however, is that "we" *are* the subjects that we need to criticize, this subjectivity is the condition of possibility for our political commitment: "I think 'we'—that crucial material and rhetorical construction of politics and of history—need something called humanity. It is that kind of thing which Gayatri Spivak called 'that which we cannot not want'" (Haraway 2004: 49).

As Spivak points out, the problem is that, in our desire to deconstruct binaries, "we must move from implied premises, that must necessarily obliterate or finesse certain possibilities that question the availability of these premises in an absolutely justifiable way" (Spivak 2001: 397). Deconstruction in this sense can be "a corrective and critical movement"; it cannot found a political program and there is no position of "a fully practicing deconstructor [. . .], the subject is always centered as a subject. You cannot *decide* to *be* decentered and inaugurate a politically correct deconstructive politics. What deconstruction looks at is the limits of this centering, and points at the fact that these boundaries of the centering of the subject are indeterminate and that the subject (being always centered) is obliged to describe them as determinate" (ibid.). We cannot *decide* to *be* open to the non-human dynamism of matter. But, given the shortcomings and violence of clear demarcations between nature/culture, human/non-human, active/passive, etc., we can be politically committed to finding and fashioning new ways of relating to alterity. Both material/ist perspectives, in their oppositional tension, offer important "sightings" for such commitment.

Historical materialism focuses on specific limits of our openness and responsiveness to alterity, and, by visualizing these limits as *social* relations, it argues that they can be practically rearranged and collectively refashioned in order to make possible other, hopefully less violent, relations to others. Marx's analysis of capitalism offers important social explanations that account for the fact that many of our relations to (human) others (and their differences) are formed as relations of competition, that many relations to ourselves and to others are formed as relations of subjects/owners/users to resources, objects of utility, commodities. This perspective makes available options of addressing the conditions set by the capitalist mode of production as globalized structural impediments to ethically adequate relations—conditions that are socially transformable. That this political commitment involves a radical questioning of human exceptionalism is an important challenge put forward by new materialism, problematizing the notion of transformation by calling attention to: "a dynamism that obeys an inhuman temporality which is incalculable by human political reason because as the condition of possibility of both, it oscillates undecidably between the passive weightiness of nature and the active variability of culture and history" (Cheah 1996: 128).

Rethinking Emancipatory Agency

Read with attention to their heretical tensions, both perspectives have valuable (in)sights to offer for emancipatory projects that want "to make a difference in material-semiotic apparatuses, to diffract the rays of technoscience so that we get more promising interference patterns on the recording films of our lives and bodies" (Haraway 1997: 16). Haraway is, in my understanding, clearly referring to social dimensions of reality that can be transformed or refashioned by collective human activity. At the same time she radically questions humanist notions of agency and emancipation. She explicitly acknowledges and problematizes that the assumption that our world can be actively arranged and transformed by human agency is a powerful heritage of modern enlightenment thought. This heritage is imbricated with all the problematic aspects of modernist thought—hierarchical dualisms, eurocentrism, androcentrism, and anthropocentrism. Any engagement with this heritage has to be a *critical* engagement, but critique cannot simply do away with its problematic conditions of possibility—it has to work through them.

Haraway's commitment to questions of materiality is focused on the natural sciences, which she seems to endorse as a "space that [she] cannot not want to inhabit and yet must criticize" (Spivak 1993: 70). Haraway even acknowledges the pleasure she takes in inhabiting this space: "A lot of my heart lies in old-fashioned science for the people, and thus in the belief that these Enlightenment modes of knowledge have been radically liberating; that they give accounts of the world that can check arbitrary power; that these accounts of the world ought to be in the service of checking the arbitrary" (Haraway 1991: 2). This could be interpreted as pleasure in engaging in practices of knowing that are, in part, responsible for what becomes real, the pleasure of being an active participant in the processes of "worlding." At the same time, this pleasure has a decidedly melancholic inflection; it has to acknowledge that our specific subjectivity, with all its violent, confining, and exclusionary implications, is all we have, it is the condition of possibility for our participation—it is that which we cannot not want, but can hope to refashion.

Haraway's specification that these practices of knowing may bring forth accounts that can *check the arbitrary* points to a critical refiguring of political commitments in terms of interventions that are not aimed at achieving certain definable goals. On the one hand, this is due to the insight that the world cannot be formed and fashioned according to a plan; it is not a passive matter that awaits human design. On the other hand, there is no singular human desire, no essential human nature or common good as benchmark for judgment and orientation. Collective action can hope to check the arbitrary by imagining and working on "the possibility of new entanglements of power, ones that do not escape power relations but that institute new arrangements of the lines of the *dispositif*" (Bell 2007: 25). We cannot escape the conditions of possibility of our participation—what we can hope is to learn to un-learn (Spivak 1985) confining assumptions and to refashion the material conditions in order to allow for less violent processes of becoming.

As a tentative conclusion I suggest that it is politically and ethically adequate to insist on representing social dimensions of our reality in order to visualize levers for transformative interventions. At the same time it is crucial to question the premises, limits, and fault lines of such a perspective. In this sense a challenge of our times would be (*pace* Chakrabarty) to hold in a state of permanent tension two contradictory perspectives: On the one side is the production of knowledge about social structures and symbolic orders, on the other side "we" should elaborate new practices of knowing that aim for a potential of fantasy, for an imaginary that could let "us" experience and respond to inaccessible heterogeneity without needing to make it directly *accessible*.

NOTES

1 Sigrid Vertommen makes a similar point in this volume.

2 As Stephanie Clare points out in this volume, the new materialist injunction to pay attention to the more-than-human world is addressed to a *human* audience. She argues that the challenge of new materialism is not so much an inclusion of more-than-human agencies into the notion of politics but, rather, a radical questioning and refashioning of human subjectivity.

3 In this volume, Banu Subramaniam and Deboleena Roy address this problem, focusing on tendencies of decontextualizing and thus universalizing the notion of the body in new materialist analyses.

REFERENCES

Alaimo, Stacy and Susan Hekman (2008 eds.). *Material Feminisms*. Bloomington and Indianapolis: Indiana University Press.

Barad, Karen (1995). "A Feminist Approach to Teaching Quantum Physics." In Sue V. Rossner (ed.), *Teaching the Majority. Breaking the Gender Barrier in Science, Mathematics, and Engineering*. New York and London: Teachers College Press, 43–75.

Barad, Karen (2003). "Posthumanist Performativity: Toward an Understanding of How Matter Comes to Matter." *Signs: Journal of Women in Culture and Society* 28(3), 801–31.

Barad, Karen (2007). *Meeting the Universe Halfway. Quantum Physics and the Entanglement of Matter and Meaning*. Durham and London: Duke University Press.

Bell, Vikki (2007). *Culture & Performance. The Challenge of Ethics, Politics and Feminist Theory*. Oxford and New York: Berg.

Butler, Judith (1992). "Contingent Foundations: Feminism and the Question of Posmodernity." In Judith Butler and Joan W. Scott (eds.), *Feminists Theorize the Political*. New York and London: Routledge, 3–21.

Castree, Noel (1996). "Invisible Leviathan: Speculations on Marx, Spivak, and the Question of Value." *Rethinking Marxism: A Journal of Economics, Culture & Society* 9(2), 43–78.

Chakrabarty, Dipesh (2000). *Provincializing Europe. Postcolonial Thought and Historical Difference*. Princeton and Oxford: Princeton University Press.

Cheah, Pheng (1996). "Mattering." *diacritics* 26(1), 108–39.

Cheah, Pheng (2010). "Non-Dialectical Materialism." In Samantha Frost and Diana Coole (eds.), *New Materialisms: Ontology, Agency, and Politics*. Durham, NC: Duke University Press, 70–91.

Chow, Rey (2006). *The Age of the World Target. Self-Referentiality in War, Theory and Comparative Work*. Durham and London: Duke University Press.

Coole, Diana (2013). "Agentic Capacities and Capacious Historical Materialism: Thinking with New Materialisms in the Political Sciences." *Millennium: Journal of International Studies* 41(3), 451–69.

Coole, Diana and Samantha Frost (2010). *New Materialisms. Ontology, Agency, and Politics*. Durham, NC: Duke University Press.

Derrida, Jacques (1981). *Positions*. Chicago: University of Chicago Press.

Dolphijn, Rick and Iris van der Tuin (2012). *New Materialism: Interviews & Cartographies*. London: Open Humanities Press.

Duvoux, Nicolas and Pascal Sévérac (2012). Citizen Balibar. An Interview with Étienne Balibar. http://www.booksandideas.net/Citizen-Balibar.html. Accessed June 5, 2013.

Haraway, Donna (1991). Cyborgs at Large: Interview with Donna Haraway. In Constance Penley/Andrew Ross (eds.), *Technoculture*. Minneapolis/Oxford: University of Minnesota Press, 1–20.

Haraway, Donna (1997). Modest_Witness@Second_Millenium. Female Man©_Meets_ OncoMouse™. New York and London: Routledge.

Haraway, Donna (2004). "Ecce Homo, Aint (Ar'n't) I a Woman, and Inappropriate/d Others: The Human in a Post-Human Landscape." In *The Haraway Reader*. New York/London: Routledge, 47–61.

Hennessy, Rosemary and Chris Ingraham (1997). "Introduction. Reclaiming Anti-capitalist Feminism." In Rosemary Hennessy/Chris Ingraham (eds.), *Materialist Feminism. A Reader in Class, Difference, and Women's Lives*. New York and London: Routledge, 1–14.

Hird, Mira (2009). "Feminist Engagements with Matter." *Feminist Studies* 35(2), 329–46.

Schneider, Joseph (2005). *Donna Haraway. Live Theory*. New York and London: Continuum.

Schueller, Malini Johar (2009). "Decolonizing Global Theories Today." *interventions* 11(2), 235–54.

Spivak, Gayatri Chakravorty (1985). "Criticism, Feminism and the Institution: An Interview with Gayatri Chakravorty Spivak." *Thesis Eleven* 10–11, 175–87.

Spivak, Gayatri Chakravorty (1988). "Can the Subaltern Speak?" In Cary Nelson and Lawrence Grossberg (eds.), *Marxism and the Interpretation of Culture*. Urbana: University of Illinois Press, 271–316.

Spivak, Gayatri Chakravorty (1993). *Outside in the Teaching Machine*. New York/London: Routledge.

Spivak, Gayatri Chakravorty (1996). "Scattered Speculations on the Question of Value." In Donna Landry und Gerald Maclean (eds.), *The Spivak Reader*. New York: Routledge, 107–40.

Spivak, Gayatri Chakravorty (2001). "Practical Politics of the Open End." In Martin McQuillan (ed.), *Deconstruction. A Reader*. New York: Routledge, 397–404.

Tuin, Iris van der (2011). "New Feminist Materialisms—Review Essay." *Women's Studies International Forum* 34(4), 271–77.

Witz, Anne and Momin Rahman (2003). "What Really Matters? The Elusive Quality of the Material in Feminist Thought." *Feminist Theory* 4(3), 243–61.

3

On the Politics of "New Feminist Materialisms"

STEPHANIE CLARE

Among the many issues raised by "new materialisms" and "new feminist materialisms" stands the question of politics. At worst, I've heard new materialisms described as the "end of feminism." At best, I've heard the repeated concern: What are the politics of the metaphysics or ontologies that new materialists posit? For although this literature calls for a move away from epistemology toward ontology, for a move away from representation toward questions of the "real," it cannot but produce representations itself; it cannot but assert particular forms and traditions of knowing through its ontological claims. "There can be no decontextualized generic body or matter," as Deboleena Roy and Banu Subramaniam put it in their contribution to this volume.[1] Michel Foucault taught us well about the entanglement of power and knowledge.[2] How might we describe the nexus of power and knowledge that runs through new materialisms?

The labels "new materialisms" and "new feminist materialisms" have been used by a range of scholars to describe a series of texts that emerged during the past ten years.[3] These texts, by authors such as Karen Barad, Jane Bennett, Rosi Braidotti, Elizabeth Grosz, Vicky Kirby, Luciana Parisi, Arun Saldanha, and Elizabeth Wilson, argue, roughly, that the linguistic or cultural turn in feminist theory, cultural theory, political theory, and, in Saldanha's case, critical race studies, is insufficient for analyzing contemporary politics and dangerous because it leaves questions of biology or "nature" to reductionist, conservative thought. Often (though not always) drawing on Gilles Deleuze's writing and often (though not always) seeking to engage rather than critique science, this scholarship argues that materiality is open to becoming or transformation, that nature and culture are inseparable, and that what is commonly taken as "culture" might, as Vicky Kirby argues, be "nature" after all.[4]

To pose the question of the nexus between power and knowledge in new materialist theories is certainly not simply to reject this scholarship. Doing so would miss its powerful repositioning of feminist thought. In a culture where science is treated as legitimate truth, new feminist materialisms make space for a feminist voice, one that does not only find the masculinist, racist, or homophobic bias in scientific knowledge, but one that develops a feminist science, a feminist ontology, or feminist metaphysics. To bring feminism to this sphere, to reject any sequestering of feminist thought, seems like a feminist move in itself. It indexes the potential of feminist thought to reach beyond itself and to speak the language of power to its own ends.

And yet what are those ends? What power dynamics are embedded in the ontologies new materialists posit? This question emerges when reading Diana Coole and Samantha Frost's introduction to their *New Materialisms* reader and noting the archive to which they turn to provide an account of materiality: Spinoza and Deleuze, particle physics and complexity theory. I am left worried about the exclusions of this archive, especially given that the authors develop a universal and totalizing account of matter. Who is the subject who knows the materiality Coole and Frost posit? How would "matter" appear differently within, for example, indigenous epistemologies whose development is key to building indigenous self-determination and governance, but which are not cited in new materialists' literature?[5] Is the account of materiality provided among new materialists an appropriation of matter? Is it a form of neocolonialism that posits its understanding of matter in the universal, all while producing a particular representation that legitimizes specific forms of knowledge and the power relations that they foster?

A similar question emerges in reading Stacy Alaimo and Susan Hekman's introduction to their edited collection, *Material Feminisms*. The authors set the stage for new materialism. They write,

> Feminist theory is at an impasse caused by the contemporary linguistic turn in feminist thought. With the advent of postmodernism and poststructuralism, many feminists have turned their attention to social constructionist models. They have focused on the role of language in the constitution of social reality, demonstrating that discursive practices constitute the social position of women. They have engaged in produc-

tive and wide-ranging analyses and deconstructions of the concepts that define and derogate women.[6]

While this certainly describes a particular story of feminist theory, this is but one story among others. Another narrative about contemporary feminist theory could be told. For instance, we might tell a story about intersectionality, and this story, which would especially highlight the contribution of black feminist thought, would seriously trouble Alaimo and Hekman's narrative. Taking Kimberlé Crenshaw's influential work as a point of reference, it would be a stretch to argue that contemporary feminist theory is defined by a "linguistic turn" which focuses on the "role of language in the constitution of reality" and which partakes in "deconstructions of the concepts that define and derogate women."[7] Even if Crenshaw focuses on law, and hence on the role of language in reality, and even if Crenshaw analyzes the categories "woman" and "woman of color," the terms by which we would describe intersectionality are quite different. Likewise, such a narrative renders invisible feminist phenomenology, such as Iris Marion Young's writing; it also makes it hard to position Donna Haraway's influential contributions.[8] Quite simply, different stories of feminist theory could be told, but Alaimo and Hekman's narrative gets repeated within new materialist work, cementing one particular—exclusionary—story of feminist thought so that new materialisms can posit itself as "new."[9]

The way, however, that I am approaching the politics of new materialisms here is ironic: I am posing the question of power, but I ask this question in relation to representation. The politics of new feminist materialisms, this initial framing suggests, lies in the representations and exclusions it produces. To insist on politics as the politics of representation is to miss new materialists' attempt, in Alaimo and Hekman's words, "to move beyond discursive construction and grapple with materiality."[10] One might respond to this argument by insisting that the politics of representation are, indeed, material, or that representations have material effects; in other words, the distinction made by Alaimo and Hekman is misleading. And yet I cannot but wonder, how can we pose the question of new materialists' politics within a new materialist frame? Posing this question, "politics" itself becomes a problem. What is a new materialist approach to politics? What counts as "politics" within new materialist thought?

Asking what counts as politics within a new feminist materialist frame is a similar question to Pheng Cheah's in his analysis of Jacques Derrida's and Gilles Deleuze's writing. Cheah acknowledges that "it is difficult to elaborate on the political implications of Deleuze's understanding of materiality as the power of inorganic life. This is partly because the various figures he employs to characterize this power do not translate easily into our conventional vocabularies of political discourse and institutional practices."[11] Rather than explore the relevance of Deleuze's and Derrida's materialisms for concrete politics, Cheah inverts the question. He incites us to ask "how they radically put into question the fundamental categories of political theory including the concept of the political itself."[12]

A similar approach was central to poststructuralist feminism, as captured in the debate between Seyla Benhabib and Judith Butler published in *Feminist Contentions*. Here, Butler examines the idea that politics requires a subject. She insists that this notion forecloses the politics both of who counts as a subject and how the subject itself is constituted. This argument draws heavily on Michel Foucault's writing on power and the subject, especially as articulated in *Discipline and Punish* and the first volume of *History of Sexuality*. In addition, it partakes in a long history of feminist thought that has been insistent on finding politics where it was not said to be.[13]

The politics of new feminist materialisms is part of this trajectory, but, I will argue, the notion of politics that emerges in new materialisms is at its best not when it redefines politics so as to include non-human or more-than-human forces but rather when it reworks understandings of human subjectivity, making it clear how the human is always enmeshed in more-than-human worlds. In this case, politics continues to center power relations between humans, but our understanding of the human itself transforms. To make this argument, I turn to two new materialist texts: Jane Bennett's *Vibrant Matter* and Karen Barad's *Meeting the Universe Halfway*.

Re-visiting "the Political": *Vibrant Matter* and *Meeting the Universe Halfway*

I focus now on particular texts so as to tease "new materialisms" apart, reading the works against each other to develop their nuances. While I have used the terms "new materialisms" and "new feminist materialisms" as shorthand to refer to a trend in contemporary scholarship, those who have been gathered under the label do not have equivalent positions and those who are considered "new materialists," such as Bennett, rarely use the term. *Vibrant Matter* traces how human agency is dependent on nonhuman forces; it theorizes a "vital materialisms" that cuts across human and nonhuman bodies, subjects and objects. In turn, *Meeting the Universe Halfway* develops a theory of what Barad terms "agential realism." This is an account of the world that, drawing on Niels Bohr's philosophy-physics, departs from representationalism, anthropocentrism, and the linguistic or cultural turn to argue that "intra-actions" constitute the "basic units of existence."[14] An agent of observation or measurement, Barad argues, cannot be clearly separated from its object; instead, the two emerge together. Such phenomena, for Barad, constitute the enfolding of matter.

While both *Vibrant Matter* and *Meeting the Universe Halfway* could be considered "new materialist," the notions of politics that emerge from their pages are quite different. Bennett attempts to develop a non-anthropocentric political theory by revisiting democratic theory in particular. The impulse behind such an attempt returns to familiar ground in feminist theory. Bennett writes, "to imagine politics as a realm of human activity alone may [. . .] be a kind of prejudice."[15] The well-known argument is that such an imagination of politics hides the question of who or what counts as human. It also hides the related question of how "the human" is constituted. But Bennett takes this line of reasoning in a slightly different direction as well. She explains, "If human culture is inextricably enmeshed with vibrant, nonhuman agencies, and if human intentionality can be agentic only if accompanied by a vast entourage of nonhumans, then it seems that the appropriate unit for democratic theory is neither the individual human nor an exclusively human collective but the (ontological heterogeneous) 'public' coalescing around a problem."[16] At issue is not quite the point that an understanding of politics built around the human forecloses the question of who or what counts as human. Rather, the issue is that humans are not separable from the nonhuman world and thus democratic theory is misguided to the extent that it imagines humans otherwise.

The problem, however, is that it is quite difficult to think of politics outside the human realm. Politics has been defined as a particularly human activity, and vice-versa, the human has been defined, in part, by his (and sometimes her) capacity for politics.[17] Bennett's penultimate chapter—the chapter, she explains, that "was the most difficult to conceive and write"—considers how the recognition of non-human agency affects "key concepts of political theory, including the 'public,' 'political participation,' and 'the political.'"[18] Following John Dewey, Bennett suggests, "a member of a public is one 'affected by the indirect consequences of transactions to such an extent that it is deemed necessary to have those consequences systematically cared for.'"[19] Within such a framework, nonhuman bodies can be easily understood as members of a public—certainly not only humans are affected by various decisions. But this is not to say that "the political goal of a vital materialism is [...] the perfect equality of actants."[20] Instead, Bennett calls for "a polity with more channels of communication between members."[21] This conclusion, however, is not quite satisfying. It raises the question of what it would mean to communicate with entities that are affected by particular "transactions," entities such as plants or rocks. Bennett herself recognizes this problem. She writes that Bruno Latour's idea of a "parliament of things" is "as provocative as it is elusive."[22] Ultimately, she moves away from Dewey's version of politics to Jacques Rancière's *Disagreement*. Even though for Rancière himself, "the public is constituted by bodies with uniquely human capabilities, talents, and skills,"[23] Bennett argues that Rancière's writing can be pushed to include a nonhuman realm. Rancière argues that the democratic act emerges when "the demos does something that exposes the arbitrariness of the dominant 'partition of the sensible.'"[24] In this case, something becomes sensible that was not previously accounted for. Building on Rancière, Bennett claims that such instigation need not simply emerge from a human. Rather, something as simple as a glove, a dead rat, or a bottle cap can change perception. Bennett explains how she is struck by the assemblage of these things, things whose presence make visible a "culture of things irreducible to the culture of objects."[25] Objects, in this case, are defined in their relation to subjects, unlike "things." From this example, Bennett concludes that things have the "power to startle and provoke a gestalt shift in perception."[26] They can therefore engage in democratic acts.

This argument does not, however, quite get away from the problem of communication. These "things" do not quite "have" the power to startle but rather they startle when they come into contact with a particular consciousness. Bennett cites her "naïve ambition" to get at the vitality or force of things by postponing a "genealogical critique of objects" and lingering in those moments of fascination with a thing.[27] But naïveté, like common sense, too easily hides the epistemic framework that makes something naïvely true. Things startle in reference to these frameworks, frameworks that make it such that an encountering consciousness is surprised by the things.

Barad's approach to politics is quite different. Whereas *Vibrant Matter* attempts to suspend the question of knowing so as to get at the power of things, *Meeting the Universe Halfway*, in a position reminiscent of feminist strong objectivity, brings attention to the process of knowing itself.[28] Whereas Bennett focuses on "things" that exist in the world—a dead rat, a bottle cap—Barad turns to subatomic particles whose being is entangled with agents of observation.

Barad's attempt to move away from what she considers the cultural or linguistic turn entails a departure from "representationalism," the belief that there exist entities in the world that words (either accurately or inaccurately) represent. Linguistic representationalism overlaps with political representationalism, which focuses on the question of how political systems might best "represent the interests of the people allegedly represented."[29] In some ways, this is Bennett's concern throughout her discussion of Dewey, and such a concern, as Barad points out, is related to the idea that "beings exist as individuals with inherent attributes, anterior to their representation."[30] This idea is implicit in Bennett's discussion of the rat, glove, and bottle cap.

In the place of such a view, Barad turns to Niels Bohr's philosophy-physics. She examines Bohr's gedanken (thought) experiment where an apparatus is used to determine the position and momentum of one electron. The problem here is that the very process of measurement affects the electron. Say light (a photon) is used to determine the electron's position. As the photon encounters the electron, this electron's movement and position will change. This means that it is impossible to measure the electron as separate from the agency of measurement, the photon. One solution to this problem is to determine the photon's own position and momentum. In this case, we could determine the photon's effect on the electron and hence calculate the electron's position prior to measurement. This, however, raises a second problem: only the position or momentum of the photon can be calculated. Not both. Why? For the photon's position to be known, the apparatus that "shoots it" has to be stable. It must remain in position. On the other hand, for the photon's momentum to be determined, the apparatus from which it emerges has to be mobile, moving with the opposite momentum of the departing photon. This means that we can't know the photon's momentum and position at the same time, and thus that it is impossible to measure an electron's position and momentum simultaneously, independent of the agent of measurement.[31] In this model, representation does not come from a position of externality from that which is representation. The photon and the electron encounter one another. To represent the electron, one must engage with it and shape it. Representation is part of the world, not separate from it. It is an event in itself.

Barad draws many conclusions from this. Popular physics has understood this experiment as pointing to an epistemological principle: Heisenberg's uncertainty principle, which states that it is impossible to determine both the place and momentum of an electron. Against Heisenberg's uncertainty, Barad argues that this experiment does not only have epistemological repercussions but also ontological ones. Drawing on Bohr, she offers a theory of indeterminacy: it is not simply that we cannot know an electron's position and momentum at the same time. It is rather that an electron *does not have* such properties simultaneously. "Things" do not exist prior to their "intra-actions" (a term Barad uses instead of "interaction" because this latter term suggests at least two separate "things" encountering rather than the entanglement of the encounter). In the case of Bohr's gedanken experiment, the electron and the photon do not have properties that are separate from one another. Instead, all we have is an intra-action between them. Barad concludes from this that phenomena, actual intra-actions, "are the basic units of existence."[32] "Phenomena" describes the wholeness of experimentation—that is, the fact that the agent of observation cannot be clearly separated from its object, and phenomena, for Barad, constitute the enfolding—not unfolding—of matter. In this model, there is no predictable nugget waiting to emerge. All we have is a becoming more complex.

Meeting the Universe Halfway does not directly address the question of politics. Indeed, Barad opens her book arguing that it "contributes to the founding of a new ontology, epistemology, and ethics"—politics is not included here. Later, Barad writes, we need an "ethics of responsibility and accountability not only for what we know, how we know, and what we do but, in part, for what exists."[33] This statement is framed as a question of ethics, but from it we might likewise draw a conclusion about politics. It seems as though from an agential realist perspective, politics concerns what becomes materialized, what bodies come to emerge. This understanding of politics is aligned with a form of poststructuralist politics that, rather than seeking to represent subjects, investigates the power relations that constitute the subject, displacing the question of politics from the power relations between subjects to the power relations that go into the subject's constitution. However, readers who might be troubled by the implicit notion of politics that emerges from *Meeting the Universe Halfway*, but not by Foucault's and Butler's writing, are forced into the recognition that, while critical of a form of politics grounded in the subject and (at least in Foucault's case) in the "human," these thinkers' versions of politics seem posited in the name of excluded human bodies. In Barad's version, the question moves beyond concern with humans and human subjects per se. She argues that Foucault and Butler, though critical of humanism and concerned with the force relations through which bodies are materialized, fail to consider the body's materiality (including its anatomy and physiology) as well as other material, nonhuman forces as well. Barad writes,

> Crucial to understanding the workings of power is an understanding of the nature of power in the fullness of its materiality. To restrict power productivity to the limited domain of the social, for example, or to figure matter as merely an end product rather than an active factor in further materializations is to cheat matter out of the fullness of its capacity.[34]

Agential realism, Barad argues, considers "the agential contributions of all material forces (both 'social' and 'natural')."[35]

However, if we understand power "in the fullness of its materiality" beyond its "limited domain in the social," must we conclude that all power relations are political? What is the difference between a power relation and a political relation? Does the force of gravity on my body constitute a form of politics? Is it even useful to maintain separate concepts of "power relations" and "politics"? These are questions that emerge when reading Barad's text.

Politics in a More-than-Human World

Although new materialisms and new feminist materialisms bring attention to the more-than-human world, their audience and authors remain human. "The (human) subject," as Hanna Meißner argues in this volume, "can be deconstructed, questioned and posited as a contingent historical figure, but it cannot be dissolved or overcome by rational decision . . . '[W]e *are* the subjects that we need to criticize, this subjectivity is the condition of possibility for our political commitment.'"[36] In this light, I suggest that we read new feminist materialisms as a project to recreate human subjectivity rather than as a project to reform politics so that it includes more-than-human actors. The texts have us recognize that human agency is imbricated with actors beyond ourselves, and this recognition puts pressure on the neoliberal subjects of self-control, self-generation, and maximization.[37]

Yet at least two dangers remain. In 1988, Gayatri Spivak argued that the "much-publicized critique of the sovereign subject actually inaugurates a Subject."[38] It conserves "the subject of the West or the West as Subject" by concealing itself, pretending it has "no geo-political determinations."[39] To the extent that new materialisms does not address the historical locatedness of its representations of materiality, its implicit critique of the subject may, in effect, inaugurate one. The challenge of new materialisms is to attend to the politics of representation while still making ontological arguments. A second, related, problem is that faith in exposing more-than-human agency and inorganic vitality can be overly optimistic. Neel Ahuja argues that posthumanist discourse "continues to invest the breakdown of species 'boundaries' with a certain idealism."[40]

Yet this fails "to recognize the violence of incorporation, the subjection inherent in drawing animality into the horizon of biopower."[41] Still more, it arrests "differences within the category of the human in order to rhetorically produce an excluded animal."[42] A similar and overlapping idealism is common in new materialist writing, which in some renditions appears positively exuberant in the rendering more-than-human worlds. *Vibrant Matter* does not address differences between humans; *Meeting the Universe Halfway* appears eager to conclude that "machinic agency is part of the ongoing contestation and reconfiguring of relations of production."[43] But this argument circumvents the agency of workers who use the spatial arrangement of machines as an opportunity for contestation.

While new materialist understandings of politics are compelling, feminist scholarship, attentive to more-than-human worlds, cannot but return to the study of power relations between humans, for it is humans whom we address in our writing and it is, arguably, human lives, enmeshed in more-than-human worlds, that we care most about. We might critique what or who counts as human, how the human has been produced, and how we understand the human, but it is to this "human" that politics remains turned toward. A new materialist understanding of politics need not find politics in the power relations between entities beyond the human but rather can turn to how power relations among humans entail more-than-human forces.

NOTES

1 Deboleena Roy and Banu Subramaniam, "Matter in the Shadows: Feminist New Materialism and the Practices of Colonialism," this volume.

2 See, for instance, Foucault, "Two Lectures," 93.

3 Scholarship that has used the term "new materialisms" includes Sara Ahmed's "Open Forum," Diana Coole and Samantha Frost's *New Materialisms*, Noela Davis's "New Materialism," Rick Dolphijn and Iris Van der Tuin's "The Transversality of New Materialism," Myra Hird's "Feminist Engagement with Matter," and Jasbir Puar's "'I Would Rather be a Cyborg than a Goddess.'"

4 Kirby, *Quantum Anthropologies*, 68–69.

5 See Cajete, *Native Science* as well as Basso, *Wisdom Sits in Places* and Battiste, *Reclaiming Indigenous Voice and Vision.*

6 Alaimo and Hekman, Introduction, *Material Feminisms*, 1.

7 Ibid. See also Crenshaw, "Demarginalizing the Intersection of Race and Sex" and Crenshaw, "Mapping the Margins."

8 See Young, "Throwing Like a Girl" and Haraway, *Simian, Cyborgs and Women* and *Modest_Witness@Second_Millenium.FemaleMan@_Meets_OnceMouse™*.

9 Sara Ahmed makes an overlapping point. She argues that "new materialisms" posits itself as new by ignoring prior feminist work on biology and in phenomenology. She concludes, "we should avoid establishing new terrain by clearing the ground of what has come before us. And we might not be quite so willing to deposit our hope in the category of 'the new'" (36). Noela Davis responds by returning to the feminist texts on biology that Ahmed cites, and arguing that these texts, unlike the new materialist work, maintain a sense of biology as distinct from the social; the new materialist point, for Davis, is that these two are inseparable. However, to make her argument, Davis must ignore Donna Haraway's work that, since the early 1990s, analyzed what Haraway termed "naturecultures."

10 Alaimo and Hekman, Introduction, *Material Feminisms*, 6.

11 Cheah, "Nondialectical Materialism," 156.

12 Ibid.

13 "The personal is political," feminists have argued. See Hanisch, "The Personal is Political" and Millett, *Sexual Politics*.

14 Barad, *Meeting the Universe Halfway*, 333.

15 Bennett, *Vibrant Matter*, 108.

16 Ibid.

17 Aristotle's *Politics*, for instance, contends, "Man is by nature a political animal" (10).

18 Bennett, *Vibrant Matter*, xviii.

19 Ibid., 103.

20 Ibid., 104.

21 Ibid.

22 Ibid.

23 Ibid., 95.

24 Ibid., 105.

25 Ibid., 5.

26 Ibid., 107.

27 Ibid., 17.

28 See Harding, "Rethinking Standpoint Epistemology," and Haraway, "Situated Knowledges."

29 Barad, *Meeting the Universe Halfway*, 47.

30 Ibid., 46.

31 Ibid., 97–131.

32 Ibid., 333.

33 Ibid., 243.

34 Ibid., 66.

35 Ibid.

36 Hanna Meißner, "New Materialist Feminisms and Historical Materialism—A Diffractive Reading of Two (Ostensibly) Unrelated Perspectives," this volume.

37 See Bondi, "Working the Spaces of Neoliberal Subjectivity," and Read, "A Geneal-ogy of Homo-Economicus."

38 Spivak, "Can the Subaltern Speak?," 271.

39 Ibid.

40 Ahuja, "Abu Zubaydah and the Caterpillar," 145.

41 Ibid., 144.

42 Ibid.

43 Barad, *Meeting the Universe Halfway*, 239.

REFERENCES

Ahmed, Sara. "Open Forum Imaginary Prohibitions: Some Preliminary Remarks on the Founding Gestures of the 'New Materialism.'" *European Journal of Women's Studies* 15.1 (2008): 23–39.

Ahuja, Neel. "Abu Zubaydah and the Caterpillar." *Social Text* 29.1 (2011): 127–49.

Alaimo, Stacy and Susan Hekman. Introduction. *Material Feminisms*. Bloomington: University of Indiana Press, 2008, 1–19.

Aristotle. *Politics*. Ed. R. F. Stalley, Trans. Ernest Barker. Oxford: Oxford University Press, 2009.

Barad, Karen. "Posthumanist Performativity: Toward an Understanding of How Mat-ter Comes to Matter." *Signs: Journal of Women in Culture and Society* 28.3 (2003): 801–31.

———. *Meeting the Universe Halfway: Quantum Physics and the Entanglement of Matter and Meaning*. Durham, NC: Duke University Press, 2007.

Basso, Keith H. *Wisdom Sits in Places: Landscape and Language Among the Western Apache*. Albuquerque: University of New Mexico Press, 1996.

Battiste, Mary. *Reclaiming Indigenous Voice and Vision*. Vancouver: University of Brit-ish Columbia Press, 1998.

Bennett, Jane. *Vibrant Matter: A Political Ecology of Things*. Durham, NC: Duke Uni-versity Press, 2010.

Bondi, Liz. "Working the Spaces of Neoliberal Subjectivity: Psychotherapeutic Tech-nologies, Professionalisation and Counselling." *Antipode* 37 (2005): 497–514.

Braidotti, Rosi. *Metamorphosis: Towards a Materialist Theory of Becoming*. Cambridge: Polity Press, 2002.

Butler, Judith. "Contingent Foundations." In *Feminist Contentions: A Philosophical Exchange*, ed. Seyla Benhabib et al. New York: Routledge, 1994, 35–58.

Cajete, Gregory. *Native Science: Natural Laws of Interdependence*. Santa Fe, NM: Clearlight Press, 2000.

Cheah, Pheng. "Nondialectical Materialism." *Diacritics* 38.1–2 (Spring-Summer 2008): 143–57.

Coole, Diana and Samantha Frost, eds. *New Materialisms: Ontology, Agency, and Poli-tics*. Durham, NC: Duke University Press, 2010.

Crenshaw, Kimberlé Williams. "Demarginalizing the Intersection of Race and Sex: A Black Feminist Critique of Antidiscrimination Doctrine, Feminist Theory and

Antiracist Politics." *The University of Chicago Legal Forum: Feminism in the Law: Theory, Practice and Criticism* (1989): 139–67.

———. "Mapping the Margins: Intersectionality, Identity Politics, and Violence Against Women of Color." *Stanford Law Review* 6 (1991): 1241–99.

Davis, Noela. "New Materialism and Feminism's Anti-Biologism: A Response to Sara Ahmed." *European Journal of Women's Studies* 16.1 (2009): 67–80.

Dolphijn, Rick and Iris Van der Tuin. "The Transversality of New Materialism." *Women: A Cultural Review* 21.2 (2010): 153–71.

Foucault, Michel. "Two Lectures." In *Power/Knowledge: Selected Interviews and other Writings 1972–1977*, ed. Colin Gordon. New York: Pantheon Books, 1980, 78–108.

———. "The Ethics of the Concern for Self as a Practice of Freedom." In *Ethics: Subjectivity and Truth; The Essential Works of Michel Foucault, 1954–1984*, ed. Paul Rabinow, trans. Robert Hurley et al. London: Penguin (1984) 1997, 281–320.

Grosz, Elizabeth. "A Politics of Imperceptibility: A Response to 'Anti-Racism, Multiculturalism, and the Ethics of Identification.'" *Philosophy Social Criticism* 28.4 (2002): 463–72.

———. *Time Travels: Feminism, Nature and Power*. Durham, NC: Duke University Press, 2005.

———. *Chaos, Territory, Art: Deleuze and the Framing of the Earth*. New York: Columbia University Press, 2008.

———. *Becoming Undone: Darwinian Reflections on Life, Politics, and Art*. Durham, NC: Duke University Press, 2011.

Hanisch, Carol. "The Personal is Political." In *Notes From the Second Year: Women's Liberation*, ed. Shulamith Firestone and Anne Koedt. New York: Radical Feminism, 1970.

Haraway, Donna. "Situated Knowledges: The Science Question in Feminism and the Privilege of Partial Perspective." *Feminist Studies* 14.3 (Autumn 1988): 575–99.

———. *Simian, Cyborgs and Women: The Reinvention of Nature*. New York: Routledge, 1991.

———. *Modest_Witness@Second_Millenium.FemaleMan©_Meets_OncoMouse™*. New York: Routledge, 1997.

Harding, Sandra. "Rethinking Standpoint Epistemology: What is 'Strong Objectivity?'" In *Feminist Epistemologies*, ed. Linda Alcoff and Elizabeth Potter. New York: Routledge, 1993, 49–82.

Hird, Myra. "Feminist Engagement with Matter." *Feminist Studies* 35.2 (2009): 329–46.

Kirby, Vicky. *Quantum Anthropologies: Life at Large*. Durham, NC: Duke University Press, 2011.

Meißner, Hanna. "New Materialist Feminisms and Historical Materialism—A Diffractive Reading of Two (Ostensibly) Unrelated Perspectives." In *Mattering: Feminism, Science and Materialism*, Ed. Victoria Pitts-Taylor. New York: New York University Press (this volume).

Millett, Kate. *Sexual Politics*. Chicago and Urbana: University of Illinois Press, 1969.

Parisi, Luciana. *Abstract Sex: Philosophy, Bio-Technology, and the Mutations of Desire.* New York: Continuum, 2004.

Puar, Jasbir K. "'I would rather be a cyborg than a goddess': Becoming-Intersection in Assemblage Theory." *philoSOPHIA* 2.1 (2012): 49–66.

Rancière, Jacques. *Disagreement: Politics and Philosophy.* Trans. Julie Rose. Minneapolis: University of Minnesota Press, 1999.

Read, Jason. "A Genealogy of Homo-Economicus: Neoliberalism and the Production of Subjectivity." *Foucault Studies* 6 (February 2009): 25–36.

Roy, Deboleena and Banu Subramaniam. "Matter in the Shadows: Feminist New Materialism and the Practices of Colonialism." In *Mattering: Feminism, Science and Materialism*, ed. Victoria Pitts-Taylor. New York: New York University Press (this volume).

Saldanha, Arun. "Reontologising Race: The Machinic Geography of Phenotype." *Environment and Planning D: Society and Space* 24 (2006): 9–24.

Spivak, Gayatri. "Can the Subaltern Speak?" In *Marxism and the Interpretation of Culture*, ed. Cary Nelson and Lawrence Grossberg. London: Macmillan, 1988, 271–313.

Wilson, Elizabeth A. *Psychosomatic: Feminism and the Neurological Body.* Durham, NC: Duke University Press, 2004.

———. "Gut Feminism." *Differences: A Journal of Feminist Cultural Studies* 15.3 (2004): 66–94.

Young, Iris Marion. "Throwing Like a Girl: A Phenomenology of Feminine Body Comportment Motility and Spatiality." *Human Studies* 3.1 (1980): 137–56.

4

Nonlinear Evolution, Sexual Difference, and the Ontological Turn

Elizabeth Grosz's Reading of Darwin

JANET WIRTH-CAUCHON

Elizabeth Grosz is an important figure in feminist readings of matter, and the conceptualization of materiality and biology as dynamic, creative forces. Grosz's work is prominent in the turn to ontology, and the shift of attention away from a discursive critique of nature as a human construct to create alternative accounts of matter and materiality (Alaimo and Hekman, 2008; Hird, 2009). As Myra Hird points out, what distinguishes this current feminist materialism from previous work on women's material conditions is not only its inclusion of nonhuman matter, but also "its keen interest in *engagements* with matter," with "affective physicality or human-nonhuman encounters and relations" (pp. 329–330).

Grosz explores matter as process and becoming, and does so in the name of feminism that needs to, as she writes, "rethink its ontological commitments," to open up what is meant by matter, biology, and the real, since social and feminist theory depend upon these. Grosz, through a reading of Deleuze, Bergson, and Darwin, creates an account of the active, dynamic processes of materiality, of "duration in matter" (Clough, 2012, p. 96). The vitality and dynamism of matter, and the attention to process and becoming, are themes taken up in Grosz's *The Nick of Time* (2004) and *Time Travels* (2005). Grosz's reading of Darwin's theory of evolution is shaped by her adoption of Deleuze's conception of life as the unfolding of difference. Grosz contends that these dynamic processes of difference and change are what Charles Darwin's theory of evolution gives to feminist and cultural theory. Darwin did nothing less than to create an historically new concept of *life* as open-ended, ongoing development and variation: "In short, life is now construed, perhaps for the first time, as fundamental becoming, becoming without the definitive features of (Aristotelian) being, without a given (Platonic) form, without human direction or divine purpose. . . . Life informs and is informed by matter, time, becoming, difference, and repetition. Life is no longer a unique quality, an essence, but a movement" (2005, p. 37). Darwin's three principles of evolution—individual variation, heritability of the characteristics of individual variation that lead to the proliferation of species, and natural selection, are the conditions for ongoing open-ended change: She argues that "When put into dynamic interaction, these three processes provide an explanation of the dynamism, growth, and transformability of living systems, the impulse toward a future that is unknown in, and uncontained by, the present and its history" (19). Further, for Grosz, the principle of natural selection is not to be read as "survival of the fittest" narrative of superiority of winners over los-ers, since it refers to a fitness for "given *and* changing circumstances," and favors "those most open and amenable to change" (21). Change in a Darwinian evolutionary model is non-teleological, open-ended; it is not to be read as the culminating in the human as its *telos* or final pinnacle (30). Rather, culture is the "increasing elaboration and complication" of nature, with nature "providing both the means and the material for [culture's] elaboration" (47).

Grosz's reading of evolution is significant because, while turning to Darwin to understand material processes and change, it is distinctly a re-reading of Darwin, a narrative that is different from the reductive or determinist story of evolutionary inevitability or hard-wiring that is predominant in some evolutionary discourse. (See Oyama's critique, in this volume, of an evolutionary model based on "immaterial informa-tion" where genetic information is construed as a set of instructions that is expressed regardless of environmental context. This contrasts with more recent developmental systems theory with which Oyama aligns her work.)

While Grosz argues forcefully for a return to ontology and to matter, it is crucial to attend to Grosz's historicizing of ontology, her conceptual-ization of matter as dynamic and indeterminate. As Grosz writes, "'The real,' 'being,' 'materiality,' 'nature,' those terms usually associated with the unchanging, must themselves be opened up to their immaterial or extramaterial virtualities or becomings, to the temporal forces of endless change, in other words, to history, biology, culture, sexuality" (2005, p. 5). Grosz provides a more open, dynamic, historical understanding of Darwin that construes evolutionary processes as themselves continuous with cultural processes of development and change. What is distinctive about Grosz's account is its focus on historicity and temporality of this dynamism—the forward propulsion and proliferation of new forms in evolution.

In spite of this radical reading of Darwin as the open unfolding of difference, Grosz's treatment of Darwin's theory of sexual selection is more confined. Here, Grosz does not rework Darwin's theory, but rather sees it as an evolutionary support for the logic of sexual difference. Grosz treats sexual difference as a political concern, arguing that Darwin's theory of sexual selection provides a confirmation of the "irreducibility of sexual difference" and "one of the ontological characteristics of life itself, not merely a detail, a feature that will pass" (2005, p. 31). In her most recent work, *Becoming Undone: Darwinian Reflections on Life, Politics, and Art* (2011), Grosz engages a detailed reading of sexual selection in her account of Darwinian evolutionary theory. She addresses the question of difference as a form of productive relationality, "as the generative force of the world, the force that enacts materiality" (45), and argues that sexual difference is the "very mechanism for the transmission from one generation to the next of all other living differences" (111). It is sexual difference that she argues is central to, and the origin of, all other variation (118). Drawing on the arguments of Luce Irigaray, Grosz argues that "Sexual difference is the question of our age: if we had to reduce philosophy to a single question, a question that would shake ontology and bring a striking transformation of epistemology, ethics, aesthetics, and politics, it would be the question of sexual difference, the first philosophy, the philosophy that founds all others, founds all knowledges" (103). Only a feminism that is "committed to the primacy of sexual difference" can gain a full appreciation for Darwin's work on sexual selection (117).

Feminist critics have pointed to this contradiction in Grosz's work between her open account of evolution alongside her "staunch support of a fundamental ontology of sexual difference" (Weinstein, 2010, p. 166). In Luciana Parisi's detailed response to Grosz's reading of sexual selection (2009), she addresses the paradox at the heart of Grosz's reading of

Darwin between her commitment to the creativity and productivity of nonlinear, open variation, and her commitment to sexual difference and sexual selection. On the one hand, Grosz explains evolution as open-ended change and potentiality, and as Parisi writes, "for a feminism open to the virtual, the indeterminate" (44), while on the other hand, her emphasis on sexual selection and reproduction narrows change along the lines of linear descent, channeling it through parental, generational inheritance. This, according to Parisi, "may simply work to reify the ontology of identity" (39).

My concern here is Grosz's reading of sexual selection within evolution, and specifically her commitment to the centrality of sexual difference as the main engine of variation and change. While Grosz's reading of evolution is indispensible for its focus on process, change, and the creative force of nature, the focus on sexual difference and sexual selection through reproduction places limits on this vision of change, reiterating a heteronormative binary view of sexuality. In so doing, it also narrows the vision of difference and variation in nature-cultures that a Darwinian account could illuminate, including the ways that a more complex, varied view of sexuality in nonhuman nature could transform our understanding of human sexuality.

Here I examine Grosz's arguments regarding sexual selection, and then turn to materialist accounts from those drawing on Whitehead's process philosophy to arrive at a different understanding of materialist becoming and change, one that does not depend on a logic of linear evolutionary inheritance. To examine this, I turn to Parisi's critical response to Grosz's work and her use of Whitehead to broach a different model of causality, leading to a more open, nonlinear account of variation and change for the future. Parisi's Whiteheadean understanding is able to address forms of asexual reproduction and evolution that contemporary evolutionary biologists are studying. Further, Whitehead's model of temporality and causality enables a more complex account of becoming and change, shaped by a wider assemblage of forces, including the technological. In this way, the theory is able to expand the understanding of change and the construction of novel forms beyond the narrow circle of the two-sex model in reproduction.

Aesthetic Evolution: Sexual Difference and Feminist Change

In Grosz's reading of Darwin's *The Descent of Man and Selection in Relation to Sex* (1871), she analyzes the principle of sexual selection as a specific form of natural selection, defined as the selection of organisms according to their fitness for survival. In Darwin's detailed observations and examination of scientific literature, he noted particular traits and characteristics that appeared to have little or no evolutionary advantage or survival value for an organism, and yet that are passed on in subsequent generations. The principle of sexual selection states that these traits function as the means of attraction of potential mates, and that (mostly female) selection of these colorful or extravagant traits in potential (male) mates will result in an intensification of these characteristics over time. In turn, their potential maladaptiveness as to survival, or their "cost" to the animal, will also increase (2011, p. 126).

Grosz's main argument emphasizes Darwin's understanding of sexual selection as part of natural selection, but distinct from it, insofar as sexual selection is based on aesthetic criteria, "and thus is relatively independent of the principles of fitness or survival that regulate natural selection" (2011, p. 118). Whereas many contemporary readings of evolution understand sexual selection and natural selection as having the same function, as a mode of survival and of passing on genetic material, Grosz champions Darwin's conclusion that sexual selection is primarily in *excess* of pure survival. The aesthetic display and ornamentation involved in sexual reproduction is either irrelevant to, or may even threaten, survival. This is central to Grosz's reading of selection, in freeing the understanding of actions and traits from a reductive frame of adaptation and fitness to make room for aesthetic expression, variation, and creativity in relations among organisms. The element of selection or choice in this process depends on "taste" and preference of qualities that may refer either to fitness (vigor, strength, or the possession of "weapons" as Darwin put it, that are used in competitive fights with rivals)[1] or to aesthetic qualities of attraction (colorfulness, performance, display). In distinguishing these, Grosz argues, Darwin opens the potential for the intensification of beauty over sheer survival (127).

A major objection to Darwin's account is that it trades on familiar cultural narratives of male competition and female passivity. On the one hand, there are elements of Grosz's analysis that help open up sexual difference beyond the limits of a heteronormative, two-sex model. Grosz follows Darwin's descriptions of the visual and aural modes of display that various species use, including his emphasis on male traits that enable these types of display. In her critical assessment of the problem of traditional heteronormative sexual scripts in Darwin's account, Grosz points out that Darwin's close observations and review of existing studies revealed numerous exceptions to the pattern of male competition and female selection. These include the existence of female competition and concomitant male choice in some species of insects, birds, and fish (122), as well as same-sex variations (129–30). Grosz notes that "over 450 species have been identified thus far where homosexual activity has been observed" (129).

Thus, she reads the account of ornamentation, display, and competition as potentially applying to either sex, though more often to males (125). Further, Grosz argues that since sexual selection need not be linked to reproduction, but to attraction and display, it could lead to a wide variety of sexual relations (130). Grosz emphasizes female preference or choice in the process, on aesthetic grounds rather than those of "fitness" (127).

While acknowledging these potentials of Darwin's theory of sexual selection, the problem of its male-centric and hetero-centric aspects is thrown into sharper relief when we examine contemporary studies in evolutionary biology. These studies are leading biologists to raise questions about the assumptions underlying studies of sexual selection, assumptions that shape the design of research studies and the kinds of questions asked. Evolutionary biologist Patricia Gowaty argues that the science of sexual selection is constrained by traditional views of sexual behavior that emphasizes male competition and rivalry and passive female choice. While Darwin had acknowledged the alternative of male choice of female mates in some species, as well as the existence of competitive females, in the subsequent studies, "focus narrowed so that modern students of sexual selection simply assumed that males were competitive and indiscriminate and females coy, passive, and discriminating" (Gowaty and Hubbell, 2009, p. 10017). One of the sources for these assumptions was an influential 1948 study by Angus Bateman, which was marked by methodological problems that Gowaty and others are now making known (Tang-Martinez and Ryder, 2005). Bateman's study, using *Drosophila melanogaster* (fruit flies) bred for specific traits, has been widely accepted as a confirmation of the Darwinian principle of female selection of visible male traits (Snyder and Gowaty, 2007).[2] This study confirmed the existence of a pattern of male promiscuity and female passivity and monogamy. Yet a major methodological problem was that Bateman's conclusions regarding reproductive behavior (greater mating frequency in males than females) were based not on direct observations of mating behavior, but only inferred from the traits of offspring (Tang-Martinez and Ryder, 2005). Yet Bateman's model and its later developments operate as a paradigm in evolutionary biology, that "provides the fundamental underpinnings for much of the research that focuses on sexual behavior, sexual selection, parental care, and evolution of mating systems" (ibid.). Commenting on Bateman's influence, Gowaty states that "Our expectations have been so strongly influenced by Bateman. It's almost as though our imaginations were limited" (Keim, 2012).

In a significant departure from these assumptions of the Darwinian model, some contemporary research turns to the importance of environmental constraints and chance in reproduction and sexual selection. Gowaty and Hubbell, for example, argue for a broader ecological model in which reproductive behavior may be attributed to such constraints as feeding niches, predators, or spatial dispersion that shape the opportunities for reproductive encounters (2009). Further, they argue that "chance variation in ecological contingencies that may induce flexible and adaptive individual reproductive decisions" are as central to reproductive encounters as sexual selection itself (p. 10,018). They make no assumptions about underlying sex differences, and instead argue for taking into account such constraining aspects as the probability of encountering potential mates, size of the population, time constraints of chance encounters, and the time period when mates are in latency due to raising of offspring (ibid.).

When these more recent evolutionary studies are considered, we see that sexual selection of traits in isolation is not the only factor shaping reproductive decision or success. Thus, while Grosz opens an important space for non-reductive readings of evolution as a theory of non-teleological growth and change, and of the production of difference and variation, Darwin's theory of sexual selection as part of natural selection can be considered too narrow a frame to encompass the very proliferation of difference that she champions. As the studies by Gowaty and others show, sexual selection is but one element in a broader system of ecological constraints and contingencies, which interrelate to produce evolutionary variation.

If sex differences and sex selection *within* species occur in a wider ecological context, then the interactions and mutual entanglements among different species and organisms—a broader relationality—come into the foreground. As Debra Bird Rose writes, the couple in two-sex reproduction exists within "situated connectivities that bind us into multi-species communities" (quoted in Kirksey and Helmreich, 2010, p. 549). It's important therefore to conceptualize forms of relationality that are not limited to a binary model of sexual difference.

Complexity of Evolution: Parisi's Anti-Genealogy of Sexual Difference

To theorize change, and the production of new modes of existence, it is important to address novelty occurring outside the logic of linear generational causality. This requires an understanding of evolution as a process that does not depend solely on an organism's fitness for survival. While sexual selection and natural selection have their place in producing variation of species, this does not define the limits of what is originary to difference, to becoming or creation, a sphere of "creativeness" that is relational and processural, in which entities relate with and transform their environment. How can we think of becoming and evolution outside of the lockstep of cause-effect, evolutionary inheritance, and in so doing, open the account to the forms of temporal chance and openness that Grosz addresses elsewhere in her ontology in *Time Travels*? Here I turn to Luciana Parisi, who has drawn on Whitehead's ontology to respond to Grosz's work, and to offer an alternative account of variation and transformation for feminist ends that does not depend solely on sexual difference as the main engine of change (Parisi, 2009, 2006).

By reading Grosz's commitment to evolutionary, generational change through Whitehead, Parisi proposes a different timeline, marked not by the evolutionary production of difference, in "sequential timelines," but by novel forms, "transitory relations" that represent a break with the past, and that occur "outside the logic of chronos" (Parisi, 2009, p. 40). Parisi confronts gradual evolutionary change with this concept of an event that allows for "rupture," "irregular diversions," novelty that breaks from past forms, rather than the "slight variations from the past to the present" represented by evolution (39).

First, Parisi addresses the technological manipulation of matter that must be included in the evolutionary account. She argues that sexual difference is not as immutable an ontological division as Grosz (and Irigaray) hold, since in an era of genetic engineering, "sex" itself has lost its certainty, a state of affairs Parisi terms "archigenetics of sex" (Parisi, 2009, 41). The ability to manipulate matter at "molecular, nano, and subatomic scales," and "the technical re-insertion of the non-organic" into organic sex, alters the temporal unfolding of sexual difference. The very ontology of sex is thus altered, and its future formations are unknown. Sarah Franklin refers to this temporal shift in the formation of matter as the "respatialisation of genealogy"—a transformation of biology—including sex—to genetic code, since "genetic information no longer necessarily passes in a one-way, linear path of descent from one generation to the next. Rewritten as information, message, code or sequence, the gene becomes newly flexible as it also becomes differently (re)productive" (Franklin, 2000, p. 190). Technology creates what Patricia Clough terms a biomediated body that is postbiological: "the biomediated body exposes how digital technologies, such as biomedia and new media, attach to and expand the informational substrate of bodily matter and matter generally, and thereby mark the introduction of a 'postbiological threshold' into 'life itself'" (Clough, 2008, p. 2). For Parisi, archigenetics "highlights an unforeseeable, un-sensed complexity of timelines, a critical point at which the genealogy of the human species" including sexual difference and evolution, are "radically transformed" (Parisi, 2009, 40).[3]

Parisi also points to forms of biological reproduction that occur outside of sexual reproduction, including asexual bacterial gene transfer, showing that genealogical evolution misses a level of biological reproduction that sexual relations depend on. "Indeed, Darwin's emphasis on sexual division as key to the evolutionary complexification of life misses a crucial—both ontological and biological—point" (Parisi, 2009, p. 46). Drawing on Lynn Margulis's work which showed that sexed organisms emerged from the symbiotic interrelations of bacteria, a process Margulis termed "endosymbiosis," Parisi argues that "Margulis maintains that there are as many varied and versatile sexes as there are colonies of bacteria passing on genes across genealogical species" (47).

The diversity of exchanges and relations at this scale, as well as the potential of genetic manipulation and transfer through biotechnology, opens a more diversified, nonlinear field of potential for radical change (Parisi, 2009, p. 47). Grosz's privileging of sexual selection and linear descent confines what is meant by feminist change to the "gridlock of lived, physically inherited positions from the past to the present" (40). Parisi instead argues for an "anti-genealogy," a nonlinear model of evolution, where: "difference is always collective and always under construction in relation to a field of potential variations in nonlinear evolution" (Parisi, 2006, p. 33).

Parisi argues that the evolution of two sexes and of sexual difference is but a moment in a broader expansion of time and space with its potential for multiple variations of sex. She notes that this immersion of experience in a wider sphere means that all embodied experience is relational, enabling multiple potential connections. Parisi draws on Whitehead's ontology that privileges relationality as the emergence of entities *through* their entanglements with one another: "Experience, then, cannot be disentangled from what happens to all particles of a body, which are at the same time entangled in what happens to the whole of nature. Experience, therefore, is always relational, pushing the body outside its lived, organic architecture entering ecologies of virtual connections" (Parisi, 2009, p. 48).

Parisi asks how a novel event emerges from this extensive continuum. Grosz stresses that only sexual difference, and only reproductive species and relations, are capable of producing novelty: "Without sexual difference there may be life, life of the bacterial kind, life that reproduces itself as the same except for contingency or random accident, except for transcription errors at the genetic level, but there can be no newness, no inherent direction to the future and the unknown" (Grosz, 2011, p. 101).

In contrast, Whitehead would not confine processes of change or novelty to sexual selection, nor to Darwinian evolutionary principles alone. Processes of creative activity are central to his ontology, part of what he termed "creative advance" (Whitehead 1929/1978, p. 21) in which novel forms emerge. "'Creativity' is the principle of novelty. An actual occasion is a novel entity diverse from any entity in the 'many' which it unifies" (31–32).

Whitehead's concept of *prehension* is central to his speculations on the nature of creative, relational processes of change. He defines prehension as the manner in which entities "take account" of each other. If perception is "*taking account* of the essential character of the things perceived" (Whitehead, 1925, p. 97), then prehension is the noncognitive awareness of an event or object which is in the immediate past (ibid.). Like Barad's concept of intra-activity, prehension places emphasis on the event or process of relating which creates the subjects and objects of knowledge. Prehension is a concept showing the specific, situated actualization of events, the manner in which they are realized (Barad, 2007).

As Steven Shaviro points out, prehension "includes both causal relations and perceptual ones—and makes no fundamental distinction between them. Ontological equality comes from contact and mutual implication" (Shaviro, 2011, 281). Prehension is an active process, in contrast to the passivity implied in perception, as Shaviro notes (286). Entities affect or change one another, and "become what they are by prehending other entities" (281). Prehension, then, is being affected by, or feeling, another. As Steve Goodman writes, "To feel a thing is to be affected by that thing. The mode of affection, or the way the 'prehensor' is changed, is the very content of what it feels. Every event in the universe is in this sense an episode of feeling, even in the void" (Goodman, 2010, 95–96). Subjects, human and non-human, emerge as an effect of this occasion of relating. Whitehead refers to the subject in this sense as a *superject*, "one that is only born in the very course of its encounter with the world" (Shaviro, 2009, p. 21).

Parisi explains prehension as a form of temporal perception: "For Whitehead, prehensions are micro-temporal modalities of perception defining not only the feeling of past occasions in present experiences but also the way the objective existence of the present lies in the future" (48). Prehension is a process by which novel forms emerge from past forms, and, in contrast to the linear inheritance implied in evolution, can be understood as another trajectory of causality that shapes events.

The relational event of affective perception—of "contact and mutual implication"—can push events (or subjects) in new, unforeseen directions. Parisi writes that "inheritance itself is never simply neutral. Every act of inheritance involves a valuation of the data inherited on behalf of the receiving entity, valuing data 'up and down'" (1978, 224, quoted in Parisi, 2009, p. 42).

From this point of view, sexual difference is not a given, inherited from the past, but rather an emergent effect of relations, a performative process within a wider material context. It is, as Hird and Roberts write, "relationality as both immanent and intra-active, producing phenomena at every turn" (Hird and Roberts, 2011, p. 111). Whitehead's concepts of prehension and nexus are congruent with feminist accounts of relational emergence. They resonate with Haraway's concepts of "becoming-with," "companion species" (2008), and sympoeisis (2013, p. 145). Haraway, who has cited Whitehead as a major influence in her work,[4] sees species reproduction as multi-species coordination—or parasitic relations—and mutual implication. Further, not only does Whitehead's ontology enable an account of potential variations and novel forms of sex, but also expands evolution to incorporate other embodied relations and assemblages, including the technological.

Conclusion

By claiming sexual difference as the origin of all other variation including that of racial difference, Grosz's analysis reduces the potential scope of that variation. The argument that sexual difference is primary reproduces the limitations of one-dimensional feminism focused only on gender that has been superseded by intersectional feminist analysis, critical race feminism, and global feminism.[5] It is therefore not clear that calls for attention to the "real" and to biology are well-served by an analysis that gives so little attention to these other differences, that are arguably as ontologically central—and contested—as the material entanglements of race, sex, and other differences.

NOTES

I would like to thank my colleagues Maura Lyons, Vibs Petersen, and Joseph Schneider, who generously read earlier drafts and provided helpful comments.

1 Darwin writes, "There are many other structures and instincts which must have been developed through sexual selection—such as weapons of offence and the means of defence possessed by the males for fighting with and driving away their rivals—their courage and pugnacity—their ornaments of many kinds" (Darwin in *The Descent of Man*, 1:257–58, quoted in Grosz 2004, pp. 124–25).

2 See commentary by biologists Brian Snyder and Patricia Gowaty: "Despite previous criticism and equivocal support from modern studies in some species, Bateman's paper retains its place as the single most important empirical observation in sexual selection." Brian Snyder and Patricia Gowaty, "A Reappraisal of Bateman's Classic Study of Intrasexual Selection, *Evolution* 61–11: 2457–68.

3 For an analysis of Parisi's treatment of the organism as informational, see Patricia Ticeneto Clough, "Feminist Theory: Bodies, Science and Technology," *Handbook of the Body*, edited by Bryan Turner, Routledge, 2012.

4 Haraway notes that the main influences in her studies of science have been from "pragmatism and the process philosophy of Alfred North Whitehead" (Haraway, 2000, p. 21).

5 Grosz, in spite of arguing against the concepts of "intersectionality" and identity, appears to make intersectionality—the experience of one form of exclusion through that of another or multiple forms—the basis of her claim for the inclusion and centrality of sexual difference as part of examination of other forms of social marginalization. While she states that she rejects the idea that race, gender, and class are "intersecting categories or structures," she goes on to argue that "they are lived through sexed bodies and the forms of living bodies are structured through the historical and cultural meanings of race, class, ethnicity, and other forms of identity. One lives one's identities, whatever they may be, however complex their intricacies, within a sexed body" (2011, p. 109).

REFERENCES

Alaimo, Stacy, and Susan Hekman (Eds.). 2008. *Material Feminisms*. Bloomington and Indianapolis: Indiana University Press.

Barad, Karen. 2007. *Meeting the Universe Halfway: Quantum Physics and the Entanglement of Matter and Meaning*. Durham and London: Duke University Press.

Clough, Patricia T. 2008. "The Affective Turn: Political Economy, Biomedia and Bodies." *Theory, Culture, and Society* 25, no. 1, 1–22.

Clough, Patricia T. 2012. "Feminist Theory: Bodies, Science and Technology." *Handbook of the Body*, ed. Bryan Turner. New York and London: Routledge.

Franklin, Sarah. 2000. "Life Itself: Global Nature and the Genetic Imaginary." In *Global Nature, Global Culture*, ed. Sarah Franklin, Celia Lury, and Jackie Stacey. London: Sage Press.

Goodman, Steve. 2010. *Sonic Warfare: Sound, Affect, and the Ecology of Fear*. Cambridge, MA: MIT Press.

Gowaty, Patricia Adair, and Stephen P. Hubbell. 2009. "Reproductive Decisions Under Ecological Constraints: It's About Time." *Proceedings of the National Academy of Science* 106, suppl. 1, 10017–24.

Grosz, Elizabeth. 2004. *The Nick of Time: Politics, Evolution, and the Untimely*. Durham and London: Duke University Press.

Grosz, Elizabeth. 2005. *Time Travels: Feminism, Nature, Power*. Durham and London: Duke University Press.

Grosz, Elizabeth. 2008. *Chaos, Territory, Art: Deleuze and the Framing of the Earth*. New York: Columbia University Press.

Grosz, Elizabeth. 2011. *Becoming Undone: Darwinian Reflections on Life, Politics, and Art*. Durham and London: Duke University Press.

Halewood, Michael. 2005. "On Whitehead and Deleuze: The Process of Materiality." *Configurations* 13, no. 1 (Winter): 57–76.

Halewood, Michael. 2011. *A. N. Whitehead and Social Theory: Tracing a Culture of Thought*. London and New York: Anthem Press.

Halewood, Michael, and Mike Michael. 2008. "Being a Sociologist and Becoming a Whiteheadian: Toward a Concrescent Methodology." *Theory, Culture, and Society* 25, no. 4, 31–56.

Haraway, Donna. 2000. *How Like A Leaf: An Interview with Thyrza Nichols Goodeve*. New York and London: Routledge.

Haraway, Donna. 2006. "Encounters with Companion Species: Entangling Dogs, Baboons, Philosophers, and Biologists." *Configurations* 14, no. 1–2, 97–114.

Haraway, Donna. 2008. *When Species Meet*. Minneapolis: University of Minnesota Press.

Haraway, Donna. 2013. "Sowing Worlds: A Seed Bag for Terraforming with Earth Others." In *Beyond the Cyborg: Adventures with Haraway*, ed. Margaret Grebowicz and Helen Merrick. New York: Columbia University Press.

Hird, Myra. 2009. "Feminist Engagements with Matter." *Feminist Studies* 35, no. 2, 329–46.

Hird, Myra and Celia Roberts. 2011. "Feminism Theorises the Nonhuman." *Feminist Theory* 12, no. 2, 109–17.

Keim, Brandon. 2012. "Traditional Sexual Values Challenged in Classic Animal Study." *Wired Magazine Online* (July 9, 2012). Accessed February 9, 2013.

Kirksey, S. Eben and Stefan Helmreich. 2010. "The Emergence of Multispecies Ethnography." *Cultural Anthropology* 25, no. 4, 545–76.

Parisi, Luciana. 2006. "Generative Classifications." *Theory, Culture, and Society* 23, no. 2–3, 32–35.

Parisi, Luciana. 2009. "The Archigenesis of Experience." *Australian Feminist Studies* 24, no. 59 (March): 39–50.

Rose, Deborah Bird. 2009. "Introduction: Writing in the Anthropocene." *Australian Humanities Review* 49: 87.

Shaviro, Steven. 2009. *Without Criteria: Kant, Whitehead, Deleuze, and Aesthetics*. Cambridge, MA and London: MIT Press.

Shaviro, Steven. 2011. "The Actual Volcano: Whitehead, Harman, and the Problem of Relations." In *The Speculative Turn: Continental Materialism and Realism*, ed. Bryant, Levi, Nick Srnicek, and Graham Harman. Melbourne: Re.Press.

Snyder, Brian F. and Patricia Adair Gowaty. 2007. "A Reappraisal of Bateman's Classic Study of Intrasexual Selection." *Evolution* 61–11 (November): 2457–68.

Tang-Martinez, Zuleyma and T. Brandt Ryder. 2005. "The Problem with Paradigms: Bateman's Worldview as a Case Study." *Integrative and Comparative Biology* 45: 821–30.

Weinstein, Jami. 2010. "A Requiem to Sexual Difference: A Response to Luciana Parisi's "Event and Evolution." *Southern Journal of Philosophy* 48, Spindel Supplement: 165–87.

Whitehead, Alfred North. 1925. *Science and the Modern World*. New York: Macmillan.

Whitehead, Alfred North. 1929/1978. *Process and Reality*. New York: Free Press.

Whitehead, Alfred North. 1933/1967. *Adventures of Ideas*. New York: Free Press.

PART II

Nature/Culture in the Twenty-First Century Sciences

5

The Lure of Immateriality in Accounts of Development and Evolution

SUSAN OYAMA

Logos, Biologos

In some cosmologies, primordial chaos was organized by a nonmaterial principle of reason and order. *Logos*, the Word, fashioned inchoate matter into a living world. This understanding is still pervasive, and persuasive to many, even in biology, the very science of life. My focus is on a manifestation I call *Biologos*. Like the Logos of philosophy and theology, Biologos is seen to invest matter with form and significance, even with life itself.

The coinage is not mine alone. Its parts fall readily into place, and two other relevant instances come from the geneticist Francis Collins, whose *BioLogos* was conceived in a radically different spirit but supports the analysis sketched below, and anthropologist Tim Ingold, who addresses a broader context with his *bio-logos*.[1] Collins became head of the United States' National Institutes of Health after directing the Human Genome Project. Neither spurning evolutionary theory for contravening Biblical teachings (as conservative creationists and believers in "intelligent design" are wont to) nor separating religion from science, he is a "theistic evolutionist," for whom Christian devotion is compatible with Darwinism.[2] Indeed, he experiences his religion as a call to celebrate the marvels of evolution. Collins's vocabulary is largely standard in secular biology as well; it exemplifies the field's *language of language,* and the seamless joining of his professional and confessional writings aids my argument that they spring from similar metaphysical underpinnings, intuitions, and impulses. Genetic *codes, transcripts,* and *translations,* far from being products of journalistic license, in fact belong to biology's laboratory lexicon, some of which has moved into informal speech, where it joins the more frankly figurative *recipes* and *libraries* in the genome. Genes "as an instructional script, a software program" are solidly mainstream, and Collins is hardly introducing a novel rhetorical frame with "the DNA language by which God spoke life into being."[3] He wishes us to take it literally, though, at least enough to dispel discomfort at his juxtaposition of devoutness and science. Unlike my Biologos, his BioLogos is thus innocent of irony. Tim Ingold, by contrast, shares my skepticism of the infocentric romance, and more generally, questions the West's approach to the natural sciences.[4]

My own qualms about Biologos came from examining a variety of informational accounts that purported to explain biological processes, but tended instead to divert attention from the very objects that needed illumination, all the while slighting those objects' interactions with their particular surrounds. In the ancient dualisms, matter is contrasted with form, idea, and mind—indeed, with language itself—and perpetually risks becoming mere medium. Yet despite such minimization, life processes are obviously intensely material: tissue propinquities, molecular conjunctions and blockages, organisms (including scientists) impinging on each other and on their inanimate surroundings.[5] *Attending* to them renders Biologos's infotalk incongrous and redundant, turning our gaze toward the constructive—and destructive—interactions (inside organisms and between them and their surroundings) by which beings and their worlds are made and remade.[6] Doing justice to life processes requires taking seriously the embeddedness and embodiment of beings. Only in material bodies and worlds can bits of nucleic acid *become* the functional complexes we call genes, and thus play a part in development, and eventually, evolution.[7]

An intriguing comparison can be made between writings from two contemporary Christian traditions (theistic evolutionists and the fundamentalist groups mentioned above), and certain biologists and philosophers of biology.[8] Despite their divergent aims, these discourses are united by several themes: information as a source of creative order; a tamer of chance; the origin of value, meaning, and direction; and as a supplement to matter and energy. I intend Biologos to encompass the terms, metaphors, assumptions, and narrative habits organized by and expressing these themes; its ruling trope is life as language, and Collins has his eyes open when he treats it literally. It's less clear what some aggressively secular neo-Darwinists are up to when they cite purportedly materialist modern biology to repudiate vitalism, essentialism, and preformationism, then present that biology's findings in terms that are curiously vitalistic, essentialist, and preformationist.[9] Richard Dawkins denies that genetic algorithms and programs are metaphorical, insisting that seeds actually carry "instructions for making themselves."[10] Like their religious adversaries, these "atheistic evolutionists"[11] populate their writings with nonphysical, prescient powers that can create organisms, apparently without the fuss of material embroilment. To Dawkins, DNA is temporal but not spatial, a "river" of "abstract instructions" coursing through bodies and affecting them while itself remaining "uninfluenced by the experiences and achievements of the successive bodies through which it flows." Life, in fact, is just digitized bytes ("and bytes and bytes"). And for George Williams, genes aren't really DNA (which is just their patterned medium) but *information*, in a "codical domain" of "bits, redundancy, fidelity, and meaning," not a material one of "color, charge, density, volume, etc." Noting the difficulties of defining life, Daniel Koshland, former editor of *Science*, did stress its kinetic, thermodynamic character. Yet the first of his seven "pillars" of life doesn't come from physics; it's a genetic program.[12]

This infophilia is conspicuous and undoubtedly overdetermined (by, for a start, entwined histories of molecular biology, systems theories, cognitive and computer science, especially artificial life and robotics, along with a dollop of physics envy). Less notice, perhaps, has been taken of the hylephobia that can attend it. Vital forces were traditionally nonmaterial, but what seems to repel Dawkins is matter itself, rank and damp: "there is no spirit-driven life force, no throbbing, heaving, pullulating, protoplasmic, mystic jelly."[13]

To some extent the atheistic evolutionists appear to be playing "anything your God can do mine can do better," but the upshot is that their privileging of the incorporeal is at odds with their materialism, marginalizing the living matter that is its ostensible subject. There's more. Biology is thought to reveal our true natures, as species and individuals, and Biologos is Nature's voice. Scientists devise refined techniques for parsing her utterances, arranging crucial comparisons and statistically distinguishing "biological bases" from mere noise.[14] Despite much critique, even dismissal, of nature-nurture dualisms, then, despite increasingly nuanced scientific reports and ever-greater public sophistication about genes,[15] the old queries about the relative importance of biological or cultural causes abound. Sometimes these are couched in "softer" terms of genetic potentials and propensities, sometimes not.[16] My question is, Why/how do these contrasts remain so tenaciously in evidence?

Infophilia and Development

Consider a mutually reinforcing triad of infocentric understandings: of heredity as transmission of genes "through" organisms; development as their "expression"; and evolution as change in gene frequencies. If ontogeny is just the read-out of preexisting genetic information, it would seem that it can have scant import in the phylogenetic drama. Recasting the triad in terms of Developmental Systems Theory (DST), however, directs us to the spatial and temporal particulars of formative interactions, and thus to organisms and their multi-scaled, mobile environments. We move from a codical biology to one more welcoming to the stuff of life and its intimate contexts.[17] *Heredity* now includes a miscellany of internal and external developmental resources (*interactants*) affecting the organism; *development* is the interdependent constructive processes that make, maintain, and alter it; and *evolution* is change in these organism-environment (developmental) systems (DSs). We needn't continue distinguishing between innate (genetic) and acquired (environmental) characters. No *interactant* (developmental resource) contains representations of what that organism will, could, or should be. None has the causal powers to create it virtually de novo, which is what a naked packet of "transmitted" information would need; nor are the nuclei (or the cells) little executive control centers. Organisms emerge in cascades of systemic contingencies. Once shifting allele frequencies are replaced by overlapping DSs, gene pools are restored to flesh—*re-incarnated* in living beings—and evolution is change in the constitution and distribution of developmental systems. Interactants become available (are inherited, in a variety of ways); traits and organisms—phenotypes—must be constructed. Nature-nurture dualities can be dismantled, and with them, Biologos's preformationism, essentialism, and nonmaterial causes.

A DS is a changing organism *and its changing developmental environments*—everything Biologos encourages us to ignore.[18] At intracellular scales, it includes bumpy molecules in crowded and graded milieus, altering their conformation, displacing each other, bringing disparate bits into conjunction. Ontogenetic processes also cross bodily boundaries: zoom out and we have organisms shading, invading, seeking each other, and engaging with their abiotic surrounds. Once we have actual chemicals, tissues, and active organisms and/with/in their worlds, discarnate programs and instructions become superfluous. Disordered oppositions cede to "natures" that are just the organisms themselves, always in flux, and to a "nurture" that is the totality of developmental interactions from which those phenotypic natures-in-transition are made: the varying products of ontogeny. Interactions are system-dependent even as they affect the system, and to develop is to help "make" a world for oneself and others, in ways benign and otherwise.

Rather than starting with Biologos's vision of discrete individuals whose basic properties exist (typically as genetic representations) without reference to their histories or surroundings, DST shows organisms in continuous, mutually transforming commerce with their environments, including other organisms. Defined as "pertaining to life," furthermore, biology embraces the social as one of its aspects, not its contrast. Pertinent environments are defined (indeed, they arise *as such*) relative to the organism, and vice versa. Boundaries can be fluid and permeable: even our experienced bodily limits are quite inconstant, sometimes including phantom limbs and prosthetics, or the car whose perimeter we experience as our own. We construct the worlds in and from which we develop, by interacting, detecting some things but not others, being a given size and in a given place, being susceptible only to certain influences.[19]

Incidence and Essence

DST primer in place, let's look at two related aspects of Biologos I call *incidence* and *essence*. *Incidence* refers to patterns of occurrence or other features thought to indicate (degrees of) genetic or "biological" causation—frequency within and among groups, correlations among relatives, presence at birth, relative fixity, etc. It is, roughly, empirical, though ambiguous nature-nurture terms make it hard to be precise about both issues and evidence.[20] *Essence* is related to incidence, but is distinguishable yet seldom explicitly mentioned, so its mischief percolates largely below critical radar. Genetic representations—information, instructions—are not only thought to explain matters of incidence (the "biologically based," "innate," "inherent," etc.), but also to specify what we most truly *are*. What's innate isn't always inevitable, we're told, so natures may not be (fully) "expressed," but because they're in our genes, they're still assumed to be *there*, even if hidden (in ways the "acquired" is not). Crude determinism can thus be avoided, while a conviction remains that the rock-bottom real is carried in textual DNA, behind the phenotypic flux.

Years ago I met a graduate student who had been inspired to go into the field of evolutionary biology by a paper presenting menstruation as a target and product of natural selection, an evolutionary adaptation. She was transported with an excitement that seemed neither ordinary intellectual enthusiasm nor drawn from the usual takes on female nature.[21] Conceiving her cycles as naturally selected seemed to have altered their meaning, even her sense of herself as a woman. Perhaps the evolutionary narrative dignified an occasionally onerous, even embarassing part of her existence, the way discovering an illustrious ancestor promises to redeem one's own sorry life. But what nature giveth, nature can take away. Philosopher Elizabeth Lloyd revived a debate on the female orgasm that dated at least to polemics on the science and politics of human evolution in the 1970s and '80s. While the male orgasm must be an adaptation, it had been argued, women's haven't been selected *for* but are mere side effects without evolutionary function, like male nipples. The dispute was highly charged, and not only in the customary manner of intellectual conflict. "Not adaptive," for some commentators, was not just about the niceties of natural selection. It was an androcentric slur. It meant "not important," "not useful," threatening to diminish the very meaning of female experience.[22] For this unhappy group, a claim that women's orgasms weren't an adaptation struck a blow at feminine nature. For some, perhaps, an adaptive story of one's own is as important as a room.

Earlier I mentioned claims that essentialist ("typological") thinking is outdated.[23] Nevertheless, people commonly assume a species core, as well as innate individual variations (your "genetic" shyness defines *you*, even after assertiveness training has stiffened your spine a bit). Such natures are treated as present whether or not they are evident, as internally represented in the DNA. In philosophers' language, representations are *intentional*: they are *about* something. They're normative, as well, for with representation comes the possibility of *mis*representation. Biologos seems to specify what nature intended, and if phenotypes can misrepresent their genotypes, some of us are surely mistakes, nature *misread*. Natures, in this view, may be hidden, or only partially manifest, and notions of genetic potential or predisposition suggest that when incidence and essence diverge, it may be essence that counts.

Essences are thus not trivial; because they bear on being and meaning, they're politically and morally loaded. I've referred to the way that genes have shed some of their air of fixity over the years, and *DNA*, at least, has arguably become less a marker of destiny and more an emblem of identity. We now hear of the DNA of the army, a nation, a corporation, even of a designer's label. Indeed, it seems increasingly to be synonymous with "brand." In both the menstruation and the orgasm examples, I believe it was an essentialist reading of Biologos that was operative, and it was anxiety about the normativity of natures that stoked some women's ire, as it has for decades. Yet like *incidence*'s often questionable messages of inevitability and intractability, *essence*'s deep and timeless truths diminish in plausibility once the genes, like other interactants, are understood as always enmeshed in developmental systems.

Is Nature Nasty or Nice?

It has become clear to many that the best antidote for a noxious account of biologically fixed sexual essence is not a set of (just as good? better? nicer?) counteressences. Nor is a view of human life organized by such inherent natures most effectively met with "social constructions," biology's mirror images, shaped from the outside rather than the inside, arbitrary, not necessary. Indeed, feminist scholars have for some time been proposing less constricting, more congenial understandings of biology and the material body.[24] This is not to say that there are no empirical regularities, only that like other research findings, they must be precisely described, treated with caution and modesty, their variability (or its lack) noted and probed; they are to be taken as occasions for further questioning, rather than as evidence for or against some privileged kind of causation (if we are focused on incidence), or for a similarly privileged intrinsic truth (if we are tracking essences instead).

Because connectedness and interdependence in nature are sometimes associated with cooperation, empathy, harmony, or stewardship, some assume that interactions of the sort described here are less aggressive or competitive than those featured in more traditional treatments, especially evolutionary ones: meta-level counterparts to romanticized femininity, perhaps, a rebuke to the mythologized masculine. DST, such people might think, offers a kinder, more collaborative world.[25]

Having contended for years with Biologos's descriptions, prescriptions, and dispensations, I would obviously balk at the idea of reading biology, including my own version, in such ways. Competition and exploitation are made possible and tempting only by interdependent circumstances and fortunes. Entrenched corruption is entrenched precisely because participants' resources, situations, and prospects are linked; it runs like a faithfully oiled machine (cooperatively and harmoniously, if you will). Empathy and generosity can and do arise in a connected world, and I would be happy to encourage them (though warily, for they too have their shadow sides and are hardly context-independent virtues). Yet the most brutal lifeboat ethics also emerge just because we're all in this together. The coupled contingencies and understandings supporting abuse and torture can be both complex and subtle: if you have never suffered from intimate, precisely calibrated cruelty, consider yourself fortunate.

People have long sought to characterize the grand panorama of nature in moral (or at least prescriptive) terms, and at times biologists have been only too eager to assist. It is thus necessary to end this excursion into Biologos, materialism, theoretical frameworks, and the metaphysics of the DNA, on this cautionary note. DST, while it has often been contrasted with standard evolutionary theory, does not, by invoking material dependencies and interconnected interactions, offer a kinder, gentler vision of life, although it doesn't regard kindness and gentleness as necessarily fraudulent or instrumental when they occur. If my work has normative "lessons," they are largely negative: blocked inferences and conclusions, invalidated implications. This is not to deny that there are subtler points to be made, or that science is infused with values and enmeshed in the micro- or macro-politics of the day; my own predilections are no doubt legible between these very lines. But such topics are for another time.[26] What I present here is a various and mutable world, by turns plastic and maddeningly recalcitrant, whose reliability can be enabled by dense relations that can turn in an instant to cascading disaster, whose fate and meaning are not to be divined in molecular runes, but must be, at every moment and in every place, made, remade. Making is neither arbitrary nor avoidable. It always takes place in ongoing enabling, constraining, growing, degenerating worlds. Intimately reintegrated with their surrounds by way of systems of living and nonliving interactants, organisms regain their full dimensions.

NOTES

1 Collins, *Language of God*; Ingold, *Perception of the Environment*.

2 Haught's term, in *God After Darwin*, 72–73, where he describes these three stances.

3 Collins, *Language of God*, 101, 123.

4 Ingold, *Perception of the Environment*, 19, 383.

5 Myers, "Animating Mechanism."

6 On interactionism see Barad, "Quantum Entanglements," note 1, 267: Oyama, *Ontogeny of Information*, 6–7 and "Terms in Tension."

7 Gottlieb, *Synthesizing Nature-Nurture*; Keller, *Century of the Gene*, ch. 1, 2; Moss, *What Genes Can't Do*; Oyama, *Ontogeny*.

8 Oyama, "Compromising Positions" and "Biologists Behaving Badly."

9 Philosopher Daniel Dennett extols "Darwinism triumphant, reductionism triumphant, mechanism triumphant, materialism triumphant" in *Darwin's Dangerous Idea*, 195; see also Dawkins, *River Out of Eden*, 17–18; and Williams, *Natural Selection*, 4. That vitalism was historically antireductionist only increases the muddle.

10 Dawkins, *Blind Watchmaker*, 111. The language, as pointed out earlier, is still current. That it is typically taken literally even without being explicitly so labeled testifies to the broad acceptance of infotalk as straightforwardly nonfigurative.

11 See Oyama, "Compromising." Criteria for inclusion in the discussion were public advocacy of standard neo-Darwinian theory, implied or explicit atheism, and, of course, ardent infophilia.

12 Dawkins, *River*, 4, 19; Williams, *Natural Selection*, 10–11; Koshland, "Seven Pillars of Life."

13 Dawkins, *River*, 17–18. Steven Pinker relegates complexity and self-organization to the vitalist trash heap in *How the Mind Works*, 4. See Hayles, *How We Became Posthuman*, 51, on the "triumph of information over materiality." For more history and analysis see Heims, *The Cybernetics Group*; Kay, *Who Wrote the Book of Life?*; Nelkin and Lindee, *The DNA Mystique*; and Rehmann-Sutter, "Genetics, Embodiment and Identity." On goo, see Grosz, *Volatile Bodies*, 194–95, and for a luxuri-

antly "involutionary"reading of chemical ecology (appreciative of pullulation *and* viscosity both), see Hustak and Myers, "Involutionary Momentum."

14 Oyama, "Speaking of Nature."

15 Condit, Ofulue, and Sheedy, "Determinism and Mass-Media Portrayals of Genetics."

16 Bateson and Mameli, "The Innate and the Acquired"; Oyama, *Ontogeny* (especially ch. 4) and *Evolution's Eye*, ch. 3, 5.

17 Van der Weele, *Images of Development*; Gilbert and Epel's (still somewhat infocentric) *Ecological Developmental Biology*. On conceptual circuits, see Oyama, "Sustainable Development," and on the transmission image, Oyama, *Evolution's Eye*, 12–14, ch. 1.

(The precise formulations in the last two sources are not necessarily shared by all Developmental Systems theorists.)

18 In *Beyond the Gene*, 49, Sapp remarks that the "genotype/phenotype distinction offered geneticists the conceptual space or route by which they could bypass the organization of the cell, regulation by the internal and external environment of the organism, and the temporal and orderly sequences during development." On the history of heredity concepts see Müller-Wille and Rheinberger, *Heredity Produced*.

19 Lewontin, "Gene, Organism and Environment"; Oyama, "Boundaries"; Sharma, *It Depends*.

20 Oyama, *Evolution's Eye*, ch. 7.

21 Takes that feminists have at various times denied, embraced, reversed, revised, even disassembled. Echols charts earlier vicissitudes of essentialism in *Daring to Be Bad*, 362–63. Some feminist scholars have found DST useful for avoiding the charms and snares of Biologos while still addressing scientifically, psychologically, and politically fraught issues; a sampling shows how this plays out in particular settings: Burlein, "The Productive Power of Ambiguity"; Fausto-Sterling, *Sexing the Body*; Waldby and Squier, "Ontogeny, Ontology and Phylogeny." Feminists' animus toward biology has largely been driven by that discipline's identification with determinism and essentialism (that is, with certain patterns of incidence and with essence), but one can, with the right headings, steer clear of fates and internally represented natures without rejecting a field that can offer much.

22 Lloyd, *Female Orgasm*. For her criticisms of such offended misconstruals of the "side effect" argument she favors, see 19, 139–42.

23 Sober, "Evolution, Population Thinking, and Essentialism."

24 Grosz, *Volatile Bodies* and *The Nick of Time*; Wilson, *Psychosomatic*.

25 Interpretations of systems are historically diverse, sometimes stressing technocratic control, sometimes analogizing organisms to ecosystems, and so on. See Hammond, *Science of Synthesis*, 150, 272; Oyama, "Terms in Tension;" Taylor, "Distributed Agency." At a different scale, see Sapp on cells as democracies or as empires ruled by master molecules, *Beyond the Gene*, 196–211. The latter view marginalized the cytoplasm, environment to those molecules.

26 Oyama, "Sustainable."

REFERENCES

Barad, Karen. "Quantum Entanglements and Hauntological Relations of Inheritance: Dis/continuities, SpaceTime Enfoldings, and Justice-to-Come." *Derrida Today* 3, no. 2 (2010), 240–68.

Bateson, Patrick and Matteo Mameli. "The Innate and the Acquired: Useful Clusters or a Residual Distinction from Folk Biology?" *Developmental Psychobiology* 49 (2007): 818–31.

Burlein, Ann. "The Productive Power of Ambiguity: Rethinking Homosexuality through the Virtual and Developmental Systems Theory." *Hypatia* 20, no. 1 (2005): 21–53.

Collins, Francis S. *The Language of God: A Scientist Presents Evidence for Belief.* New York: Free Press, 2006.

Condit, Celeste M., Ofulue, Nneka, and Sheedy, Kristine M. "Determinism and Mass-Media Portrayals of Genetics." *AJHG* 62 (1998): 979–84.

Dawkins, Richard. *The Blind Watchmaker.* New York: Norton, 1986.

———. *River Out of Eden: A Darwinian View of Life.* New York: Basic Books, 1995.

Dennett, Daniel C. *Darwin's Dangerous Idea: Evolution and the Meanings of Life.* New York: Simon & Schuster, 1995.

Echols, Alice. *Daring to Be Bad: Radical Feminism in America 1967–1975.* Minneapolis: University of Minnesota Press, 1989.

Fausto-Sterling, Anne. *Sexing the Body: Gender Politics and the Construction of Sexuality.* New York: Basic Books, 2000.

Gilbert, Scott F. and David Epel. *Ecological Developmental Biology: Integrating Epigenetics, Medicine, and Evolution.* Sunderland: Sinauer Associates, 2009.

Gottlieb, Gilbert. *Synthesizing Nature-Nurture: Prenatal Roots of Instinctive Behavior.* Mahwah, NJ: Lawrence Erlbaum Associates, 1997.

Grosz, Elizabeth. *Volatile Bodies: Toward a Corporeal Feminism.* Bloomington and Indianapolis: Indiana University Press, 1994.

———. *The Nick of Time: Politics, Evolution, and the Untimely.* Durham, NC: Duke University Press, 2004.

Hammond, Debora. *The Science of Synthesis: Exploring the Social Implications of General Systems Theory.* Boulder: University Press of Colorado, 2003.

Haught, John F. *God after Darwin: A Theology of Evolution.* Boulder, CO: Westview Press, 2000.

Hayles, N. Katherine. *How We Became Posthuman: Virtual Bodies in Cybernetics, Literature, and Informatics.* Chicago: University of Chicago Press, 1999.

Heims, Steve J. *The Cybernetics Group.* Cambridge, MA: MIT Press, 1991.

Hustak, Carla and Natasha Myers. "Involutionary Momentum: Affective Ecologies and the Sciences of Plant/Insect Encounters." *d i f f e r e n c e s: A Journal of Feminist Cultural Studies* 23, no. 3 (2012): 74–118. DOI: 10.1215/10407391-1892907

Ingold, Tim. *The Perception of the Environment: Essays on Livelihood, Dwelling and Skill.* London and New York: Routledge, 2000.

Kay, Lily E. *Who Wrote the Book of Life? A History of the Genetic Code*. Stanford: Stanford University Press, 2000.

Keller, Evelyn F. *The Century of the Gene*. Cambridge, MA: Harvard University Press, 2000.

Koshland, Daniel E., Jr. "The Seven Pillars of Life." *Science* 295 (March 22, 2002): 2215–16. DOI: 10.1126/science.1068489

Lewontin, Richard C. "Gene, Organism and Environment." In Derek S. Bendall, ed., *Evolution from Molecules to Men*, 273–85. Cambridge: Cambridge University Press, 1983. Reprinted in Susan Oyama, Paul E. Griffiths, and Russell D. Gray, eds., *Cycles of Contingency: Developmental Systems and Evolution*, 59–66. Cambridge, MA: MIT Press, 2001.

Lloyd, Elizabeth A. *The Case of the Female Orgasm: Bias in the Science of Evolution*. Cambridge, MA: Harvard University Press, 2005.

Moss, Lenny. *What Genes Can't Do*. Cambridge, MA: MIT/Bradford, 2003.

Müller-Wille, Staffan and Hans-Jörg Rheinberger, eds. *Heredity Produced: At the Crossroads of Biology, Politics, and Culture, 1500–1780*. Cambridge, MA: MIT Press, 2007.

Myers, Natasha. "Animating Mechanism: Animations and the Propagation of Affect in the Lively Arts of Protein Modelling." *Science Studies* 19, no. 2 (2006): 6–30.

Nelkin, Dorothy and M. Susan Lindee. *The DNA Mystique: The Gene as a Cultural Icon*. New York: W. H. Freeman, 1995.

Oyama, Susan. *The Ontogeny of Information: Developmental Systems and Evolution*, 2nd ed. Durham, NC: Duke University Press, 2000.

———. *Evolution's Eye: A Systems View of the Biology-Culture Divide*. Durham, NC: Duke University Press, 2000.

———. "Terms in Tension: What Do You Do When All the Good Words Are Taken?" In Susan Oyama, Paul E. Griffiths, and Russell D. Gray, eds., *Cycles of Contingency: Developmental Systems and Evolution*, 177–93. Cambridge, MA: MIT Press, 2001.

———. "Boundaries and (Constructive) Interaction." In Eva M. Neumann-Held and Christoph Rehmann-Sutter, eds., *Genes in Development. Re-reading the Molecular Paradigm*, 272–89. Durham, NC: Duke University Press, 2006.

———. "Speaking of Nature." In Chuck Dyke and Yrjö Haila, eds., *How Does Nature Speak? Dynamics of the Human Ecological Condition*, 49–65. Durham, NC: Duke University Press, 2006.

———. "Compromising Positions: The Minding of Matter." In Anouk Barberousse, Michel Morange, and Thomas Pradeu, eds., *Mapping the Future of Biology: Evolving Concepts and Theories*, 27–45. Boston Studies in the Philosophy of Science, Vol. 266. Dordrecht: Springer Verlag, 2009.

———. "Biologists Behaving Badly: Vitalism and the Language of Language." *History and Philosophy of the Life Sciences* 32 (2010): 401–24.

———. "Sustainable Development: Living in Systems." In Bruce Clarke, ed., *Earth, Life & System:Evolution and Ecology on a Gaian Planet*, 203–24. New York: Fordham University Press, 2015.

Pinker, Steven. *How the Mind Works*. New York: Norton, 1997.

Rehmann-Sutter, Christoph. "Genetics, Embodiment and Identity." In Armin Grunwald, Mathias Gutmann, and Eva M. Neumann-Held, eds., *On Human Nature: Anthropological, Biological, and Philosophical Foundations*, 23–50. Berlin: Springer Verlag, 2006.

Sapp, Jan. *Beyond the Gene: Cytoplasmic Inheritance and the Struggle for Authority in Genetics*. Oxford: Oxford University Press, 1987.

Sharma, Kriti. *It Depends: Contingent Existence and Life As We Know It*. New York: Fordham University Press, 2015.

Sober, Elliott. "Evolution, Population Thinking, and Essentialism." *Philosophy of Science* 47 (1980): 350–83.

Taylor, Peter J. "Distributed Agency within Intersecting Ecological, Social, and Scientific Processes." In Susan Oyama, Paul E. Griffiths, and Russell D. Gray, eds., *Cycles of Contingency: Developmental Systems and Evolution*, 313–32. Cambridge, MA: MIT Press, 2001.

van der Weele, Cor. *Images of Development: Environmental Causes in Ontogeny*. Albany: State University of New York Press, 1999.

Waldby, Catherine and Susan Squier. "Ontogeny, Ontology and Phylogeny: Embryonic Life and Stem Cell Technologies." *Configurations* 11 (2003): 27–46.

Williams, George C. *Natural Selection: Domains, Levels, and Challenges*. Oxford: Oxford University Press, 1992.

Wilson, Elizabeth A. *Psychosomatic: Feminism and the Neurological Body*. Durham, NC: Duke University Press, 2004.

6

Embodying Intersectionality

The Promise (and Peril) of Epigenetics for
Feminist Science Studies

LISA H. WEASEL

Intersectionality has been a powerful concept for feminist theorizing. Developed and brought to the fore by generations of black feminist theorists and activists (e.g., Combahee River Collective 1978; Collins 1990; Crenshaw 1989) and expanded upon ever since, the notion of interlocking oppressions constituted within matrices of domination has provided a nuanced, three-dimensional understanding of the differences in privilege and power that manifest in women's individual and collective lived experiences. The recognition that oppressions and privileges along intersecting vectors of gender, race, class, sexuality, ability, and other categories are intermeshed and cannot be isolated from one another or understood as simply additive has sometimes been challenging within feminist analytical frames focusing exclusively on social construction. Even when the tensions of multiple vectors of privilege and oppression can be held simultaneously in social analyses, their origins and diffractions are nonetheless still considered to stem from different sources, such as sexism and racism, albeit theorized as coalesced and inseparable in the experience of the individual.

While the social analysis of intersectionality has received a great deal of attention within feminist theorizing, far less attention has been given to the material manifestations of intersectionality, particularly the embodiment of intersectional experience. Certainly, mainstream conceptions of the material and embodied associations of frequently invoked social categories such as gender, race, class, sexuality, and ability activated in intersectional analyses have a long and distasteful history, dominated by a reductionist science and medical discourse. But, I will argue, retaining intersectionality primarily as an artifact of social construction, and ignoring the co-construction of material, embodied manifestions of intersectional identities, limits theory and constrains efforts to combat the very intertwined oppressions and injustices that intersectionality brings to light.

In the same way that intersectionality as a tool of social analysis has proven powerful for dismantling binaries and oppositions envisioned within social realms, we can also draw on its conceptual strength to reimagine and reconfigure the relationship between the social and material in the analysis of power and oppression, transforming the relationship between social and material from one of binary opposition to one of mutual co-construction and interstitial enactment. As Karen Barad says, "we need a method for theorizing the relationship between 'the natural' and 'the social' together without defining one against the other or holding either nature or culture as the fixed referent for understanding the other" (2007, 30).

Here, I want to posit an unsuspecting source for the seeds of such an intersectional, socio-material revisioning of power, privilege, and identity: science itself. While feminist science studies has emerged as a subdiscipline within the feminist academic canon and has generated a substantial body of discursive critique of mainstream science, there is a need to continue to theorize from an intersectional, feminist perspective within the scientific realm of materiality. As Stacy Alaimo and Susan Hekman state in their introduction to the anthology *Material Feminisms*, "While no one would deny the ongoing importance of discursive critique and rearticulation for feminist scholarship and feminist politics, the discursive realm is nearly always constituted so as to foreclose attention to lived, material bodies and evolving corporeal practices" (2008, 3). Even interdisciplinary social science fields (such as geography) that attempt to integrate the social/natural divide, have "black-boxed the material, biochemical body" (Guthman & Mansfield 2012, 2). There is a deep and serious need to identify productive interstices within the natural sciences for feminist participation and engagement. Without a critical, intersectional feminist lens and framework that meets science (and scientists—whether feminist or not) where they are at—with materiality solidly at the fore—feminist science studies will remain limited in its ability to participate in the co-construction of scientific knowledge.

Prominent feminist science studies theorists have contributed, and indeed brought to the forefront, the need to understand matter (Barad 2007), and specifically biological matter as well as non-human actors (Haraway 1989, 2003, 2008) as active agents and equal participants in material-semiotic interactions. Yet there remain few examples of how such theoretical frameworks might find expression in, or be extrapolated to, the everyday practice of the natural sciences. Such a translation of feminist science studies theorizing of the intersectionality of material and social forces into actual scientific practice is politically important for feminists who value social change and justice, as the natural sciences, in theory and in practice, hold significant power to impact and shape both policymaking and the lived existence of the collective material-semiotic actorship to which we belong.

Here, I want to draw on epigenetics, an emerging discipline within molecular biology and genetics, as a resource for an intersectional socio-material theory and practice of feminist science that integrates the interplay between internal and external forces in the enactment and experience of power and privilege. Epigenetics has generated a great deal of attention from the media and through it, the general public (e.g., Cloud, 2010; Davey Smith 2012; Paul 2010); from scientists who often proclaim it a "new paradigm" (e.g., Vineis, 2009; Ebrahim 2012); and from science and technology scholars who have critically interrogated its unfolding and trajectories (e.g., contributors in Richardson and Stevens 2015; Landecker 2011; Mansfield 2012; Mansfield and Guthman 2015). Intersectional feminist engagement with epigenetics becomes all the more important as the expanding embrace and landscape of epigenetics continues to forge forward.

From Critique to Co-Construction: The Path to the Post-Genomic Era

What has come to be known as the "post-genomic" era has emerged in parallel and consistent with feminist critiques of the reductionist, essentialist constraints of the strict genetic determinism symbolized by the prior decades—plus "race" to sequence the human genome. Feminist scholars, many of them trained in the natural sciences, including Evelyn Fox Keller, Ruth Hubbard, Anne Fausto-Sterling, Ruth Bleier, and Bonnie Spanier, have provided direct and incising critiques of how an insistence on a rigid, fixed, and predeterministic material genome constrains and reinforces social categories such as gender, race, class, and the attendant socio-material consequences of such views. Such criticisms have not been limited to feminists; Richard Lewontin, a Harvard geneticist, has been one of the most prominent critics of the reductionist molecular biology paradigm that prioritizes the material sequence of DNA above all else in the determination of identity.

If we are to believe in the validity of our feminist critiques within a materialist context, then we must also anticipate that there could be "outs," alternative cuts through the same messy terrain, enabling new materializations of meaning that take us beyond critique and into the territory of [re]construction. And, we must hope that these routes will emerge eventually and spontaneously, not only at feminist insistence, but because materiality, as an agent in and of its own making, will resist the constraints of a singular social construction. As Barad states, such "changes in the apparatuses of bodily production matter for ontological as well as epistemological reasons: different material-discursive practices produce different material configurings of the world . . . they do not merely produce different descriptions" (Barad 2007, 184).

The rumblings of such a shift are now beginning to be heard within what is commonly called "post-genomic" science. The limitations of the discursive practices of genomic science and their associated materially enacted boundaries, properties, and meanings have become clear not just to the critical eye of feminists, but even to experimentalists committed to a reductionist DNA-driven genomic paradigm. The promises of the human genome project have largely failed to materialize; its nucleotide sequence has not provided the divined insight into human identity, nor has it adequately explained the legion of health conditions it was presumed to control (notwithstanding the saliency and legitimacy of such framings in the first place). Emerging out of these limitations, new material-discursive practices are being enacted within and through the science of epigenetics, producing not merely different descriptions of the world, but indeed different material configurations with the potential to participate in the active unfolding of political outcomes important to feminists. Biologists Richard Lewontin and Richard Levins preface this theoretical shift away from the scientific construction of the material exclusivity of DNA as a self-reproducing manufacturer of a determinist social fate, to a more complex, intersectional understanding of life. "A living organism at any moment in its life is the unique consequence of a developmental history that results from the interaction of and determination by internal and external forces. The external forces, what we usually think of as "environment," are themselves partly a consequence of the organism itself as it produces and consumes the conditions of its own existence. Organisms do not find the world in which they develop. They make it" (Lewontin and Levins 2007, 242).

As Sara Shostak and Margot Moinester (2015) point out, the integrative, intersectional potential of epigenetics is not uniformly embraced nor realized within scientific theorizing and practice. Tensions and varying interpretations exist between what they characterize as the more reductionist "exposome" model prominent in molecular epidemiology, and "neighborhood" effect–based studies typical of sociological and social epidemiological approaches to gene-environment interactions. In this context, feminist participation and intervention are necessary, to direct the potential of the expanding views proffered by various strands of epigenetic theory and research, toward a shift in material-discursive practices that can more fully illuminate how intersectionality becomes materialized and embodied.

Asking New Questions: Epigenetics at the Intersection of the Social and Material

A specific such potential shift in material-discursive practices is evidenced by renewed interest and refinement in the clinical (re) construction of health and disease through the clinical focus on Developmental Origins of Health and Disease (DOHaD). Where the genomic paradigm cast the material structure of the gene and DNA as arbiters and engineers of social enactments, strictly separating one from another in hierarchical containment, epigenetics and its associated DOHaD paradigm trace a contour potentially much more closely aligned with Barad's agential realism. Although what might be called the "weak" epigenetic program tinkers only slightly with the reductionist genomic paradigm, asserting that epigenetic "marks" atop the fixed genome merely fine-tune its singular expression, on a deeper level, a stronger version of the science of epigenetics holds more revolutionary implications for re-imagining the relationships entwined and emerging out of naturecultures, and the political potentials of such.

Within its most encompassing interpretation, epigenetics "is concerned with the broader study of the determinants of individual development as conditional, inductive interactions among the organism's constituent components and structures and between these and external forces. These determinants are both temporal and spatial, related to various time-scales and various organizational layers . . . the genome tends to be seen more and more as a complex dynamic system of which the characteristic cohesion, flexibility, changeability, and evolvability are the focus of study" (Van de Vijver et al., 2002). "As such, this new science presents a completely new, dynamic, iterative, and open-ended model of relations between environments, genes, cells, bodies, and health status" (Guthman and Mansfield, 2012). Unraveling and reweaving these previously disparate strands requires an interdisciplinary understanding and revision of both conceptions of the material, as privileged in the discourses of the natural sciences, and social forces, as interrogated by feminist projects lying within the social sciences and humanities.

Whereas the genomic paradigm focuses on the fixity and determination of the inherited sequence of the DNA genome in dictating physical traits and material physiologies as well as cognitive and mental proclivities of individuals, epigenetics offers a more flexible, temporal and plastic framework to explain the emergent properties of phenotype and embodied material shaping of organisms through relational, context-dependent interactivity within environmental contexts. While the units of determination in the genomic paradigm are the inherited nucleotide base pairs in the DNA sequence, epigenetics focuses instead on the ways in which environmental exposures and experiences, including dietary intake, chemical contamination, and psychosocial stressors, interact within a physiological milieu to toggle tiny methyl and acetyl groups tagging DNA nucleotides and the proteins that wrap and unwind DNA, opening it to expression or closing off its potential transcription or translation. In this way, epigenetics as a model traces an intersectional and continuously interacting course between social experiences and contexts (including those that arise out of intersectional race, class, and gender positionality) and their material enactment through neurons, hormones, nutrients, methylation, and acetylation. In contrast to the genomic emphasis on the single individual DNA code, within an epigenetic frame, there are many possible de-, un-, and re-codings of the material potentialities contained within a single sequence of DNA depending on how, when, and where its shaping by methylation and acetylation takes place along a space-time continuum that varies throughout the developmental trajectory of the organism. Epigenetic remodeling through methylation and acetylation is labile, particularly during liminal lifestages such as oogenesis and fetal development, as well as the "slow growth" period in preparation for puberty and as an organism ages. At the same time, epigenetic modifications are also capable of imprinting and inhering across generational boundaries. Crews and Gore (2012) describe these different molecular manifestions of epigenetic marks as epigenetic context-dependent (Ec) versus epigenetic germline-dependent (Eg) modifications, with an emphasis on their interaction: "Beyond additivity or synergism, of greatest importance is the emergent property of the interaction: that is, how transgenerational germline-dependent modifications alter the organism such that it responds to proximate stimuli, such as context-dependent environmental stressors, in a different manner" (3).

This breach between social and physiological in epigenetic models that blur boundaries between experiences defined as external and/or social and phenomena considered internal and/or material properties of an organism has important implications for a feminist revisioning of socio-material intersectionality.

Epigenetics, meaning literally "on top of" genetics, provides a scientific model of an intra-active socio-material interface that traces a reflexive continuum between social and material. Whereas in the genomic paradigm, DNA served as a "master molecule" to be sequenced and decoded, in epigenetics, DNA, the same molecule, becomes a flexible form of material agency, the multiple potentialities of which are manifested in relationship with both itself and external actors, along a socio-material continuum. In epigenetics, DNA is not a single sequence, but a collection of multiple, overlapping, and intra-active expressions that are un- and re-coded in relational process along multiple time and space continuums. In this way, the body is re-envisioned as an ongoing form of relational becoming; "the existence of epigenetic processes (as well as undifferentiated stem cells) suggests that beings are always in a state of becoming . . . rather than an organism adapting to an external environment by passively thriving, the environment actively comes into the body and shapes how genes express" (Guthman & Mansfield 2012, 10).

Relational events occurring along intersecting pathways stemming from such socio-material phenomena as diet, psychological experiences of stress, and environmental chemical exposures, themselves complex and intra-active processes, literally shape and re-shape the potentiality of DNA, no longer a singular master but an agential partner in physiological becoming. Epigenetics brings into focus the plasticity of the genome, as a flexible interface that is sculpted and shaped by socio-material influences and experiences as well as through its own, tentative translations and transcriptions. This "sculpting" is accomplished by three primary (and often overlapping) molecular pathways: methylation, in which small biochemical tags are affixed to CpG nucleotides in DNA, blocking that region from transcription; acetylation, in which slightly larger biochemical tags are tacked onto histones, the spool-like proteins that DNA is wound around, releasing regions of the DNA thread and opening it up to genetic transcription; and micro-RNAs, small transcripts copied off of open regions of the DNA which double back and bind to previously transcribed mRNA sequences, and prevent their translation into protein. In these processes, the line between social and material isn't just blurred; these forces are tangled and entwined in a way that makes it impossible to draw lines between them. At this level, the genome transitions from a singular, deterministic code to a selective reading, subject to local molecular fluctuations and internal cellular agency.

However, it would be a mistake to end a discussion of epigenetics at the level of the cell. Methylation, acetylation, and microRNA activity are not isolated events purely in the material realm. They are important mediators along a socio-material pathway that ties lived social experiences in the "macro" world to shifting palettes of protein expressions and activities at the "micro" realm and back again in performative engagement, across a wide landscape of cell types involved in the ongoing becoming of the body. Epigenetic processes have been shown to serve as sites of integration and interface between intersectional socio-material phenomena such as stress, diet, and environmental chemical exposures and their embodiment in differential material enactments of gene expression and protein translation, which in turn cycles back to influence our perception, enactment, and embodiment in the world.

In concert with the molecular elucidation of the socio-material continuum in the form of methylation, acetylation, and microRNA, the broader perspective on intersectionality between social and material in determining lifecourse stories is also undergoing significant shifts consistent with feminist attempts to devise intra-active visions of becoming. "In simple terms, the process of development is now understood as a function of 'nature dancing with nurture over time,' in contrast to the longstanding but now outdated debate about the influence of 'nature versus nurture.' This is to say, beginning prenatally, continuing through infancy, and extending into childhood and beyond, development is driven by an ongoing, inextricable interaction between biology (as defined by genetic predispositions) and ecology (as defined by the social and physical environment)" (Shonkoff et al., 2012).

Accompanying the shift toward epigenetics in the post-genomic era, in the clinical realm a theory known as Developmental Origins of Health and Disease (DOHaD) has also emerged, with a focus on the plasticity that goes beyond the inherited DNA genome and serves as a developmental interface between the social and material at both individual and transgenerational levels. The DOHaD paradigm began with an observation of an intriguing correlation between birthweight and health disparities emerging later in life, such as cardiovascular disease and diabetes, that were geographically stratified within the UK and associated with rising "prosperity" at all but the highest levels (Barker, 2007). Further research focused on maternal nutrition and stress as prenatal forces shaping fetal growth and subsequent birthweight, and it was hypothesized that this developmental plasticity in birthweight reflected an adaptive feedback between social and environmental conditions in the maternal generation, and the subsequent material shaping of the fetus. Additional research on generational diet, birthweight, and risk for CVD showed that it was not just the experience of the maternal generation that influenced birthweight, but paternal experience as well, with effects of both maternal and paternal experience sometimes extending back several generations (Kaati et al., 2002; Pembrey et al., 2006; Painter 2008). This was a totally new view of how material bodies are shaped during development, predicated not simply on the DNA sequences individuals inherit, the focus of the genomic paradigm, but also on how experiences in the social realm, such as raced, classed, and gendered configurations of stress and diet, both during and prior to—sometimes many generations prior to—conception and birth are active co-participants in the material formation of the fetus and later adult body. Importantly, it expanded the focus on maternal effects of prenatal life (prone to "good mother"/"bad mother" dichotomies) to also include paternal contributions, not just genetic but also experiential.

Once again, the need for feminist intervention and active participation in the construction of epigenetic science is clear. As Sarah Richardson (2015) and colleagues (2014) warn, "careless" and miscontextualized interpretations and presentations of mothers in DOHaD and epigenetics threaten to reify the reductionism inherited from the genomic paradigm, and further problematize and stigmatize the maternal body as an epigenetic "vector." Becky Mansfield and Julie Guthman (2015) contend that epigenetics, echoing past forms of eugenics, is being shaped as a reproductive science, in which women's bodies and behaviors become the target, and women of color in particular are held personally responsible for the prevention or propogation of "abnormal" fetuses.

From an intersectional feminist perspective, there is a need to more deeply probe and problematize such emphasis and definition of maternal causation, as well as paternal effect, within DOHaD and epigenetics. After all, gendered maternality and paternality are not homogeneously constituted, socially or materially. Race, class, gender, and sexuality (as well as other forces) intersect forcefully in parental images and experiences. The maternal epigenetic concerns that Annie Murphy Paul, a privileged white woman, characterizes in her book *Origins* (2010), detailing her pregnancy on the Upper West Side of Manhattan (cruising Whole Foods for the most epigenetically favorable meal, for example) differ dramatically from the characterizations and oppressions generated by "welfare queen" mythology that continues to haunt the pregnancies of poor women of color (Gilman, 2014). Indeed, the ways that racism, classism, and sexism intersectionally tinker with each other in an epigenetic context are illustrated by the case of Kim Anderson, a wealthy black attorney and executive profiled in the California News Reel series *Unnatural Causes*, who enacted many of the same privileged epigenetic concerns during her pregnancy that Paul documents, but who nonetheless falls into the stratified statistic that places the birth outcomes of highly educated black women on par with white women without a high school diploma. Intersectional experience matters, not just socially, but also materially.

The socio-material context of paternality in the United States is no less intersectional. What Michelle Alexander terms "the new Jim Crow" and its mass incarceration of black men; the "invisible presence" of black fathers (Connor & White, 2006); and the specifically embodied nature of racism against black fathers detailed by Ta-Nehisi Coates (2015) all speak to the ways in which the intersectional socio-materiality of gendered and classed racism are woven into paternality as an important potential contributor to DOHaD.

At the time that the DOHaD paradigm emerged, it was already clear that social experiences stemming from intersectional oppressions based on race, class, and gender—such as discrimination, poverty, and social isolation and marginalization—have significant overall health costs for both individuals and groups (Adler & Rehkopf, 2008). In the past, these associations remained statistically robust, yet physiologically murky. For example, data consistently show that African Americans across gender, class, and age boundaries experience different and more detrimental health outcomes than either European Americans or recent African immigrants to the United States, in similar strata for a variety of outcomes—including heart disease, hypertension, diabetes, obesity, and low birth weight (CDC, 2011). Without attention to socio-material intersectionality and within the genomic paradigm there has been much hunting and gathering of DNA samples under the premise that race is genetically encoded, that a materially determined physical "race" presupposes any social signification. On the other hand, deconstructing race, class, and gender as solely social constructions, even when intersectional, ignores the individual and collective physical embodiment of health disparities that crosses social and material lines and integrates them in a complex entanglement.

Not unexpectedly, when birthweight appeared to strongly correlate with race in U.S. populations, regardless of socioeconomic status, explanations were sought within the genomic paradigm that posited explanations based on genetic differences between race groups (Green et al., 2005; Dizon-Townson, 2001). The limitations of the genomic paradigm were betrayed by intriguing data that showed, time and time again across different groups, that members of the same "racial" groups had strikingly different birthweight outcomes based on whether they were recent immigrants to, or had been born and raised in, the United States (Singh & Yu, 1996; Acevedo-Garcia, Soobader, & Berkman, 2005). Birthweight disparities didn't correlate with race; they correlated with a generational history of experiencing embodied, intersectional racialization leading to the formation of race-gender-class disparities in the sociomaterial temporal and spatial context of the postcolonial United States.

With the emergence of epigenetics and DOHaD, some of the missing puzzle pieces linking the intersection of the social and the material in these cases has emerged, providing a flexible model of a physiological pathway through which socially constructed stressors associated with discrimination and social inequalities work together with material configurations to produce particular patterns of gene expression which then manifest themselves as "racial" embodiments of epigenetic health (Kuzawa and Sweet 2009). This in turn has led to new questions, and intriguing observations, about how environments and physiologies work together, across time and space, to shape being. For example, associations between low birthweight, race, and nation are present not just for maternal experience, but also correlated with father's race, nation, and immigrant status (Krishnakumar et al., 2011). Attention to the intersectional nature of both social and material being, as well as conventional feminist conceptions of intersectionality in the social realm in which race, class, and nation, amongst other categories, are co-theorized along with gender, are necessary and extremely important in these forays.

Epigenetics and DOHaD has the potential to enable an intersectional, socio-materialist approach to phenomena such as these, by holding multiple strands of social differences and inequalities simultaneously tethered to the material, physical body, and seeking to integrate their points of intersection and diversion. Thus, the intersectional forces of race, class, and gender (as well as other categories) that occur in the social realm, themselves informed and shaped by material significations related to physical bodies and conditions, are integrated and intersect in material, epigenetic enactments of those experiences through networks in and through the body that include cortisol stress responses, nutrient cycling, methylation and acetylation patterns. Importantly, these material networks are engaged in a process of constant, dynamic remodeling, while at the same time they can persist in doppelganger traces that cross multiple generational boundaries. The body doesn't possess separate receptors or signals for gender discrimination or the stress of racism; in the material enactment of intersectional social constructions, embodiment serves as a means of integration and enmeshed performativity.

Fighting Social Disparities with Subversive Resignifications: Politics and the Reconfiguring of Socio-Material "Reality"

Epigenetics and DOHaD offer a lens through which social and biological phenomena form an intersectional matrix within which the potentiality of multiple meanings is materially embodied and disembodied through plasticity and remodeling. Of course, the scientific literature on epigenetics and DOHaD does not necessarily read in this fashion, although it lends itself to such interpretations in a way that the genomic paradigm did not. "The key issue now in the post-genomic era is to consider a number of possible models in which these two streams of influence—genetics and environmental—intersect to either express the consequences of risk or provide some buffer against adverse developmental outcomes" (Rende, 2012).

This is where the critical task of feminist participation in post-genomic science plays such an important role. Epigenetics and post-genomic science in general offer a constructive window through which well-developed intersectional feminist frameworks can be applied, but only if we are willing to cross the threshold from critique to participation; from theory to practice. Extending the feminist analysis of intersectionality into the material realm via epigenetics is an important and undertheorized avenue for exploration. Feminist participation in further conceptualizing and interrogating the socio-material intra-actions and agency that shape health outcomes along intersectional axes is not just intellectually compelling; it may also provide important avenues for feminist social change.

In that regard, as a feminist scientist, I am concerned not just with intersectional reworkings of epigenetics as a science that draws different cuts through the material-discursive space of becoming, but also with "accountability for the consequences of the construction of [epigenetic] subjectivity" (Barad, 2007) that such an epigenetic material-discursive (re)configuring enacts. In the focus of epigenetics on re-envisioning the socio-molecular process of becoming, we must not render the living, breathing, subject invisible, as technoscientific processes are prone to (Barad 2007, 215; Casper 1994, 844). What could epigenetics embody in practice, not only within the boundaries of science, but importantly, outside and along its borders? Can epigenetics enact an intersectional sociomaterial politics consistent with feminist goals and experience?

The revisioning that epigenetics enables as a scientific signification of the intra-activity that occurs at the socio-material interface reveals interactions that hold political power for social change. Epigenetics and DOHaD provide a socially sanctioned route imbued with the power of science, to bring to light the socio-material consequences of intersectional disparities, as physical embodiment unfolds and re-folds under, around, and into the intersectionality of race, class, and gender not only through means such as differential access to healthcare treatments, interventions, and services—themselves sociomaterial intra-actions—but also through the daily physical embodiment and enactments of intersectionality as lived material becoming. And this is just at the surface. Below the surface, epigenetics reveals a collaborative sociomolecular trace, a material sedimentation, in Barad's terminology, of lived intersectional existence in the form of methylation and acetylation patterns that refract and react to the networked interface of socio-material differences.

What of these sedimentary (but not sedentary) marks? What political power do they hold that a nature/culture binary does not? Within the U.S. political system, focusing solely on the social side of such a binary frequently leaves everything to individual change. If it is all just socially constructed, by all means change your social situation. Pull yourself up by the bootstraps! As long as we leave an active and self-assembling socio-material interaction out of the picture, the insidious nature of socio-material disparities will remain resistant to change.

What epigenetics and DOHaD offer politically, empowered by the cloak of science, is a set of data that connects the social and the material as integral and co-constructed partners, enabling an assignment of responsibility for this co-construction. Ontological and epistemological responsibility is a key element of Barad's agential realism; as she says, "realism, then, is not about representations of an independent reality but about the real consequences, interventions, creative possibilities and responsibilities of intra-acting within and as part of the world" (2007, 37). Within the current U.S. political environment, socio-material intra-activity holds power, although perhaps not recognized on those terms, but important for feminists to recognize nonetheless. For example, as long as smoking was constructed as a lifestyle choice, a social phenomenon, policy languished as the tobacco industry assigned responsibility to individual smokers. But once the social phenomenon of smoking, and the tobacco industry's role in its social promotion, was cut a different way, through the lens of the electron microscope which revealed the intra-active socio-material presence of physical benzopyrene adducts from tobacco smoke bonded onto the p53 tumor suppressor gene, the socio-material circuit was completed, responsibility was assigned, and lawsuits were settled and policies changed. Different cuts through the race-class-gender space yield differing socio-material pictures within this example, of course, and this does not mean that the problem has been solved. But it does illustrate that socio-material cuts that take as their starting point feminist intersectionality at the discursive socio-material interface could have "real" consequences, politically and personally, for social change.

Yet the potential power of the emerging paradigms of epigenetics and DOHaD for change may never be realized if feminists do not rise to the call and engage with and in the science as it develops. Science is a social construction—on that we likely all can agree—but one with definitive political and material consequences. Epigenetics on its own will not be liberatory or lead to change; as a social practice, it is just as susceptible to "epi-eugenics" as the prior human genome paradigm was. The DOHaD literature, with its focus on maternal impacts on fetal developmental plasticity and adaptive arguments about socially stratified populations, is already replete with plenty of fodder for feminist criticism (Richardson et al., 2014; Bliss, 2015; Mansfield & Guthman, 2015; Richardson, 2015). Without direct feminist engagement and participation, we are likely to see feminist science studies remain, in Banu Subramaniam's words, "moored to the mode of critique of science" (2009), while opportunities for re- and co-constructive change pass us by.

I want to end with a call for continued engagement with a persistent problem—the need to understand and ameliorate the difficult relationship between feminism and the practice of science that seems to persist in communities of both women's studies and the sciences. We need more intersectional feminist work that engages and participates at the socio-material interface, troubled and complex as it may be, if we want to effect change consistent with feminist goals. This will necessarily require both embracing science not as enemy but as ally in our movements for socio-material change, as well as reshaping the cuts and contours that define science within and beyond its borders.

REFERENCES

Acevedo-Garcia, Dolores, Mah-J Soobader, and Lisa F. Berkman. 2005. The Differential Effect of Foreign-Born Status on Low Birth Weight by Race/Ethnicity and Education. *Pediatrics* 115(1): e20–e30.

Adler, Nancy E. and David H. Rehkopf. 2008. U.S. Disparities in Health: Descriptions, Causes, and Mechanisms. *Annual Review of Public Health* 29: 235–252.

Alaimo, Stacy and Susan Hekman. 2008. *Material Feminisms*. Bloomington: Indiana University Press.

Alexander, Michelle. 2011. *The New Jim Crow: Mass Incarceration in the Age of Color-blindness*. New York: Free Press.

Barad, Karen. 2007. *Meeting the Universe Halfway: Quantum Physics and the Entanglement of Matter and Meaning*. Durham, NC: Duke University Press.

Barker, D.J.P. 2007. The Origins of the Developmental Origins Theory. *Journal of Internal Medicine* 261 (5): 412–417.

Casper, Monica. 1994. Reframing and Grounding Nonhuman Agency: What Makes a Fetus an Agent. *American Behavioral Scientist* 37 (6): 839–856.

Centers for Disease Control and Prevention. 2011. Health Disparities and Inequalities Report—United States, 2011. MMWR volume 60 (Supplement).

Cloud, John. 2010. Why Your DNA Isn't Your Destiny. *Time*, January 6.

Coates, Ta-Nehisi. 2015. *Between the World and Me*. New York: Spiegel & Grau.

Collins, Patricia Hill. 1990. *Black Feminist Thought: Knowledge, Consciousness and the Politics of Empowerment*. New York and London: Routledge.

Combahee River Collective. 1978. The Combahee River Collective Statement. Reprinted in Barbara Smith, ed., *Home Girls: A Black Feminist Anthology*. New York: Kitchen Table Press.

Connor, Michael and Joseph White. 2006. *Black Fathers: An Invisible Presence in America*. Mahwah, NJ: Lawrence Erlbaum Associates.

Crenshaw, Kimberle. 1989. Demarginalizing the Intersection of Race and Sex: A Black Feminist Critique of Antidiscrimination Doctrine, Feminist Theory and Antiracist Politics. *University of Chicago Legal Forum*, 139–167.

Crews, David and Andrea Gore. 2012. Epigenetic Synthesis: A Need for a New Paradigm for Evolution in a Contaminated World. F1000 *Biology Reports*. 4:18. http://f1000.com/reports/b/4/18, accessed June 26, 2014.

Davey Smith, George. 2012. Epigenetics for the Masses: More Than Audrey Hepburn and Yellow Mice? *International Journal of Epidemiology* 41(1): 303–308.

Dizon-Townson, Donna S. 2001. Preterm Labour and Delivery: A Genetic Predisposition. *Paediatric Perinatal Epidemiology* 15(suppl 2):57–62.

Ebrahim, S. (2012) Epigenetics, the Next Big Thing. *International Journal of Epidemiology* 41(1): 1–3.

Gilman, Michele Estrin. 2014. The Return of the Welfare Queen. *Journal of Gender Social Policy and Law* 22, no. 2: 247–279.

Green N. S., K. Damus, J. L. Simpson, et al. 2005. Research Agenda for Preterm Birth: Recommendations from the March of Dimes. *American Journal of Obstetrics and Gynecology* 193:626–635.

Guthman, J. and Mansfield, B. 2012. The Implications of Environmental Epigenetics: A New Direction for Geographic Inquiry on Health, Space, and Nature-Society Relations. *Progress in Human Geography* 37, no.4: 486–504.

Haraway, Donna. 1989. *Primate Visions: Gender, Race, and Nature in the World of Modern Science*. Routledge: New York and London.

Haraway, Donna. 2003. *The Companion Species Manifesto: Dogs, People, and Significant Otherness*. Chicago: Prickly Paradigm Press.

Haraway, Donna. 2008. *When Species Meet*. Minneapolis: University of Minnesota Press.

Kaati, G., Bygren, L. O., and Edvinsson, S. 2002. Cardiovascular and Diabetes Mortality Determined by Nutrition During Parents' and Grandparents' Slow Growth Period. *European Journal of Human Genetics* 10 (11): 682–688.

Krishnakumar, Ambika et al. 2011. The Paternal Component of the "Healthy Migrant" Effect: Father's Natality and Infant's Low Birth Weight. *Maternal and Child Health Journal* 15: 1350–1355.

Kuzawa, C. and E. Sweet. 2009. Epigenetics and the Embodiment of Race: Developmental Origins of US Racial Disparities in Cardiovascular Health. *American Journal of Human Biology* 21(1): 2–15.

Landecker, Hannah. 2011. Food as Exposure: Nutritional Epigenetics and the New Metabolism. *Biosocieties*, 6(2): 167–194.

Lewontin, Richard and Richard Levins. 2007. *Biology Under the Influence: Dialectical Essays on Ecology, Agriculture, and Health*. New York: Monthly Review Press.

Mansfield, B. 2012. Race and the New Epigenetic Biopolitics of Environmental Health. *BioSocieties* 7(4): 352–372.

Mansfield, B. and Guthman, J. 2015. Epigenetic Life: Biological Plasticity, Abnormality, and New Configurations of Race and Reproduction. *Cultural Geographies* 22(1): 3–20.

Painter, R. C., C. Osmond, P. Gluckman, M. Hanson, D. I. Phillips, and J. T. Roseboom. 2008. Transgenerational Effects of Prenatal Exposure to the Dutch Famine on Neonatal Adiposity and Health in Later Life. *BJOG: An International Journal of Obstetrics and Gynaecology* 115 (10): 1243–129.

Paul, Annie Murphy. 2010. *Origins: How the Nine Months Before Birth Shapes The Rest of Our Lives*. New York: Free Press.

Pembrey, M. E, L. O. Bygren, G. Kaati, S. Edvinsson, K. Northstone, M. Sjöström, and J. Golding. ALSPAC Study Team. 2006. Sex-Specific, Male-Line Transgenerational Responses in Humans. *European Journal of Human Genetics* 14(2): 159–166.

Rende, Richard. 2012. Behavioral Resilience in the Post-Genomic Era: Emerging Models Linking Genes with Environment. *Frontiers in Human Neuroscience* 6: 50.

Richardson, Sarah S. 2015. Maternal Bodies in the Postgenomic Order: Gender and the Explanatory Landscape of Epigenetics. In Sara S. Richardson and Hallam Stevens, eds. *Postgenomics*. Durham, NC: Duke University Press.

Richardson, Sarah S., Cynthia R. Daniels, Matthew W. Gillman, Janet Golden, Rebecca Kukla, Christopher Kuzawa, and Janet Rich-Edwards. 2014. Don't Blame the Mothers. *Nature* 512: 131–132.

Richardson, Sarah S. and Hallam Stevens, Eds. 2015. *Postgenomics*. Durham, NC: Duke University Press.

Shonkoff, Jack P., Andrew S. Garner, and The Committee of Psychosocial Aspects of Child and Family Health, Committee on Early Childhood, Adoption and Dependent Care, and Section on Developmental and Behavioral Pediatrics. 2012. The Lifelong Effects of Early Childhood Adversity and Toxic Stress. *Pediatrics* 129 (1): 232–246.

Shostak, Sara and Margot Moinester. 2015. The Missing Piece of the Puzzle?: Measuring the Environment in the Postgenomic Moment. In Sarah Richardson and Hallam Stevens, eds. *Postgenomics: Perspectives on Biology After the Genome*. Durham, NC: Duke University Press.

Singh, G. & S. M. Yu. 1996. Adverse Pregnancy Outcomes: Differences Between US- and Foreign-Born Women in Major US Racial And Ethnic Groups. *American Journal of Public Health* 86(6): 837–843.

Subramaniam, Banu, 2009. Moored Metamorphoses: A Retrospective Essay on Feminist Science Studies. *Signs: Journal of Women in Culture and Society* 34(4):951–980.

Van de Vijver G., L. Van Speybroeck, and D. De Waele. 2002. Epigenetics: A Challenge for Genetics, Evolution, and Development? *Annals of the NY Academy of Sciences* 981:1–6.

Vineis, P. 2009. The Research Program in Epigenetics: The Birth of a New Paradigm. In *Epigenetics and Human Health: Linking Hereditary, Environmental and Nutritional Aspects*, A. G. Haslberger, ed. Weinheim, Germany: Wiley-VCH Verlag GmbH & Co. KGaA, doi: 10.1002/9783527628384.ch1.

7

Sex/Gender Matters and Sex/Gender Materialities in the Brain

ANELIS KAISER

The materiality of *sex/gender*[1] has been a contested arena of debate in Gender Studies, not only since Judith Butler's *Bodies That Matter* (1993), but, as we know, also before (e.g., Haraway 1986). Since then, we have moved forward, on one side, with the understanding of how science constructs the truth about sex/gender in human corporeality and its behavioral materiality. On the other, we have also made headway in understanding the biological logics and illogics of genes, gonads, genitals, and their interplays with the brain and other sexed/gendered parts of the body. Despite the accumulation of knowledge in each of these two discourses—the metatheoretical reflection on the construction of sex/gender on the one hand and the critical bio-medical production of sex/gender-related knowledge on the other—the transfer of insights between these two domains has progressed rather slowly. From my vantage point as a queerfeminist cognitive neuroscientist currently working in the lab, there is still an enormous disconnection between those who think in terms of a "symbolic" (or linguistic) signification of a sexed/gendered materiality on the one side, and those who believe in the "real" and objectifiable matter of sex/gender on the other. Further, scholars who examine how matter comes to meaning (e.g., scholars from Science Studies, Gender Studies, the Arts and Humanities) and researchers who conduct empirical hands-on investigations on matter (e.g., physicians, neuroscientists, biologists, physicists, chemists) still do not engage in exchange as often as interdisciplinary enterprise would require.

What complicates the communication between these two discourses was and still is that both groups of academics are trapped in their own disciplines: the Humanities, the Social and Cultural Sciences on one side and the Natural Sciences on the other. The transmission of knowledge on theoretical and methodological levels is considerably hampered by disciplinary power. For instance, we can ask: Who from Genetics has ever read Haraway's *Primate Visions* (1989) and who from Gender Studies has ever glanced at Joel's "Male or Female? Brains Are Intersex" (2011)? Or who in Gender Studies would spend months conducting "reductionist" experiments and evaluating biology based data? In parallel, who from Chemistry would visit the archives to read what medical scientists published about gonads in the nineteenth century?

There are, of course, some who have engaged in such transgressive endeavors, e.g., Fausto-Sterling (2012a, b), Bleier (1984), Birke (1986), Haraway (1984), Roy (2008), Schmitz (2012), Jordan-Young (2010) and several others, Karen Barad being one of them. As a physicist and philosopher, Barad knows *what* matters when materiality materializes itself. She has dedicated considerable attention to the inextricable entanglement between what we would colloquially call "things" and their meaning (e.g., 2003, 2007, 2012), and, as I will discuss here, her revision of Judith Butler's concept of performativity helpfully advances a materialist-semiotic understanding of sexed/gendered matter. However, I argue that even Barad fails to fully address the question of how and where exactly sex/gender is instantiated in intra-active bodily materiality. In this chapter, I aim to delve into another type of materiality than that commonly studied in physics, namely into the matter of the brain. I will show the intransigence of dichotomously mattered sexed/gendered brain regions in neuroscientific practice, and argue that in contrast to the "non-vital" materiality of physics, addressing the brain's sex/gendered materiality requires a distinct approach to the "bio" of neurobiological matter.

With this goal in mind, the structure of this chapter will revolve around five main points: I begin with (1) my point of departure,[2] Butler's understanding of materiality, which is primarily concerned with surfaces, I argue, as opposed to what lies beneath them, and Barad's materialist intervention. Barad's conceptualization of agency at the depth of materiality is particularly valuable in enabling me to examine a very specific micro level of matter. However, I distinguish Barad's agential realist notion of (physical) matter from what I call bio-matter or more specifically neuro-matter, which is the main concern when studying the brain. This will bring us to examine the agency of neurobiological matter of the brain (2) and the role sex/gender plays in it (3). I then ask (4) how much independent agency we want to ascribe to the specific subcortical matter itself, and I make (5) the applicability of an agentic materiality in neuroscientific empiricism a subject of discussion. In the following, I will apply a diffractive reading of feminist theories of the body and matter through Neuroscience in order to examine the entanglement of matter and agency in sexed/gendered brains.

(1) Performativity and the Subsurface of Non-Vital and Neurobiological Matter

Relations of power are, as Foucault as well as Butler and others have demonstrated, inevitably entangled with the materiality of our bodies; a strict separation of these categories is untenable (Foucault 1976; Butler 1990, 1993). One of Butler's most important contributions to the theory of sex/gender is her understanding of sex/gender performativity, according to which being a woman or man is understood as a product of repeated activities within a system of sexed/gendered power relations and not as inevitable, natural materializations (1990). Through the iteration of normed statements, performativity has the *effect of materiality* and can therefore not be understood as a single, willful act, but rather as a practice of constant repetition and citation. To address the body's materiality in relation to sex/gender, Butler proposes

> [...] the return to the notion of matter, not as site or surface, but *as a process of materialization that stabilizes over time to produce the effect of boundary, fixity, and surface we call matter"* (1993, 9; emphasis in original)

In this context, the very materiality of our bodies has always been criss-crossed by binary sex/gender norms and can never be viewed as sex/gender-neutral. I would argue that exactly the same is true for our brains: in neuroscientific experiments, the "hard" and "independent" variable sex/gender, marked as F and M, is understood as a preliminary determinant and not a resulting factor. For instance, many MRI empirical settings are prepared by default so that the experiment could not even start without checking the box for F or M, thus making participants into sexed/gendered subjects even before the study begins. This suggests that regulatory norms, sex/gender, and matter constitute an indivisible triad that finds its materialization in neuroscience too. But what if we turn the focus away from subjects (as individuals) and point at the cortical matter *itself*? Is there a sexed/gendered constitution of the materiality of the brain or does the term "constitution" not entail the idea of subject status, a status that only one piece of "bio-matter" cannot sustain? Past and present investigations on the regulation and constitution of the self through and in neuroscientific discourse confirm that neuroscientific research is part of a power/knowledge complex (Rose 2003; Maasen and Sutter 2007; Lettow 2008; Schaper-Rinkel 2012). However, when we are not referring to the neurosciences as discourses that enable the constitution of subjects, but to the brain itself, to this 1.3 kilograms of cerebral biology, this piece of material facticity with its own rules and which is a part of the subject and not the whole of it, how exactly do sexed/gendered discourses fit in, and how do they become material reality?

Butler's articulation of performativity as having the effect of materiality is insufficient to address these questions. While some have argued that Butler (1990, 1993) disregards or even dissolves material bodies into discourse or language (Duden 1993; Landweer 1994; Alaimo & Hekman 2008), I do not share this opinion. But I do want to note that she uses a very specific understanding of the body, namely a *human* body which constitutes and acts out sex/gender in its performative behavior and everyday interaction and social practice. On this point, Barad argues:

> Butler's concern is limited to the production of human bodies (and only certain aspects of their production, at that), and her theorization of materalization is parasitic on Foucault's notions of regulatory power and discursive practices, which are limited to the domain of human social practices. (2007, 145)

In this sense, in Butler's analyses, the body and its materiality only reach a human-biological surface, a point to which Barad also draws attention, claiming, like others, that matter cannot be only a "kind of citationality" nor a product of discursive acts (2007, 151).

It is true that we actually learn very little from Butler about the matter of the body and body parts, the transgression *underneath the skin* and the associated sex/gender constructions *within* the body. Butler does not examine *where* and *why* these processes take place, or *why* they take place where they do. With respect to certain entities of "biological-material" manifestations *under the skin*, we only get a vague hint, which is moreover hard not to label as a subversive or inassimilable rest.

> It must be possible to concede and affirm an array of "materialities" that pertain to the body, that which is signified by the domains of biology, anatomy, physiology, hormonal and chemical composition [. . .]. None of this can be denied. (Butler 1993, 66–67)

By limiting the gaze to the body's border rather than into its inside, Butler loses sight of a certain materiality, the materiality of interest to science and particularly to biomedical science. Ironically, at the same time, she creates a close proximity to materiality within the body by equalizing sex and gender. This closeness to, and distancing from, a body-under-the-skin elides the material-"biological" body examined through the methods of all biomedical sciencies. And it is exactly this paradoxical situation of closeness and distancing to corporeal matter that keeps appearing and reappearing for those gap workers at the edge of science and gender studies.

Barad takes us one step further here: We pass through the body's border and get to the inside of materiality, where our attention is drawn to material processes and forms of agency. "[A]ny robust theory of the materialization of bodies would necessarily take account of *how the body's materiality*—for example, its anatomy and physiology—*and other material forces actively matter to the processes of materialization*" (2003, 809, emphasis in original).

If performativity is material, matter is active. Barad assumes that matter is a part of its own process of construction, it is generative and involved in the creation of its own meaning—albeit not prediscursively. Materiality is a doing that creates itself onto-epistemologically (Barad 2007). Following Haraway's (1995) idea of factuality or organisms taking an active part in creating its meaning by referring to it as "material-semiotic actors" (96), Barad's materialist conceptualization of agency allow an analysis of sex/gender materialization at a very specific micro level, at the level of neuro-matter.

However, it is important to keep in mind that while Barad's concept of materiality refers extensively to materialities and bodies in general, the main focus of her work is limited to *physical* material manifestations. In her posthumanist vision, Barad insists on the similarities between different materialities. In contrast, I would like to call attention to some specific characteristics of neurobiological matter. Contrary to most of the physical bodies to which Barad refers, neurobiological matter is a type of matter that we carry in our bodies and which is very much *alive*. Hence, the question becomes: How can this neurobiological, this living matter that we *have* in our bodies and that we at the same time also *are*, be comprehended in its active-agential and performative doing?

(2) Agential Doing in Neurobiological Matter

In the brain, agential doing is in full swing! Neurons are firing, metabolic processes are taking place in and between cells, blood is circulating, action potentials are being activated and inhibited, brain fluid is flowing, old tissue is being removed, synapses are forming, the frontal lobe is "communicating" with the parietal lobe, subcortical structures are sending information to the cortex, and much, much more. Usually, these processes are signified by biology; it is the discipline of neurobiology that claims the sole power to define and explain these processes. However, I believe it could be interesting to examine exactly these processes diffractively, through the lens of queerfeminist theories of sex/gender, the body, and materialization.

Neurobiological Plasticity and Performativity

In addition to these permanently ongoing processes, activity in the brain also displays another feature: the dynamic adaptability of the brain, expressed as *brain plasticity*.[3] Neurological plasticity represents lifelong adaption processes in the brain, and the whole nervous system, which depend on new experiences made by the individual.

The networks of neural cells and synapses in the brain, in the cortex and everywhere else, are constantly being stabilized, destroyed, and rebuilt—always depending on what is going on in our minds, body, and environment. The cortex in particular is therefore not determined from the outset, neither in its structure and connectivity, nor in its patterns of functional activation. Instead, in the process of developing and while dealing with its environment, biological matter is constantly changing. The enormous dynamic of brain plasticity can explain the diversity of brains, because each person has different experiences. In the context of neurological plasticity, what happens in this material dimension is this: we learn. Or would it be more correct here to say: the brain learns agentially, and we learn along?

From the viewpoint of the neurosciences, learning necessitates modulation of existing neuronal networks and/or the formation of new networks. This process occurs at several levels. At the level of electrophysiology, the signal strength at the single activated synapse is increased—this is called *long-term potentiation* (Bliss & Lømo 1973). This sensitized transmission is accompanied at the biochemical level by the production of new molecules that stabilize well-used synapses, while at the same time creating new synapses and, in parallel, probably also pruning unused connections. Together this results, at the structural level, in new or more efficient connectivity. At the level of neurons or neuronal networks, learning is therefore nothing more than a change in connectivity patterns dependent on experience-driven synaptic activity (Kandel 2001).

The concept of neuronal plasticity introduces dynamism into our understanding of our mental organ. Consequently we have come to see the structure and function of the brain as increasingly receptive and responsive to the environment. In light of this idea, brain materiality becomes something that is always in the "doing" or in the process of "becoming," matter in which new neuronal networks are constructed as an effect of learning or "matter" is "mattering." A central aspect of these processes of neuro-material "becoming" is the repeated or frequent performance of similar or identical experiences outside the brain. We see now how *repetition* gains crucial significance at the point of materialized becoming— also for the functioning of the brain.

The neuroscientific view of brain plasticity as an outcome of learning, as a repetitive and iterative product of an interaction, can be understood as equivalent to the concept of performativity, specifically at the level of the neuronal subsurface.[4] I argue here that, analogous to performativity, neuronal plasticity has the effect of materiality. Materiality as becoming, materiality as an iterative loop, can be associated in its own performativity with neurobiological plasticity. The notion that the substance of matter is not a thing but a doing (Barad 2007) also corresponds to the concept of a plastic brain.

(3) Stumbling Across Sex/Gender in an Active Neurobiological Matter

So far, we have dived and delved into the neuro matter of agential neurobiological doing. We have considered the building of networks and how neuronal plasticity becomes manifest. At this point we need to ask: What about sex/gender? How is this "brain-matter-in-the-doing" or "brain mattering" of interest to gender theory? In my opinion, there are two areas of interest in which sex/gender come into play here.

First, "brain-mattering" is relevant in that *sex/gender socialization* comes into effect in an evident manner through neurobiological learning. Binary sex/gender socializations are learned by the brain and— roughly speaking—can result in similar or "typical" sex/gender specific neuronal networks of brain structures. An example for this is sex-/ gender-related language lateralization in the brain. Women seem to activate the language centers on both sides of their brains, whereas men tend to show only a left-hemispheric activation (e.g., Philipps et al. 2001; Baxter et al. 2003; Bitan et al. 2010; Phillips et al. 2013). Even though the question of sex/gender-specific language lateralization in the brain is still under debate in cognitive neuroscience (Sommer et al. 2004; Kaiser et al. 2009), as is the further issue whether this sex/gender difference can in fact be generalized beyond the domain of language (Ihnen et al. 2009), this example may illustrate the palpable impact of socialization. It would only be logical that sex/gender differences are represented in our receptive and adaptive brains, considering that we are made into women and men right from birth and that our brains are practicing and learning sex/gender all day, day in and day out—also in terms of neurobiologically dealing with language. From this point of view, social norms are materially embodied in the brain. Such an understanding of *embodiment* is certainly nothing new and has been repeatedly outlined, most prominently, by Anne Fausto-Sterling (2000) and Fausto-Sterling and colleagues (2012a, 2012b).

Second, "brain mattering" is of interest insofar as the brain tends to remain sexless/genderless at the micro-level of neurobiological intra-active processes of mattering—as regarded from a Baradian perspective. In the depths of neurobiological agency, neurons fire, brain fluids circulate, and synaptic connections and new neural networks form. At this micro-neurobiological level of activity, sex/gender seems to disappear, giving us the impression that sex/gender gets lost deep down in bio-matter. At second glance, however, we *do* find entities that are actually highly sexed/gendered. And they cannot be easily eliminated. When continuing to examine the material life of depths of the brain, we find substances such as hormones and genes, phenomena predominantly signified by the disciplines of biology and neurology, which certainly place a sex/gender on specific parts of brain[5] matter in a quite dichotomous manner. For these substances, as we know from biology, sex/gender not only matters at the level of a person's socialization, but already at a level of unlearned processes of mattering within significant parts of the human brain. While for inorganic physical matter, agency is free from sexed/gendered units such as hormones and genes, the same does not hold true for the bio-material brain. In the hypothalamus and hypophysis, for example, steroids are given a significant role. In a very matter-like way, they are said to form a dichotomous (Swaab et al. 2001; Morris et al. 2004) sexed/gendered neuroanatomical "facticity". Such facticity is in turn inseparably linked to the neurobiological basis of reproductive capacities and to the reproductive function in life.[6] In other words, there are these places in the brain that have, at a high probability, sex/gender neurophysiological and neuroanatomical dimorphic layout, a "difference" that virtually uncontestably originates in its own dimorphic agency. More explicitly, research has demonstrated a clear "distinction" between what we call "female" and "male" neuroanatomical correlates of reproductive properties in (a specific part of) the hypothalamus (e.g., García-Falgueras et al. 2011), and the pituitary gland plays an important role as well. Biologically, this is said to be a material reality, or indeed a "fact." Since biology is the discipline that gives signification here, there is no other approach to understand bio-material processes at this level of neuromaterial depth. Despite this fact, I nevertheless ask: Are there other ways of dealing with this dichotomized character of the hypothalamus and hypophysis? I argue for a diffractive reading, one that addresses this biologically powerful facticity through a materialist but also through a queer, feminist, and constructivist lens.

(4) How Agentic Can Neurobiological Matter Be?

Barad describes the nervous reactions some people display in response to an account of agency that ascribes agency not only to human subjects (2012, 55). Through Barad's accreditation of agency to the very materialities that make up these subjects, somehow, I personally feel nervous, too. Such alarm is justified by the ways in which some people still use a sex/ gender-difference based neurobiology of our brain, in a social context, to justify various forms of purported inability of men to look after children; of denying people in same-sex relationships their rights; or of pathologizing transgender people. For this reason I regard as very productive Barad's notion of agency in a materiality without sex/gender, a notion which she develops in relation to physical bodies. However, in a bio-materiality like the brain and as an example the hypothalamus that is constitutively so strongly crossed by binary power discourses, the situation is a different one. Here the question arises: what type of self-contained, independent, and subversive *agency* do we want to ascribe or attribute to this specific subcortical matter itself? And what should such agency look like so that the very determinisms which deconstructivist approaches over the last decades helped us to get rid of do not sneak in again? To preempt misunderstanding: from a queerfeminist perspective such as mine, the subcortical interplay of some steroids in the hypothalamus and hypophysis cannot and should not be denied.[7] To give an example, after ingesting testosterone for a few months, certain material effects would surely manifest in my brain—they would make a "difference" in my body. This might include effects such as growing facial hair or muscles, which with all probability would be associated with the attribution of being "male." Thus, when recapturing material agency in the body and brain, I want to consider when corporal "differences" are agentic and what we mean by that. And for that we continue with the example of the hypothalamus.

I suggest we understand the hypothalamus (as well as the hypophysis and other brain regions closely embedded in what is called "sexual

difference" and later "sexual categorization") as "dimorphically agentic" insofar as their effects on neurophysiological, neurostructural, and
bodily features can be detected, measured, and registered by means of
scientific methods. When framing these measurable and quantifiable
characteristics in a responsible ethical onto-epistemological context in
which matter can materialize itself, I would however hesitate to call their
characteristics "dimorphic" or "different." Rather, I suggest to continue
searching for new terminologies and to build new onto-epistemological
units that do not necessarily correspond one-to-one to existing material
items and current entities of signification. Since practices of difference
continue to be inextricably interwoven with the purpose of segregation,
division, and exclusion,[8] in the field of interdisciplinary queer feminist
neuro-research, we have yet to reach a point where we could operate
with terms such as "different" from a neutral perspective or with "male"
or "female" as coequal—also not in/for the brain. In the same vein, I
suggest employing a more fitting term than "male" or "female" when describing neurostructures or the effects that neurostructures can trigger.
For instance, the fact that injecting steroids leads to a specific ("different" and "real") neurostructure, which in turn leads to beard growing,
should not make queer feminists feel uncomfortable, since there is nothing dismissive about this; rather, it is the moment that a specific brain
structure or the beard is signified, labeled, and in the following perceived as only and always "male" (with all implications for the rest of the
body and one's behavior) that we should attend to. Again, the problem
is not about negating changing or "different" brain structures or functions we can measure using specific scientific methods; the problem
is about, for instance, thinking of a larger INAH3 or a beard as being
solely "male" expected to be found in a correspondent, complete, and
constantly "male" behaving body and mind. This is precisely the point
where we need, in the empirical labs, to create new onto-epistemological
units and to name them in a new form applying new methodological
and statistical tools. This is also exactly the point of scientific production
where we could indeed reach out to neuroscientific researchers working
on what they still call "sexual differentiation"[9] and work together with
them on shifting knowledge. That would indeed be a productive interdisciplinary approach to building new onto-epistemological assemblies.
Thus, to me, introducing "agency" into neuromatter urgently needs the

reframing of the very specific signification practices—in each and every step of neuroscientific experimentation. It is not enough to give matter its agency back. At the same time, we need to work on the epistemological aspect of the newly emerging onto-epistemologies.

(5) Agentic Neuromateriality in Empirical Research?

I see the true value of agency for a queer gender-sensitive neurobiology in empirical, experimental investigations rather than in theoretical analyses. There is an urgent need to include and integrate insights developed in Barad's agential realism approach into *empirical research within the brain sciences*. Similar to Butler, Barad has been claiming that "Epistemology, ontology, and ethics are inseparable" (2012, 69). This raises the question: How are Barad's concepts ethically transmittable into the operationalization of what active material sex/gender *is* within an experimental setting? What would a hands-on bioscientific research praxis on the agency of materiality look like? How can we be "objective" (Barad 2012, 57) so that we can responsibly conduct experiments in which matter can materialize itself in an ethico-ontoepistemological manner? Some of these questions have been touched on in the preceding paragraphs; others still need further reflections and interdisciplinary exchange.

The issue of experiment-based scientific research is crucial in order to avoid what happened to a scientifically approached body against the backdrop of the Butlerian sex/gender deconstruction, i.e., to the role the natural sciences played in Gender Studies of the last decades. This "deconstructed" category made it, casually speaking, to the empirical edge of the neuroscientific laboratory but it was not able to transgress the experimental boundary of scientific research within the *natural* sciences. This means there is for instance research *about* the construction of sex/gender in the Neurosciences, but no research *with* deconstructed sex/gender *in* neuroscientific experiments. So how should we handle Barad's theory in order to already situate it *inside* the empirical and experimental production of gender-related bio-materialities? Or, in provocative terms and to return to the topic of *power* mentioned at the beginning: Why should we not use the power of science to create newly sexed/gendered biology?

NOTES

I would like to thank Sigrid Schmitz, Cordula Nitsch, Victoria Pitts-Taylor, and Stephan Meyer for their substantial comments that helped improved this chapter in this and previous versions.

1 *Sex/gender* is used here to demonstrate that, in the eyes of the author, we still need to use these two terms together to remind ourselves about their intertwinement when examining matter in the context of science (Kaiser et al. 2007, 2009, 2012).

2 In line with Haraway (1988) and Harding (1991), I would like to position this chapter so as to clarify my theoretical background as well as my original questions and to avoid the illusion of a perspective from nowhere. What was at the bottom of the thoughts I am presenting here? And what are the thematic threads and the significant theories and concepts that inform my questions?

3 With *neurobiological plasticity* I refer here to structural plasticity. It was long believed that the brain can only alter its function in an otherwise structurally stable network. Paradigmatic research a few decades ago opened a completely new view of the brain as an organ capable of changing its constitution, i.e., its structure or anatomy, during all phases of (human) life as an effect to shifting circumstances (see also Rubin 2009).

4 It is not surprising that the neuroscientific concept of *plasticity* and the gender studies-based approach of *performativity* both show similar characteristics. Both Gender Studies and the Neurosciences are relatively new disciplines. Emerging concepts within both fields underlie contemporary zeitgeist, trends, and scientific policies (Kaiser 2010). Others have shown how the emergence of neuronal plasticity can be regarded in a framework of political economy (Malabou 2008), governmentality (Pitts-Taylor 2010), or neoliberal politics of meritocracy (Schmitz 2012).

5 Some researchers argue that there are not only a few specific brain regions (areas predominantly involved in reproduction or sexual behavior) that are dimorphic and that the rest of the brain has not only one unsexed/ungendered form (McCarthy and Arnold 2011). Rather, this research postulates that (chromosomal) sex/gender is everywhere in the brain, and thus plays a crucial role in many or even most brain regions (McCarthy and Arnold 2011; McCarthy et al. 2012).

6 Here, I deliberately come very close to an understanding of sex/gender difference as "unlearned" or "natural" that some regard so much as "biological" and obvious that it has nothing to do with *the* (social) sex/gender of the brain *they* are talking about, or others regard it as "biological" so much that they could appear to be "essentialists" when dealing with it and thus totally omit this question altogether. These two different attitudes toward a final and definite answer to the sex/gender question of the brain are based on the fact that although we have managed to decouple many "gendered" characteristics from the brain by demonstrating how contiguous they are to socialization or context (e.g., Rippon et al. 2014), "sex" differences, i.e., reproduction-based features, still represent and substitute *the* (biological) "sexual difference" (Kaiser 2012) in neuroscience. From this under-

standing of "sexual difference" as final, reproduction-related difference mandatorily follows a dualistic sex/gender categorization in bio-scientific experimentation. And thus suddenly we not only "admit," "see," "observe" a pure and evident reproduction-based sex/gender difference in the brain and body during empirical reserach, but we are in midst of (scientific) signification practices through categorization. As Ayala and Vasilyeva (2015) have shown, sex/gender categorization is never based solely on differential reproductive roles. The capacity or property of playing one of two (or more) roles in reproduction does not force us to play this role. Reproductive capacities are also rarely really what we are interested in when we signify/call something or someone "male" or "female" in scientific research and society. For instance, when we look for "male participants" in the frame of a cognitive neuroscientific experiment, we are certainly not interested in the (potential or already proved) property of men to produce fertile sperm. In addition, we necessitate many other biological (not to mention the cognitive and social) factors to act successfully in terms of reproduction. Thus, the (potential) property of producing eggs and sperm is in fact not distinctive or specific enough to categorically split (a study's) population and signify them as two groups. At this point, a "female" or "male" categorization does not keep the accuracy or precision such terms should have in the highly complex interdisciplinary endeavor of neuroscience and gender theory.

7 In addition, we should broaden our approach of either "denying" or "negating" sex/gender differences or similarities since things are more complicated than that (see also Jordan-Young 2010, Maney 2016). It is about finding new, empirically measurable units and affording them with new and productive significations.

8 . . . and empirical science is axiomatically bound to practices of difference.

9 McCarthy and Arnold (2011) argue for a new parallel-interactive model of "sexual differentiation" rather than relying on the old linear model. My personal vision of interdisciplinary research is that this type of knowledge and all the knowledge behind could be productively tied to ongoing queerfeminist work in the neurosciences. However, this should be done diffractively, i.e., by using this empirical and measurable data to build new onto-epistemological units in an interdisciplinary exchange. Through this process, some empirical and measurable data that, for instance, McCarthy and others provide may need to be re-captured in a way that allows it to become signified by a new term in dialogue and accordance with queer feminist and gender theory. In this way—rather than through the mere integration of knowledge produced in neuroscience into gender scholarity—I see a possibility of appropriating new materialities and coupling them with sex/gender theories, thereby contributing to the formation of new onto-epistemological knowledge in which "agency" is thinkable and productive.

REFERENCES

Alaimo, Stacy, and Susan J. Hekman. 2008. *Material Feminisms.* Bloomington: Indiana University Press.

Ayala, Saray, and Nadya Vasilyeva. (2015). Extended Sex: An Account of Sex for a More Just Society. *Hypatia: A Journal of Feminist Philosophy.*

Barad, Karen. 2003. Posthumanist Performativity: Toward an Understanding of How Matter Comes to Matter. *Signs: Journal of Women in Culture and Society* 28, no. 3: 801–31.

Barad, Karen. 2007. *Meeting the Universe Halfway.* Durham, NC: Duke University Press.

Barad, Karen. 2012. Interview with Karen Barad. In Rick Dolphijn and Iris van der Tuin, eds. *New Materialism: Interviews and Cartographies.* Open Humanities Press. An Imprint of MPublishing—University of Michigan Library, Ann Arbor: 48–70.

Baron-Cohen, Simon. 2003. *The Essential Difference: Men, Women and the Extreme Male Brain.* London: Allen Lane.

Baxter, Leslie C., Andrew J. Saykin, Laura A. Fleshman, Sterling C. Johnson, Stephen J. Guerin, D. R. Babcock, and Heather A. Wieshart. 2003. Sex Differences in Semantic Language Processing: A Functional MRI Study. *Brain and Language* 84, no. 2: 264–72.

Birke, Lynda. 1986. *Women, Feminism and Biology: The Feminist Challenge.* Hemel Hempstead: Wheatsheaf.

Bitan, Tali, Adi Lifshitz, Zvia Breznitz, and James R. Booth. 2010. Bidirectional Connectivity between Hemispheres Occurs at Multiple Levels in Language Processing but Depends on Sex. *Journal of Neuroscience* 30, no. 35: 11576–85.

Bleier, Ruth. 1984. *Science and Gender: A Critique of Biology and Its Theories of Women.* New York: Pergamon Press.

Bliss, Timothy V., and Terje Lømo. 1973. Long-lasting Potentation of Synaptic Transmission in the Dentate Area of the Anaesthetized Rabbit Following Stimulation of the Prefront Path. *Journal of Physiology* 232, no. 2: 331–56.

Butler, Judith. 1990. *Gender Trouble: Feminism and the Subversion of Identity.* New York: Routledge.

Butler, Judith. 1993. *Bodies That Matter: On the Discursive Limits of "Sex."* New York: Routledge.

Duden, Barbara. 1993. Die Frau ohne Unterleib: Zu Judith Butlers Entkörperung. Ein Zeitdokument. *Feministische Studien* 11, no. 2: 24–33.

Fausto-Sterling, Anne. 1992. *Myths of Gender: Biological Theories About Women and Men* (2nd ed.). New York: Basic Books.

Fausto-Sterling, Anne. 2000. *Sexing the Body. Gender Politics and the Construction of Sexuality.* New York: Basic Books.

Fausto-Sterling, Anne, Cynthia Garcia Coll, and Meghan Lamarre. 2012a. Sexing the Baby: Part 1—What Do We Really Want to Know About Sex Differentiation in the First Three Years of Life? *Social Science & Medicine* 74, no. 11: 1684–92.

Fausto-Sterling, Anne, Cynthia Garcia Coll, and Meghan Lamarre. 2012b. Sexing the Baby: Part 2—Applying Dynamic Systems Theroy to the Emergences of Sex-related Differences in Infants and Toddlers. *Social Science & Medicine* 74, no. 11: 1693–702.

Foucault, Michel. (1976) 1998. *The History of Sexuality Vol. 1: The Will to Knowledge.* London: Penguin.

García-Falgueras, Alicia, Lisette Ligtenberg, Frank Kruijver, and Dick Swaab. 2011. Galanin Neurons in the Intermediate Nucleus (Inm) of the Human Hypothalamus in Relation to Sex, Age, and Gender Identity. *Journal of Comparative Neurology* 519: 3061–3084.

Haraway, Donna. 1984. Primatology Is Politics by Other Means. *PSA: Proceedings of the Biennial Meeting of the Philosophy of Science Association* 2: 489–524.

Haraway, Donna. 1986. Primatology Is Politics by Other Means: Women's Place Is in the Jungle. In Ruth Bleier, ed., *Feminist Approaches to Science.* New York: Pergamon Press, 77–118.

Haraway, Donna. 1988. Situated Knowledges: The Science Question in Feminism and the Privilege of Partial Perspective. *Feminist Studies* 14, no. 3: 575–99.

Haraway, Donna. 1989. *Primate Visions: Gender, Race and Nature in the World of Modern Science.* New York and London: Routledge.

Harding, Sandra. 1991. *Whose Science? Whose Knowledge?: Thinking from Women's Lives.* Ithaca, NY: Cornell University Press.

Ihnen, S.K.Z., Jessica A. Church, Steven E. Petersen, and Bradley L. Schlaggar. 2009. Lack of Generalizability of Sex Differences in the FMRI BOLD Activity Associated with Language Processing in Adults. *NeruoImage* 45, no. 3: 1020–32.

Joel, Daphna. 2011. Male or Female? Brains Are Intersex. *Frontiers in Integrative Neuroscience* 5 (20 September): 57.

Joel, Daphna. 2012. Genetic-gonadal-genitals Sex (3G-sex) and the Misconception of Brain and Gender, or, Why 3G-males and 3G-females Have Intersex Brain and Intersex Gender. *Biology of Sex Differences* 3 (17 December): 27.

Jordan-Young, Rebecca. 2010. *Brain Storm: The Flaws in the Science of Sex Differences.* Cambridge, MA: Harvard University Press.

Kaiser, Anelis. 2010. The Cortical Power of Gender. *Paper presented at the Conference "NeuroGenderings."* Uppsala, Sweden (March).

Kaiser, Anelis. 2012. Re-conceptualizing Sex and Gender in the Human Brain. *Journal of Psychology* 220, no. 2: 192–98.

Kaiser, Anelis, Sven Haller, Sigrid Schmitz, and Cordula Nitsch. 2009. On Sex/Gender Related Similarities and Differences in fMRI Language Research. *Brain Research Reviews* 61, no. 2: 49–59.

Kaiser, Anelis, Esther Kuenzli, Daniela Zappatore, and Cordula Nitsch. 2007. On Females' Lateral and Males' Bilateral Activation During Language Production: A fMRI Study. *International Journal of Psychophysiology* 63, no. 2: 192–98.

Kandel, Eric R. 2001. The Molecular Biology of Memory Storage: A Dialogue Between Genes and Synapses. *Science* 249, no. 5544: 1030–38.

Kuria, Emily Ngubia (2012). The Challenge of Gender Research in Neuroscience. In F. Vander Valk, ed., *Essays in Neuroscience and Political Theory; Thinking the Body Politic,* New York: Routledge, 268–87.

Landweer, Hilge. 1994. Jenseits des Geschlechts? Zum Phänomen der theoretischen und politischen Fehleinschätzung von Travestie und Transsexualität. In Institute for Social Science Frankfurt a. M., ed. *Geschlechterverhätnisse und Politik.* Frankfurt am Main: 139–67.

Lettow, Susanne. 2008. Flexibilization and Determinism. Neurosciences and the Naturalization of Subjectivity. *Forum Wissenschaft* (April 2008): 10–13.

Maasen, Sabine, and Barbara Sutter, eds. 2007. *On Willing Selves: Neoliberal Politics and the Challenge of Neuroscience.* Hampshire and New York: Palgrave Macmillan.

Malabou, Catherine. 2008. *What Should We Do With Our Brain?* Translated by Sebastian Rand. New York: Fordham University Press.

Maney, Donna L. 2016. Perils and Pitfalls f Reporting Sex Differences. *Philosophical Transactions of the Royal Society B* 371: 20150119.

McCarthy, Margaret M., and Arthur P. Arnold. 2011. Reframing Sexual Differentiation of the Brain. *Nature Neuroscience* 14, no. 6: 667–83.

McCarthy, Margaret M., Arthur P. Arnold, Gregory. F. Ball, Jeffrey. D. Blaustein, and Geert J. Vries. 2012. Sex Differences in the Brain: The Not So Inconvenient Truth. *Journal of Neuroscience* 32, no. 7: 2241–47.

Morris, John A., Cynthia L. Jordan, and S. Marc Breedlove. 2004. Sexual Differentiation of the Vertebrate Nervous System. *Nature Neuroscience* 7, no. 10: 1034–39.

Palm, Kerstin. 2012. Räumliches Vorstellungsvermögen—von Natur aus Männersache? Kritische Anmerkung zu biologischen Forschungen über geschlechtsspezifische Kompetenzen. In Wenka Wentzel, Sabine Mellies, and Barabara Schwarze, eds. *Generation Girls' Day.* Berlin: Budrich UniPress: 211–34.

Phillips, Michael, Mark Lowe, Joseph T. Lurito, Mario Dzemidzic, and Vincent P. Mathews. 2001. Temporal Lobe Activation Demonstrates Sex-based Differences During Passive Listening. *Radiology* 220, no. 1: 202–7.

Phillips, Owen R., Kirsti A. Clark, Eileen Luders, Ramin Azhir, Shantanu H. Joshi, Roger P. Woods, John C. Mazziotta, Arthur W. Toga, and Katherine L. Narr. 2013. Superficial White Matter: Effects of Age, Sex, and Hemisphere. *Brain Connectivity* 3, no. 2: 146–59.

Pitts-Taylor, Victoria. (2010). The Plastic Brain: Neoliberalism and the Neuronal Self. *Health (London)* 14, no. 6: 635–52.

Rippon, Gina, Rebecca Jordan-Young, Anelis Kaiser, and Cordelia Fine. 2014. Recommendations for Sex/Gender Neuroimaging Research. Key Principles and Implications for Research Design, Analysis and Interpretation. *Frontiers in Human Neuroscience* 8 (28 August): 650.

Rose, Nikolas. 2003. Neruochemical Selves. *Society* (November/December): 46–59.

Roy, Deboleena. 2008. Asking Different Questions: Feminist Practices for the Natural Sciences. *Hypatia: A Journal of Feminist Philosophy* 23, no. 4: 134–57.

Rubin, Beatrix P. 2009. Changing Brains: The Emergence of the Field of Adult Neurogenesis. *BioSocieties* 4 (December): 407–24.

Schaper-Rinkel, Petra. 2012. Auf dem Weg zu einer neurowissenschaftlichen Gouvernementalität? Zu den Konturen einer neuen Emotionen-Politik. In Felix Heidenreich, and Gary S. Schaal, eds. *Politische Theorie und Emotion*. Baden-Baden: Nomos: 255–69.

Schmitz, Sigrid. 2012. The Neurotechnological Cerebral Subject: Persistence of Implicit and Explicit Gender Norms in a Network of Changes. *Neuroethics* 5, no. 3: 261–74.

Sommer, Iris E. C., André Aleman, Anke Bouma, and René S. Kahn. 2004. Do Women Really Have More Bilateral Language Representation Than Men? A Meta-analysis of Functional Imaging Studies. *Brain* 127, no. 8: 1845–52.

Subramaniam, Banu. 2009. Moored Metamorphoses: A Retrospective Essay on Feminist Science Studies. *Signs* 34, no. 4: 951–80.

Swaab, Dick F., Wilson C. J. Chung, Frank P. Kruijver, Michel A. Hofman, and Tatjana A. Ishunina. 2001. Structural and Functional Sex Differences in the Human Hypothalamus. *Hormones and Behavior* 40, no. 2: 1845–52.

8

The Communicative Phenomenon of Brain-Computer Interfaces

SIGRID SCHMITZ

Current developments at the nexus of neuro-technologies apparently fragment the border between body, technology, culture, and society. Bodies and brains incorporate technology via connectivity with machines or prostheses. Although Brain-Computer Interfaces and neuro-prosthesis have been developed primarily in the medical sector, further applications currently enter society as a whole. In consequence, these neuro-technological apparatuses not only transgress the border between the biology and technology but they are also deeply embedded in socio-cultural contexts, norms, and discourses.

From my background in feminist Science Technology Studies and in particular by taking the perspective of *feminist materialism*, I question the dynamic becomings of these hybrid phenomena in this chapter. How can we grasp the bio-techno-socio-cultural entanglements, including brains, bodies, EEG-caps, brain implants, connected computers and technical devices, all embedded in scientific and medical research, in markets, in the military field, as well as in societal power relations?

I use Karen Barad's onto-epistemological framework of agential realism (Barad 2007, Barad 2003) as an analytical perspective to consider the agential forces of matter, technologies, and meanings in course of the intra-active realization of Brain-Computer Interfaces. I understand the *notion of agency* as an enactment that is not necessarily bound to consciousness or intentionality, attributes that are commonly aligned to human subjectivity. As Barad states, agency

> is the enactment of iterative changes to particular practices—iterative reconfigurings of topological manifolds of spacetimematter relations— through the dynamics of intra-activity. Agency is about changing possibili-

ties of change entailed in reconfiguring material-discursive apparatuses of bodily production, including the boundary articulations and exclusions that are marked by those practices in the enactment of a causal structure. (Barad 2007: 178, italics taken from the original)

I use this concept of agency to account, in particular, for the agential cuts (Barad 2003) that materialize the hybrid phenomenon of Brain-Computer Interfaces, where brainbodies intra-act with technological components. Being aware of setting agential cuts myself by conceptualizing these components, I take their communicative dynamics as a starting point to develop questions for further research. This in-depth analysis of the mutual enactments between brainbodies, computer hard- and software, and technical devices allows for a reflection on the entanglements of meanings and decisions that frame the particular becomings of these neuro-technological phenomena in current society. Using the term *brainbodies*, I highlight the twofold notion of the brain in western culture: the brain as part of our body, i.e., as organic materiality, and the brain as a core of our thinking, of our rationality, and of our communicative actions with the outer world. Brainbodies are not only centered at the node between body and mind; they already represent material-discursive entanglements of both body and mind.

If technologized brainbodies materialize through continuous intra-actions, and if they constitute and constantly re-constitute during processes of information transfer and codes of communication, these modern cyborgs (Haraway 1991) may bear the potential to disrupt concepts of reductionist biological determinisms, of seemingly *natural* brain causes that are again and again used to legitimize gendered (and intersected) societal orders and norms. However, these cyborgs always carry particular meanings. Their becoming is conceptualized by scientists and designers, who themselves are guided by particular discourses, norms, and aims in medical, societal, or even in military contexts. Therefore, I will also question the role of actors within these material-semiotic networks and consider the relations of power and cultural symbolism that may be manifested in and through the development of neuro-technological apparatuses, such as Brain-Computer Interfaces.

My wandering through the landscapes of these current neuro-technologies will follow three pathways. *First*, I refer to the multifaceted concept of brain plasticity that has stimulated critical feminist neuroscience. I elaborate how this concept, to my view, has to be re-formulated for debates on agential materiality. I also refer to its apparently contradictory use in the notion of modern neurobiological determinism. This oscillating understanding is important for my following analysis of Brain-Computer Interfaces in the *second* part, where I look more closely at the dynamic processes of communicative intra-actions between brainbodies and technical apparatuses. My *third* pathway leads to reflections on the role of actors and power relations in the agential realization of neuro-technologized brainbodies and on the consequences of their socio-cultural embedding.

This is a first attempt to grasp several components and constitutions between brainbodies, neuro-technologies, and discursive entanglements, which lead to further questions for additional research.

The Multifaceted Meanings of Brain Plasticity

Critical gender analyses of brain research's methodological and empirical background uncovered its underlying binary sex concepts and heteromatrices (for overview see Schmitz and Höppner 2014b). These analyses showed how methodological distortions influence the assessment of findings, and feminist neuroscience, in particular, challenged the drawing of simplified homogenizations regarding sex categories or generalized cognitive abilities. The inclusion of meta-studies that uncovered methodical influences and contradictory findings (Kaiser et al. 2009; Sommer et al. 2004; Wallentin 2009) into scholarly neuroscientific journals attests the increasing sensitization toward critical reflections of methods within this scientific discourse (Rippon et al. 2014).

Maybe even more important was the use of the brain plasticity concept to deconstruct neurosexisms, i.e., the manifestation of sex differences by brain causes, in this field of research. The notion of brain plasticity extended the narrative field by referencing the influences of experiences and social interactions on the structural and functional developments in the brain. These concepts are now discussed widely within the neuroscientific literature as well as in popular media. Scholars in feminist neuroscience—including myself—have outlined plasticity concepts for years to point out the inseparability of biology and socio-cultural experiences throughout a lifetime (Jordan-Young and Rumiati 2012; Schmitz 2010; Vidal 2012). In consequence, the brain is not only seen as the determining source and fate for individual behavior, but as malleable and changeable during the subject's societal becoming. From the perspective of feminist neuroscience, the concept of brain plasticity offered important value to criticize reductionist biological determinisms, and particularly to question the gendered constructions of behavior and cognition, of rationality and emotionality, or of sexual preferences (for overview see Bluhm et al. 2012; Dussauge and Kaiser 2012). The NeuroGenderings expert network (https://neurogenderings. wordpress.com/) further elaborates these approaches (for overview, see Schmitz and Höppner 2014a).

In narrating plasticity stories, however, scholars of feminist neuroscience mostly stressed a return of genealogies of cause and effect, arguing that social experiences and power relations impact the brain's structure and function. In this notion, culture acts on behavior by forming and shaping the biology of the brain. This use of the brain plasticity concept is important but also leads to at least two challenges. *First*, the materiality of the brain remains to be framed as a more or less passive reactor to the attribution of gendered (and intersected) significations. Instead, in the perspective of a feminist materialist approach, we should discuss brain plasticity rather as an intra-active phenomenon. It has to be questioned how brain networks matter and how they enact in cognition and behavior. If we understand brain and culture as being indivisibly intertwined in an assemblage of reciprocal exchange, constituting and continuously reshaping each other, the phenomenon of the brainbody-in-culture is not only passively awaiting its shaping and forming from outside. The disclosure of the impartible entanglements of brainbodies, mind, behavior within socio-cultural contexts and meaning-makings inspired the feminist neuro-discourse to account for the brain's agency in a non-essentialist manner. Elizabeth Wilson started this debate in her book *Neural Geographies* (Wilson 1998) and I study her ideas in greater detail in the next section.

Second, the expansion of the domains of neuroscientific knowledge into other disciplines (e.g., education, economics, sociology, or philosophy) has led to an abundance of current neurocultures. They mostly account for the individual as a *cerebral subject*—the anthropological figure of the human according to which all decisions and actions are explainable and predictable from the brain (Ortega and Vidal 2007). This notion of the cerebral subject is deeply connected to a modern *neurobiological determinism* (Schmitz 2012). Irrespectively of its innate or experience-based formation, the brain's materiality at a particular moment of acting is again taken to determine, explain, and predict to the fullest extent all processes of human thinking and acting. In consequence, the brainbody is not seen as a material-discursive phenomenon, but instead is again framed as the essential entity, as the origin and cause for behavior, cognition, and decision-making.

This concept of neurobiological determinism is intertwined with that of the plastic brain—a contradiction only at first sight. We can disclose the interrelated and simultaneous effectiveness of both concepts in the current framing of a *neuro-governmentality.* This form of governmentality refers to the implementation of technologies of power and the market economy into technologies of the self in the field of brain optimization. Neuro-governmentality seems to emerge as a central paradigm in biopolitical regulation in current western society (Maasen and Sutter 2007; Rose 2005). One's own brain, and the human brain in general, should be trained, modulated, enhanced, and tuned to optimize human capabilities on the neoliberal market. The enhanced brainbody evolves into a critical success factor for the subject that aims for marketing one's labor profitably and to take a successful position in social hierarchies within the normative notion of modern meritocracy. Brainbodies are taken as a resource in following these demands of "biomedical neoliberalism" (Pitts-Taylor 2010). Albeit malleable for particular aims and outcomes through tuning treatments, it seems that the notion of an essential and enclosed bio-materiality at a particular time of acting is conceptualized to ensure predictability and control of these manipulations (Schmitz 2014).

These concepts also stand in the center of the development of neuro-technical approaches, in the medical sector as well as in those approaches that aim to use the brainbody as a resource for individual and societal optimization. I will now focus on the question of how to grasp the neuro-technologized brainbodies without falling into the trap of modern neurobiological determinism, but by taking the dynamics and entanglements between agential brainbodies, technologies, and meaning-making into account.

Communicative Intra-Actions in Brain-Computer Interfaces

Brain-Computer Interfaces (BCI) are conceptualized to detect and extract the activity pattern of particular movement information out of the brain and to transform this output into computer-generated algorithms. The latter then should be converted into signals to navigate the connected technical devices, e.g., computer cursors, wheelchairs, or prostheses, in order to replace human organs and activities. Superficially, this popular description stresses two notions of BCI. First, they seem to be based on linear concepts of information transfer from the inside of the brain to the outer world. Second, the computer apparently represents a form of transfer module for the commands in order to be executed by the devices. Both computer and devices appear to be neutral and not enacted in the quality of the information itself, which is taken from the brain. The term *thought translation* that is mostly used in publications and public discourses to present these forms of BCI strengthen the impression of a conscious and linear (inside-to-outside) process that is facilitated by technologies (Schmitz 2012).

I will refer to some prominent examples of BCI to show that these phenomena do not follow such simple and linear rules of information transfer; instead, they currently re-constitute due to mutual processes of communication and learning. In combining the terms of *communication* and *learning*, I start to shed a more differentiated light on the processes of exchange of information between the brainbody, technologies, and the environment, and on their reciprocal impacts throughout the intra-active forming of the BCI phenomena.

Non-invasive BCI use EEG signals to operate external devices, for example to help paralyzed patients to communicate, at least in part, with the outer world. With the help of the so-called Thought-Translation Device a patient with amyotropic lateral sclerosis who was unable to communicate otherwise was trained to move a cursor up and down on a computer screen to select letters for writing a text (Birbaumer et al. 1999). Meanwhile the patient can choose websites and links with the so-called Descartes Web-Browsing System (Karim et al. 2006). Again, this may sound easy and linear at first sight. The communicative BCI assemblage, however, embraced his brainbody with its neural tissues, physiological processes, and neural activities, his attempts to raise or lower his slow cortical potentials, the corresponding changes in EEG activity that were detected from his scalp by using an EEG-Cap with particular sensor points, the chains to the computer, the computer hardware, the software algorithms, the screen layout and the movements of the cursor, the recognition of the results of the patient's actions by the software, by communication partners and by himself, and the continuous re-shaping of further actions. In consequence, the successful realization of this brainbody-computer-communication required learning processes and decisions at various sites.

At this point, I will cut only two of the intra-acting components out of this assemblage, the patient with his brainbody and the computer software, although there are additional components that have to be taken into account (see next section). The computer software had to be designed for a complex array of algorithms for data analyses and for new, so-called learnable algorithms that should emerge to translate the communication pattern of the brainbody into binary commands for the cursor: the computer had to learn. The patient also had to learn new forms of communication with the machine in order to reach the desired BCI outcome. The changing of his cortical potentials could not be performed immediately. The patient needed one year of training to adapt his cortical activity to understandable signals for the computer.

The most interesting aspect throughout the agential realization of this phenomenon arises from the patient's descriptions about his efforts and challenges with respect to the communicative and learning processes. The patient wrote these explanations down with the help of the BCI system (Neumann 2001: 61–63). The visual feedback from the moving cursor on the computer screen was necessary for him to acquire the skill for lowering or raising his cortical potentials. However, this visual feedback seemed to operate more as a positive reinforcement in a longlasting process of operant conditioning (Schwartz et al. 2008) than as an informative pattern that the patient could have consciously analyzed. This is the first hint to a form of unconscious agency in the communicative process between the patient's brainbody that processes the visual feedback and the computer setup. As well, the performing of changes in his slow cortical activity to get the cursor to move up and down was *not* simply based on conscious decisions. Instead, the patient described his efforts as producing a feeling of a "pressure in the brain" to select a letter, respectively he tried to "empty his thoughts" in order to achieve a letter rejection (Neumann 2001: 61–63). Albeit being inseparably intertwined with his conscious desire to move the cursor, these images were not consciously controllable or repeatable by his thoughts, as the patient mentioned.

These descriptions support a differentiated view on the brainbody-computer-communication that seems to realize in a network of entanglements between sensory inputs from the computer screen, materialities and functions of the brainbody, unconscious and conscious processes of meaning making, and of producing particular outputs to the EEG-cap. For the patient it was not the controllable production of his "thoughts" (as a metaphor of the rational mind) but the inseparable entanglement with brain activities and even sudden emotions (Neumann 2001: 62) that guided the communication process. Remarkably, current developments of EEG-based Brain-Computer Interfaces address such processes of operant conditioning and affective stimulation (De Massari et al. 2013; Silvoni et al. 2011) to improve the communication between brainbody and computer. Moreover, they try to use brain plasticity on the "human" side and learnable algorithms on the "computer" side to modificate this communication more effectively.

The former example of non-invasive BCI first touches the agential intra-actions of brain dynamics and the connected technology. With a second example I will further elaborate these entanglements. Invasive BCI are developed in the area of neuro-prosthetics to support *direct* interaction between the brain and external devices (arm or leg prostheses). The grounding work for developing neuro-prostheses was done with apes and thus crosses the *humanimal border*. Interestingly, the references to *thoughts* that should direct the technical devices are taken in this field without challenging the question of thoughts or *mind* as being particular human characteristics (Nicolelis 2003). I will focus next on the intra-actions between (also animal) brainbodies and computers.

Miguel Nicolelis and his research group worked with Macaques to develop neuro-prostheses. A 320-electrode array was implanted in the brain of an ape, while she moved a joy-stick in a computer game to put a ball in a cube for a food reward. The brain implant was connected to a computer. The neuronal pattern in multiple cortical areas of the ape's brain that accompanied the arm and hand movements was analyzed and particular movement information was extracted and transferred into a set of computer algorithms. Along the way, a parallel control of a robotic arm was conducted with the same action: the movement of a ball in a cube in the real-world environment. This robotic arm was closely attached to the computer and visible for the ape. Then the researchers removed the joy-stick and after a while the ape decreased her arm and hand movements. But the movement of the robotic arm continued, and the ape got her food reward. The authors concluded that the ape learned to operate the robotic arm solely by neuronal activity; *by her thoughts*, as they frame it (Nicolelis 2003).

Nevertheless, the communicative intra-actions between brainbodies and technical apparatuses are not conceptualized only in one direction. The prerequisite for a successful communication is the so-called closed loop (Lebedev & Nicolelis 2006). Multiple feedbacks during training were most important for the ape to *learn* successful regulation of the prosthetic arm, i.e., food reward, visual and also sensory feedback redirected in her brain. Brain plasticity is stressed as the basic requisite for the learning capability of the brainbody on the one hand. At the counterpart, the development of learnable algorithms of the computer software is analogized similar to brain plasticity.

These two examples show that the BCI discourse itself breaks up the apparent linearity from inside the brainbody (the cause) to the outside world (the effect). The framing of BCIs as intra-active phenomena may change notions of brainbodies and computers as self-contained entities. Due to the mutual intra-actions it may not even be possible to separate lines of linear causalities. It is the *communication between* these components that matters, and this leads to the question how the exchange of information reciprocally impacts the involved components of these intra-actions.

I again set agential cuts to extract some of the codes and types of information that enact in these forms of communication. Brainbodies, in my view, are material-discursive formations that emerge out of biological and meaning-making processes, which are constantly performed and situated in environmental (including societal) contexts. I will start with the intra-actions between molecular, cellular, nerve, and tissue components that already comprise a set of material agencies ranging from molecular transformations, modulations of membrane potentials, and electrical activity to physiological and chemical intra-actions of transmitters with membranes. These fine-grained material underpinnings are actively engaged in forming the codes of brain communication, and they already develop a high grade of complexity. Although particular functions are often attributed to specific brain areas, communication patterns are not closed up in particular nerve cells, small networks, or even in particular brain areas. The nervous system seems to be highly interconnected within a circuitry of intercommunications between cortical areas, between cortical and sub-cortical regions, between brain and body, and also between brainbody and the outside world.

An even more complex pattern arises, if I refer to the phenomenon of *information* that emerges of such multitude aspects of physiological, chemical, and electronic intercommunicative processes. Concepts of connectionist neurosciences question whether the informative content of brain activity can be reduced to single entities as neurons or to an electrical on/off tuning. Elizabeth Wilson determined that these approaches "figure cognitive processing as the spread of activation across a network of interconnected, neuron-like units. . . . It is the connections between these units, rather than the units per se, that take on the pivotal role in the functioning of the network" (Wilson 1998: 6). That is to say, "individual units have no representational status as such, it is the overall pattern of activity across the network in total [that counts]" (156). "Knowledge is implicit, stored in the connections rather than the units" (160).

However, we cannot understand the brainbody as an entire system characterized only by autopoetic or solely biomaterial dynamics. The dynamics of brain codes, communication, and information patterns are always open to environmental entanglements. Following plasticity concepts, the brainbody realizes and integrates sensory inputs or behavioral patterns through learning processes. Agential changes in network connections, neuronal and synaptic reorganizations, variations in signal processing, and transmitter regulation as well as changes in inter- and intra-cellular molecular processes down to gene regulations always intra-act with unconscious and conscious experiences, information from the environment, meaning-making and discursive settings. All of them re-form communication patterns and constitute new forms of *information*. In this perspective, neither the brain's materiality nor the conscious mind can be conceptualized as a passive recipient or pure actor. It is their agential convergence that constitutes behavior and communication.

Coming back to the brainbody-computer-communication, I also consider the components of the computer hardware and software (its algorithms) that intra-act with the brainbodies via the multitude of visual and senso-motoric feedback loops, via screen layouts, implanted chips, EEG-electrodes, and chains. The computer "communicates" via a binary code. Although this code for communication can reach high forms of complexity, it is grounded in another form of logic than the brainbody's communication. This aspect is important for the following considerations: The brainbody has to intra-act with the mathematical-logical machine. On the one hand, the neuro-functional *pattern of information* emerges of a complex and multitude setting of electronic and bio-chemical signals associated with unconscious and conscious meaning-making dynamics. On the other hand, the computer works within a logic framework of binary codes.

The computer has to understand and to translate the brainbody's communication into its binary code (on/off, up/down, yes/no) in order to regulate the movement of a cursor on the screen or that of a prosthetic device. In this conception, the machine should learn through these forms of communication and it should change its algorithms to develop a more complex output for its actuators. Although these outputs meanwhile allow for more degrees of freedom, i.e., they permit movements of cursors or prostheses in various directions (Karim et al. 2006), the machine cannot change its principle of binary coding. In consequence, the mutual learning exchanges between the computer and the brainbody, which are necessary requisites for the materialization of BCIs, foster questions regarding how the differing codes re-form the information-generating processes in all the biological and technological components, and how they frame and re-constitute the emerging and dynamic communicative processes in technologized brainbodies.

My upcoming research interest is to analyze further and in more detail how brain activities and computer codes intra-act and with what outcomes. Current dedates in BCI development take the intra-action of both brain plasticity and learnable algorithms into consideration to sharpen the accuracy of "brain commands" (Leuthardt et al. 2009) and to improve the algorithms for neuroprosthetic control (Cunningham et al. 2011). Furthermore, these intra-actions constitute modifications of the technologized bodybrain: observing a touch of an avatar arm already changes activity in sensoromotor brain areas of a monkey (Shokur et al. 2013), and even impossible arm movements can be "learned" by humans (Moseley and Brugger 2009).

Recent approaches even enlarge the assemblage of components enacted within these intra-active developments. Brain-to-Brain Interfaces (BBI) are coming under development, which try to connect two (or more) brainbodies via technological devices and Internet facilities (Rajesh et al. 2014). Although referring to a seemingly linear transmission of information, BBI approaches already account for the shaping effects of communication on the biological formations: "A BBI rests on two pillars: the capacity to read (or "decode") useful information from neural activity and the capacity to write (or "encode") digital information back into neural activity" (Rajesh et al. 2014: 1) Furthermore, not only taking conscious exchange of information into focus, the developers target "information that is available to our brain [but] is not introspectively available to our consciousness" (ibid.: 1). There is need to develop further in-depth research to assess the agential codes of bodybrains and the digital software codes that are addressed and extracted, how these components are put into exchange, and how they intra-actively frame the BBI developments.

At this point, it is important also to account for additional components that interact in the current BCI (and BBI) phenomena. As the computer's translation depends on binary information, it also has to be questioned how this logic frames the decisions of researchers and designers, which components of the brainbody-code they consider, extract, and adopt for the communication with the computer, or via digital codes with other bodybrains. In the next section I discuss who decides on the arrangements and the framing of these forms of communication.

Intra-Actors, Power Relations, and Further Questions for Research

BCI phenomena do not realize (in the sense of a "coming into existence") in a neutral vacuum. They realize within medical, social, political, and economic settings, discourses, and power relations. How do these entanglements change the phenomenon of BCI and to which targets and aims? Who decides on intelligible codes, on form, content, and processes of these communications? Who has the power to define which information processing is more favorable than others?

The medical sector at first glance aims for an improvement of the *patients' autonomy* with the help of computer-facilitated communication. However, the decisions on how this communication should be advanced are made by scientists with a particular expertise, by physicians, and technical experts. They localize target brain areas and decide on particular brainbody-codes to be extracted while installing the BCI networks. They construct the sensor implants and program the computer basic algorithms from which the machine should develop further algorithms. All these actors negotiate how the communication between the brainbody and the computer should be performed. Although there are first considerations for the machine to adapt its learnable algorithms alongside with changing brain signals (Castermans et al. 2014), most researchers ask for the brainbody to adapt the forms of communication that the technology requires (Lebedev et al. 2005). The brainbody is targeted to plastically reframe its neuronal and synaptic connectivity and efficiency down to the cellular and molecular levels. How then do these adaptions civilize the brainbody concerning particular forms of agency or even particular forms of thinking?

I have analyzed elsewhere the current framing of Brain-Computer Interfaces that are developed and implemented in wider societal contexts (Schmitz 2012). EEG-caps and other BCI products are advertised on the commercial market to facilitate *thought-communication* between subjects, to improve mobile communication, to control avatars in computer games *with one's mind*, or to enable hands-free control of mobilization aids or home devices. These first analyses have shown how the framing of the neuro-technologized subject refers to the paradigm of optimizing human capabilities for the neoliberal market. Enhancement of flexibility, connectedness, mobility, operationability, and rationality turned out to be at the center of these developments. I have also worked out the gendered connotations of these targets following a constant framing of masculinized rationality over feminized emotionality (ibid.: 273–274).

Here I juxtapose three argumentative figures that highlight the ambivalences in these discourses. First, the popular representation of BCI in the commercial field particularly points to seemingly autonomous and rational processes that the subject could realize in communication with the technology. The repeated references to *thoughts* and *minds* as the driving forces produce an image of the conscious and self-confident subject that *uses* the technologies for her/his aims and needs. The apparently autonomous setting of human decision-making and controlled communication masks the embedding of theses self-technologies in current neuro-governmental bio-politics and its connectedness with research policies, markets, the military field, and state politics (Pickersgill 2013). The military sector, for example, takes a predominant role in financing the development of BCI, neuro-prosthesis, and further neuro-technologies (e.g., the work of the Nicolelis research group was financed by the Defense Advanced Research Projects Agency—DARPA; see Hoag 2003).

Second, the brainbody seems to remain a resource, tamed and trained for particular targets, which the technologized human should aim for. In my view, this framing re-signifies the classical concepts of a more or less passive nature as a resource, in this case the bodybrain as an instrument for realizing techno-hybrid demands and to optimize her-/himself for the neoliberal market.

The third figure currently arises in the discursive arena of BCI developments. The recently launched EU-based "Human Brain Project" (https://www.humanbrainproject.eu/discover/the-project/overview) and the Swiss "Blue Brain Project" (http://bluebrain.epfl.ch/cms/lang/en/pid/56882) fund approaches to map the whole brain's networks on computer hardware and software at a cost of approximately 1 billion Euro. Superficially argued for use in improving the information exchange and networking between neuroscientific research groups, another opinion bypasses these approaches: the aim to create the virtual brain, and perhaps even to make the individual brain immortal in digital worlds. There is currently a very controversial discussion within Europe's neuroscientific community about the scientific policies in handling this project, its aims, and participating groups (cf. http://news.sciencemag.org/brain-behavior/2014/07/updated-european-neuroscientists-revolt-against-e-u-s-human-brain-project). Consequently, the intra-action of discourses on transhumanity and technological singularity with current neuro-technological developments should be a topic of in-depth analyses of feminist materialism, as they touch upon the deeply gendered question of what should be *virtualized for eternity*.

These three concepts leave those agential intra-actions more or less out of sight that constitute the analyzed BCI phenomena and the upcoming BBI developments. The framework of feminist materialism offers the possibility to regard these intra-actions between brainbodies, technological apparatuses and software facilities, meaning-making processes, and power relations in more detail. I began to analyze the relation of conscious and unconscious enactments of brainbodies and computer technologies as well as the question, which agential intra-actions have which part in the constitution of these communicative assemblages. Further research is needed to gain a deeper insight into the possibilities for eroding boundaries between nature, technology, and culture in the dynamic realizations of neuro-technological phenomena. Further study is also required for analyzing negotiations of communication rules, and the role of various actors and power relations that frame these developments along current societal norms and values.

REFERENCES

Barad, Karen. 2003. Posthumanist Perfomativity: Toward an Understanding of How Matter Comes to Matter. *Signs: Journal of Women in Culture and Society* 28, no. 3: 801–831.

Barad, Karen. 2007. *Meeting the Universe Halfway*. London: Duke University Press.

Birbaumer, Nils, et al. 1999. A Spelling Device for the Paralyzed. *Nature* 398: 297–298.

Bluhm, Robyn, Anne J. Jacobson, and Heidi L. Maibom, eds. 2012. *Neurofeminism: Issues at the Intersection of Feminist Theory and Cognitive Science*. New York: Palgrave Macmillan.

Castermans, Thierry, Matthieu Duvinage, Guy Cheron, and Thierry Dutoit. 2014. Towards Effective Non-Invasive Brain-Computer Interfaces Dedicated to Gait Rehabilitätion System. *Brain Sciences* 4: 1–48.

De Massari, Daniele et al. 2013. Brain Communication in the Locked-in State. *Brain* 136: 1989–2000.

Dussauge, Isabelle, and Anelis Kaiser, eds. 2012. Special Issue Neuroscience and Sex/Gender. *Neuroethics* 5, no. 3.

Haraway, Donna. 1991. A Cyborg Manifesto: Science, Technology, and Socialist-Feminism in the Late Twentieth Century. In *Simians, Cyborgs and Women: The Reinvention of Nature*, ed. Donna Haraway. New York: Routledge, 149–181.

Hoag, Hanna. 2003. Remote Control. *Nature* 423: 796–798.

Jordan-Young, Rebecca, and Raffaella I. Rumiati. 2012. Hardwired for Sexism? Approaches to Sex/Gender in Neuroscience. *Neuroethics* 5, no. 3: 305–313.

Kaiser, Anelis, Sven Haller, Sigrid Schmitz, and Cordula Nitsch. 2009. On Sex/Gender Related Similarities and Differences in fMRI Language Research. *Brain Research Reviews* 61: 49–59.

Karim Ahmed A. et al. 2006. Neural Internet: Web Surfing with Brain Potentials for the Completely Paralyzed. *Neurorehabilitation and Neural Repair* 20: 508–515.

Lebedev, Mikhail A. et al. 2005. Cortical Ensemble Adaptation to Represent Velocity of an Artificial Actuator Controlled by a Brain-Machine Interface. *Journal of Neuroscience* 25, no. 19: 4681–4693.

Lebedev, Mikhail, and Miguel A. L. Nicolelis. 2006. Brain-Machine Interfaces: Past, Present and Future. *Trends in Neuroscience* 29, no. 9: 536–546.

Leuthardt, Eric C. et al. 2009. Evolution of Brain-Computer Interfaces: Going Beyond Classic Motor Physiology. *Neurosurgical Focus* 27, no. 1. Doi: 10.3171/2009.4.FOCUS0979.

Maasen, Sabine, and Barbara Sutter, eds. 2007. *On Willing Selves. Neoliberal Politics vis-à-vis the Neuroscientific Challenge.* New York: Palgrave McMillan.

Moseley, Lorimer G., and Brugger, Peter. 2009. Interdedendence of Movement and Anatomy Persist When Amputees Learn a Physiologically Impossible Movement of Their Phantom Limb. *PNAS* 106, no. 44: 18798–18802.

Neumann, Nicola. 2001. *Gehirn-Computer-Kommunikation. Einflüsse der Selbstregulation langsamer kortikaler Hirnpotentiale.* PhD Thesis. Tübingen: University of Tübingen.

Nicolelis, Miguel A. 2003. Brain–Machine Interfaces to Restore Motor Function and Probe Neural Circuits. *Nature Reviews* 4: 417–422.

Ortega, Francisco, and Fernando Vidal. 2007. Mapping the Cerebral Subject in Contemporary Culture. *RECIIS* 1, no. 2: 255–259.

Pickersgill, Martin. 2013. The Social Life of the Brain: Neuroscience in Society. *Current Sociology*, online first. doi: 10.1177/0011392113476464.

Pitts-Taylor, Victoria. 2010. The Plastic Brain: Neoliberalism and the Neuronal Self. *Health: Interdisciplinary Studies in Health, Illness and Medicine* 14, no. 6: 635–652.

Rajesh, P. N. Rao, Andrea Stocco, Matthew Bryan, Devapratim Sarma, Tiffany M. Youngquist, Joseph Wu, and Chantel S. Prat. 2014. A Direct Brain-to-Brain Interface in Humans. *PLOS ONE* 9 (11), e111332. doi: 10.1371/journal.pone.0111332.

Rippon, Gina, Rebecca Jordan-Young, Anelis Kaiser, and Cordelia Fine. 2014. Recommendations for Sex/Gender Neuroimaging Research: Key Principles and Implications for Research Design, Analysis, and Interpretation. *Frontiers in Human Neuroscience* 8. doi: 10.3389/fnhum.2014.00650.

Rose, Steven. 2005. *The Future of the Brain: The Promise and Perils of Tomorrow's Neuroscience.* Oxford: Oxford University Press.

Schmitz, Sigrid. 2010. Sex, Gender, and the Brain—Biological Determinism versus Socio-Cultural Constructivism. In *Gender and Sex in Biomedicine. Theories, Meth-*

*odologies, Results,*ed. Ineke Klinge and Claudia Wiesemann. Göttingen: Universitätsverlag Göttingen, 57–76.

Schmitz, Sigrid. 2012. The Neuro-technological Cerebral Subject: Persistence of Implicit and Explicit Gender Norms in a Network of Change. *Neuroethics* 5, no. 3: 261–274.

Schmitz, Sigrid. 2014. Feminist Approaches to Neurocultures. In *Brain Theory: Essays in Critical Neurophilosophy,* ed. Charles Wolfe. New York: Palgrave Macmillan, 195–216.

Schmitz, Sigrid, and Grit Höppner, eds. 2014a. *Gendered Neurocultures: Feminist and Queer Perspectives on Current Brain Discourses.* Vienna: Zaglossus.

Schmitz, Sigrid, and Grit Höppner. 2014b. Feminist Neuroscience: A Critical Review of *Contemporary Brain Research. Frontiers in Human Neuroscience* 8. doi: 10.3389/fnhum.2014.00546.

Schwartz, Barry, Edward A. Wasserman, and Steven J. Robbins. 2008. *Psychology of Learning and Behavior.* (5ᵗʰ ed.). Part II: Behavior-Event Learning: Operant Conditioning. New York: Norton, 132–164.

Shokur, Solaiman et al. 2013. Expanding the Primate Body Schema in Sensorimotor Cortex by Virtual Touches of an Avatar. *PNAS* 110, no. 37: 15121–15126.

Silvoni, S. et al. 2011. Brain-Computer Interfaces in Stroke: a Review of Progress. *Clinical EEG aand Neuroscience* 42, no. 4: 245–252.

Sommer, Iris E., André Aleman, Anke Bouma, and René S. Kahn. 2004. Do Women Really Have More Bilateral Language Representation Than Men? A Meta-Analysis of Functional Imaging Studies. *Brain* 127: 1845–1852.

Vidal, Catherine. 2012. The Sexed Brain: Between Science and Ideology. *Neuroethics* 5, no. 3: 295–303.

Wallentin, Mikka. 2009. Putative Sex Differences in Verbal Abilities and Language Cortex: A Critical Review. *Brain and Language* 108: 175–183.

Wilson, Elizabeth A. 1998. *Neural Geographies. Feminism and the Microstructure of Cognition.* New York: Routledge.

PART III

Biopolitics and Necropolitics

9

Technologies of Failure, Bodies of Resistance

Science, Technology, and the Mechanics of
Materializing Marked Bodies

JOSEF BARLA

Asking for technology and the body at the same time almost inevitably evokes the question of what kinds of connections extend between the two. But what if it is not so much a question of connections but of entanglements? What if the terms "technology" and "the body" do not refer to two distinct phenomena that somehow interact with one another but rather technologies are always embodied technologies (even more so if technology is also understood as a particular mode of knowing and being) and material bodies have to be understood as always already technologized bodies—yet in different ways and with very different ethical and political consequences? What would it mean to understand the entanglement of technology and the body not so much as a matter of epistemological but of ontological indeterminacy? That is, what would it mean to argue that the boundaries and properties of bodies and technologies are performatively enacted through particular material-discursive practices in which ontological indeterminacy is resolved locally and temporarily? What would it mean to "read" technology and the body diffractively through one another?

If technicity and corporeal materiality are deeply entangled with one another, the question arises how to analyze and understand the effects of technologies and technoscientific practices on material bodies. That is, how to understand the processes through which differently (re)configured bodily materialities are enacted through particular technologies and technoscientific practice? And what can be said about the role of material bodies themselves within these very processes?

Stories about the power of technologies and technoscientific practices to shape, discipline, and to objectify the body have been and still continue to be of fundamental importance for the feminist critique of power relations and social inequalities. But what if it is not only too easy but also limiting, both philosophically and politically, to assume that technologies function precisely according to particular interests or social power relations that have been inscribed into them, disciplining and objectifying a mere passive body? What if what is needed today is perhaps *also* a story of technological failure instead of the same old tales of the domination and disciplining of the body through the means of science and technology?

Rosi Braidotti (2013) stresses the need for new stories, new methods, and new figures to emerge in order to be able to analyze our present world, which is a world thoroughly transformed by technobiopower and biocapitalism. It is in this sense that figures and concepts are not mere tools to make an otherwise mute and inaccessible world intelligible but, on the contrary, active re(con)figurings of the world with far-reaching consequences. The apparatus of bodily production—a concept deeply rooted in feminist contestations of fundamental dichotomies and certainties—might just be such a figure, such a "materializing narrative" (Haraway 1997: 151), that allows for new stories about technologies and bodies to emerge, contesting a thinking that differentiates between original and illegitimate copy, the natural and the artificial, dynamic language and passive ahistorical matter.

Departing from these questions, in this chapter, I will put forward a technophilosophical re(con)figuring of the concept of the apparatus of bodily production as both a figure referring to objects of philosophical inquiries—in the sense of particular sites where biological, technological, social, economic, and political forces intra-act and in doing so mutually materialize certain phenomena—and as a tool for feminist and other critical analyses of narratives centering on questions of power and becoming-with-technologies. Thoroughly informed by the work of Donna Haraway and Karen Barad, I will argue that such a technophilosophically reworked concept of the apparatus of bodily production might provide us with a deeper understanding of how not only particular knowledges about bodies but simultaneously also specifically (re)configured bodies—meaning, bodies marked by race, ethnicity, nationality, and sex/gender—are performatively enacted through particular technologies and technoscientific practices, along with particular ethical and political consequences. Most importantly, rather than understanding the bodies involved as mere objects or as sites on which powerful technologies and technoscientific practices act, I will argue that such a technophilosophical account promises to provide us with a counternarrative to stories emphasizing the omnipotence of science and technology, allowing us to philosophically take into account material bodies as generative and as potentially unruly.

Mapping the Terrain

It is no coincidence that feminist theorists, scholars of color, and those speaking from marginalized locations in particular put questions of materiality and material bodies at the center of critical analyses, given their historically longlasting identifications with nature. Queer and feminist scholars have not only deconstructed the idea of the gendered and sexed (female) body as a matter of fate but also shifted the focus toward questions of the body and embodiment. The concept of the apparatus of bodily production is only one outcome of these endeavors, although a highly promising one for analyzing questions centering on biology, politics, power, and agency in their entanglement with one another.

The term "apparatus of bodily production" can be traced back to the feminist literary scholar Katie King, who employed her figure of the apparatus of literary production to shed light on the question of how literature comes into existence at the crossroads of global capitalism, art, and technology (King 1991: 92). In "The Promises of Monsters," Donna Haraway takes up King's figure of the apparatus of literary production and reframes it as a tool for feminist analyses of technoscientific practices, highlighting the objects of knowledge as active entities. It is against this backdrop that Haraway puts forward the argument that organisms and, for that matter, bodies are not born but rather produced "in worldchanging technoscientific practices by particular collective actors in particular times and places" (1992: 297). This, however, does not mean that bodies and organisms are mere *social* constructions. Referring to biology, Haraway illustrates that organisms, as material-semiotic entities, emerge through specific apparatuses of bodily production—that is, arrangements consisting of human and nonhuman entities, discourses, technologies, as well as technoscientific and other practices.

Influenced by Haraway's insights, in *Meeting the Universe Halfway* (2007), Karen Barad shifts the focus to questions of matter and materiality, foregrounding the ontological implications of the concept of the apparatuses of bodily production. In contrast to the belief that matter is simply ahistorically given, and only mechanically following Newtonian laws, Barad encourages us to rethink matter as a process rather than a mere end product. Matter, for Barad, is never settled but constantly in becoming.

It is precisely against this backdrop that, by drawing on the work of the quantum physicist Niels Bohr, Barad reframes the notion of the apparatus as an instrument for feminist analyses of technoscientific practices centering on questions of agency, materiality, and power. By understanding apparatuses as all the material-discursive practices that help constitute phenomena, of which they simultaneously form a part, Barad argues in what follows that not only meanings but also boundaries and properties manifest through particular apparatuses. For Barad, apparatuses are thus neither static arrangements nor are they "external forces that operate on bodies from the outside; rather, apparatuses are material-discursive practices that are inextricable from the bodies that are produced and through which power works its productive effects" (Barad 2007: 230). As parts of phenomena as well as phenomena themselves, apparatuses function as "boundary making practices," determining "what matters and what is excluded from mattering" (ibid.: 148).

Re(con)figuring the Apparatus

Following the Latin roots of the term apparatus as "to bring forth something" (*apparare*), I propose an understanding of the apparatus of bodily production as both a metaphor and a method, a figure and an analytical tool. Figures and figurations (that is, the methodological and theoretical use of figures) are, as Donna Haraway (1997: 11) reminds us, "performative images"; "condensed maps of contestable worlds" with the power to "trouble identifications and certainties." Although figures are images, they do not merely represent or mirror pre-existing phenomena. Rather, figures are also always performative and therefore generative. The

potential of the apparatus of bodily production as a technophilosophical figure and method lies precisely in "the join between the figurative
and the factual" (Haraway 2000, 24).

However, as with Haraway's (1992: 298) theorization of the object of
knowledge as material-semiotic actor, I do not want to imply an immediate presence of apparatuses of bodily production as actual, discrete
objects "out there." Apparatuses of bodily production, in my reworked
understanding, are neither necessarily concrete objects nor specific
spatiotemporally localizable places, but rather relational, generative
phenomena or "sites" where specific material-discursive reconfigurings and processes of coming-to-being-and-meaning occur. Following the idea that concepts are material reconfigurings (Barad 2007),
the technophilosophically reframed concept of the apparatus of bodily
production that I propose here refers to both objects of philosophical
inquiry—in the sense of particular sites where biological, technological,
social, economic, and political forces intra-act[1] and in doing so mutually
materialize a certain phenomenon—and to an analytical tool for technophilosophical inquiries of narratives centering on questions of power
and becomings. It is for this reason that such an understanding of the
apparatus of bodily production not only demands a rethink of epistemology, incorporating the objects of knowledge as actively involved in
the process of knowledge production, but also of ontology: The fixed
modernist ontology as essentially given and therefore as fate is deconstructed and reframed as a specific effect of intra-actions of humans
and nonhuman entities—be they organic, technological, discursive, or
textual. Ontology becomes visible as never solid but constantly in flux,
and thus as a contested ground.

I believe that such an understanding of the apparatus of bodily production, in particular as a technophilosophical tool of investigation into
the nature of becoming-with-technology, allows for deeper understandings of how particular technologies and technoscientific practices performatively enact specifically reconfigured—that is, marked—bodies.
What is more, I believe that such an account allows us to take into account material bodies as generative and unruly, and therefore as actively
involved in the processes of their own reconfigurings, rather than understanding them as mere objects or inert matter that powerful technologies and technoscientific practices act upon. Finally, I believe that

such a technophilosophically re(con)figured notion of the apparatus of bodily production may also allow the taking into account of the ever-changing topologies of power, yet precisely without overemphasizing the omnipotence of science and technology, or ignoring the potential of bodies and organisms to be unruly, as I will demonstrate by turning to a concrete worldly example.

Materializing Authentic Bodies: UK Border Agency's Human Provenance Pilot Project

Against the background of the so-called War on Terror and recent global migration movements, new biometrical identification technologies are increasingly used to complement traditional methods of border and identity control. Biometric technologies function by collecting information about the body, or more precisely about parts of the body, and translating this information into mathematical variables. Operating from the premise that bodies do not lie, biometric technologies are increasingly deployed for monitoring and controlling migration flows and the movement of individuals. In the early twenty-first century, borders are progressively becoming technologized borders: satellites surveying suspicious movements from their orbit, drones spotting small boats on the Mediterranean Sea, and instruments detecting the heat emitted by the bodies of refugees hiding in vessels, to name but a few. At the same time biometric technologies relocate the borders deep into the body as biometric analyses and DNA tests exercise surveillance from within. Even though it is important not to lose sight of the fact that borders are not democratic, meaning that not everyone can pass through every border at any time, borders today seem to be nowhere and everywhere at the same time. They can be portable, such as ID cards and biometric passports, or virtual and thus accessible from everywhere, as is the case for biometric and genetic databases. This development not only transforms the meaning of migration but also that of bodies in a very material sense.

In September 2009, the UK Border Agency announced the launch of its *Human Provenance Pilot Project* (hereafter referred to as the *HPPP*). In the wake of debates about the alleged "abuse of the UK asylum system" (UK Border Agency 2009a: 3) as well as worries about so-called nationality swapping—that is, the accusation that refugees would often claim to come from certain war-torn regions such as, for example, Somalia in order to increase their chances of receiving asylum—UK authorities had sought new methods to "identify a person's true country of origin" (UK Border Agency 2009b). As a microscopic regime of seeing-knowing-materializing, the *HPPP* ought to reveal truths about the very essence of material bodies by reading off "ethnic origin" and even "nationality" (UK Border Agency 2009a, 2009b) from the bodies of African asylum-seekers using genetic testing and biometrical identification technologies. As the UK Border Agency considered nationality swapping to be widely common especially among African asylum-seekers, the project exclusively targeted refugees from Africa, in particular those claiming to come from Somalia.

The *HPPP* operated following the assumption that bodies cannot lie, and neither can isotopes and genes. Consequently, the UK Border Agency believed that a combination of DNA ancestry testing—which included mitochondrial DNA as well as Y chromosome and single nucleotide polymorphisms (SNP) testing—along with isotope analysis could reveal an applicant's "true country of origin." Applicants were asked to provide a mouth swab and hair and nail samples, which then were tested for DNA and certain isotopes. Mitochondrial DNA tests are used to scrutinize the genetic information stored in mitochondria. Mitochondria are organelles, subunits located in the cells of animals and plants that not only provide energy to body cells by converting food into a form that can be consumed by the cell but also possess their own, distinct DNA. Y line tests look at specific markers on the Y-chromosome that are passed down paternal lines. Both tests, mitochondrial DNA analysis and Y-chromosome analysis, can, under specific circumstances, provide information about a person's ancestral heritage since certain genetic variations are more common in certain geographical areas of the world than others. Single nucleotide polymorphisms are subtle variations in the genetic code of a person's chromosomes that can also correlate to "ethnic origin." However, none of these tests are particularly accurate and only provide very limited information (see Nature 2009). Isotope analysis is used in archaeology, anthropology, and human geography to date material cultural artifacts, to track historical movements of people, and more recently also to study migration movements of endangered animals as well as environmental influences on them. In the case of the *HPPP* it was believed that certain isotopes could determine the "true country of origin of an applicant" (UK Border Agency 2009a: 8) as well as the possible routes the applicant took to get to the United Kingdom. The UK Border Agency never revealed details about the isotopes under examination. However, the use of skin and nail tissue samples suggests that the tests focused most likely on lighter element isotopes such as strontium, oxygen, and hydrogen (see Travis 2009).

Strontium is a chemical element that belongs to the group of alkaline earth metals and is mostly found in inorganic materials such as rock. Weathering allows the isotopes to trickle into the groundwater, and from there they find their way into plants, animals, and the human body. Similar to calcium, strontium then becomes embedded in bones, hair, and nail tissue. As signatures of isotopes—that is the number of particles in the atomic nucleus—vary according to geographical location and because the isotopes incorporated are in constant exchange with the surrounding environment, analyzing the isotopic ratios in nail and hair tissue and matching them against comparison ratios from the country of which the asylum-seeker claims to hold nationality should have allowed the UK Border Agency to draw conclusions about the place of birth as well as recent migration movements of the applicants.

After two years, the project was terminated in summer 2011. The announced final report was never published, the planned international review was suspended, and the UK Border Agency said that it has no intentions of continuing the project in the near future, without providing any explanation for this decision (see UK Home Office 2011).

What does it mean now to consider the UK Border Agency's *HPPP* as an apparatus of bodily production? In an important sense, the *HPPP* as an apparatus of bodily production was as much concerned with the goal of producing knowledge (about the supposed essence of particular bodies) as it was concerned about enacting specific bodily materialities. As a nexus where power-knowledge-materiality in their entanglement concentrates and intra-actively materializes a certain phenomenon, namely, the alleged authentic Somali body that is eligible to receive asylum in the UK, the project materialized bodies that were allowed to legally remain in the country and those that were not. In a certain sense, thus, the *HPPP* has not so much revealed supposed truths about the bodies analyzed but rather reconfigured them by short-circuiting technology and technoscientific practices with biology, race, ethnicity, and nationality, determining—but at the same time also materializing—what counts as an authentic Somali body. Barad reminds us that measurements have material and ontological consequences. Measurements are not "simply revelatory but performative; they help constitute and are a constitutive part of what is being measured. In other words, measurements are intra-actions [. . .] material-discursive practices of mattering" (Barad 2012: 6–7). In fact, it is only through these very technologies and practices that the phenomenon the *HPPP* sought to measure came to matter. To put it bluntly, there was no authentic (biological or ethnic) Somali body before its enactment through the *HPPP*.

The *HPPP*, as an apparatus of bodily production, not only translated flows of data into material bodies and vice versa; in addition, the bodies the *HPPP* enacted were not just any bodies but bodies marked by ethnicity, nationality, and race. What is more, the fact that in the case of the *HPPP* exclusively male[2] black bodies came into focus illustrates that some bodies are obviously less trustworthy than others. The male black body claiming to come from Somalia itself became a document—one which, it was thought, not only could not lie but also one whose true essence could be unveiled by means of certain technologies and technoscientific practices.

It is against this background that it is important to recall Donna Haraway's urge not to ignore the potentially dangerous consequences that entanglements of informatics, biology, and politics bring with them. Haraway makes this point especially clear, arguing that "lives" are what are "at stake in curious quasi-objects like databases; they structure the informatics of possible worlds, as well as of all-too-real ones" (1995: xix). And indeed, in a certain sense the *HPPP* falls in the racist history of the reification of certain human beings constructed as passive, subordinated objects for technoscientific investigations that aim at revealing their supposed truths.

Theorizing race, and even more the materiality of race, is never innocent. It took a very long time for scholars of color as well as other critical thinkers and political activists to deconstruct the belief that race is a naturally occurring attribute of the human species. However, the question remains whether or not this means that race and racialized bodies are mere socio-cultural and linguistic constructions?

For Haraway (1997: 213) it is clear that "race is the kind of category about which no one is neutral." Race clearly matters in both senses of the word and it would be shortsighted to believe that racialized bodies are mere linguistic constructions. Understanding the UK Border Agency's *HPPP* as an apparatus of bodily production illustrates this by demonstrating *how* bodies marked by race, ethnicity, and nationality were enacted through particular material-discursive practices (which are by far not only technological or technoscientific in nature), and in doing so that neither the category race nor racialized bodies are epistemologically or ontologically transcended ahistorical phenomena. Rather than being preexisting—that is, transcendental and supposedly natural— phenomena or, on the contrary, mere social and linguistic constructions, racialized bodies are reframed as effects of material-discursive relations; not matters of fact but matters of concern.

What is more, as a generative site where specifically (re)configured bodies—that is, bodies marked by race, ethnicity, nationality, and sex/ gender—come to matter in both senses of the word, the case of the *HPPP* illustrates that it would be a mistake to believe that with/in genomics race would become "less meaningful" on a subdermal or molecular scale as, for example, the critical race scholar Paul Gilroy (2000: 37) argues. Analyzing the *HPPP* as an apparatus of bodily production rather suggests that genomics is far away from making race less meaningful. In fact, it could be said that race, today, does not only enter through the skin, as Frantz Fanon has put it with the notion of epidermalization, or Stuart Hall has seen it in the writing of difference on the skin of the other, but is increasingly read off from the very "interior" of the body— that is, of the DNA, mitochondria, and the isotopes incorporated into the body.

Technologies of Failure, Bodies of Resistance

Donna Haraway reminds us that at the heart of what she terms speculative fabulation—that is, "the practice that studies relations with relations"—lies the idea that it "matters what matters we use to think other matters with; it matters what stories we tell to tell other stories with; it matters what knots knot knots, what thoughts think thoughts, what ties tie ties. It matters what stories make worlds, what worlds make stories" (2011). Stories, in an important sense, are not fictions or made up but are rather, as Haraway (1997: 230) emphasizes, "devices to produce certain kinds of meanings" and materialities. "Stories and facts do not naturally keep a respectable distance; indeed, they promiscuously cohabit the same very material places" (ibid.: 68).

It has to be understood in this sense that theorizing the *HPPP* with a Baradian informed and technophilosophically re(con)figured concept of the apparatus of bodily production as both a figure and a method allows for a different story to emerge; one that foregrounds the *limited* rather than *pervasive* power of technologies and technoscientific practices, and in doing so might open up a different perspective on science, technologies, and bodies in their entanglements with one another. Rather than as a case for the technological and technoscientific colonization, disciplining, and objectification of material bodies, the *HPPP* becomes apparent as a failed attempt of silencing the forces and flows of material bodies.

Considering UK Border Agency's *HPPP* as an apparatus of bodily production thus not only provides us with an understanding of how bodies marked by race, ethnicity, and nationality come to matter in their entanglement with technologies, technoscientific practices, and political discourses but also—rather than regarding material bodies as mere passive moldable matter, as not much more than a kind of information storage device that can be accessed through the means of genetic and biometric technologies—puts forward an understanding of material bodies as potentially agentic and consequently as generative parts of the very apparatus through which they come to matter. It is in this sense that analyzing the *HPPP* as an apparatus of bodily production suggests that the attempts of technologically reading "ethnic origin" and nationality from the bodies of African asylum-seekers failed. And it would be too easy to see this as an outcome of the circumstance that the *HPPP* was scientifically flawed or that the technologies applied were not accurate enough, for such an account would only remain caught in the logics of the myths of technological progress and determinism, reproducing the very same belief in the omnipotence of science and technology that feminist and other critical scholars have been contested for decades. Rather, such a technophilosophical perspective outlined in this chapter puts to the fore the idea that neither did the technologies function according to the political interests inscribed into them nor did the bodies concerned play along as expected; meaning, neither could the bodies involved have been fixated on mere passive objects of knowledge, nor were the isotopes under investigation incorporated in the ways expected.

It is for this reason that theorizing the *HPPP* as an apparatus of bodily production demonstrates, on the one hand, that biometric identification technologies such as DNA and isotope testing represent new technologies of surveillance, especially in the process of migration, raising serious political and ethical questions—not only because these technologies and technoscientific practices tend to reessentialize and rebiologize race (for example, by reworking race as referring to genotype), but also because they might lead to an understanding of kinship and family as a primarily biological relation. What is more, the project—as an integral part of the UK's border machine—demonstrates that the border neither begins nor ends at the geographical or political borders of the EU, but is relocated into the depths of the body. On the other hand, however, a technophilosophical understanding of UK Border Agency's *HPPP* as an apparatus of bodily production also suggests that even a powerful, repressive, and anti-democratic technology of control such as the *HPPP* was not powerful enough to mute the forces and flows of material bodies (human and nonhuman ones). In doing so, such an account disrupts both the idea that political interests and beliefs could be inscribed into technologies with the intended effects and the idea that material bodies would be mere passive objects on which technologies and technoscientific practices act.

"There is no need to fear or hope, but only to look for new weapons," Gilles Deleuze (1992: 4) reminds us. Yet these weapons of thinking, these practices of developing new concepts and figures that, for example, allow us to take into account the potential of bodies—be they human or nonhuman—to be unruly and to "kick back" (Barad 2007: 215), as well as the fact that technologies can always fail, are precisely what gets lost in theories that emphasize the omnipotence of science and technology.[3] Shifting the focus toward the question of what technologies do, rather than what technology is, what bodies can do, rather than what (the supposedly natural) body is, however, may provide us with an understanding of how technologies and material bodies in their entanglement with one another constitute the very material our world is made of—instead of only assuming that powerful invasive technologies would increasingly dominate, manipulate, and dissolve the body (whose?) or even nature itself (whatever that might be). Disrupting the belief in the omnipotence of technologies and technoscientific practices, the figure of the apparatuses of bodily production as an apparatus of investigation into the nature of becoming-with-technologies precisely allows us to turn to these questions, and in doing so "to work toward 'more promising interference patterns', both between words and things (allowing for things and bodies to be active in processes of signification)," as Iris van der Tuin (2011: 26–27) puts it.

NOTES

1 Barad's neologism of intra-action highlights that objects and agencies do not exist prior to the intra-actions. In contrast to the term interaction, "which presumes the prior existence of independent entities or relata" (2007: 139), the notion of intra-action implies an ongoing becoming. Intra-active agencies and forces "emerge from, rather than precede, the intra-action that produces them" (ibid.: 128).

2 UK Border Agency's case owner manuals state that females "were unable to be DNA tested using the Y chromosome analysis method because they have two X chromosomes in their cells and not an X and a Y" (2009a: 3). Even though the manual also states that females "can be tested using the mitochondrial analysis method and in the near future it will be possible to test women using SNPS, which is expected to begin during the life of this pilot" (UK Border Agency 2009a: 3), it remains entirely unclear whether or not females were tested during the run-time of the pilot project.

3 Acknowledging the potential of material bodies and things to "kick back" does not mean to open up a dualism between technology and the body once again, for both technologies and bodies are always multiplicities themselves which are in various ways entangled with one another.

REFERENCES

Barad, Karen. 2007. *Meeting the Universe Halfway. Quantum Physics and the Entanglement of Matter and Meaning*. Durham, NC: Duke University Press.

Barad, Karen. 2012. "'Matter feels, converses, suffers, desires, yearns and remembers': Interview with Karen Barad," in *New Materialism: Interviews & Cartographies*, Rick Dolphijn, Iris van der Tuin, eds. Ann Arbor, MI: Open Humanities Press, 48–70.

Braidotti, Rosi. 2013. *The Posthuman*. Cambridge/Malden: Polity Press.

Deleuze, Gilles. 1992. "Postscript on the Societies of Control," *OCTOBER* 59 (Winter): 3–7.

Gilroy, Paul. 2000. *Against Race. Imagining Political Culture Beyond the Color Line*. Cambridge, MA: Harvard University Press.

Haraway, Donna. 1992. "The Promises of Monsters: A Regenerative Politics for Inappropriate/d Others," in *Cultural Studies*, Lawrence Grossberg, Cary Nelson, and Paula Treichler, eds. New York/London: Routledge, 295–337.

Haraway, Donna. 1995. "Cyborgs and Symbionts: Living Together in the New World Order," in *The Cyborg Handbook*, Chris Hables Gray, ed. New York/London: Routledge, xi–xx.

Haraway, Donna. 1997. *Modest_Witness@Second_Millennium.FemaleMan©_Meets_OncoMouse™*. New York/London: Routledge.

Haraway, Donna. 2000. *How Like a Leaf: An Interview with Thyrza Nichols Goodeve*. New York: Routledge.

Haraway, Donna. 2011. *SF: Science Fiction, Speculative Fabulation, String Figures, So Far*. Pilgrim Award Acceptance Comments, http://people.ucsc.edu/haraway/ Files/ PilgrimAcceptance-Haraway.pdf (accessed January 30, 2014).

King, Katie. 1991. "Bibliography and a Feminist Apparatus of Literary Production." *Text* 5: 91–103.

Nature. 2009. "Editorial: Genetics without borders," *Nature* 461: 697.

Travis, John. 2009. "Key Questions on Nationality Testing." *Science Online* (September 29), http://news.sciencemag.org/2009/09/key-questions-nationality-testing (accessed February 24, 2012).

UK Border Agency. 2009a. *Nationality Swapping—Isotope Analysis and DNA Testing*. http://news.sciencemag.org/scienceinsider/entry-assets/nationality-swapping-DNA-testing.pdf (accessed December 12, 2011).

UK Border Agency. 2009b. *Stakeholders Letter from 11.9.2009*. http://news.sciencemag. org/scienceinsider/entry-assets/stakeholder%2Bletter.11.9.09.doc (accessed December 12, 2011).

UK Home Office. 2011. "FOI release 20818 Human Provenance Pilot Project," *Gov. uk* (December 12), https://www.gov.uk/government/publications/20818-human-provenance-pilot-project (accessed March 5, 2012).

van der Tuin, Iris. 2011. "A Different Starting Point, a Different Metaphysics: Reading Bergson and Barad Diffractively." *Hypatia*, 26 (1): 22–42.

10

The Enactment of Intention and Exception through Poisoned Corpses and Toxic Bodies

TEENA GABRIELSON

Lively, mobile, disruptive, and intimate, toxic substances make frequent appearances in the literature of feminist new materialism (Alaimo 2010; Bennett 2010; Chen 2012; Tuana 2008). Offering a peculiar example of the liveliness of the inanimate, toxic substances traverse the world through wind currents, food chains, bloodstreams, water pathways, a sea of industrial and consumer products, and the circulations of global capital, to name a few. This mobility is accompanied by a permeability that illuminates the porosity of corporeal bodies and the interdependencies among humans and between humans and their natural/built worlds. Inherently slippery, the polysemous root of the adjective "toxic," *pharmakon*, refers not only to poison, or philter, but also to remedy, medicine, drug. The constitutive conceptual unruliness of toxic substances is amplified by the ability of many substances to continue to make change far into the future either through persistence or impacts at the genetic level. With visceral, affective force, toxic substances subvert traditional binaries such as nature/culture, violate the integrity of long-standing categories like the human body and its environment, and traffic in the social, political, material, technological, scientific, and discursive.

Yet, as Deboleena Roy and Banu Subramaniam remind us (this volume), there is some danger in weighing too heavily the abstract or general features of materiality without also attending to the specific contexts and histories that define the contours of material-discursive phenomenon. Whether rooted in the literature Stacy Alaimo refers to as "materialist memoirs" (2010), the natural-geo-political disaster of Hurricane Katrina that Nancy Tuana considers (2008), or the racially malleable material-discursive phenomenon of lead examined by Mel Chen (2012), these groundings reveal the extent to which the materialization of toxic substances in bodies (both human and non), the visibility of those bodies, and the differential experiences created are deeply political processes.[1] Like Josef Barla, I am particularly interested in the plurality of toxic human bodies and adopt Barad's agential-realist approach to address the question of "how differently configured bodies emerge in their very materialities through intra-actions of material, discursive, [political], technological, and technoscientific forces and practices?" (this volume).

In response, I interject a focused comment intended to give greater definition to the toxic body by tracing its historical production through practices of toxicology.[2] Interdisciplinary, applied, and entrenched in politics from its founding, the field of toxicology has had a profound influence on our changing understandings of toxicity, while its evolution offers a provocative point of entry into the larger socio-political anxieties that quite often drive efforts to tame and contain the wild vitality of toxic substances. Most immediately, I want to suggest that we cannot adequately understand contemporary toxic bodies, the political manipulations of them, and their constitution in the co-constituted discursive/material hierarchies of power without some familiarity with the articulation of these bodies through the practices of toxicology.

In what follows, I draw primarily upon toxicological textbooks and symposia to trace the emergence of two different historical, material-discursive configurations of the toxic body. I focus on two specific apparatuses of bodily production (see Barla, this volume) critical to the assembling and orchestration of the various human and nonhuman actors and practices through which these bodies were enacted. The first is the apparatus of early lab-based analytical methods of chemical detection, as deployed in the courts. Through these methods, the nineteenth-century "poisoned corpse" materialized as a victim that sought to affirm the dualisms of good and evil, innocence and guilt, and, crucially, purity and contamination. By the mid-twentieth century, advances in industrialization and toxicology led to the development of the apparatus of the dose-response curve and the materialization of the "toxic body" within a newly configured association of actors and practices dedicated, not to justice, but to managing the public good. In working through these examples, we begin to see not only that politics "are literally inscribed into our bodies" (Roy and Subramaniam, this volume) but that such bodies, materialized through socio-material enactments, can come to further elaborate, consolidate, or bolster emerging and contestable political ideals.

The Poisoned Corpse

Across nineteenth-century Europe and the United States, the availability of poisonous substances, the difficulties of detection, and the intimate character of the crime had made murder by poisoning a matter of significant concern (Essig 2000). In the United States, early toxicology built upon the successes of individual European toxicologists such as Mathieu Orfila, considered the "grandfather" of toxicology for his advances in chemical detection, and followed British academic institutions in locating toxicology within the larger field of medical jurisprudence. While drawing from pathology, physiology, and chemistry, early American toxicology was primarily an endeavor of forensic medicine initially concerned with the prosecution of homicide and the determination of the cause of growing numbers of suicides and accidental deaths by the ingestion of poisons. Long considered a "hidden" crime, murder by poisoning "could be accomplished without a direct confrontation between murderer and victim; since it was thought to leave no marks on the surface of the body, poison effected an invisible violation of flesh; and since its recognized physiological and pathological signs often simulated natural disease processes, poison's murderous course lent itself to interpretative obscurity" (Burney 2002, 293). The toxicologist, then, was to attend to the patient's history, symptoms, physical and toxicological evidence, and any suspicious human behavior surrounding the onset of symptoms in an effort to make the crime visible. Toxicologists were to learn the language of chemistry (Burney 2006) and thereby "speak for the dead" (Essig 2000, 169).

As toxicology developed with physiology over the course of the late nineteenth and early twentieth centuries, the clinical manifestations or *symptoms* of poisoning came to play a central and critical role in determining the particular substance that may have been ingested (convulsants, excitants, depressants, nerve poisons, blood poisons), and the route of exposure (inhalation, ingestion, absorption). Yet, a clever poisoner might easily mask her work by adopting a potion that mimicked the symptoms of disease.[3] Here, quantitative chemical analysis of post-mortem blood and organ tissue proved incredibly useful in identifying the ingestion of a poisonous substance and demonstrating that it worked its magic chemically, rather than mechanically (arsenic versus crushed glass). However, for both the toxicologist and the legislator, one could not conclude a poisoning had occurred from the mere presence of a poisonous substance in the patient's lifeless body; one must also determine the "fatal dose."

The oldest (and one of the most enduring) of toxicological problems was how to define a poison. As Jacques Derrida describes the inherently slippery root of "toxic," *pharmakon* "partakes of both good and ill, of the agreeable and the disagreeable"; without an essence of its own, it merely marks the boundary of outside and inside, "always springing up from without, acting like the outside itself, [it] will never have any definable virtue of its own" (99, 102).[4] Thus, the thorny problem of defining a poison begins with the elusive character of substances, since the same substance might produce no effect, a therapeutic effect, a toxic effect, or a lethal effect at different dosages and in different persons. As John Reese, the most prominent toxicologist in the United States in the 1870s and '80s explains, "the law makes no distinction between a murder committed by the administration of a grain of strychnia and one resulting from taking an ounce of oxalic acid, provided both were given with the same evil *design*; which is equally fatal, although they differ so widely in their fatal dose" (1874, 16, emphasis added).

Yet, revealing the design Reese references is a complicated affair. The question for coroners and toxicologists was whether there was sufficient evidence to find "proof of poisoning" before the law so as to hold one individual accountable for the death of another. Reese explains that the main object of proof was to establish the *connections* among the "*symptoms, lesions,* and *chemical analysis*—directly with the substance employed, and with the *intention* of the person employing it" (Reese 1874, 16). As this quote suggests, the material-discursive phenomenon of the nineteenth-century poisoned corpse emerges in the intra-actions of a robust association comprised of a host of actants, both human and nonhuman.[5] The association is knit with practices, such as the medical evaluation of patient symptoms, the toxicological lab work of chemical detection, the coroner's report, the evidentiary standards of crime scene investigation, the interviewing of potential suspects, the legal practice of expert witness testimony, and the sensational reporting of the incident, to name a few.[6] Following medical philosopher Annemarie Mol (2002), the poisoned corpse is multiple. It is produced through different practices that are distributed in different places and conducted by different people; each of which could be unraveled and parsed in detail, and many of which could come into conflict, jeopardizing the coherence of the corpse and the verdict of the trial.

Despite these potential conflicts, where the evidence converges, the poisoned corpse "hangs together" (Mol 2002, 55). And, while the adversarial legal process of obtaining expert witness testimony at times dealt a blow to the credibility of early chemical detection processes, over the course of the century, these methods improved in sensitivity and reliability and became increasingly important to securing a guilty verdict at trial. While Reese goes to great lengths to suggest that there are instances where sufficient proof of poisoning can be made *without* chemical detection, he admits "it is usually considered the most satisfactory evidence of the crime, by both court and jury" (1874, 69). In the 1832 case of Lucretia Chapman, a defense expert stated it more bluntly: "If there is no arsenic found, all symptoms and exhumations go for nothing. In a word, no poison—no poisoning,—no cause—no effect" (quoted in Essig 2000, 158). Thus, at least two seemingly linear causal chains were entwined to enact the poisoned corpse: a chain of physical reactions designed to produce scientific reliability and a chain of reasoning designed to produce confidence in the legal process (Burney 2006).

In the first, the credibility of the apparatus of chemical analysis depended upon the consistent success of the process through which identifiable poisons were reliably refined from contaminated viscera. Taking what is considered to be one of the most significant achievements of nineteenth-century toxicology, James Marsh's test for arsenic (one of the most popular poisons of the period), the chain looked like this: a mixture of presumably contaminated bodily fluids from the alimentary canal—the addition of zinc—the release of hydrogen—the combination of hydrogen and arsenic to produce arsine gas—ignition—and, finally, the deposition of metallic arsenic on a white porcelain surface held in the flame (Reese 1874, 232–233). In contrast to the reagent tests of the period, where arsenic was added to another solution resulting in the "throwing down" of a precipitate of a particular color, like "canary yellow" or "*Scheele's green*" (ibid., 230), Marsh's reduction process reproduced the poison in material form, offering an ontological assurance of credibility that could be demonstrated in the courtroom.

In the second, chemical detection provides a forceful link in the chain of reasoning that connects the intentions of a perpetrator to the death of a victim. The reconstructed chain looks like this: evidence intention—poisonous substance—victim—symptom—harm/death—chemical detection—legal determination of guilt/perpetrator. It begins with evidence of individual intention, followed by the victim's exposure to a substance with the result of bodily harm initially identified by the appearance of a symptom, and concludes with the post-mortem detection of a poisonous substance in the victim's bodily tissue or fluids. Through this conjoined toxicological-medical-legal apparatus, those unruly substances, long wielded by unhappy spouses, impatient heirs, and assassins in their revolutionary plots, became ordered and legible through a linear story of causality cast upon a background of dualities of purity and contamination; good and evil; victim and perpetrator; guilt and innocence. Thus, as the poisoned body is enacted through increasingly reliable methods of chemical detection, it is laced with the logic of intention. To state it otherwise, the body cannot congeal where there is chemical evidence but no intention or intention without chemical evidence—Justice is achieved as chemical detection confirms, in the context of the court, the conceptual categories of a purposive perpetrator and a passive victim, while the poison itself remains a mere tool.

Transitioning

In contrast to texts of the early to mid-twentieth century that defined toxicology as the "science of poisons" and explicitly focused on substances, today, the Society of Toxicology defines the field as "the study of the adverse effects of chemical, physical, or biological agents on people, animals, and the environment" (www.toxicology.org). While both use of the term "poison" and wrangling among toxicologists over its definition continued well into the twentieth century, by century's end "poison" had shifted to "agent" and toxicologists' focus of inquiry from "substances" to "effects." Here, I want to take just a moment to parse the semantic subtleties of this shift, particularly for our understandings of intention and causality.

The word "poison" can be used as a noun or a verb. As an adjective it becomes "poisonous." As such, the term conveys an ontology and intentionality largely absent from the word "toxic." This inherent intentionality may be most clear in the expression "accidental poisoning" where the verb must be qualified in order to *remove* intent. In contrast, the term "toxic" is primarily used as an adjective. While some now use the words "intoxicant" or "toxin" as related nouns, the first is primarily still popularly associated with pleasure and drugs (particularly alcohol), while the second refers specifically to a poisonous substance that is the product of a living organism (for example snake venom, not inorganic chemicals). Finally, while "detoxify" is widely recognized as a verb, toxify is not. Thus, one might intentionally, but probably not accidentally, remove toxic agents from a body, but we would not talk of either accidentally or intentionally toxifying someone or something.[7]

In the following rather lengthy quote, subtleties like these are fairly explicitly at work. In the foreword to William D. McNally's 1937 text, *Toxicology*, Carey P. McCord, a medical doctor, states the following:

> In some measure it may be maintained that the number of toxic agents surrounding a people constitutes an index of its cultural development . . . Theirs [toxicologists] is the duty to detect the nature and mechanism of poisonings with such exactness that the guilty may be punished as a deterrent to others who might elect similar activities; to guide therapeutists as to the thresholds demarking safe and beneficent actions of man's natural and synthetic agents from those direful actions associated with use in larger amounts; to plan with industry and commerce for the controlled use of baneful substances and machines, lest the human elements of industry and commerce be damaged in the performance of their obligations. Thus the toxicologist takes a place alongside the lawmaker, the educator, the healer, the minister, the engineer, as a unit in the orderly organization of mankind—all participating in the conservation of the public well being. (McNally 1937, i–ii)

In this passage, McCord offers three different duties of the toxicologist. In the first, he explicitly references "poisonings" and places the toxicologist within the medical-legal association described above. In the second and third, toxicologists take their place within the fields of industry and commerce as key partners in managing toxic agents for the public good, defined in terms of both economic advancement and public health. Toxic substances are now separated into poisons which become the means for killing someone and synthetic agents and baneful substances which must be managed for public health and safety—the one an individualized weapon, the other a potential public hazard that also holds great promise. In this shift, deaths by poisoning are laden with intention, as deaths by exposure become mere accidents.

The Toxic Body

As Christopher Sellers has brilliantly documented, by the early twentieth century the industrial workplace had become a place of both uncertainty and hazard (1997). First and foremost, industrial poisonings were not the product of intentional individual actions; exposure to hazardous substances was part and parcel of the work. As workers reported for physicals conducted by company doctors, their bodies became the site for determining acceptable concentrations of pollutants in the environment. As such, *exposure* to poisonous substances was no longer understood as an aberration, but as endemic to the processes of industrialization. The conditions of the industrial workplace challenged toxicologists with a whole new level of ambiguity that included chronic and cumulative effects stemming from long-term exposures (in addition to acute effects), the mixing of chemical substances in the environment, the interaction of social factors such as nutrition, fatigue, or home location with exposure to workplace pollutants, and the continuing enigmas of human variability and susceptibility. For progressive-era industrial hygienists like Alice Hamilton, fieldwork and environmental surveys complemented the analytical chemistry of earlier toxicologists. However, by the 1940s, the laboratory offered new possibilities for gaining some traction with this dizzying array of variables.

In the newly rarified realm of the lab, the key question for toxicologists through the mid-twentieth century was: how much? In 1960, K. J. Olson, a toxicologist with the Biochemical Research Laboratory of Dow Chemical Company, stated the following: "A degree of being poisonous.

This is a good basic concept, because toxicity entails a definite dimension, that of quantity or amount. On this basis, then, any chemical is more or less toxic dependent upon amount. In a broad sense, everything is toxic. No chemical is non-toxic" (9). This statement reflects the more general tendency to identify the centrality of dosage to poisoning, but in rather loose terms. During this period, dose was often linked to values reflecting the inherent toxicity of a substance. One of the first key values was the LD50 or the "amount of poison per unit of body weight which will kill 50 per cent of the particular species of animals employed for the tests" (Dubois and Geiling 1959, 26). Building on the concept of the lethal dose, by the late 1940s toxicologists had established a scale designed to describe the toxicity of various chemical agents based on dosage. An "extremely toxic" chemical was so at 1mg, whereas a "moderately toxic" chemical would produce adverse effects only at 50–500 mg, and a "relatively harmless substance" would allow more than 15 gm (ibid., 28–29).[8]

What had been a rule of thumb since Paracelsus' work in the fifteenth century gained increasing support through the lab work of the mid-twentieth century such that by the 1980s, it had become the iron law of toxicology: it is the dose that makes the poison. This glib phrase is the crystallization of years' of lab work culminating in the dose-response curve, which tracks a linear relationship that presumes that, as dosages increase, so does the harmfulness of the substance's effect. Within the carefully constructed space of the lab, toxicologists focused on the internal, cellular ecology of exposure by testing individual chemicals on animals and then extrapolating the results to identify what was initially referred to as the Maximal Allowable Concentration level of a substance, or what later became Threshold Limit Values (Sellers 1997, 153–186). As Michelle Murphy explains, this limit was specifically designed "for human workers daily exposed to that chemical at work five days a week, eight hours a day" (2006, 90). Thus, the dose-response curve presumes that the human body, initially the male industrial worker, can withstand exposure to harmful substances and suffer "no observable adverse effects."

The end result was that exposure to a toxic substance does not necessarily create a toxic body. As Horace W. Gerarde explains in his 1960 article "Chemicals in Industry," "The presence of the chemical or its metabolites in the body fluids is prima-facie evidence that some of the chemical has been absorbed. This indicates that exposure has occurred, but does not mean that injury has resulted from the absorption of this amount of chemical in the body" (24). As such, the toxic body was *definitionally* a rarity. Among all bodies exposed, and there were many, only those bodies that *tell* of symptoms, at either the macro or micro level, were deemed toxic. More specifically, to establish a body as toxic, one must show that a specific chemical regularly produces specific symptoms (when a worker is exposed at a particular threshold level) through a specific diagnostic test, such as a blood test. As Murphy explains, "The dominant assemblage in toxicology not only rendered perceptible the specific bodily effects of chemicals, it also set up criteria by which one could exclude a bodily condition from the category of occupational disease" (2006, 91).

In this way, the toxic body of the twentieth century emerged in the intra-actions of a thickly populated association comprised of traditional and newly devised, potentially toxic, industrial substances, legislators, laboratory animals, industrial physicians, public health advocates, regulatory officials, symptoms of illness, industrial machinery, toxicologists, factory managers, insurance adjusters, industrial laborers, and a host of others. Mediating this association were practices as seemingly divergent as congressional hearings, industrial production processes, union meetings, risk-benefit analysis, litigation, the two-year rat bioassay, media reports, worker compensation forms, profit analyses, professional lobbying, and the management of chronic health conditions. Yet, while all of these practices contributed to the enactment of the toxic body, I have focused on the apparatus of the dose-response curve because of its central role in the orchestration of this assemblage and in its power as a boundary-making device. As Barad explains, the apparatus both "helps produce and is part of the body it images," and, critically, it is a "device for making and remaking boundaries" (2007, 201–2). It is through the dose-response curve that the toxic body emerged as a by-product of industrialization and as exception to the rule that ultimately legitimized the very conditions of its production.

In the history of contaminated bodies, the logic of exception, as actualized through the dose-response curve, has been a critical element in the normalization of toxic exposures and the underwriting of distributive inequalities in exposure that continue to, perhaps increasingly, mark contemporary life. Most obviously, this logic was critical to the legitimation of the dramatic expansion of chemical production that took place in the United States after World War II, such that by the 1960s some could refer to the *necessary or essential* exposures of life "in the chemical age" (Dubois and Geiling 1959, 209; Geiling and D'Aguanno 1960, 3). For twentieth-century toxicologists, lawmakers, and industry representatives, the key to maintaining human health and economic progress was to manage the environments in which exposure took place to limit the proliferation of toxic bodies. As long as toxicology, regulatory agencies, and industry prevented mass acute poisonings (like the 1948 smog of Donora, Pennsylvania, the 1984 Union Carbide release in Bhopal, and the 1986 Chernobyl disaster), the logic of exception worked to cast all other instances of acute poisoning as accidents, aberration, or the product of human variability, and exposures were normalized (Harrison 2011). Clearly, as the logic of exception minimized the perceived frequency of such events, the segregation of the workforce further obscured the problem from the public view by curtailing exposures to the socially marginalized working class. The effort to establish thresholds and quantify human risk to hazards also tended to abstract and individualize human bodies through a universal language based upon a fictional body (the average body) rooted in the industrial workplace but created through the extrapolation of animal studies to an unvaried human population. Constructed in this way, threshold levels tend to erase particularities of the human body (such as age, gender, pregnancy, and cultural practices) and to uproot the body from the social and geographical landscapes of exposure (Murphy 2006). In the last two decades there have been a growing number of social science analyses, like Murphy's, that work to challenge and expose the exclusions created by concepts of modern toxicology such as the dose-response curve. Joined by scientific research, public epidemiology, and community-based participatory research, this work underscores both the politicization of toxicology and the need for preventative policy (Brown 2007; Frickel 2004; Fischer 2000; Shostak 2013; Vogel 2013).

To return to the twentieth century, as the language throughout the last section suggests, in contrast to the nineteenth-century poisoned corpse, the toxic body was cast as a mere by-product of industrial processes that were widely considered to drive economic (and, often, cultural) progress. As such, exposures that produced acute responses, and toxic bodies, were conceptualized, for the most part, as inadvertent. Through the dose-response curve, human perpetrators were replaced by toxic agents that became the actants that produce, at some dose, adverse effects. In doing so, responsibility was displaced from specific individuals, corporations, or institutions to regulatory processes and individual citizens who may now expect to experience (and try to avoid) exposure. Rather than rely directly on individual human symptoms and chemical analyses that could determine an absolute "fatal dose," as in the case of the poisoned corpse, the normal and pathological came to be determined by threshold levels that defined toxicity by human populations' responses (extrapolated from animal studies) to particular environments. The chief objective for toxicologists, industry representatives, and government regulators was then to manage environments so as to profitably use toxic substances while minimizing and socializing risks to public health. As Timothy Luke explains, "Recognizing that science might deliver fairly reliable probabilistic statements about the types of health effects, their relative severity, and the population that will be affected simultaneously naturalizes risk (turns it into an unavoidable background condition), socializes it (reduces it to a collective cost born by all), and personalizes it (transforms it into a matter of lifestyle choice)" (2000, 248–249).

To conclude, I want to suggest the value of distinguishing between these two bodies and the meanings they carry by focusing on the structuring of intention in their materialization. Both of these bodies continue in our midst (while neither receives the attention they once did). Husbands continue to be poisoned by their wives and workers continue to experience exposures to chemical agents, some deemed toxic, others not. Thus, the contaminated body is plural. But, as Mol demands we recognize, each of these bodies is also multiple; cohering and dissolving in the mesh of practices through which they are materialized. Among those practices are the organization and articulation of the political.

In the case of the poisoned corpse, through the methods of chemical detection and the chain of reasoning that establishes guilt, the dead body becomes a victim and the perpetrator can be blamed, upholding sovereignty, justice, and human agency. Such clean distinctions become useful in the politics of self/nation and other, the maintenance of clearly demarcated boundaries, the articulation of innocence, the assertion of autonomy, and the search for solutions. In the example of the toxic body, the dose-response curve and the logic of exception socialize risk and responsibility, enliven toxic agents, and obscure the uneven distribution of toxic exposure and harm. A key constituent in the politics of personal responsibility and in the campaigns to produce doubt, uncertainty, and imperceptibility, the toxic body contributes to what Rob Nixon calls the "slow violence" inflicted, primarily, on the poor (2011). Neither the problems of discipline nor security, as Foucault would identify them, prevail in contemporary political life, but they do endure. And, to rework and take responsibility for the boundaries that are created by the apparatuses that produce each of these contaminated bodies, we must first carefully attend to their construction.

NOTES

1 This is a point developed more fully by Stephanie Clare in this volume.

2 To be sure, there are other critical practices through which these bodies are enacted, including environmental justice activism, to name just one.

3 I adopt the female pronoun here as a marker for the rich literature on female poisoners and the gendering of poisoning as a form of murder.

4 One of the chief similarities between the poisoned corpse and the toxic body is the understanding that the toxic substance is external to the body. This assumption gains credibility with the germ theory of bacteriology in the late nineteenth century, but has come under increased scrutiny in contemporary toxicology as more is learned regarding processes of metabolism and detoxification.

5 For Latour, Actor-Network-Theory (2005) offers a means of tracing the social in the congealing of new associations, where mediators form and maintain the relations that give shape to gatherings of both human and nonhuman actants. For my research, Latour's approach is useful because it provides a means of distinguishing among the quite different associations within which contaminated bodies emerge.

6 In his excellent essay, Burney positions the work of the legal advocate and the toxicologist within similar although different "rule-bound and highly stylized modes of signification" (2002, 309).

7 I want to thank my colleague, Erin Forbes, for her insights here.

8 While this scale conceptualized the inherent toxicity of a substance, toxicologists acknowledged that interpretation was still required to determine the particular hazard or risk of any particular substance.

REFERENCES

Alaimo, Stacy. 2010. *Bodily natures: science, environment, and the material self.* Bloomington: Indiana University Press.

Barad, Karen. 2007. *Meeting the universe halfway: quantum physics and the entangle-ment of matter and meaning*. Durham, NC: Duke University Press.

Bennet, Jane. 2010. *Vibrant matter: a political ecology of things*. Durham, NC: Duke University Press.

Brown, Phil. 2007. *Toxic exposures: contested illnesses and the environmental health movement*. New York: Columbia University Press.

Burney, Ian A. 2002. Testing Testimony: Toxicoogy and the Law of Evidence in Early Nineteenth-Century England. *Studies in History and Philosophy of Science* 33: 289–314.

Burney, Ian A. 2006. *Poison, detection and the Victorian imagination*. Manchester: Manchester University Press.

Chen, Mel Y. 2012. *Animacies: biopolitics, racial mattering, and queer affect*. Durham, NC: Duke University Press.

Derrida, Jacques. 1981. Plato's Pharmacy. *Disseminations*. Translated by Barbara John-son. Chicago: University of Chicago Press.

DuBois, Kenneth P. and E.M.K. Geiling. 1959. *Textbook of toxicology*. New York: Ox-ford University Press.

Essig, Mark Regan. 2000. *Science and sensation: poison murder and forensic medicine in Nineteenth-Century America*. PhD Dissertation, Cornell University.

Fischer, Frank. 2000. *Citizens, experts, and the environment: the politics of local knowl-edge*. Durham, NC: Duke University Press.

Frickel, Scott. 2004. *Chemical consequences: environmental mutagens, scientist activism, and the rise of genetic toxicology*. New Brunswick, NJ: Rutgers University Press.

Foucault, Michel. 2007. *Security, territory, population: lectures at the College de France, 1977–1978*, ed. Michel Senellart. New York: Palgrave Macmillan.

Geiling, E.M.K. and William D'Aguanno. 1960. Our Man-Made Noxious Environment. "Problems in Toxicology," ed. J. M. Coon and Elliott A. Maynard. Federation of Ameri-can Societies for Experimental Biology: Symposium in Chicago, Illinois, April 13.

Gerarde, Horace W. 1960. Chemicals in Industry. "Problems in Toxicology," ed. J. M. Coon and Elliott A. Maynard. Federation of American Societies for Experimental Biology: Symposium in Chicago, Illinois, April 13.

Harrison, Jill Lindsey. 2011. *Pesticide drift and the pursuit of environmental justice*. Cambridge, MA: MIT Press.

Latour, Bruno. 2005. *Reassembling the social: an introduction to Actor-Network-Theory*. Oxford: Oxford University Press.

Luke, Timothy. 2000. Rethinking Technoscience in Risk Society: Toxicity as Textuality. In *Reclaiming the environmental debate: the politics of health in a toxic culture*, ed. Richard Hofrichter. Cambridge, MA: MIT Press, 239–254.

McNally, William D. 1937. *Toxicology*. Chicago: William D. McNally.

Mol, Annemarie. 2002. *The body multiple: ontology in medical practice*. Durham, NC: Duke University Press.

Murphy, Michelle. 2006. *Sick building syndrome and the problem of uncertainty: environmental politics, technoscience, and women workers*. Durham, NC: Duke University Press.

Nixon, Rob. 2011. *Slow violence and the environmentalism of the poor.* Cambridge, MA: Harvard University Press.

Olson, K. J. 1960. Toxicity of Chemicals—Basic Concepts. *Symposium on Toxicology: Its Effect Upon Our Industrial and Domestic Lives.* Midland, MI: Dow Chemical Company.

Reese, John James. 1874. *A manual of toxicology: including the consideration of the nature, properties, effects, and means of detection of poisons, more especially in their medico-legal relations.* Philadelphia: J.B. Lippincott & Co.

Sellers, Christopher. 1997. *Hazards of the job: from industrial disease to environmental health science.* Chapel Hill: University of North Carolina Press.

Shostak, Sara. 2013. *Exposed science: genes, the environment, and the politics of population health.* Berkeley: University of California Press.

Tuana, Nancy. 2008. Viscous Porosity: Witnessing Katrina. In *Material feminisms*, ed. Stacy Alaimo and Susan Hekman. Bloomington: Indiana University Press.

Vogel, Sarah. 2013. *Is it safe? BPA and the struggle to define the safety of chemicals.* Berkeley: University of California Press.

11

Neurofeminism

An Eco-Pharmacology of Childhood ADHD

JULIAN GILL-PETERSON

In October 2012, the *New York Times* profiled a doctor in a county north of Atlanta who routinely diagnoses low-income white children with Attention Deficit Hyperactivity Disorder (ADHD) in spite of doubting its empirical existence. Dr. Michael Anderson administers Adderall to his middle school patients as pure performance enhancement, a pharmaceutical treatment aimed at quantitatively and qualitatively improving the life chances of children who, in his mind and the minds of their parents, are biologically and culturally impaired by an education system dismantled by decades of state disinvestment. "I don't have a whole lot of choice," Anderson explains, "We've decided as a society that it's too expensive to modify the kid's environment. So we have to modify the kid" (Schwarz 2012).

Following Anderson's prognosis, this chapter considers childhood ADHD and its pharmacological treatment with amphetamine drugs as a case of biopolitical performance enhancement. It foregrounds the child's body in the historical extension of psychiatry from an institutional to a pharmaceutical mode to accent the increasingly dominant role of chemical molecules in managing human development and capital. The ubiquity of pharmacology within psychiatry indexes a recalculation and re-contracting of the value of the human organism within which childhood represents a newly vital period of investment and enhanceable development. The protocols of psychiatry laminate the crisis of neoliberal state disinvestment in education and healthcare resultant in a generation of American children currently coming of age with a diminished expectation to live better or longer than their parents' generation (an expectation severely unequally distributed by race, sex, class, citizenship, and ability). Psychiatry is, in this context, generalized from the self-enclosed spatiotemporality of the asylum and hospital through its ascendant marriage to pharmacology since World War II, a process consolidated in the global neoliberal economies of the 1980s and 1990s. In lieu of an individualizing architecture of confinement for the psychotic or mentally ill, pharmacological psychiatry makes itself pervasive in a generalizable prognostics of endemic risk factors for mental disorder and a neurobiological enhancement of bodies either impaired in reference to a norm of capitalist performance or deemed, through racialized and sexed standards of plasticity, eligible for eugenic improvement. Drugs offer the promise of performance enhancement to increase the holistic life chances of children like Dr. Anderson's patients under the strained material relation to futurity emblematic of financial capitalism, where the value of education and labor diminishes even as the demand for them increases.

Within these processes the child's body plays a decisive role in the investment in and the measure, activation, and exchange of, the value of the human organism's body and mind as discrete capacities, as human capital (Adamson 2009). This emergent logic of value amounts to a normative redefinition of what it means to "grow up": rather than moving iteratively from the enclosure of the home to the school, to the clinic and then to the army, factory, or office, the child's body is a site of continuous investment practice and a demand for austere self-autonomy that can perform with greater probability of success in a volatile labor market. Child development is entrenched in the United States—and particularly dramatically so post-2008—in a crisis of modernity's disciplinary molds that authorizes the implementation of a more supple apparatus of performance enhancement as governance that, importantly, extends from the neurobiological to the cognitive and conscious scales of bodies. Every year, hour, and second, even, of investment in the biological and mental capacities of the child can be expected to yield a predictable future return of value relative to the contingency of the market (Foucault 2008, 230). Only with this sweeping, global reach of investment in and enhancement and mortgaging of children's bodies and brains that begins with its matter and extends to mental performance in tests scores does it become possible to realize the Bush-era slogan of "No Child Left Behind." As a complement to state disinvestment in education, psychiatry and the pharmaceutical industry are called upon to assume the liability of invest-ment practices in the human capital embodied in children. Dr. Anderson in Georgia is called upon to prescribe Adderall to re-contract the risk of nurturing the capacities of children for a future in which enhancement cannot be expected from an impoverished education system alone.

The active involvement of both soma and psyche in the biopolitics of childhood ADHD calls upon a *neurofeminism*[1] that does not privilege culture over nature, or specifically culture over the brain and nervous system, since Adderall and its cognates confusingly treat biologically a loosely defined set of behavioral disorders. The controversy and con-tinued disagreement within psychiatry, education, and popular culture over what constitutes ADHD animates this chapter's turn to Elizabeth Wilson's "gut feminism" to avoid a somatophobic theory symptomatic of interactional formulae of brain and culture. Instead, this chapter pursues a more "intra-actional" (see Barad 2007) mode that can account for the logical contradiction of the simultaneity and interval of pure difference between social behavior and neurobiology expressed in the phenom-enon of childhood ADHD. A neurofeminism can agree to work with, rather than refuse or resolve, this logical impasse through an ecological mode of distributed causes and effects that are both natural and cul-tural, though irreducible to either. What follows deduces from Wilson's framework a speculative method that engages the complexity of the his-torical extension of psychiatry via the mass medication of children: an *eco-pharmacology*. Eco-pharmacology attends to what an anti-biological feminism and a homologous Cartesian psychiatry and behavioral psy-chology remain unable to do with childhood ADHD: read attention as a variable capacity of body *and* mind, activated and animated affectively, while also differentially distributed by forms of biopolitical measure and capitalist value.

Gut Feminism and Neurofeminism: An Eco-Pharmacology of Drugs

In "Gut Feminism," Elizabeth Wilson (2004a) outlines her discomfort with somatophobic and especially anti-biological forms of feminism, which tend to define the body as culturally malleable and knowable only as psychically ideational, so that any material substrate animating it is implicitly passive. Wilson returns to Freud and the unresolved legacy of women hysterics, whose treatment was divided during his lifetime between purely psychic conceptions of anatomy independent of biology and neurobiologically interested approaches, particularly evident in Freud's sometimes uneasy contrast with his contemporary Sandor Ferenczi. In the latter's work, Wilson accents an immanent animacy of matter, its capacity for *mattering* (Cheah 1996) that incorporates an endogenous psychic vocabulary in Ferenczi's notions of "the biological unconscious" and "organic thought," which he proposes are most evident in moments of trauma where higher consciousness breaks down in favor of somatic modes of knowing and acting (Wilson 2004a, 75, 77).

Wilson grows Ferenczi's work into a project of "gut feminism" through a reading of the bulimic body. Her gambit is that the causal confusion over the treatment of bulimia by antidepressants, the fact that it remains unclear why or how it is that antidepressants are effective in treating the symptoms of bulimia, is a productive confusion for feminist theory. That the pharmacological treatment of mood has desirable effects on a disorder of gut, in her words, may "speak to an ontological organization that is at odds with organic rationality" (2004a, 83). In an instructive moment, Wilson reframes this apparent confusion of mood and gut, one that a somatophobic feminism is no better than doctors at explaining, offering in lieu of an interactional model between the two terms what, following Karen Barad, could be termed an "intra-actional" reading: "I am arguing that antidepressants alleviate bullemia [*sic*] because there is no radical (originary) distinction between biology and mood. Mood is not added onto the gut, secondarily, disrupting its proper function; rather, temper, like digestion, is one of the events to which enteric substrata are naturally (organically) inclined" (85).[2] This is not a purely monist reading, though; it does not propose that psyche and soma are identical units in the symptomatology of bulimia. Instead, though they do not have an originary distinction worth attempting to preserve analytically, there is some intra-actional process at hand through which gut is always already inclined toward expression through mood and mood is always already inclined toward expression through the gut—or, rather, the distinctive expressions of gut and soma are derivative, secondary effects of a psychosomatic system's life. It is this psychosomatic simultaneity, which nevertheless relies on a notion of pure difference or interval between the psychic and somatic in bulimia, that accounts for antidepressants' effectiveness in treating bulimia.

In Wilson's reading of bulimia and her larger project (Wilson 2004b) resides the potential of a neurofeminism. In the case of neurofeminism, the diagramming of the psyche and soma takes shape in the interval between neurobiology and behavior. Somatophobic feminism would read ADHD as neurobiologically unreal to the extent that its epistemological invention is remarkably recent and its treatment, especially in childhood, is without a doubt organized by the most brute of capitalist measures of the productive body. Psychiatry, on the other hand, would argue, in an inversion of that Cartesian presumption, for the medical, brain-based veracity of ADHD as organic disorder to which medicine merely empirically reacts with increasing precision and rationality. Both thereby remain incomplete in that they cannot account for their opposed and excluded other, be it the brain, or culture and capital. A neurofeminist eco-pharmacology works to avoid their mutual exclusion.

The playful and deliberately non-empirical phrase "eco-pharmacology" aims to imagine a neurofeminism through an analysis of affective ecologies, one nested in Gilles Deleuze and Félix Guattari's (1987, 283) suggestive concept of "pharmacoanalysis" in *A Thousand Plateaus*. If affects are understood as real increases or decreases in what a body can do, its relative degree of power, then drugs can be analyzed according to whether they increase the relative degree of power of a body in its milieu or decompose it by amplifying its toxicity. A body, in this context, is defined as a consistency of unequal forces at multiple scales, from the physical to the psychic, a metastable system within a milieu in which drugs either amplify that consistency, tending toward what Deleuze and Guattari term its "optimal" threshold, or else decompose it, tending toward the "pessimal" threshold after which it dies or becomes something different (283–284). In a pharmacoanalysis, drugs are evaluated in terms of what they can make a body do or impair it from doing. Deleuze and Guattari invoke "drugs" mostly in the recreational, hallucinogenic sense, but the point they make applies to prescription pharmaceuticals: while drugs contain the potentiality to encourage forms of life that radically decompose the human ego, "Drug addicts continually fall back into what they wanted to escape: a segmentarity all the more rigid for being marginal, a territorialization all the more artificial for being based on chemical substances" (285).

It is telling, in this regard, that Selective Serotonin Reuptake Inhibitors (SSRIs), mass prescribed for a range of conditions including depression and anxiety, are classified as non-addictive by the Food and Drug Administration in order to justify their long-term use (Nash 2012). Adderall and other ADHD drugs, on the other hand, are classified as potentially addictive (the difference between addiction and chronic use seemingly being a doctor's prescription). Their long-term effects on the bodies of children, especially, remain mostly unknown. The arbitrariness of psychiatry's epistemological designations, but for social norms of capitalist performance, underscores Deleuze and Guattari's point: the assumption that prescription drugs are inherently life-giving, tending toward the optimal threshold of a body's degree of power, whereas recreational drug use inherently tends toward the pessimal, is not reflected in their actual effects. Pharmaceuticals, like recreational drugs, are better thought in terms of their deployment and dosage. As an iteration of the *pharmakon* whose apertures Jacques Derrida (2004) carefully dilates in "Plato's Pharmacy," drug compounds are simultaneously the poison and the remedy, and the indecision between these two modes is in some important sense irreconcilable. Rather than preventing a decision, however, as Angela Mitropoulos (2012) demonstrates, capitalism makes use of this originary confusion to authorize a contract relation that makes an increase in the attentional capacity of a child's body through Adderall linked to the demand for increased quality and quantity of output at school and work.

Eco-pharmacology is hence a useful tool for a neurofeminism because it matches the complexity of the phenomena it engages: ecological thought imagines bodies, drugs, and larger milieu like biopolitical and capitalist apparatuses within a system whose variation emerges in discrete capacities like attention.[3] This is not only a feminist or materialist project because it involves the sexed body and sexuality, but as an analysis of how life's value is cultivated from birth it opens onto the racialized imaginary of contemporary eugenics. Consider the utility of eco-pharmacology, in a larger project, for engaging something like what I term "model minority psychosis": the apparently rising diagnosis of psychosis in international students in the United States, young immigrants, and their children from Asia and South Asia, who are prescribed an array of drugs to return them to the mythologized ability to outperform other ethnic groups in earnings and assimilation. Then consider this eugenic pharmacology of mental health alongside the violently disproportionate incarceration of black and brown youth for minor possession of marijuana and other "recreational" drugs considered of no value to the laboring body (see Alexander 2012, 59–96). To return to Georgia, Dr. Anderson's prescription of Adderall to poor white children is an element in a strategy of the retention of whiteness as carrying a biological entitlement to upward mobility, even after the abandonment of the public school as an institutional equalizer of opportunity for poor whites in the South. The contemporary eugenic, enhanceable body of chemicals, hormones, and neurons, is the plastic body of a project of sex and hygienic whiteness.[4] In naming the child as a eugenic form, however, we are taken into a longer genealogy of the racial cultivation of life by medicine.

ADHD and Amphetamines: A Genealogy

Amphetamine sulfate–based compounds like Adderall and Ritalin are designed to affect the neurotransmitters of the autonomic and central nervous systems by releasing stored norepinephrine, a hormonal neurotransmitter, which has two contradictory but generalizable effects: the stimulation of the nervous system, but in a manner that induces physical calm and mental focus (Kaplan 1992, 3, 7, 15). Amphetamines were first synthesized in the pharmaceutical boom of the 1930s and their initial experimental use was in treating narcolepsy (Dub and Lurie 1939, 40). Charles Bradley, doctor at a Rhode Island home for children with behavioral disorders, was the first American to conduct clinical research into amphetamine treatment in children, research funded by Smith, Kline, & French, which actually hoped to market amphetamines as a cognitive performance enhancer (Strohl 2011, 29). Bradley was interested in seeing if the drug Benzedrine could alleviate the headaches of 40 of his patients aged 5–12. In a 1937 article describing his findings, he reported that quite by accident he found that although the Benzedrine did nothing to address headaches, the stimulant did have two consistent effects: a vast improvement in the children's "drive" to complete schoolwork, and a "subdued" embodied emotional state that dramatically reduced acting-out (578–79). A larger study of 100 children under his care four years later (Bradley and Bowen 1941) corroborated these results.

Even after the two studies, Bradley remained ambivalent about the promise of amphetamines in the treatment of childhood behavioral disorders for several reasons: he could not find any organic basis for the behaviors he was by accident treating pharmacologically; the effects of the drugs were temporary, co-extensive only with chronic use, instead of curative; and ultimately he felt that Benzedrine was not ethically or therapeutically equivalent to changes in a child's environment if the goal was behavioral modification or improved school performance (102). Bradley remained haunted by the interval between the social and biological that amphetamines manipulate, foreshadowing, while disavowing, their potential as a performance enhancer. Amphetamines did not take off in the 1940s as a treatment for behavioral disorders in children after the publication of his research. Tranquilizers remained the standard treatment for unruly kids, while amphetamines tended to be prescribed, with a notable clinical success that has faded from view in the contemporary era of SSRIs, primarily for depression and other non-psychotic mood disorders in adults (Dub and Lurie 1939, 582–84). The mass medication of children was unthinkable during the decades leading out of the Depression and World War II in which the state was massively increasing its institutional investment in education, public health, and the welfare of children.

Amphetamines ascended to their contemporary predominance through neoliberal market and cultural forces. Although the drug named Ritalin became available in 1956 and the *Diagnostic and Statistical Manual* (*DSM*) first included an entry on "Attention Deficit Disorder" in 1980, it remained little admired until the 1990s, when psychiatry became irreversibly attached to pharmacology, and psychodynamic therapy and psychoanalysis were firmly displaced in the United States (see Healy 2002). Ritalin's marketing essentially mimicked the runaway success of Prozac, capitalizing on the state-corporate consensus around a new apparatus of normalizing technologies for the emergent field of mental health. Drawing on the "silver bullet" theory of treatment in which drugs selectively target individual conditions, the pharmaceutical industry took control of the development, clinical trials, and marketing of prescription drugs. In this paradigm, the mass marketing of drugs is predicated not on curing disease per se, but rather by modulating individual risk factors for disease, disorder, or other forms of impairment. Drugs can be prescribed chronically and with the view of maximizing the largest possible proportion of the population that can be medicated for the longest period of time (Dumit 2012, 8). Ritalin fits this model because ADHD is not a disease; as Bradley noted, the set of behavioral deviations from social norms that hyperactivity or an inability to focus name can only be partially improved by chronic amphetamine dosage, rather than "cured." As performance enhancement, there is a seemingly infinite market demographic for these drugs, including a large black market. When childhood and education are being reorganized according to the logic of financial capitalism, so that every moment, down to the hour, that a child can focus in school will yield a calculable return in future productivity as a worker, ADHD drugs create a consumer appeal theoretically as wide as contemporary antidepressants or anti-anxiety medications. The recent expansion of pharmaceutical marketing campaigns to potential "adult ADHD" patients suggests an even further generalization of its market demographic.

Though the magic bullet theory of selective drugs was never practically realized according to psychiatry's own operational protocols during the first few decades after the Second World War, the idea nevertheless became a consensus, one diluted but recapitulated in contemporary popular understandings of depression and anxiety: the receptor model of pharmacology. The logic of the receptor model is to synthesize chemical molecules that bind with an increasingly perfectible selectivity to a single neurotransmitter receptor. Once combined with the discovery of dopamine and seratonin, a hypothesis formed that many mental illnesses or disorders are simply a product of "too much" or "too little" of these chemicals acting upon the nervous system. If specific drug compounds could bind with the right receptors to increase or decrease dopamine or seratonin reception as the case may require, then seemingly everything from mild depression to schizophrenia could be cured pharmacologically—purely biologically, without the need for psychotherapy. These hypotheses have never been satisfactorily verified on the terms of scientific research protocols, and yet have drifted into the cultural expectation of what drugs can do, as well as the U.S. FDA's regulation that requires "specific drugs for specific diseases" (Healy 2002, 28, 204–24).

A feminist eco-pharmacology is well suited to complicate psychiatry's solely molecular explanation of body, mind, and disorder. As Antonio Damasio (2003, 73, 85) explains, drawing on his expertise as a neuro-biologist with mutually informing readings of Spinoza, there is a miss-ing empirical step in the explanation of how drugs "treat" depression, anxiety, or ADHD. The nervous system cannot in practice be isolated—that is, the selective attachment of a drug molecule to a specific neuron receptor cannot predictably and reliably change the operation of that neuron (and do nothing else). This is, to summarize, because pharma-cology does not account for the interval between body and mind in that it remains Cartesian, separating mind and matter as isolated ac-tionable fields. From a Spinozist reading of neurobiology in which body and mind are attributes of the same substance, thereby simultaneous but expressed differentially through modalities like consciousness and sensation, Damasio argues that the reason why drugs have been unable to produce consistent effects in medical research is that the feedback of the mind upon the body through its neural mapping has been ignored. Put differently, in the idiom of Barad's (2007, 33) feminist materialism, the body, on drugs, is the sum total phenomenon of the "intra-actions" of the mind, body, and pharmacological compounds that in a metastable system modulate mood, feelings, and other body and conscious states.

Nervous systems are a widespread biological form, utilizing electrical signals to animate a huge spectrum of life, sometimes in close conjunc-tion with endocrine systems. Brains, in turn, are an incredibly complex iteration of nervous systems, but neither exceptional to humans nor pre-programmed organs that operate in isolation or with a telos (Malabou 2008). What the sciences and philosophy aim to capture under the ref-erent "mind" (see Prinz 2012) arises in an even more complex system, when the body, *in its entirety, not just "in" its brain*, activates the capacity for self-representation through thought and what neurobiologists like Damasio term "neural mapping." In this systems-theory-derived ac-count, when a body can think about its thinking, as well as represent its bodily processes to itself as a perceptual image or thought, it has devel-oped a capacity that significantly modifies the way it reacts and inter-venes into its milieu, itself, and the relation between each. The point is not to oppose and hierarchize consciousness over bodily processes, or the inverse, as pharmacology does, for example, in its attempt to manage the runaway animacy of a given drug's "primary" effect versus its litany of so-called side effects.

What a feminist, eco-pharmacological reading of neuroscience can do is attend to the intricate, reciprocal causes and effects of *all* of the scales of the individuated body and mind on drugs—perception, affection, thought, and the feedback loops that transduce them. As Damasio (2003, 120, emphasis added) summarizes, "The molecular mechanisms that result from the introduction of a drug into the system account for the beginning of a chain of processes that lead to the alteration of feeling *but not for the processes that eventually establish that feeling*," meaning that the eventual feeling is always an open-ended, indeterminate result. To transplant this insight back to the case of ADHD: while psychiatry may claim to know how the molecular modulation of the nervous system by amphetamines *can* affect the composing of the distribution, intensity, and duration of the body's perceptual capacities and their parallel self-representation in the mind, it cannot know how those effects are accomplished in chemical isolation without accounting also for the existence of the mind's feedback effects on the body's neural mapping.

A neurofeminism is thereby able to diverge from the common assumption of all of the fields of knowledge mobilized thus far: that of the rational human organism, a homeostatic ideal that self-regulates or self-governs according to a telos or plan. Pharmacology and psychiatry most explicitly invest in this model through the idea of ADHD as a verifiable disorder whose impairment can be compensated for in near real-time by amphetamines, supplements that restore a rational brain to rule over the body. Damasio's neurobiological perspective, in a sluggish reading of Spinoza's *conatus*, also reproduces this model by suggesting that the point of the Spinozist frame of body and mind is the homeostatic achievement of self-regulation indicated by the feeling of joy (36). And in contemporary philosophy, Bernard Stiegler's *Taking Care of Youth and the Generations* (2010, 127), a thoughtful meditation on the breakdown of the normative relation between adults and children marked by the contemporary degradation of circuits of transindividuation founded upon deep attention, unfortunately also relies on a technophobia whose implicit claim is that deep attention is the proper homeostatic norm of humans, a norm short-circuited by television, advertising, and digital culture (a diagnosis, still, that is accurate).

If the child's body on amphetamine drugs cannot be taken for granted as an impaired but otherwise rationally organized and sovereign organism, and instead indexes the intra-actional iterations of body, mind, and chemicals, the effects of ADHD drugs return us to the undecidable tensions in Bradley's 1930s experiments. What remains unresolved is the definition of attention.

Attention Without Opposition

This chapter's diagramming of childhood ADHD affirms N. Katherine Hayles's (2007, 187) argument that the Enlightenment-derived, modern form of "deep attention," which in her words "is characterized by concentration on a single object for long periods . . . ignoring outside stimuli while so engaged, preferring a single information stream, and having a high tolerance for long focus times," is becoming to an as yet unpredictable degree laminated over, generationally, by what she terms "hyperattention," which in contrast "is characterized by switching focus rapidly among different tasks, preferring multiple information streams, seeking a high level of stimulation, and having a low tolerance for boredom." In the competing discourses of truth surrounding childhood ADHD, "deep attention" tends to remain an unquestioned norm in relation to "hyper attention." Still, the idea that attention *should* be organized for depth, whether justified by the chemistry of the brain, the supposed evolutionary "function" of the nervous system and mind, or the historical fact of the pedagogization of children through education, seems more resentful of hyperattention's expressiveness about something of the contemporary than it seems based on a mode of evaluation as complex as the organization of childhood ADHD. Given the contemporary mortgaging of futurity by financial capitalism in which children's bodies are cultivated as open-ended, extractable vital resources, it would also miss the function of the nostalgia for deep attention within neoliberal disinvestment in education to author yet another critique of hyperattention.

An eco-pharmacology of childhood ADHD casts doubt on whether deep attention is in any way more natural, more desirable, or even a better political goal, than hyperattention, but it also desires to dispense with the imperative to have to decide the question once and for all. In that way it diverges from the tendency toward the opposability of deep- and hyperattention. Attention can be conceptualized by neurofeminism instead as a much more labile and variable capacity produced and culti- vated across a continuum of forms of historical social entrainment of the physical, affective, and cognitive dimensions of body *and* brain.

Genealogically, attention can be anchored in a much longer *durée* than the discourses participating in anxieties over children and digital tech- nology permit. The Western and European entrainment of bodies and minds begins at least in the Greek city-states with the simultaneous foun- dations of the physically disciplined phalanx army (Protevi 2009, 153–55) and mental academies of philosophy (Protevi 2001, 133–35). Foucault's (1990, 1988) work on the care of the self in early Christianity constitutes a second archive of a set of practices that trace the embodied and cogni- tive entrainment of attention and spirit in the West. Deep attention is not established as hegemonic until long after both of these moments, with the advent of capitalist modernity and colonialism. A matrix of attention that extends from its most physical tendencies of expression, in the army, gymnastics, and organized sport, through the transmission of affect in musical ritual, performance, and dance, and then into the more cognitive or mental realms of reading and writing, does not sustain the opposability of deep- and hyperattention. For instance, dance, like Wilson's example of bulimia, does not fit easily in Hayles's framework, neither obviously "deep" nor "hyper" in its configuration. Yet dance, especially in its public and ritualized iterations, is a form of entrainment of attention that oper- ates through the rhythmic affectivity of bodies in unison and can prompt a collective mental focus on a common idea (Ehrenreich 2007).

Childhood ADHD similarly relies on an ecology of neurobiological, mental, and affective dimensions in its pharmacological treatment as a technology of performance enhancement. Adderall and Ritalin, as with Dr. Bradley's findings on Benzedrine in the 1930s, produce simultane- ously mental (focus) and biological (reduced hyperactivity) effects. As with Wilson's reading of the treatment of bulimia by antidepressants, the alleviation of the symptoms of ADHD cannot be separated, causally, into mental and behavioral given their simultaneity; at the same time, they are expressed differentially, rather than being either a single entity or two combined entities. ADHD drugs amplify the attentional capacities of children's bodies; as performance enhancement, this increase in what the child's body and mind can do is intelligible according to a form of measure derivative of capitalist success: focus and concentration lead to improved output and value. The mass medication of children for ADHD is both a supplement to and potential future replacement for the molding of the public school that, in crisis after decades of disinvestment, can no longer ensure the future productivity of children's bodies on its own. The liability for investment in education must be assumed by children themselves, in their bodies, now that the state no longer will—a shouldering of risk and debt not without its costs.

All this is not to say that Adderall could not be deployed differently, in a way that increases what children's bodies can do on their own terms rather than solely for the purposes of creating better human capital and enhanced biological futures. Recreational use of amphetamines, or buying Ritalin on the black market to study for exams, however seemingly subversive of the law of their prescription, is not a realization of that potentiality. Rather than continuing to have to decide the veracity of ADHD, the enabling or regulatory effects of pharmaceuticals writ large, or whether attention ought to be deep- or hyper- in organization, a neurofeminism affirms the complexity of the neurobiological, mental, and pharmacological in a system without efficient causality. The loss of efficient causality, of course, also marks a loss of certainty of what counts as the political. If the "new maladies of the soul" (Kristeva 1995) of which ADHD, like allergies, autism, depression, anxiety, or model minority psychosis, is a symptom, are to be addressed differently, it will be by engaging, rather than dismissing, pharmacology. After all, "for better," or "for worse," Dr. Anderson's kids are already on drugs.

NOTES

This chapter benefited from the generous attention of everyone who participated in Mattering: Feminism, Science and Materialism and the CUNY Graduate Center. I thank Karen Barad, Susan Oyama, Jesse Prinz, and John Protevi for catalyzing feedback. This work would never have grown without Rebekah Sheldon, who I am so grateful to have met at Mattering. I am also indebted to Victoria Pitts-Taylor for all of her hard work on this volume, as well as to my fellow contributors. Any shortcomings in this chapter are, of course, my own.

1 There is an edited collection with this title already: Robyn Bluhm, Anne Jaap Jacobson, and Heidi Lene Maibom, eds., *Neurofeminism: Issues at the Intersection*

of Feminist Theory and Cognitive Science, London: Palgrave MacMillan, 2012. To be clear, my use of the term is unrelated to that volume, nor do I make any claim on coining it.

2 Wilson (2006) follows up in a subsequent essay, "The Work of Antidepressants: Preliminary Notes on How to Build an Alliance Between Feminism and Psychopharmacology," as well as her book *Psychosomatic* (2004). This chapter endorses her proposition that "some biologically reductionist demands have the potential to expand our theories of the body in important, innovative, and sometimes exhilarating ways" (3). Wilson's book, *Gut Feminism* (2016), will undoubtedly greatly enrich the broader project of feminist science studies.

3 Ecological thought encompasses a much larger field than I can address here. I emphasize the affectivity of ecologies in order to attend to the specificities of pharmaceuticals across multiple scales of being. In that sense, I am particularly indebted to Félix Guattari's work (1989) in "The Three Ecologies," as well as Gilbert Simondon's (1989) work on individuation.

4 And there are other drugs that could be analyzed as part of the broader historical process of "pharmaceuticalization," as Simon J. Williams, Stephen Katz, and Paul Martin (2011, 8) underline in considering ADHD medication alongside the "wakefulness promoting" medication Modafinil.

REFERENCES

Adamson, Morgan. 2009. "The Human Capital Strategy." *Ephemera* 9:271–284.

Alexander, Michelle. 2012. *The New Jim Crow: Mass Incarceration in the Age of Colorblindness* (New York: New Press).

Barad, Karen. 2007. *Meeting the Universe Halfway: Quantum Physics and the Entanglement of Matter and Meaning* (Durham, NC: Duke University Press).

Bradley, Charles. 1937. "The Behavior of Children Receiving Benzedrine." *American Journal of Psychiatry* 94: 571–88.

Bradley, Charles and Margaret Bowen. 1941. "Benzedrine (Amphetamine) Therapy of Children's Behavior Disorders." *American Journal of Orthopsychiatry* 11: 91–103.

Cheah, Phengh. 1996. "Mattering." *Diacritics* 26: 108–139.

Damasio, Antonio. 2003. *Looking For Spinoza: Joy, Sorrow, and the Feeling Brain* (New York: Harcourt).

Deleuze, Giles and Félix Guattari. 1987. *A Thousand Plateaus* (Minneapolis: University of Minnesota Press).

Derrida, Jacques. 2004. *Dissemination* (London: Bloosmbury).

Dub, L. M. and L. Lurie. 1939. "Use of Benzedrine in the Depressed Phase of the Psychotic State." *Ohio State Medical Journal* 35: 39–45.

Dumit, Joseph. 2012. *Drugs for Life: How Pharmaceutical Companies Define Our Health* (Durham, NC: Duke University Press).

Ehrenreich, Barbara. 2007. *Dancing in the Streets: A History of Collective Joy* (New York: Macmillan).

Foucault, Michel. 2008. *The Birth of Biopolitics: Lectures at the Collège de France, 1978–79* (New York: Palgrave MacMillan).

———. 1990. *The History of Sexuality, Vol. 2: The Use of Pleasure* (New York: Vintage).

———. 1988. *The History of Sexuality, Vol. 3: The Care of the Self* (New York: Vintage).

Guattari, Félix. 1989. "The Three Ecologies." *new formations* 8: 131–147.

Hayles, N. Katherine. 2007. "Hyper and Deep Attention: The Generational Divide in Cognitive Modes," *Profession*: 187–199.

Healy, David. 2002. *The Creation of Psychopharmacology* (Cambridge, MA: Harvard University Press).

Kaplan, Stanley H. 1992. *Pharmacology Notes* (New York: Stanley H. Kaplan Center).

Kristeva, Julia. 1995. *New Maladies of the Soul*. Translated by Ross Guberman (New York: Columbia University Press).

Malabou, Catherine. 2008. *What Should We Do With Our Brain?* (New York: Fordham University Press).

Mitropoulos, Angela. 2012. *Contract and Contagion: From Biopolitics to Oikonomia* (New York: Minor Compositions).

Nash, John. 2012. "Ritalin calms hyperactive child and prescriptions soaring—but experts warn of serious side effects." *Daily Mail*, May 7. http://www.dailymail.co.uk/health/article-2141044/ADHD-Ritalin-prescriptions-soaring-experts-warn-effects.html.

Prinz, Jesse. 2012. *The Conscious Brain* (Oxford: Oxford University Press).

Protevi, John. 2009. *Political Affect: Connecting the Social and the Somatic* (Minneapolis: University of Minnesota Press).

———. 2001. *Political Physics: Deleuze, Derrida and the Body Politic* (London: Athlone Press).

Schwarz, Alan. 2012. "Attention Disorder or Not, Pills to Help in School." *New York Times*, October 9. http://www.nytimes.com/2012/10/09/health/attention-disorder-or-not-children-prescribed-pills-to-help-in-school.html?pagewanted=all&_r=1&.

Simondon, Gilbert. 1989. *L'individuation psychique et collective* (Paris: Aubier).

Stiegler, Bernard. 2010. *Taking Care of Youth and the Generations* (Stanford, CA: Stanford University Press).

Strohl, Madeleine P. 2011. "Bradley's Benzedrine Studies on Children with Behavioral Disorders." *Yale Journal of Biology and Medicine* 84: 27–33.

Williams, Simon J., Stephen Katz, and Paul Martin. 2011. "The Neuro-Complex: Some Comments and Convergences." *Media Tropes* 3: 1–12.

Wilson, Elizabeth A. 2016. *Gut Feminism*. Durham, NC: Duke University Press.

———. 2006. "The Work of Antidepressants: Preliminary Notes on How to Build an Alliance Between Feminism and Psychopharmacology." *BioSocieties* 1: 125–131.

———. 2004a. "Gut Feminism." *differences* 15: 66–94.

———. 2004b. *Psychosomatic: Feminism and the Neurobiological Body* (Durham, NC: Duke University Press).

12

Female Bodily (Re)Productivity in the Stem Cell Economy

A Cross-Materialist Feminist Approach

SIGRID VERTOMMEN

This chapter is—like Hanna Meißner's chapter—the product of ambiguous yet productive feelings of excitement and astonishment while exploring the recent literature on feminist materialism. On the one hand, I am greatly enthused about the return of the material in feminist theory after decades of (un)divided feminist attention to cultural and discursive turns. At the same time, I am surprised by the lack of interaction between adherents to newer interpretations of feminist materialist theory and older traditions of historical materialism. As Sara Ahmed (2008, 32) aptly remarked: "The new materialism does not take as its point of entry a critique or engagement with historical materialism, which does not haunt this emergent field even in its absence." Of course—as Meissner rightly stated in this book—it is far from productive, and even problematic, to assume the existence of two well-delineated paradigms within feminist materialist theory and to "close up" authors within the labels and subcategories of either of the two perspectives. That said, I do find it imperative to transcend the uncomfortable silence between these strands of feminist materialism and to analyze if and how they can mutually reinforce each other. I will do this through a well-defined case study that has emanated from my research on the political economy of egg donations in Palestine/Israel. This chapter offers a cross-materialist feminist analysis of the ways in which female bodily productivity is being mobilized in twenty-first-century bio-economies, using a *diffractive* reading of historical materialist and new materialist feminist contributions. Diffraction refers to "reading texts intra-actively through one another, enacting new patterns of engagement, attending to how exclusions matter" (Barad 2010, 243). I will elucidate on the (dis)continuities between both perspectives on the use of women's reproductive tissues in stem cell economies. By focusing on various themes such as reproductive labor, the nature-culture divide, and the position of biology and critique within feminist studies, I will examine if and how old and new materialist feminist perspectives can cross-fertilize and "interrupt each other productively" (Haraway in Meissner, this volume).

Female (Re)productivity in the Stem Cell Economy

The bio-economy is increasingly pushed forward to become an important niche in the global knowledge economy. In the policy discourses of the Organization for Economic Cooperation and Development (2009) and European Commission (2012), the bio-economy is envisioned as an opportunity to develop "a more competitive yet sustainable economy based on the commercial development of biotechnologies that capitalize the latent value underpinning biological materials."[1] In his book *The Politics of Life Itself* (2007), Nikolas Rose reminded us that capitalizing life and capturing the "biovalue" in biological processes has indeed turned into a very globalized and profitable industry in which living entities such as bacteria, genes, viruses, plants, and even animals are increasingly subjected to forms of intellectual property. According to Melinda Cooper (2008, 23) this has radically transformed the life sciences and biomedical research "into a lucrative area of investment for the increasingly volatile forms of financial and venture capital that have dominated the global economy since the 1970s." The stem cell industry constitutes an important sector in the bio-economy. This burgeoning yet still highly experimental sector is developing medical technologies and therapies based on stem cells, intended to treat degenerative and chronic diseases such as Parkinsons, multiple sclerosis, and Alzheimer's, as well as organ damage, through in vivo, tailor-made tissue growth instead of organ transplant (Gottweis et al. 2009). Pharmaceutical and biotech giants, but mostly smaller start-up companies—often emanating from university spinoffs—from countries as diverse as the United States, the UK, Israel, India, China, and Singapore—are investing large sums in human embryonic stem cell research for the development of "promissory" cell therapies and technologies (Thompson 2005).

Stem cells are immature, unspecialized cells that possess two main qualities that make them very desired "bio-objects" in the research market (Waldby 2008. First of all, they are pluripotent, which means that they can be induced to become any mature bodily cell. Second, they are self-regenerative, meaning that they can renew themselves for long periods through cell division. The most viable sources of human embryonic stem cells are still female reproductive tissues such as embryos (and by proxy egg cells), placenta, umbilical cord blood, and even fetuses.[2] This has urged Margaret Lock and Sarah Franklin (2003, 7) to place reproductive processes at the core of the biosciences "as the primary generator of wealth, agency and value." They rightly remarked that the new, experimental knowledge resulting from stem cell research can only be *invented* and produced with the help and participation of tissue providers who are increasingly procuring the biomedical research sector (consisting of universities, research institutions, R&D departments of biotech and pharmaceutical companies) with their raw reproductive resources. Overall, the provision of reproductive tissues for research purposes is organized through a gift system.[3] To avoid the exploitation of underprivileged women who could be unduly induced to sell their bodily materials for financial reasons, women are restricted to donate for altruistic reasons—for the progress of science and humanity—without getting any financial compensation in return. Even in rare cases such as in the State of New York or Israel, where women are reimbursed for providing their tissues to biomedical research, they are still framed as altruistic donors who provide tissues through bioethical rather than economic frameworks (Waldby 2008; Waldby and Cooper 2010).[4] Intellectual property law stipulates that donated reproductive materials are either biological waste or *res nullius*, i.e., nobody's property (Dickenson 2007). While spare embryos and egg cells from fertility treatments, umbilical cords, placentas, and even aborted fetuses are donated as "nature's gifts to science," they are eventually transformed into patentable products such as stem cell lines, stem cell technologies, and therapies.

The bio-economy, and the prevalent legal framework on tissue donations, is underpinned by sharp dichotomies between reproduction-production, nature-culture, resource- invention, gift-commodity. Consequently, women—who are traditionally associated with reproduction and nature—have been relegated to disadvantaged socioeconomic and cultural positions by these prevailing dichotomies. In what follows I will argue that a materialist feminist approach can offer crucial insights in the debate on female bodily (re)productivity in the twenty-first-century bio-economy. By diffracting a Marxian feminist perspective with a new materialist feminist one, I will examine how the two perspectives converge and diverge in their analysis of female tissue donations for the stem cell industry.

Feminist Materialism: What Materiality Matters?

Marxian feminism and new materialist feminism have both been adamant in putting the material back on the feminist agenda. They criticized the so-called cultural/linguistic turns in feminist studies which focused on how genders, sexualities, and bodies are discursively and socially constructed. In her Cyborg Manifesto, Donna Haraway (1991, 152) wrote: "The textualization of everything in poststructuralist theory should be criticized for its utopian disregard for the lived relations of domination that ground the play of arbitrary reading."[5] New materialist feminist Karen Barad (2003, 1) seconds this when stating that "language has been granted too much power (. . .) It seems that at every turn lately everything—even materiality—is turned into a matter of language or some other form of cultural representation." She continues: "Matter is not support, location, referent, or source of sustainability for discourse. It does not require the mark of an external force like culture or history to complete it (. . .) nor is it an uncontested ground for scientific feminist or Marxist theories" (821).

Even though both feminisms are labeled as materialist, there is a significant difference in the way materiality is conceptualized within Marxian and new materialist feminist theory. For Marxian feminists, who grew strong during the second feminist wave in the 1970s, materialism refers to the socio-historical circumstances in which unequal social and economic power relations between men and women arose within a capitalist world economy (Barrett 1980). New materialist feminist conceptualizations of materiality diverge from Marxian and post-Marxian perspectives that perceive it as strictly economic or social. According to Barad, "agential realism advances a new materialist understanding of naturalcultural practices that cut across these well-worn divides" (2007,

226). Accordingly, postmillennial feminist materialists have introduced a broader ontological vision on materialism that takes into consideration corporeality, non-human agency, the physical substance of bodies and of the world more generally (Alaimo & Hekman 2008). Because of this fundamentally different conceptualization of the material, Marxian and new materialist feminists have tended to focus on different issues within the debates on female bodily (re)productivity. Marxian feminists, for instance, have addressed topics such as property rights and (re)productive labor, while new material feminists have been attentive to more ontological debates such as the nature-culture divide, post-humanism, and the position of biology within the feminist studies. Since many of these topics matter in a materialist discussion of the position of women and their bodies in the twenty-first-century bio-economy, I will elaborate a bit further on them.

Marxian Feminism, Reproductive Labor, and the Mind-Body Split

Focusing primarily on relations of production within capitalist economies, Marx himself did not pay much attention to matters of reproduction. According to Marx, what a woman does when giving birth and life is "merely" natural, not social. It was not deemed to produce any use-value nor add any surplus value. Therefore it could not belong to the sphere of production and was banned in stepmotherly fashion to the sphere of reproduction or even consumption (Dickenson 2007). One of the major accomplishments of Marxian feminism has been to emphasize how women's unpaid domestic labor has been indispensable for the social reproduction of capitalism. Christine Delphy, Michelle Barrett, and Mariarosa Dallacosta, for instance, have convincingly reconceptualized women's domestic and maternal work as a form of productive labor that complemented the industrial labor of the male breadwinner within the Fordist accumulation regime and household model (Waldby & Cooper 2010). More recently, Marxian feminist scholars are identifying similar forms of unacknowledged feminized labor within the post-Fordist bio-economy. Specifically for the stem cell market, feminist authors such as Donna Dickenson (2007), Charis Thompson (2005), Catherine Waldby and Melinda Cooper (2010, 2014) have argued that women who donate their reproductive tissues to the stem cell sector are actually laboring, each of them putting forward their own specificities and accents. Dickenson (2007), for instance, perceives tissue donations as a form of reproductive labor in which women are alienated from their own biological materials. Thompson (2005) introduced the concept of *biomedical mode of reproduction* to refer to the ways in which reproductive tissues are industrialized to become standardized entities such as cell lines. Waldby and Cooper (2010) opt for the term *regenerative or clinical labor*, emphasizing not so much the reproductive capacities of donated embryos, egg cells, umbilical cords, and placentas, but their regenerating capacities within stem cell therapies. All these scholars emphasize that even though the biological capacities of human bodies and the reproductive labor of female donors are indispensable for biocapitalism, they are never recognized as such within the labor process. Gambardella (1995) already posited that the valorization mostly goes to the productive, innovative, scientific labor of the scientist who transforms biological matter into patentable products.

There is a fundamental division of labor between scientific production and biological life in the organization of intellectual property in the life sciences. As Waldby & Cooper (2010, 8) phrase it: "It [intellectual property law] recognizes the cognitive, highly skilled labour of the researcher, the scientist and the clinician, but it systematically undermines the constitutive nature of the biological material." Patent law was shaped this way since the landmark American court case of Chakrabarty versus Diamond in 1980. Chakrabarty was a genetic engineer working for General Electric who received the right to patent a bacterium that was capable of breaking down crude oil. His patent application was initially rejected because living things were not patentable according to patent law. After 1980, the U.S. Congress allowed to patent "anything under the sun that is made by man," including stem cell lines (Waldby & Mitchell 2007). This implies that embryos or egg cells as such cannot be patented, yet the stem cell lines derived from human embryos can easily enter intellectual property regimes.[6] Until recently, the European patent law took another path. In 2011, the European Court of Justice decided—against all odds—that procedures involving human embryonic stem cells cannot be patented given that this type of research is based on the destruction of the human embryo, and thus consequently of human life. This inflicted a major blow to the European stem cell sector. In December 2014, the European Court of Justice partially backtracked this decision, after a series of complaints from stem cell scientists and companies alike. It ruled that human embryonic stem cells made from unfertilized eggs can be patented—on the basis that they lack the capacity to turn into a human being (Callaway & Abbott 2014). However, tissue provisions in the EU are organized through a gift system. The European Union Tissue Directive from 2004 states that "as a matter of principle, tissue and cell application programmes should be founded on the philosophy of voluntary and unpaid donation (. . .), altruism of the donor and solidarity between donor and recipient." The valorization of labor in the stem cell economy is underpinned by a Cartesian dichotomy between mind and body. In the logic of the binary only the mind is considered capable of producing surplus value while the female body is nothing but dumb and passive matter that merely brings forth "natural" products such as embryos, egg cells, and placentas.

The aforementioned Marxian feminist scholars have tried to counter the misogynist effects of the mind-body split by arguing that women also *labor* to create bodily tissues for stem cell technologies. For instance, on egg cell donations Donna Dickenson (2007, 65) wrote, "there is nothing remotely natural about the process of ovarian stimulation and egg extraction. It involves a lot of emotional and physical labour." She refers to the fact that becoming an egg donor is quite an arduous process. First, potential candidates have to go through time-consuming physical and psychological tests. Then, egg cell donors have to undergo hormonal treatments to overstimulate their ovaries to produce multiple follicles, which are ultimately surgically removed and *harvested*. Dickenson aims to upgrade the reproductive labor of egg cell donors by removing it from the natural sphere, which all too often has been equated with passive and taken-for-granted femininity. Even though she rightly demonstrates how disadvantageous the Cartesian mind-body split is for women within the stem cell economy, she does so by holding on to the ontological separation between nature and culture. Rather than foregrounding the *inherent* agency or productivity of the natural reproductive body, what is a primary focal point in the new feminist materialist research agenda—Dickenson revalues egg donations by relegating them to the cultural/labor sphere. In this sense, Vicki Kirby (2008, 216) remarked how many intellectual critiques into Cartesian logic are "much more likely to preserve the assumption that nature is deemed to be thoughtless by expanding the category culture to include whatever is defined against."

The Biological In/and the Social: From Hybrid Inter-Actions to Intra-Active Agency in the Stem Cell Economy

The new materialist turn is in part motivated by the perceived status of the biological within feminist thought. Even though the groundbreaking work of feminist biologists such as Lynda Birke (1986), Donna Haraway (1991), Anne Fausto-Sterling (1992, 2000), and Evelyn Fox Keller (1995) underscores the long and continuous feminist engagement with/on biology and ontological matters, certain strands within feminist thought have remained rather reluctant to engage with biological data or to use biological arguments in defining what constitutes a woman (Davis, 2009).[7] This hostility toward the biological as a scientific discourse is not surprising. Elisabeth Grosz (2005, 13) acknowledges that feminists may have good reasons to mistrust the ways in which biology as a scientific discipline has been put forward, since it has been "actively if unconsciously used by those with various paternalistic, patriarchal and class commitments to rationalize their various positions." However, Grosz (2005, 13) argues that it is absurd to repudiate biology and nature as such since "this is what we are and will always be." New materialist feminists such as Grosz, Kirby, Wilson, and Birke are trying to re-engage with biology in a positive and affirmative way, without falling into the pitfalls of socio-biological determinism and essentialism that would legitimize or naturalize social inequalities. The main ambitions of new materialist feminists are twofold. First, they want to refute any implicit feminist assumption that biological matter is a passive, thoughtless, fixed, and stable entity by emphasizing its open, dynamic, intelligent, and agential character. Second, they want to engage with biology and materiality in such a way that doesn't not separate it conceptually and ontologically from the social realm. New materialist feminists view the artificial separation between the social and the biological to be detrimental for a correct and just understanding of the world and science. Donna Haraway (1991, 170) has been particularly critical toward those "who continue to see deepened dualisms of mind and body, animal and machine, idealism and materialism in the social practices, symbolic formulations and physical artifacts associated with high technology and scientific culture." She actually holds these dialectics responsible for the practices of domination of women, people of color, nature, workers, animals. Instead of seeing the two spheres of the biological and the social *inter-act*, which presumes the pre-given existence of independent entities, new feminist materialists perceive it as an intra-active entanglement, "a non-separability of biology with/in sociality" as Noela Davis (2009, 75) phrases it. To underline this intimate entanglement between the social and the biological, Barad introduced the notion of *intra-active becoming*. By doing this, she proposed an onto-epistemology in which "knower, known, and laboratory instrument act and come into being simultaneously, in their mutual entanglement." According to Barad (quoted in van der Tuin 2011, 31), "none of the three has the definitive say or agency in the coming into being of the eventual knowledge claim; they are co-constitutive, and all of them, including the known that is haunted by being objectified and thus feminized, are agential." Adopting this explicitly post-humanist reasoning to my case study—stem cell research—suggests that it is not just the stem cell researcher but also the embryo as such (or other raw biological materials that are used for stem cell research) and the microscope, the freezer and other lab tools needed for stem cell research that are co-producing new knowledge and eventually a human embryonic stem cell line. Although this is a fundamental critique on the prevailing mind-body split in the stem cell sector's labor regimes, the one who appears to be vanishing in this post-humanist rationale is the woman and her embodied agency (Dickenson 2007). This remark raises important questions of how to interpret this "agentification" of biological matter, even when it is not essentialized or "thingified." This question of agential power becomes all the more relevant when one starts to think about how to put the onto-epistemological recognition of bodily productivity into practice within the twenty-first-century bio-economy with its gendered, classed, and racialized labor and property regimes. I will address and illustrate the ambivalence surrounding the issue of intra-active agency and biology with/in sociality by analyzing how it has been put forward by feminist scholars who are studying women's bodily (re)productivity in the stem cell economy. I will focus particularly on the work of Sarah Franklin and Catherine Waldby, both of whom have critically analyzed the relation between capitalism and stem cell science and who—according to my reading—have been inspired yet also criticized by both strands of feminist materialism. The question of political engagement and praxis will be explicitly addressed in a final and separate paragraph.

Anthropologist Sarah Franklin's research has focused on the changing relations of gender, kinship, and sex with the introduction and mainstreaming of reproductive technologies and repro-genetics. Her work can also be viewed as a continuous work-in-progress to come to terms with the shifting relation between materiality and sociality in the field of reproductive biology. As a new materialist feminist *avant la lettre* she has always been very careful not to take matters of reproduction as natural laws. In early work with Helena Ragoné (1998: 2), for instance, she cautioned against "the relegation of 'reproduction' to a domain of 'natural' or biological facts . . . considered prior to, and separate from, sociality." In her latest book "Biological Relatives" (2013) in which she conceptualized "biology as a technology" and "technology as a biology" through the window of IVF, she described how reproductive substances such as eggs and sperm were never "merely" biological, but always (even before assisted reproductive technologies) necessitated activation through technologies of gender and kinship. However, according to Noela Davis (2009), Franklin's (2003) understanding of the intricate relation between the biological and the social is one of *hybridity* or a "joining together of two unlike things that belong to different orders," which is in direct opposition to the new materialist notion of inseparability (Davis 2009: 75). Davis claims that Franklin's analysis is rooted in Marilyn Strathern's concept of merographic connections, which refers to a "co-mingling of parts that belong to different wholes" (Strathern quoted in Franklin 2003, 66). Davis (2009) insists that this is a major divergence from new feminist materialism's theorization of a holographic intra-acting of the biological with/through the social.

Throughout her work, Franklin has also shown a keen interest in reproductive matter not only as a physical relation, but also as a social one. She has explored the capitalization of reproductive processes in/by contemporary bio-science by engaging with concepts such as bio-wealth and bio-capital. In his enlightening classification of the research on biocapital, Stefan Helmreich (2007) catalogued Franklin's work in the Marxist feminist cluster that has shown particular interest in the shifting binaries of production versus reproduction and the remaking of the boundaries between nature versus culture under bio-capitalism. In her work with Margaret Lock (2003: 8), Franklin defined bio-capital as "wealth depending on mobilizing the primary reproductive agency of specific body parts, particularly cells, in a manner not dissimilar to that by which, as Marx described it, soil plays the 'principal' role in agriculture." This definition closely resembles Catherine Waldby's (2000, 2002, 2007, 2008) understanding of bio-value as "a surplus of biological vitality." In her analysis of tissue economies, she (together with Robert Mitchell and Melinda Cooper) suggests that bio-value is produced wherever the generative and transformative productivity of living entities, such as stem cells, can be used and instrumentalized for human projects. Marxian political economists, such as Kean Birch and David Tyfield (2012), have fundamentally critiqued Waldby's (and to a lesser extent Franklin's) theories for their techno-scientific focus on the presumed "novelty" of the relation between biotechnology and capitalism without paying attention to financial processes of post-Fordist capitalism. They problematized various aspects of these theories, including their "fetishization of biological matter" (all things "bio" such as bio-capital/ism, bio-value, and bio-economies) as the source of value, rather than labor or economic process as well as the "problematic adoption of Marxist language in these bio-concepts without the necessary adoption of Marx's theoretical formulation of the labor theory of value underpinning key terms like value, capital, and surplus value" (Birch and Tyfield 2012: 299). Going back to Marx's labor theory of value, it posits that value is realized through the (exploitable) capacities of workers, as embodied labor power, rather than any latent characteristic of biological matter. Birch and Tyfield question Waldby's presumed notion of biological generativity as a form of accumulated labour power. Stefan Helmreich (2007, 2008: 464) agrees that by viewing the biological process itself as a form of surplus value and profit production, much of the STS research on bio-capital actually tends to "naturalize" biotech. He clarifies: "This belief is based on a metaphor: that organisms are labourers. We must be careful not to imagine reproduction as a transparently 'natural' process (. . .), as though their productivity is the essence of their species being. To see matters this way is to see organisms as natural factories or assembly lines, when in fact they only become so in certain relations." He uses the example of stem cells as pluripotent and self-regenerating tissues as an example to illustrate this. "One might argue that stem cells are animated by a double fetishism—infused with vitality because of the erasure or the labour and regulation that allow them to appear 'in themselves' in such places as laboratories and simultaneously imbued with life because of their origin in living things" (Helmreich, 2008: 464).

The point of disagreement between the historical and the new materialist literature on bio-capitalism boils down to the question of who/what produces value and of—even more fundamentally—who is the political subject. Historical materialists criticize new materialism's posthumanist understanding of biological matter as an agential power. In a strict application of Marx's labor theory of value, it is not the body or biological matter as such that labors and produces value, but human labor power. In Birch and Tyfield's interpretation, there would be no value in a stem cell "without the effortful and waged application of knowledge and work" to transform that biological matter into a product or commodity. Contrary to Waldby and Franklin's perspective on biological productivity, Birch and Tyfield (2012, 221) believe that "value results from the application of knowledge to nature, and the subjection of that knowledge to intellectual property rights, and not from nature itself or from particular biological material. In discussing these political-economic concepts here, we have shown how value, capital, and surplus value are constituted by some form of labor—whether this is knowledge, immaterial, cognitive, or what-have-you labor—and not to some characteristic latent within biological matter." Again, the one who appears to be vanishing is the lady (Dickenson 2007). What I believe is missing in Birch and Tyfield's "old school" analysis of the bio-economy, as well as in their critique of Waldby's work, is a feminist reading of the labor theory of value. By focusing only on knowledge labor, they reaffirm the misogynist mind-body split in the (bio-)economy and bluntly dismiss the notion of reproductive (or clinical or regenerative) labor as it has been put forward by Marxian feminists like Dickenson and—as well—Waldby. According to my reading, their work centers around the notion of reproductive labor of female tissue donors, and not around the inherent generativity of the reproductive material. Dickenson (2001, 2007), for example, understands bodily productivity as an expression of the donor's agency and not of her body as such. The generated "bio-value" is derived from her agential power even though her body serves as a medium. Also, Waldby (2008) puts the embodied productivity and agency of the donor at the core of her analysis of the stem cell economy. She criticizes the ontological mind-body split, but keeps a close eye on the current political economy of tissue donations and the gendered division of labor within the stem cell economy, which often places female tissue providers in a disadvantaged position.

Even though Franklin and Waldby have been chastised by both materialist sides for not being "old" or "new" enough, there is a lot to learn from their work and the "trans-materialist" critique on their work, as I will conclude in the last section on critique and praxis.

The Question of Critique, Praxis, and Engaged Feminism

Feminism, particularly during the second wave, has always been both an intellectual and a political prescriptive project. Even though this conflation has also produced the necessary ambivalence and tension, feminists agreed that as a critical theory, feminism should also involve a politically transformative and emancipatory practice. In the broadest sense, this implied that feminist scholars were to produce knowledge and develop conceptual tools that could destabilize the hegemonic status quo.

Marxian feminist scholars in particular focused on producing knowledge that could help transform the institutions that distribute economic resources and political power asymmetrically according to gender lines (Ebert 1992). Therefore, "old" materialist feminist theory has always been an engaged intellectual project, anchored in a well-defined critique on the uneven distribution of power along class, gender (and ethnicity) lines. Teresa Ebert argued that "by perceiving the body as both a means of productive labour but also as a site acted on by labour, Marxist feminism has offered possibilities for social and political struggle over the way women's bodies are produced, used and even exploited by specific historical forms of the division of labour on the basis of gender differences" (1992, 23). Within the debate on women's participation in the stem cell economy, the Marxian feminist critiques are manifold: the commodification of what should not be commodified, the performance of medical procedures which contravene the physician's duty of *first do no harm*, the non-recognition of women's reproductive labor and the co-opting of their altruism into the process. These critiques have been politically translated into various demands, ranging between a moratorium on certain tissue donations until the long-term medical effects are properly investigated, to the recognition of the reproductive labor of female donors by financially compensating them or giving them other forms of *property rights* within the body, such as the right to transfer, waive, and exclude others from the use of one's body parts (Munzer 1990; Dickenson 2007).

New feminist materialism's critical engagement mainly crystallizes around its post-humanism and its ability to disturb anthropocentric thought and practice, which is deeply entrenched in Western traditions of liberalism and Enlightenment. It is characterized by a greater and highly necessary concern and care for human relationships and interdependencies with other non-human species and inhabitants of the earth, such as animals, plants, and the planetary environment in general (McNeil 2010). However, according to my new materialist reading of the bio-economy, it remains unclear how the proposed concepts and values (including sociality with/in biology, post-humanism, and a renewed focus on ontology) can disrupt or challenge the global asymmetries of power that shape our post-Fordist economy. Moreover, it has been questioned if political engagement is even part of the new feminist materialist agenda. According to Maureen McNeil (2010, 432), there can be no doubt that new feminist materialism "is a clear turn away from Marxist (Hegelian) theorising and from the forms of left culture which heavily influenced second-wave feminism." She also sees a definitive break with feminist theory which aimed at "tracing masculinist bias, the neglect of women or patriarchal norms in intellectual discourses and academic disciplines" (ibid.). Indeed, Grosz and other neo-materialists believe that the feminist strategy of critique "has run out of steam." They view it as excessively negative, restricting and even counterproductive in terms of producing social change (McNeil 2010). As such, they have opted for the strategy of *reparative reading* of some authors who from a feminist point of view have been considered to be misogynist, such as Darwin, Freud, and Bergson. I argue that this reparative approach could be fruitful insofar as it does not lose sight of the global power dynamics that are at play in the socio-material world. For instance, new material feminists are very interested in the question of what defines human or biological life. They share this post-humanist interest with intellectual property law-yers from biotech and pharma moguls who have never been more con-cerned by the ontological problem of our humanness in their crusade to patent everything that can be categorized as *not human* (Slater 2002). I already referred to the landmark case of Chakrabarty versus Diamond in 1980, after which the U.S. Congress allowed to patent "anything under the sun that is made by man" (Waldby and Mitchell 2007). Another fa-mous case was the Moore versus US Regents case. In 1990, Moore, who had been treated by Dr. Golde for hairy-cell leukemia and had his spleen removed in the process, sued Dr. Golde and the University of California for stealing "his property," i.e., his spleen cells that turned out to have a huge therapeutic and thus commercial value. Dr. Golde patented the cell line from Moore's spleen cells, and sold the patent to Genetics Institute Inc. and Sandoz Pharmaceuticals, who transformed it into a commer-cial product. When Moore demanded part of the profits, the California Supreme Court decided he had no property rights to his own biologi-cal cells.[8] These cases illustrate how onto-epistemic turns in the field of molecular biology, but as well in feminist theory are taking shape in an era of neoliberal financial capitalism in which intellectual property mo-nopolies have become primordial assets (Cooper 2008; Zeller 2008). To be very clear, I don't mean to suggest that neo-materialists should stop questioning the nature-culture binary out of fear that their knowledge might be hijacked by commercial science and high finance. That would be as silly as claiming that feminists should refrain from questioning the practice of tissue donations for the stem cell sector given that they are often backed up by pro-life, anti-abortion activists who oppose use of human embryos for stem cell research. A critique doesn't lose its politi-cal relevance because it's supported by "strange bedfellows." However, that doesn't mean one shouldn't be attentive to with whom she or he is sharing the bed. To avoid processes of political recuperation and co-optation, I believe it is imperative to be aware of one's obvious and less obvious "friends and foes," and to engage with them in a clear and ar-ticulated way.

When asked in an interview how feminist technoscience and STS could be reoriented in a meaningful way, Lynda Birke (Birke and Åsberg 2010, 421) replied: "One of my concerns for all these fields [referring to feminist biology and new feminist materialism, SV] is precisely that they so easily become removed from grassroots political activism, as they become more and more absorbed in the navel-gazing of academia. Yes, I'm part of all that, having always been an academic. But it saddens me to see how the ideals of the women's liberation movement so rarely seem to drive research. So perhaps that is a (re)orientation I would like to see more of." I believe that with a more articulated interaction and dialogue between "older" and "newer" approaches to materialism, feminist theory could radically expand its emancipatory horizons and imaginaries in the twenty-first century. Considering that there is no possibility or desirability to develop universal and comprehensive theories, I fully agree with Hanna Meißner's proposal (this volume) to productively and diffractively use the permanent tension and ambivalence between these two materialist paradigms by continuing to produce knowledge about the socioeconomic structures of the stem cell economy with its problematic labor and property regimes, while at the same time engaging with "new practices of knowing that aim for a potential of fantasy," that transcend our Eurocentric, anthropocentric, and Cartesian notions of agency.

NOTES

1 European Commission. 2012. "Innovating for Sustainable Growth: A Bioeconomy for Europe."

2 Since 2006, a lot of stem cell research is based on induced pluripotent cells which are not necessarily stemming from women's bodily tissues, but from adult cells such as stomach, liver, skin cells, and blood cells (Takahashi & Yamanaka 2006). As such, induced pluripotent stem cell research has evaded certain bio-ethical issues surrounding the use (and destruction) of human embryos for stem cell research. Yet, certain problems have come up around the potential clinical use of IPS cells, and human embryos are still considered to be the "gold standard" within stem cell research. Another non-reproductive source of stem cells is bone marrow.

3 There are flourishing black markets in reproductive tissue such as embryos and egg cells in countries such as the Ukraine, Romania, Spain, South Africa, and India (Waldby 2008).

4 There are of course exceptions. For instance, in New York or Israel it is allowed for healthy women, who are not undergoing fertility treatment themselves, to sell their egg cells for reproductive or research purposes in return for financial compensation. But even in these rare cases, women are compensated for their time and discomfort, not for the sale of their reproductive materials as such.

5 I thank Victoria Pitts-Taylor for reminding me that Haraway's *Cyborg Manifesto* offered a critique of Marxist theory along with linguistic theories. She critiqued Marxism not only for its totalizing character, but also for its humanism, its distinction between human and technology, and machines, and human and animal.

6 In 2011, the European Court of Justice decided that procedures that involve human embryonic stem cells cannot be patented given that this type of research is based on the destruction of the human embryo, and thus potentially of human life. This inflicted a major blow to the European stem cell sector. In December 2014, the European Court of Justice partially backtracked this decision by ruling that human embryonic stem cells made from unfertilized eggs can be patented—on the basis that they lack the capacity to turn into a human being. The decision of the European court clears the way for stem cell patents (Callaway and Abbott 2014).

7 For a thorough discussion on the history of feminist engagement with and critique on biology as a physical substance and as a scientific discipline, see Ahmed (2008), Davis (2009), van der Tuin (2008).

8 http://www.kentlaw.edu/perritt/courses/property/moore-v-regents-excerpts2.htm.

REFERENCES

Ahmed, Sarah. 2008. "Open forum imaginary prohibitions: Some preliminary remarks on the founding gestures of the New Materialism." *European Journal of Women's Studies* 15 no. 23: 23–39.

Alaimo, Stacy and Hekman, Susan. 2008. *Material Feminisms*. Bloomington: Indiana University Press.

Barad, Karen. 2003. "Posthumanist performativity: Toward an understanding of how matter comes to matter." *Signs: Journal of Women in Culture and Society* 28 no. 3: 801–831.

Barad, Karen. 2007. *Meeting the Universe Halfway: Quantum Physics and the Entanglement of Matter and Meaning*. Durham, NC: Duke University Press.

Barad, Karen. 2010. "Quantum entanglements and hautological relations." *Derrida Today* 3.2: 240–268.

Barrett, Michele. 1980. *Women's Oppression Today: Problems in Marxist Feminist Analysis*. London: Verso.

Birch, Kean. 2013. "The political economy of technoscience: An emerging research agenda." *Spontaneous Generations: A Journal for the History and Philosophy of Science* 7 no. 1: 49–61.

Birch, Kean and Tyfield, David. 2012. "Theorizing the Bioeconomy, Biovalue, Biocapital, Bioeconomics or . . . What?" *Science, Technology and Human Values* 38 no. 3: 299–327.

Birke, Lynda. 1986. *Women, Feminism and Biology: The Feminist Challenge.* Hemel Hempstead: Wheatsheaf.

Birke Lynda and Åsberg, Cecilia. 2010. "Biology is a feminist issue: Interview with Lynda Birke." *European Journal of Women's Studies* 17 no. 4: 413–423.

Callaway, Ewen and Abbott, Alison. 2014. "European court clears way for stem-cell patents." *Nature.* 18/12/2014 http://www.nature.com/news/european-court-clears-way-for-stem-cell-patents-1.16610 (last entry 10/07/2015).

Cooper, Melinda. 2008. *Life as a Surplus: Biotechnology and Capitalism in theNeoliberal Era.* Seattle: University of Washington Press.

Davis, Noela. 2009. "New materialism and feminism's anti-biologism: a response to Sara Ahmed." *European Journal of Women Studies* 16 no. 1: 67–80.

Dickenson, Donna. 2001. "Property and women's alienation from their own reproductive labour." *Bioethics* 15 no. 3: 205–217.

Dickenson, Donna. 2007. *Property in the Body: Feminist Perspectives.* Cambridge: Cambridge University Press.

Directive 2004/23/Ec of the European Parliament and of the Council of 31 March 2004 on setting standards of quality and safety for the donation, procurement, testing, processing, preservation, storage and distribution of human tissues and cells. http://eur-lex.europa.eu/LexUriServ/site/en/oj/2004/l_102/l_10220040407en00480058.pdf (last consulted 07/02/2013).

Ebert, Teresa. 1992. "Ludic feminism, the body, performance and labour: bringing materialism back into feminist cultural studies." *Cultural Critique* 23: 5–50.

European Commission. 2012. Innovating for Sustainable Growth: A Bioeconomy for Europe. http://ec.europa.eu/research/bioeconomy/pdf/201202_commision_staff_working.pdf (last consulted 14/01/2016).

Fausto-Sterling, Anne. 1992. "Building two-way streets: the case of feminism and science." *National Women's Studies Association Journal* 4: 336–349.

Fausto-Sterling, Anne. 2000. *Sexing the Body: Gender Politics and the Construction of Sexuality.* New York: Basic Books.

Fox Keller, Evelyn. 1995. *Refiguring Life: Metaphors of Twentieth-century Biology.* Irvine: Columbia University Press.

Franklin, Sarah. 2003. "Rethinking nature-culture: anthropology and the new genetics." *Anthropological Theory* 3: 65–85.

Franklin, Sarah. 2013. *Biological Relatives: IVF, Stem Cells, and the Future of Kinship.* Durham, NC, and London: Duke University Press.

Franklin, Sarah and Lock, Margaret. 2001. *Remaking Life & Death: Toward an Anthropology of the Biosciences.* Santa Fe: School of American Research Press.

Franklin, Sarah and Ragoné, Helena (eds.). 1998. *Reproducing Reproduction: Kinship, Power, and Technological Innovation.* Philadelphia: University of Pennsylvania Press.

Gambardella, Alfonso. 1995. *Science and Innovation: The U.S. Pharmaceutical Industry During the 1980s.* Cambridge: Cambridge University Press.

Gibbon, Sarah and Novas, Carlos. 2008. *Biosocialities, Genetics and the Social Sciences: Making Biologies and Identities.* London: Routledge.

Gottweis, Herbert, Salter, Brian, and Waldby, Catherine. 2009. *The Global Politics of Human Embryonic Stem Cell Science: Regenerative Medicine in Transition.* New York: Palgrave Macmillan.

Grosz, Elizabeth. 1994. *Volatile Bodies: Toward a Corporeal Feminism.* Indianapolis: Indiana University Press.

Grosz, Elizabeth. 2005. *Time Travels: Feminism, Nature, Power.* Durham, NC: Duke University Press.

Haraway, Donna. 1991. *Simians, Cyborgs and Women: The Reinvention of Nature.* New York: Routledge.

Helmreich, Stefan. 2007. "Blue-green capital, biotechnological circulation and an oceanic imaginary: A critique of biopolitical economy." *BioSocieties* 2: 287–302.

Helmreich, Stefan. 2008. "Species of biocapital." *Science as Culture* 17 (4): 463–78.

Kirby, Vicki. 2008. "Natural convers(at)ions: or, what if culture was really nature all along?" In Alaimo, Stacy and Hekman, Susan, *Material Feminisms.* Bloomington: Indiana University Press, 214–236.

McNeil, Maureen. 2010. "Post-millennial feminist theory: encounters with humanism, materialism, critique, nature, biology and Darwin." *Journal for Cultural Research* 14 no. 4: 427–437.

Munzer, Stephen. 1990. *A Theory of Property.* New York: Cambridge University Press.

OECD. 2009. "The bioeconomy to 2030: designing a policy agenda." http://www.oecd.org/futures/long-termtechnologicalsocietalchallenges/42837897.pdf (last consulted 14/01/2016).

Rose, Nikolas. 2007. *The Politics of Life Itself: Biomedicine, Power, and Subjectivity in the Twenty-First Century.* Princeton, NJ: Princeton University Press.

Slater, Dashka. 2002. "Humouse." *Legal Affairs* (November-December): 21–28. http://www.legalaffairs.org/issues/November-December-2002/feature_slater_novdec2002.msp (last consulted 14/01/2016).

Takahashi Kazutoshi and Yamanaka Shinya. 2006. "Induction of pluripotent stem cells from mouse embryonic and adult fibroblast cultures by defined factors." *Cell* 126 no. 4: 663–676.

Thompson, Charis. 2005. *Making Parents: The Ontological Choreography of Reproductive Technologies.* Cambridge, MA: MIT Press.

Van der Tuin, Iris. 2008. "Deflationary logic: Response to Sara Ahmed's imaginary prohibitions: Some preliminary remarks on the founding gestures of the New Materialism." *Journal of Women's Studies* 15 no. 24: 411–416.

Van der Tuin, Iris. 2011. "A different starting point, a different metaphysics: reading Bergson and Barad diffractively." *Hypatia* 26 no. 1: 22–42.

Waldby, Catherine. 2002. "Stem cells, tissue cultures and the production of biovalue." *Health* 6: 305–323.

Waldby, Catherine. 2008. "Oocyte markets: women's reproductive work in embryonic stem cell research." *New Genetics and Society* 27 no. 1: 19–31.

Waldby, Catherine and Cooper, Melinda. 2010. "From reproductive work to regenerative labour: the female body and the stem cell industries." *Feminist Theory* 11 no. 3: 3–22.

Waldby, Catherine and Mitchell, Robert. 2007. *Tissue Economies: Blood, Organs and Cell Lines in Late Capitalism*. Durham, NC: Duke University Press.

Zeller, Christian. 2008. "From the gene to the globe: Extracting rents based on intellectual property monopolies." *Review of International Political Economy* 15(1): 86–115.

13

Prisons Matter

Psychotropics and the Trope of Silence in Technocorrections

ANTHONY RYAN HATCH AND KYM BRADLEY

A scream, a cry, a laugh—these exhortations signify a lively process in which a body is responding to the world, to other bodies within the world. Bodies that are alive make noise; bodies that are inanimate are silent. Under unjust conditions, live bodies are forced into silence and dead ones can shout. Feminist and critical race science studies scholars have remained all too silent about the prison industrial complex as a site for the enmeshing of natures and cultures, made possible through technoscience. By allowing the technoscientific practices that support the prison industrial complex (and hence the U.S. police state) to remain beneath a shroud of silence and naturalism, science studies remains politically disengaged from one of the most important struggles for human freedom in the contemporary moment (Davis 2003). This oversight is curious given Michel Foucault's centrality to political analyses of technoscience. Foucault initially theorized the prison as a complete or austere institution through which docile bodies were manufactured through a tightly coordinated system of architectures, practices, and procedures (Foucault 1977). Prison functions as a disciplinary institution that severs social relationships between people on the inside and those on the outside and efficiently quiets the objections of political dissidents and those who oppose the prison state.

Whereas science studies have yet to focus their attention on the prison as a site for the enmeshing of natures and cultures, they have examined pharmaceutical drugs as biotechnologies that manipulate the boundaries between bodies and cultural systems, particularly along the axes of gender and race (Dumit 2012; Kahn 2013; Orr 2006; Pollock 2012). One particular group of drugs bears a special strategic relationship to the prison:

psychotropics. There is a substantial body of medical literature that connects the use of psychotropic drugs (hereafter, psychotropics) to aggressive and violent behavior. Doctors routinely prescribe psychotropics to manage a wide range of psychosocial symptoms and psychiatric disorders, given their pronounced biochemical effects on the brain and the nervous system. While their specific mechanisms of action on the brain remain elusive, psychotropics represent a powerful and widely distributed set of drugs that change thought, mood, and social behavior. Even when they are prescribed and used in ways consistent with sound psychiatric practice, psychotropic medications have been associated with suicide, homicide, and other forms of interpersonal violence (Healy, Herxheimer, and Menkes 2006; Moore, Glenmullen, and Furberg 2010; Breggin 2008, 2010). When overused and abused, psychotropics can literally be deadly both for users and for those with whom they come in contact.

Beyond their ostensibly legitimate purpose to treat psychiatric disorders, psychotropics are also a part of the field of technocorrections, the strategic use of biotechnologies to manage prisoners' bodies and to facilitate unjust policies that reproduce mass incarceration. The term "technocorrections" represents the application of new technologies in the effort to reduce the costs of mass incarceration and minimize the risks prisoners pose to society. Psychotropics, electronic tracking and location systems, and genetic and neurobiological risk assessments encompass the field of technocorrections. Tony Fabelo, a U.S. government prison policy strategist, outlines the great potential for psychotropics as a technique of technocorrections:

> Pharmacological breakthroughs—new "wonder" drugs being developed to control behavior in correctional and noncorrectional settings—will also affect technocorrections. Correctional officials already are familiar with some of these drugs, as many are currently used to treat mentally ill offenders. *Yet these drugs could also be easily used to control mental conditions affecting behaviors considered undesirable even when the offenders are not mentally ill* . . . These drugs could become correctional tools to manage violent offenders and perhaps even to prevent violence. (Fabelo 2000, 2)

Also known as "chemical restraints" within psycho-legal discourse, psychotropics are biotechnologies whose production and consumption are shaped by racial and gendered meanings (Ettore & Riska 1995; Orr 2003, 2006). What kinds of new materialities does the use of psychotropics in the prison create?

In this chapter, we argue that the use of psychotropics in prisons creates new forms of material existence in which prisoners' bodies are silenced. First, we sketch two political contexts, biopolitics and necropolitics, which can account for the new realities of technocorrections in prisons. Psychotropics transform the silencing function of prisons by manufacturing a new kind of interior silence within the spirit/soul/psyche of prisoners. This experience of spirit murder (Williams 1991) is mediated through a necropolitics that fosters a violent separation of human material existence from the spirit/soul/psyche of the prisoner, a new form of material existence that we both illuminate and challenge in this chapter. Then, we develop an interpretation of the trope of silence within feminist and critical race theories as a framework for analyzing the distribution of psychotropics as a process within the domain of technocorrections.

Prison Bodies and Social Death

The prison industrial complex serves as a central institutional location for the operation of a gender-segregated and racially coded system of power, an apparatus designed to rearticulate the ostensibly natural body of the prisoner through the grid of prison culture (Rhodes 2004; Brown 2009). The culture of prisons relies on and constitutes relations of institutionalized racism and sexism. Feminist scholars have carefully analyzed how the institutional practices and cultural meanings that define prison life are articulated through discourses of race and gender (Resnik and Shaw 1980; Davis 2003; Brewer and Heitzeg 2008; Sudbury 2013; Lawston and Meiners 2014). Intersectional frameworks that analyze race, gender, sexuality, class, and citizenship as intersecting axes of domination and resistance shape these arguments by highlighting the ways in which these systems of power draw upon each other for meaning and operate simultaneously to maintain injustice. As scholars like Angela Davis and Michelle Alexander have strenuously argued, the prison industrial complex and the criminal injustice system that feeds it both rely on and inform these systems of power as they impact prisoners, their families and communities, and the entire nation (Davis and Shaylor 2001; Davis 2003; Alexander 2010).

The prison industrial complex requires dehumanizing forms of political logic that can justify the legalized disappearance of millions of people, and the suppression of prison abolitionist movements that actively oppose it. Prisoners living within the prison industrial complex are not literally dead (yet) or missing, but rather are experiencing a kind of "spirit murder" that ignores their humanity in the name of security. Patricia Williams defines spirit murder as the "disregard for others whose lives qualitatively depend on our regard" (Williams 1991). We submit that this spirit murder is accomplished, at least in part, through the unquestioned use of psychotropics within prisons, brokered by new relations of biopower that have turned against life. As Paulo Freire notes, "More and more, the oppressors are using science and technology as unquestionably powerful instruments for their purpose: the maintenance of the oppressive order through manipulation and representation. The oppressed, as objects, as 'things' have no purposes except those their oppressors prescribe for them" (Freire 2000). It is tempting to circumscribe materiality in such a way as to exclude the spirit life of people in favor of an understanding of life that is anchored in a hard, fleshy, and thus material body. Using psychotropics to act on the spirit life of people requires that prison agents (administrators, guards, medical care providers, officers) treat the spirit as if it is a material thing that can be manipulated to coercive ends, as Freire suggests.

The ontological transformation of nature and persons into "things" that allows groups to become points of contact within both biopolitics and necropolitics is a central feature of institutionalized state violence (Scott 1999; Césaire 2000; Freire 2000). Michel Foucault developed the term biopower as an analytic term for the synthesis of disciplines and social regulations that take biological life and the improvement of health as their target. Whereas discipline operates at the level of an individual body, biopower operates through "massifying" strategies that deal strictly with *populations* as "a political problem, as a biological problem, and as power's problem" (Foucault 2003 [1976], 245). The practices of biopower involve the construction of knowledge about and the widespread use of demographic averages, comprehensive and comparative measures, and statistical assessments that are derived from the surveillance of populations. Similar to the mechanism of discipline, institutions use these population measures recursively to establish further regulations that are intended to act on the population as a whole. Whereas discipline makes docile bodies so as to increase their utility, the regulatory component to biopower constructs populations so as to maximize their health and life. While we recognize the dynamic that discipline creates for individual bodies, we draw on a biopolitical framework to analyze how prisons use psychotropics in the name of health of the imprisoned population as a whole.

Importantly, Foucault sees the institutions of medicine, the state, and capitalism as central to the operation of power and interprets both the institutional knowledge they manufacture and social practices in which they engage through the analytic of biopower. Foucault argues that states historically exercised their right to kill their enemies, both foreign and domestic, and that this management of death was central to the extension of the power of the sovereign. While states continued to kill as a means to controlling unruly bodies (and they still do this, of course), during the historical transition to a biopolitical organization of state power, nations began to do something different. Beginning in the late eighteenth century, European nation-states started producing their own scientific knowledge about their populations through surveys, implementing new forms of social medicine designed to improve the health of their populations, and monitoring the labor force conditions of their populations, all in terms of strengthening the nation-state through the mechanisms of health. To explain the significance of this new political relationship, Foucault writes, "One might say that the ancient right to *take* life or *let* live was replaced by a power to *foster* life or *disallow* it to the point of death" (Foucault 1978, 138).

What is known about psychotropic use is hobbled by their embeddedness within a field of biopower which means that they only have meaning within discourses of biomedicalization. Biomedicalization refers to a theoretical framework for understanding the historical processes through which human lives and social behaviors fall under the jurisdiction of an increasingly technological and biological approach to health and the clinical practice of medicine (Clarke et al. 2003). Given their centrality to prisons, surprisingly little is known publically about the conditions under which psychotropics are distributed, to whom, their biological effects on prisoners' bodies, and what they might mean as biotechnologies that simultaneously serve diverse social, medical, and political purposes. It is especially challenging to evaluate the claim that psychotropics are used to control prisoners because there is little systematic knowledge of the extent and nature of their use in prisons and, yet, what is known is limited by the context of biopower. Population studies of psychotropic drug prescribing practices and utilization, effectiveness, side effects, and adherence are all carried out under the assumption that the provision of psychotropics is always legitimate because it is carried out in the interests of managing or improving prisoners' mental health. For example, several recent studies examine psychotropic prescribing practices in U.S. prisons, but they only sample prisoners who have been clinically diagnosed with psychiatric disorder (Wilper et al. 2009). This strategy makes it impossible to discern if psychotropics are prescribed to prisoners who do not have clinically defined psychiatric disorder, and they do not capture specific instances where prisoners are forcibly administered psychotropics.

Then, as a technique within *biopolitics*, psychotropics are distributed to persons living within prisons in the name of improving their mental health. In this context, the distribution of psychotropics within prisons, however excessive or unregulated such distribution might be in practice, is legitimate and even rational in the context of high levels of serious mental illness and trauma among prisoners. Psychotropics are viewed as legitimate medical therapies that are more or less effective in managing the symptoms associated with psychiatric and emotional disorders. While this biopolitical narrative grounded in the legitimacy of health-promoting practices may permit and justify the distribution of what may ultimately be *billions* of doses of psychotropics annually to persons living and dying within prisons, we question the extent to which psychotropics may also serve as new technological means to illegitimate ends sought by these institutions.

Initially articulated as an extension of and response to the limitations of biopower to account for political processes that continued to mobilize death through European transnational slavery and colonialism, necropower is an analytic term that refers to "the generalized instrumentalization of human existence and the material destruction of human bodies and populations" (Mbembe 2003, 14). In contrast to biopower, which is enabled principally through the mechanism of law, Achille Mbembe argues that necropower operates within "a state of exception"—an extra-legal space in which serialized, mechanized, and impersonal murder can be carried out without regard for legal prohibitions against execution or assertions about individual rights under law (Agamben 2005). Necro-power functions by designating a population for destruction through instantiating a discourse of enmity, herding that enemy population into an isolated territory that is severed from any viable social infrastructure, and using overwhelming technoscientific force to create death. "Death worlds" result from this process of instrumental murder, a "new and unique form of social existence in which vast populations are subjected to conditions of life conferring upon them the status of the living dead" (Mbembe 2003, 40).

Accordingly, as a technique within *necropolitics*, psychotropics are distributed to persons living within prisons in the name of human psy-chic and social destruction. Here, the distribution of psychotropics is problematic and illegitimate in terms of the purpose of prisons to con-fine, discipline, and exterminate unwanted social groups. Psychotropics are viewed as instruments of a mutant variation of psychobiopower that mobilizes biotechnology in the process of achieving social death (Orr 2003). In other words, psychotropics are used inside prisons to destroy humans, in a particular sense, that have already been socially seques-tered for eventual disposal and who already exist in a state of social abandonment.

These two approaches to the relationship between human material existence and biotechnologies, and the political systems in which they are embedded, help us evaluate scientific and legal claims about the le-gitimacy or illegitimacy of social practices. These social processes are centered on the body and the kinds of rationality offered by prisons in carrying out those practices. Determining whether a particular medical practice is understood as legitimate because it promotes life and good health, or, conversely, is understood as illegitimate because it accelerates death and suffering is contingent on the form of political rationality that justifies the enactment of the practice itself. The conceptual boundary between what is legitimate or not, like the theoretical contiguity of bio-power and necropower, is porous and indeterminate, as is the ontological space that separates waking life from certain death (Timmermans 2006).

While stories of therapeutic legitimacy may justify the distribution of psychotropics to populations living within these institutions, we theorize that this meaning of psychotropics may obscure their great potential as instruments of social control that are made possible by power relationships that mobilize biotechnology in the name of human psychic destruction. The question should not be whether these practices are legitimate, but rather how power functions to obliterate any meaningful distinction between what is normal medicine and what is abnormal killing. As rates of psychotropic use have increased inside these institutional spaces, they have also steadily increased in so-called free society, making it more difficult to interpret the meaning of institutionalization, or at least the uses of biotechnologies as a means to control surplus populations housed inside prisons.

Tropes of Silence

As an analytic device to make sense of this boundary between imprisoned bodies that need to live (biopolitical) or die (necropolitical), we position the trope of silence as a way of talking about the epistemic effects of biotechnologies on the body. Silence is both an effect and instrument of power, and is as important to the meaning and practices of subordination as the discursive statements that envelop it. Critical theorists often deploy a discourse of silence to define the effects of unequal power relationships on disadvantaged social groups. Silencing oppressed groups is a direct mechanism of achieving oppression and also an indirect means of suppressing any opposition to those conditions of oppression. People living under oppressive social conditions are actively silenced through violent acts of murder and genocide, imprisonment and internment. Groups' oppositional voices are contained through marginalization and exclusion from media landscapes, communicative exchanges, and intellectual conversations. Feminists have long mobilized silence to explain and oppose women's oppression within literary space (Olson 1978; Belenky et al. 1986; Cameron et al. 1992; Romano 1993; Hedges and Fishkin 1994).

Social theorist Avery Gordon tells us to examine the ghosts in our societies, social figures who embody hidden unequal power relationships and suffering. While the figure of the ghost may seem immaterial and ephemeral, finding and interrogating these ghosts can help us put a name to the power relationships that function in our societies, a precursor to combating systemic injustice. The lived experiences of prisoners and the meaning of their institutionalization lie at the boundary of their continued traumatic existence and their fully anticipated, if not accelerated and purposeful, death. Avery Gordon's figural analysis of ghosts raises the importance of analyzing silence and why the silence exists (1997). According to Gordon, "the ghost always carries the message . . . that the gap between personal and social, public and private, objective and subjective is misleading in the first place. That is to say it is leading you elsewhere, it is making you see things you did not see before . . . your relation to things that seemed separate or invisible is changing" (Gordon 1997, 98). While Gordon posits the ghost as a visual figure, we can *see* if we examine the interstitial space between social structures and subjection, we ask if ghostly figures also require aural analysis, one that attunes our ears to *hear* differently. Does the specter of the ghost make noise? Yes and no. For Gordon, ghostly haunting is "an animated state in which a repressed or unresolved social violence is making itself known" (Gordon 2011, 2). It is the white noise within our lives that, for some, is easily ignored and after a while seems to disappear. For others, white noise screams loudly. White noise instills a sense of "something-has-to-be-done" within us. Despite the push to reinterpret materialism away from questions of voice and power, we have to remain committed to a discursive understanding of materialism that permits oppressed groups to speak their truth about conditions of subordination. Speaking out about experiences of injustice does not, by definition, make those experiences somehow more real for the persons and groups who went through it, but refusing to remain silent about oppression serves to validate those experiences in a substantive way.

Black feminist scholars also mobilize the trope of silence as a way to discuss the process of black women's coming to voice within racialized forms of capitalist patriarchy. Having been made silenced within the public sphere and civil society, black women have struggled to be heard against forces of sexism within black communities and racism vis-à-vis white communities. Patricia Hill Collins establishes the necessity to "break the silence" through forms of dominant knowledge and containment practices that prevent individuals and groups to "escape from, survive in, and/or oppose prevailing social and economic injustices" (Collins 1998, xiii). For Collins, people living in conditions of injustice must break the silence that keeps them marginalized, come to voice and speak out against institutional knowledge. Coming to voice is one important tool that formerly silenced groups can use as a form of resistance against oppression. Nonetheless, Collins warns that as useful as it is to speak out and "break the silence," we must be careful that the voices of disadvantaged groups do not become co-opted by institutions of power or turned back against ourselves. In the existing hegemony, our words can be co-opted through the incorporation of "toothless identity politics in which difference becomes a hot commodity" (1998, 57). The same dangers lurk when calls to refurbish materialism require that we forget the role that speech acts play in establishing and justifying social hierarchies (Lawrence, Crenshaw, Matsuda, and Delgado 1993).

Mel Chen's work articulates the structure that organizes the human and non-human animate world through discursive hierarchies of race, gender, sexuality, and ability (Chen 2012). Through an analysis of his relationship with a couch, Chen points to the absurdities of the belief that inanimate objects do not have affect or animation. Chen brings to life and to voice these foreseeably inanimate objects. Humans justify their self-appointed position atop animacy hierarchies by reference to discursive utterances they deploy to classify and rank both themselves and other purportedly inanimate objects, which fill categorical space below humans and are thus assumed to "speak" less. However, Chen queers this assumption and animates inanimate objects with recognition that they speak through symbols and assumptions placed upon them that make them intelligible. Language brings concepts and objects to life and it is misleading to assume that immaterial signs do not have a material existence in their own right. We ought to interpret questions of silence in a material sense that permits us to see clearly the relationships between social power and voice.

Case Studies of Psychotropics and Silence

The practice of dispensing psychotropics in prisons is a necropolitical technique that controls prisoners' mentation and silences their voices. The boundary between distributing psychotropics as therapy for psychiatric problems and as punishment for unruly behavior and speaking out is porous and permeable, drawn by the subject who listens to the voices of prisoners and prisoners' advocates. In this last section, we present a set of historical cases, and the legal discourse about them, in which psychotropics were used explicitly for the purposes of controlling and silencing prisoners.

The police powers of the state and the civil rights of prisoners are in constant tension within prisons and with respect to psychotropics. Not fully citizens with all of the rights and entitlements guaranteed thereto, prisoners maintain a precarious social location in U.S. law and political economy. Prisoners have functioned as the principal research subjects in biomedical experiments and pharmaceutical clinical trials, as loyal consumers and hard-working producers of privatized prison commodities, and as the abject objects of state power. A complex of laws and policies, penal procedures, scientific techniques, and corporate contracts ensures that prisoners will remain rigidly disciplined, thoroughly regulated, and hugely profitable. By receiving healthcare, prisoners are exercising their constitutional right not to die via deliberate indifference in prison. At the same time, by exercising their rights to healthcare, prisoners open themselves up to poor treatment, ethical abuses, medical negligence, and forced treatment. The state often asserts its interests in maintaining social control and power within prisons by forcing potentially dangerous, legally incompetent, or mentally ill prisoners to take psychotropics (Winick 1977), which it can do if the prisoner is classified as dangerous and if the forced drugging is in the best medical interest of the prisoner (Floyd 1990, Herbel and Stelmach 2007; Zonana 2003). Prisoners can also refuse to take psychotropics to protect their rights to free speech (Sindel 1991), bodily integrity (Gostin 2003), due process (Zeigelmuller 1993), and other constitutional grounds. According to recent noteworthy analyses, prisoners can legally contest forced medication on constitutional grounds (Floyd 1990; Cichon 1992; Dute 2001).

In the 1970s, the use of tranquilizers in state mental hospitals and prisons became known through journalists' investigations and high-profile legal cases (Mitford 1974). In the 1970s, several legal analysts (Spece 1972; Shapiro 1974; and Singer 1977) also drew attention to the problematic use of psychotropics in prisons, a topic that has only received scant coverage in the years since (Floyd 1990; Auerhahn & Dermody Leonard 2000).

In 1974, Ted Morgan of the *New York Times* visited a notorious New York City male detention facility literally called "The Tombs," because it was said to resemble an Egyptian tomb. There, he described the main function of the psychiatrist to "drug the inmate into submissiveness and prevent suicide attempts" to the detainees who were awaiting trial:

> [t]he psychiatrist has become the successor of the brutal guard. Both men work toward the same goal: to produce a model prisoner, quiet and passive, who answers when he is spoken to and does what he is told. Where the brutal guard used rubber hoses, the psychiatrist relies on powerful tranquilizers like Thorazine. (Morgan 1974)

The double function of psychotropics is also mirrored in Morgan's observations about the cavalier practice of drugging: "A sure way to quiet down a man who is 'acting out' is to put him on 1,100 milligrams of Thorazine a day. It turns him into a zombie. Or, in clinical terms, it screens off the amount of input so the inmate can reorganize his psychic structure" (Morgan 1974, 276).

Women prisoners are more likely to receive psychotropics during incarceration (Shaw 1982; Spieglman 1997). Their presumed criminality is also understood within the context of gender ideology organized around femininity and the female body (Allen 1987; Faith 2011). In 1976, a group of imprisoned women at the Bedford Hills Correctional Facility were strip-searched, shackled, and then transferred to the Mattewean State Hospital in New York because they represented "disciplinary problems" for the prison. There, the women were drugged with antidepressants, antipsychotics, sedatives, and tranquilizers (Jones and Latimer 1982). None of the women were ever diagnosed with any mental disorders and subsequently filed and won a civil case against the prison and hospital, settling out of court for $4,857.14 each (Auerhahn and Dermody Leonard 2000, 605). At the civil trial, the hospital officials openly admitted that "medication often serves a dual purpose in the physical and mental rehabilitation of patients and inmates . . . toward both effective custody and effective rehabilitation" (Jones and Latimer 1982, p. 7 fn. 19).

A group of Leavenworth prisoners wrote to the U.S. Congress in 1980, protesting unjust treatment by prison officials. They reported,

The Leavenworth prison authorities utilize widespread forced drugging for completely inappropriate reasons; it could be fairly viewed as a prevention measure utilizing chemical strait jackets . . . Some of us have tried to physically resist the injections—believing it is inherently unjust to be given dangerous medication for certified psychotics when we're not psychotic—only to be assaulted by their "goon squad," beaten, held down, injected with Prolixin and confined in the neuropsychiatric ward. Some are resigned to our fate and regard it as futile to resist this mad technototalitarianism. We merely acquiesce to their demands and take our periodic injections quietly. (Source Select Committee on Narcotics Abuse and Control 1980)

In 1988, officials at Stateville Prison and Menard Hospital in Illinois forced Mr. Albert Sullivan, a black prisoner, to take large doses of Haldol, an anti-psychotic drug. In legal proceedings, Mr. Sullivan alleged that Dr. Parwatikar, a psychiatrist, and Mary Flannigan, the superintendent at Menard, forced him to take powerful drugs "because of [his] black race, male sex, poverty and because I am a prisoner and mental patient and sex-offender" (*Sullivan v Flannigan and Parwatikar*). At trial, Dr. Parwatikar stated,

The need for Mr. Sullivan being on anti-psychotic medication is quite clear from the past history. During the period of 1972 thru 1982 [he] had 59 assaultive episodes. Thus, it is quite essential that Mr. Sullivan must be on some sort of anti-psychotic medication for the rest of his life.

Given the legal rules governing forced medication in Illinois, Mr. Sullivan is not able to come off the forced medication long enough to prove that he does not need it.

Conclusion

In 1962, Rachel Carson's landmark text *Silent Spring* harkened a future present in which ecological disaster created a spring without birdsong (Carson 1962). Today, we are witnessing the subjection and silencing of an entire generation of persons, who are subjected to technocorrections in the era of mass incarceration. The coercive ways that psychotropics serve to manufacture prisoners' silence is hidden behind practices of state secrecy, medical complicity, and corporate profiteering that result from and protect policies of mass incarceration. These two theses, biopower and necropower, help us evaluate claims about the legitimacy or illegitimacy of social practices centered on the body and the kinds of rationality offered by total institutions in carrying out those practices. Determining whether a particular social medical practice is understood as legitimate because it promotes life and good health, or, conversely, is understood as illegitimate because it accelerates death and suffering is contingent on the form of political rationality that justifies the enactment of the practice itself. The conceptual boundary between what is legitimate or not, like the theoretical contiguity of biopower and necropower, is porous and indeterminate, as is the material space that separates waking life from the walking dead.

The biopolitical context for psychotropic distribution in prison obfuscates the boundary between what practices constitute benevolent therapy and mean-spirited efforts at achieving political control. Psychotropic treatments are, by definition, intended to control patients' symptoms under the assumption that such symptoms are behavioral and cognitive expressions of underlying biochemical processes in the brain. So, psychiatric treatment with psychotropics is always controlling, regardless of whether the intention is to heal or to control. While questioning whether the psychotropic management of prisoners is effective is indeed important in a therapeutic sense, if the only questions asked about psychotropics are therapeutic, it becomes exceedingly difficult to ask questions about psychotropics that pertain to control or domination. Despite the fact that the provision of psychotropics takes place under the jurisdiction of medical officials and the aegis of medical treatment, these drugs are still dispensed in prisons, whose sociopolitical functions are to deprive prisoners of liberty and to punish. The boundary between therapy and control is effectively meaningless in the context of prisons.

REFERENCES

Agamben, Georgio. 2005. *State of Exception* (translated by Kevin Attell). Chicago: University of Chicago Press.

Alexander, Michelle. 2010. *The new Jim Crow: mass incarceration in the age of color-blindness.* New York: New Press.

Allen, Hilary. 1987. Rendering them harmless: The professional portrayal of women charged with serious violent crimes. *Gender, crime and justice*, 81–94.

Auerhahn, Kathleen, and Elizabeth Dermody Leonard. 2000. Docile bodies? Chemical restraints and the female inmate. *Journal of Criminal Law and Criminology* 599–634.

Belenky, Mary Field, Blythe McVicker Clinchy, Nancy Rule Goldberger, and Jill Mattuck Tarule. 1986. *Women's ways of knowing: The development of self, voice and mind.* New York: Basic Books.

Breggin, Peter Rogers. 2008. *Medication madness: A psychiatrist exposes the dangers of mood-altering medications.* New York: St. Martin's.

———. 2010. Antidepressant-induced suicide, violence and mania: Risks for military personnel. *International Journal of Risk and Safety in Medicine* 22.3: 149–157.

Brewer, Rose M., and Nancy A. Heitzeg. 2008. The racialization of crime and punishment: criminal justice, color-blind racism, and the political economy of the prison industrial complex. *American Behavioral Scientist* 51, 5, 625–644.

Brown, Michelle. 2009. *The culture of punishment: Prison, society, and spectacle.* New York: New York University Press.

Cameron, Deborah, Elizabeth Frazier, Penelope Harvey, M.B.H. Rampton, and Kay Richardson. 1992. *Researching language: Issues of power and method.* New York: Taylor & Francis.

Carson, Rachel. 1962. *Silent Spring.* Greenwich, CT: Fawcett Publications.

Césaire, Aimé. 2000. *Discourse on Colonialism.* New York: Monthly Review Press.

Chen, Mel. 2012. *Animacies: Biopolitics, racial mattering, and queer affect.* Durham, NC: Duke University Press.

Cichon, D. 1992. The right to "just say no": a history and analysis of the right to refuse antipsychotic drugs. *Los Angeles Law Review* 53:283–426.

Clarke, Adele E., Janet K. Shim, Laura Mamo, Jennifer Ruth Fosket, and Jennifer R. Fishman. 2003. Biomedicalization: Technoscientific transformations of health, illness, and U.S. biomedicine. *American Sociological Review* 68 (2): 161–194.

Collins, Patricia Hill. 1998. *Fighting words: Black women and the search for justice.* Minneapolis: University of Minnesota Press.

Davis, Angela Y. 2003. *Are prisons obsolete?* New York: Seven Stories Press.

Davis, Angela and Cassandra Shaylor. 2001. Race, Gender, and the Prison Industrial Complex: California And Beyond. *Meridians: Feminism, race, transnationalism* 2:1–25.

Dumit, Joseph. 2012. *Drugs for life: how pharmaceutical companies define our health.* Durham, NC: Duke University Press.

Dute, J. 2001. Compulsory medication within the prison system. *Medicine & Law* 20:221–226.

Ettore, Elizabeth and Elianna Riska. 1995. *Gendered moods: Psychotropics and society.* London: Routledge.

Fabelo, Tony. 2000. "Technocorrections": The promises, the uncertain threats. Sentencing & corrections issues for the 21st century. Department of Justice, Office of Justice Programs, National Institute of Justice, No. 5, pp. 1–6, 2.

Faith, Karlene. 2011. *Unruly women: The politics of confinement & resistance*. New York: Seven Stories Press.

Floyd, Jami. 1990. The administration of psychotropic drugs to prisoners: state of the law and beyond. *California Law Review* 78, 1243–1285.

Foucault, Michel. 1977. *Discipline and punish: The birth of the prison*. London: Vintage.

Foucault, Michel. 1978. *The history of sexuality, an introduction: volume I*. Translated by R. Hurley. New York: Vintage.

Foucault, Michel. 2003 [1976]. *Society must be defended: lectures at the College of France, 1975–1976*, edited by F. Ewald, A. Fontana, and M. Bertani. Translated by D. Macey. New York: Picador.

Freire, Paulo. 2000. *Pedagogy of the oppressed*. Translated by Myra Bergman Ramos; with an introduction by Donald Macedo. New York: Continuum, 59–60.

Gordon, Avery. 1997. *Ghostly matters: Haunting and the sociological imagination*. Berkeley: University of California Press.

Gordon, Avery. 2011. Some thoughts on haunting and futurity. *Borderlands* 10.2: 1–21, 2.

Gostin, L. O. 2003. At law: compulsory medical treatment. the limits of bodily integrity. *Hastings Center Report* 33:11–12.

Healy, David, Andrew Herxheimer, and David B. Menkes. 2006. Antidepressants and violence: problems at the interface of medicine and law. *PLoS Medicine* 3.9: e372.

Hedges, Elaine, and Shelley Fisher Fishkin. 1994. *Listening to silences: New essays in feminist criticism*. New York: Oxford University Press.

Herbel, B. L., and H. Stelmach. 2007. Involuntary medication treatment for competency restoration of 22 defendants with delusional disorder. *Journal of the American Academy of Psychiatry and the Law* 35:47–59.

Jones, Charles H., and Stephen M. Latimer. 1982. Liles v Ward: A case study in the abuse of psychotropic drugs in prison. *New England Journal of Prison Law* 8:1–38.

Kahn, Jonathan. 2013. *Race in a bottle: the story of BiDil and racialized medicine in a post-genomic age*. New York: Columbia University Press.

Lawrence III, Charles R., Kimberle Williams Crenshaw, Mari J. Matsuda, and Richard Delgato. 1993. *Words that wound: critical race theory, assaultive speech, and the First Amendment*. Boulder, CO: Westview Press.

Lawston, Jodie M., and Erica R. Meiners. 2014. Ending our expertise: Feminists, scholarship, and prison abolition. *Feminist Formations* 26.2: 1–25.

Mbembe, Achille, and Libby Meintjes (Trans). 2003. Necropolitics. *Public Culture* 15.1: 11–40.

Metzl, Jonathan Michel. 2001. *The Freud of Prozac: Tracing psychotropic medications through American culture, 1950–2001*. Ann Arbor: University of Michigan Press.

———. 2003. *Prozac on the couch: Prescribing gender in the era of wonder drugs*. Durham, NC: Duke University Press.

Mitford, Jessica. 1974. *Kind and usual punishment: the prison Business*. New York: Vintage Press.

Moore, Thomas J., Joseph Glenmullen, and Curt D. Furberg. 2010. Prescription drugs associated with reports of violence towards others. *PLoS One* 5.12: e15337.

Morgan, Ted. 1974. Waiting for justice—8th floor: homicides; 9th floor: addicts; 10th floor: suicidal: ENTOMBED." *New York Times*, February 17, pp. 273–278.

Olson, Tillie. 1978. *Silences*. New York: Feminist Press at City University of New York.

Orr, Jackie. 2003. *Touching feeling: Affect, pedagogy, performativity*. Durham, NC: Duke University Press.

Orr, Jackie. 2006. *Panic diaries: A genealogy of panic disorder*. Durham, NC: Duke University Press.

Pollock, Anne. 2012. *Medicating race: Heart disease and durable preoccupations with difference*. Durham, NC: Duke University Press.

Resnik, Judith, and Nancy Shaw. 1980. Prisoners of their sex: Health problems of incarcerated women." *Prisoners' Rights Newsletter*, 319–413.

Rhodes, Lorna. 2004. *Total confinement: madness and reason in the maximum security prison*. Berkeley: University of California Press.

Romano, Susan. 1993. The egalitarianism narrative: Whose story? Which yardstick? *Computers and Composition* 10: 5–5.

Saukko, P., and L. S. Reed. 2010. Introduction: Governing the female power. *Governing the Female Body: Gender, Health, and Networks of Power*: 1–16.

Scott, James. 1999. *Seeing like a state: how certain schemes to improve the human condition have failed*. New Haven, CT: Yale University Press.

Shapiro, Michael H. 1974. Legislating the control of behavior control: Autonomy and the coercive use of organic therapies. *Southern California Law Review* 47(2): 237–356.

Shaw, Nancy. 1982. Female patients and the medical profession in jails and prisons: a case of quintuple jeopardy," in *Judge, lawyer, victim, thief, women, gender roles, and criminal justice*, ed. N. H. Rafter and E. A. Stanko. Chicago: Northeastern University Press.

Sindel, P. E. 1991. Fourteenth Amendment: the right to refuse antipsychotic drugs masked by prison bars. *Journal of Criminal Law and Criminology* 81:952–980.

Singer, Richard. 1977. Consent of the unfree: Medical experimentation and behavior modification in the closed institution part 1. *Law and Human Behavior* 1(1): 1–43.

Source Select Committee on Narcotics Abuse and Control, 96th Congress, Second Session. 1980. United States Bureau of Prisons study: institutional drug abuse treatment programs and utilization of prescription drugs at five institutions. House of Representatives, Washington, DC.

Spece, Roy G. 1972. Prisoners and mental patients. *Southern California Law Review* 45:616–681.

Spieglman, Richard. 1997. Prison drugs, psychiatry, and the state, pp. 146–167 in *Corrections and Punishment 8: SAGE Criminal Justice Annuals*, ed. David S. Greenberg.

Sudbury, Julia. 2013. *Global lockdown: Race, gender, and the prison industrial complex*. New York: Routledge.

Sullivan v. Flannigan and Parwatikar 91–3416. 1993. United States Court of Appeals, Seventh Circuit. Retrieved January 1015. https://law.resource.org/pub/us/case/reporter/F3/008/8.F3d.591.91–3416.html.

Timmermans, Stefan. 2006. *Postmortem: How medical examiners explain suspicious deaths*. Chicago: University of Chicago Press.

Williams, Patricia. 1991. *The alchemy of race and rights: Diary of a law professor*. Cambridge, MA: Harvard University Press.

Wilper, Andrew, Steffie Woolhandler, Wesley Boyd, Karen Lasser, Danny McCormick, David Bor, and David Himmelstein. 2009. The health and health care of US prisoners: a nationwide survey. *American Journal of Public Health* 99:1–7.

Winick, B. J. 1977. Psychotropic medication and competence to stand trial. *American Bar Foundation Research Journal* 2:769–816.

Zeigelmuller, W. P. 1993. Sixth Amendment due process on drugs: the implications of forcibly medicating pre-trial detainees with antipsychotic drugs. *Journal of Criminal Law and Criminology* 83:836–867.

Zonana, H. V. 2003. Competency to be executed and forced medication: *Singleton v. Norris*. *Journal of the American Academy of Psychiatry and the Law* 31:372–376.

PART IV

New Materialism and Research Practices

14

Urban Api-Ethnography

The Matter of Relations between Humans and Honeybees

MARY KOSUT AND LISA JEAN MOORE

Humans describe honeybees as "social insects" because the species is created and sustained through the collective labor of the hive.[1] A single honeybee—queen, drone, or worker—cannot live independently of the larger colony that bees co-create together. But as their existence continues to be threatened due to the elusive syndrome Colony Collapse Disorder (CCD), honeybees have become eco-political insects—discursively and materially. In May 2013, an ominously titled article "Russia Warns Obama: Global War Over 'Bee Apocalypse' Coming Soon," explained that Russian president Putin delayed a meeting with U.S. Secretary of

Beekeepers conduct hive check on Crown Heights, Brooklyn rooftop. Photo by Lisa Jean Moore.

State John Kerry due to his "extreme outrage" over President Obama's protection of global biogenetic seed manufacturers Monsanto and Syngenta, who use insecticides known as neonicotinoids that are believed to be responsible for the deaths of bees and other species.[2] Many European countries have already banned the use of neonicotinoids, which could threaten national food supplies if bees are not available to pollinate industrial agriculture. While the "bee apocalypse" may not lead to war, the rhetoric underscores how valuable the bee population is to the human population. Our interventions in the biosphere—globalization, trade, urbanization, industrial pollution, monocroping, biogenetic engineering—radically alter the conditions under which all species live and complicate our ability to co-exist in common worlds.

As honeybees are thrust into the arena of global environmental politics, they have simultaneously been invited into another, more local human-dominated landscape—the metropolis. In the context of CCD, locavore food movements, urban farming, and sustainability, novice beekeepers are establishing hives on detritus-filled rooftops and in backyards flanked by concrete in major U.S. cities like LA, San Francisco, and New York. Bees have always been present in cities, but only recently have been cast as trendy urban pets to be fostered and saved.[3] Because they are integral to our current system of agricultural production, and have metaphorical value (industrious, busy, social), they function well as an eco-political insect mascot; a new cause célèbre to champion. Bees' fragility has become part of the collective consciousness in many human social worlds. In the 1970s, Americans rallied to save the dolphin and the whale, and now we turn toward the bee, an insect that humans are dependent upon and with whom we are physically connected. They have become even more valuable to us since they have gone missing.

In this chapter, we draw from our three-year multispecies ethnography of urban beekeeping[4] conducted in New York City amidst bees and their human caretakers. Our fieldwork began with urban beekeepers, our primary key informants who introduced us to rooftop hives and colonies located near clogged expressways. We quickly became acutely aware of our other nonhuman informants who populated the field and challenged our senses—thousands of insects that careened and whirled around our bodies; buzzing vibrantly in our ears, stinging us, landing quietly on our skin. How would we translate our intersections with a species that we cannot communicate with through a commonly shared language? Being in the field with beekeepers was relatively easy; we understood what they said and their behaviors were familiar, but being with bees—a species that is doubly othered as both animal and insect—was a more complex and ambiguous undertaking.

Here we interrogate our api-ethnography through diffraction—and our own feminist empiricism in an attempt to get closer to the bee as a productive species that co-creates the culture of the city. Bees' material production of honey, propolis, royal jelly, and beeswax as well as their being, the very body, enable social worlds to exist. Our work explores the iterative intra-activities of bees and beekeepers and the particular materiality of these insect-human relationships. We highlight our own transformations again through intra-actions—both physical and epistemological/methodological—as we seek to reposition bees as active and lively subjects rather than passive objects, or othered species. In the doing of our api-ethnography, beekeepers and bees have come to matter as members of the metropolis and local ecologies, as well as in larger systems of agriculture and politics. Drawing from the political theorist Jane Bennett (2010), we conceptualize bees as "vibrant matter" to complicate how we consider "life" and "matter" and to blur the distinctions between human and nonhuman.

We began by asking how bees become meaningful to human life, and how humans have created conditions that make them feel indispensable to bees' survival. A "follow that bee" approach has led us from the culture(s) of New York City beekeeping and field sites where the air is filled with swirling, diving bees, to networks of military engagements that utilize drone and swarm warfare, medical practices such as medihoney™ and apitherapy, classrooms where bees are models of heterosexuality and domestication, and immigration policies. Here we return to the bee itself, within the act of collecting ethnographic data to bring it closer into focus as a nonhuman actor, rather than an insect-object defined by its humanness (i.e., the bee as a social insect, the hive mind) or utility to humans as pollinators and honey producers.

This work is situated as part of the growing contributions in multispecies ethnography, located at the intersections of environmental studies, science and technology studies, and animal studies, focusing on understudied organisms. Multispecies ethnography is a new genre and mode of anthropological research seeking to bring "organisms whose lives and deaths are linked to human social worlds" closer into focus as living co-constitutive subjects, rather than simply relegating them to "part of the landscape, as food for humans, (or) as symbols" (Kirksey and Helmreich 2010: 545). Drawing from our embodied fieldwork, we consider some of the challenges of doing multispecies ethnography, and how our lively insect subjects compelled us to reconsider our human positionality. In some cases, while performing hive inspections, the bees' cacophony and kinetic activity muffled everything human. These insects captured our attention and redirected our thoughts and impulses.

Troubling the Anthropomorphic Impulse

In conducting our fieldwork, we were constantly entangled in the material-discursive relations of human-insect interactions. Bees are a species we rely on; their pollination makes our contemporary diets possible, and their honey, venom, and pollen are revered for holistic nutrition and alternative health treatments. They are literally a part of our bodies, and we tend to describe their behaviors in anthropocentric terms—insects that become too much like us. Humans' descriptions and interactions with honeybees produce gendered and raced interpretations of the insect species' performances and activities. Our informants have described queens as "promiscuous," "bitches," and "loose women," drones as "lazy" and "incompetent," and workers as "feminist sisters." Queen bees are often sold with their wings clipped to limit their ability to swarm with the hive, as a way of "pinning her down."

Bees are also made meaningful through ethnic and racial characterizations. For example, Africanized bees are framed as dangerous, aggressive "killer bees'" that breach national borders and threaten populations—human and bee. At the same time, certain European honeybees are narrated as sweet and docile, bees that we welcome into human "contact zones" (Haraway 2008) as co-present and co-mingling organisms. When we invite other species into our spaces they may be projected onto systems of human stratification, but they are also subject to scientific taxonomies and descriptions that label them as a distinctly nonhuman species. Simultaneously, bees are understood as animals (non-humans) who curiously "waggle dance" and populate "democracies" that are comparable to the ones that govern our lives (Seeley 2010).

Moving beyond anthropomorphic interpretations is a challenge. We grapple with the urge to simply see bees as a pure expression of the natural and humans (ourselves included) as wholly layering the cultural on top of bees' behaviors. As feminists, this urge is troublesome but as humans it is almost automatic. We want to resist the dichotomizing impulse. As Karen Barad writes, "Nature is neither passive surface awaiting the mark of culture nor the end product of cultural performances" (2003:827). But we have found this tricky, as metaphor is so seductive, particularly for describing bees, our social insect other. In our work, we attempt to interpret material and discursive realities as they emerge through observing the interactions between bees and the humans who care for them. Throughout this process, we have wrestled with the challenges of the ontology of bees and how to account for them in our research—particularly at a time of eco-catastrophe and Colony Collapse Disorder. What is the being—materially and existentially—of the bee?

We worked to get out of our own way as we conducted an api-ethnography that considers bees as cultured beings that traffic between worlds of the hive, and the urban landscape. Yet, at the same time we were corporeally enmeshed with bees, as their smells, sounds, and stings energized our bodies, and our human feelings and emotions lingered long after we left the field. For the first time, we experienced saving our research subjects (from drowning in fountains and kiddie pools) but also killed bees by inadvertently pinning and squishing them while inspecting hives, or through getting stung, which left us hurt and the bee lifeless. While we did not have to get IRB approval to conduct research on bees, it is clear that they were vulnerable as a result of our presence.

Animal studies scholars address the role of interactions and inter-subjective exchanges between human and animals in social worlds and within the research process (DeMello, 2012; Raffles 2011; Taylor, 2007; Arluke, 2003; Alger and Alger, 1997, 2003; Myers, 2003; Sanders, 1993). Much of the important work in this area focuses on pets like dogs and cats, domestic companion animals we are intimately connected with (Haraway, 2003, 2008).[5] However, as feminist sociologists we were never trained to interpret the actions of any nonhuman species, certainly not insects. We knew them as pests who lurched or flew uninvited into our space, creating disruptions, rather than as pets, who are fairly predictable and present. Critical animal studies, which does inform our work, suggests that we become advocates for the animal and set aside our human impulses, and yet as ethnographers we are limited, with few tools to inhabit that space of bee-ness (Best 2009).

It is decidedly more difficult to interpret these nonhuman actors. We don't speak their language, share their culture, or engage in mutually negotiated intimate acts with them. Since we cannot have a direct relationship to the bee, we engage in practices of circulating reference. Our only access to bees, other than direct observation as we walk the streets of New York City and happen upon an individual bee, has occurred through the urban beekeepers translating what they do for us. In turn, our work is then translating what they do for our audience. And on still another level of mediation, we all (humans) are translating for the bees. The directionality of translations appears to be from human to human or from bee to human but not from bee to bee about human—that we can ascertain. We had to adjust our other senses of perception outside of the verbal and textual toward the somatic. We also had to imagine the ways that human expectionalism limits our ability to understand bees. Simple changes such as squatting on all fours to observe the landing strip of a hive, or breathing in the pungent smells from a freshly opened Langstroth box, provided us with different ways of intra-acting with bees. In what follows, we examine how this approach opens us up to more productive mattering.

Becoming with Bees: Embodied Fieldwork

When we were in the field with bees and beekeepers we participated in hive checks, the most physical aspect of our fieldwork.[6] While the bees build comb, reproduce, and make honey contained within the hive box, part of the beekeepers' responsibility is to periodically inspect the hive to assess whether or not the bees are healthy and productive. We don't necessarily "check in" with traditional pets, because they are usually intertwined with our private spaces and part of daily routines. If they are mobile, responsive, tails wagging or purring contently, traditional pets have been implicitly checked. Checking in on bees is more of an event and ritual—you don't do it daily but it often requires more physical engagement. Bees demand that you go to them, which can mean time, money, travel, and physical effort (particularly if the hives are on a rooftop three stories high). So, unlike with traditional pets, there is a different type of site- specific and time-sensitive labor that takes place. This places an onus on the beekeeper to be present and even officious in a particular way, and acquiring this embodied knowledge extended to us as researchers struggling to be co-present with bees in the field. Our fieldnotes reveal our limitations as we attempted to plunge ourselves into the practice of multispecies ethnography:[7]

I begin to hear voices and see makeshift boxes, crooked wood and metal structures. These are the beehives, and like old buildings, you wonder if they are strong enough to house anything. People are working the bowed hives, bent over. Lisa Jean has a white veil on and is bent over and helping split up hives, looking for queens, eyeing up any signs of life—both good and bad. The good signs are a full even bar loaded with honey and nectar and brood . . . some of the top bars are a bit broken and uneven and break and fissure a bit when she pulls a bar up from the boxes. She's moving purposefully and finds a Queen somehow amidst a full healthy frame of bees that is overflowing with larval gooey activities . . . but I'm going to have to touch all this mess without gloves, veil, suit. Fuck. Within ten minutes I am sweaty, coated with dirt and starting to itch, just from looking, I haven't even moved towards the bees yet, just away from them as they breach the space around my body. Out of my league/space.

Bees are looping around in circles—some rapidly, others more crazed, they are like toddlers, flying in the air and they cross and crisscross the hives and the trees and us and make the air sometimes clogged with zigzagging. Try not to focus on all of the careening and I can imagine bees accidentally banging head on into each other and dying in mid air. I learn that long hair is not a good idea as bees can get caught in it, become angry and confused, and sting. Sam lends me his hat and I feel a bit more protected when I shove my hair into it—maybe he sees that I am nervous and tells me to talk with Lisa Jean in the shade. Guess they are more calm in the shade or I become more of a muted target. Who knows. I want a veil. Somehow, miraculously, I am not getting stung. Watch bees land softly on my wrist, see them on my legs, shoulder, feel them bump into my head (the rapidly careening ones) and even had one bounce straight off my nose. Remain pretty calm I think (except later when the roach crawled off the frame and up my arm). Others back a few feet away when the bees take over the local airspace. As I get updated by Lisa Jean I see her swollen lip, and hands and I see in her eyes that she has been stung hard and it hurts.

As we endeavored to work with beekeepers, and stay out of the way of the bees—we paid attention to what the bees were doing to us humans and the physical objects and sensations they produced. When we assiduously focused our awareness toward the bee, it was apparent that their actions co-directed the inspections and checks. As much as beekeepers attempt to keep the bees calm and docile by using smokers,[8] humans do disrupt them and we observed that the bees may be the ones that were managing human interventions. Their energies regulated us—if they were hot and angry we worked fast to leave them alone, and if they were more calm and compliant the bees seemed to allow us to stay longer and glean more from our participant observations. The hive inspection may have been initiated by humans, but its length and outcome was very much dependent upon the bees' actions. Angry bees dive-bomb, sting, and buzz very loudly—they are intimidating and most informants worked swiftly to get out of their space, even those wearing full protection—a veil, suit, and gloves designed to protect the skin from multiple stings. We looked to what the bees made and did, fine-tuning all of our senses.

As the fieldnotes above narrate, when we went on our first hive inspections we were acutely aware of the possibility of being stung. This awareness was an obvious and ever-present embodied and emotional concern. However, part of learning to work with bees and observing the labor of others involves not only learning what to look for, but studying how the bees smell. It was not simply an act of observing human/bee exchanges, but making contact with the bee through our own bodies. Our first encounters with honeybees was surprisingly sensual, specifically, we were introduced to the intoxicating feral smell of the bee. Sometimes when the hive box was opened, a slightly fetid, almost pleasantly rotten odor overtook us; other times is was lemony and faint. The beekeepers told us that we were drinking in the bees' pheromones. Informants talked about how the scent of the hive drew them physically closer to bees, their rhythms and sensibilities. B. J., a Brooklyn backyard beekeeper and chicken caretaker, explicitly talked about the seductive nature of the smell, likening it to fragrant truffle oil and human pheromones:

> I love the smell. Like if I am weeding and near the side of the hive and I get a whiff of it and I am like oh my god, it is like truffle oil or something. It gets right here and you are like, Whoa, lovely. And you know they are working. And it is oh, so like um, a heady good sex smell.

Meg Paska, an urban homesteader, professional beekeeper and blogger, reflected not only on the pleasure of smelling the bees, but like B. J. above, on the significance of the smell as a sign of content and healthy bees, as "it usually indicates colony health." For Paska, it is an aroma that similarly calls to mind human intimacies and memories. She described it as "a slight fermentation scent, very subtle. The bees wax and propolis. For me, it is the most intoxicating smell I can think of. In the wintertime I find myself craving that smell. It is kind of comforting, like home or something. I just want to put my face in it." These narratives unearth the embodied nature of beekeeping, and the levels of physical exchange through the labor of beekeeping. In this case, the particular scents that permeate the hive space bring the bees closer to us. Some beekeepers inhale the hive; its energy and emissions.

Numerous beekeepers confirmed that they try to determine what the bees might need based on their buzz. A hive can produce thunderous clatter as if the bees are yelling, but other times the bees' collective sound is more like a whir or hum. Beekeepers listen carefully to the buzzing to assess what they may be feeling or trying to communicate. B. J. listens to the bees and what their sounds might mean, "It gets higher and lower based on their activity. When they are angry it gets higher pitched and louder. If I am in there too long, they give me signs. They can be smoked again or get out and leave them alone." Similarly, Eric Rochow, beekeeper and creator and producer of Gardenfork.tv, a videoblog, said, "You can tell when they are mad by the sound changing. It gets louder. When you open it up they are kind of looking out at you. Then when something agitates them the tone changes and when you smoke them the tone changes right away. It gets busier—you can hear this ring—they are sending a signal out. And then when they are bonking you it is a much higher-pitched sound. They are warning you and trying to get you to go away." Humans interpret bee sounds as if they are auditory codes to decipher insect behavior, but there is also an energy in the bee buzz which, like music, fills the body. You hear the bees not only in your ears, but also as sonic vibrations reverberating through your arms, legs, hands. The buzz is somatic and it materializes through the bodies of insects and humans.

While the different pitches, notes, and levels of buzzing can sometimes be alarming to human ears, the noise emitted by bees may also be meditative. The noise depends upon the bees, the person, the site, the weather, and the moment. In the fieldnotes below, we describe how "working" with bees involves tasting fresh honey stores in addition to being caught up in a cacophony of sounds:

> All the splitting up and re-queening is the work that Sam does. His co-labor with and for the bees. Today he is working with an audience (us). He is patient and upbeat and genuinely excited to see an overflowing frame, or to stick his fingers in the honey or break off a piece of comb. He makes jokes—"taste this, this is awful!" (jocular and ironic). And I shyly put my finger forward around some oozing clear honey literally being made now. I keep it in one cell of the comb because there are active bees, squirming, caked and chunky/clunky all around. Sam just goes in with confidence and ease and the bees keep doing their thing. Swirling and whirling—their buzzing coming closer, darting and arching by my face and ears, but I hear a distant hum when the bees and the boxes are opened up. When he forcefully shook some of the frames and the bees dropped to the bottom of a new home (wooden box), they get more vocal and move faster and even with people talking around me all I heard was the bees' noise. I say "it sounds like water." I think that's the best way to describe it. It is a uniform noise—as a whole—but if you listen closely there are ebbs and flows and the sound moves like water around and inside your ears.

Through the movement and the numbers of insects who overpopulated the air, we struggled to listen to bees. It was important to observe what they were doing, to see them, and also to hear them. We wondered exactly what we were hearing—was it noise, a directed communication from the bees—was the buzz the bees' way of speaking to us? Or are we irrelevant and just get to listen in to private, collective chatter? We cannot provide answers to these questions, but we can describe the intense vibrations that reverberated through our bodies and directed us to move slowly and cautiously as we observed and conducted hive checks. When the hive box is opened, the bees' work, comb, wax, larvae, honey, as well as the colony itself, are temporarily exposed and both species become more vulnerable in the presence of each other.

Intraspecies Mindfulness

Engaging in the intersections between humans and bees, and entertaining the possibility of an ontology of other objects, enables us to reposition them (the bees) through decentering ourselves (Bennett, 2009; Morton, 2010). Our fieldwork among beekeepers and bees calls for an ethics of *intraspecies mindfulness*, a concept that itself is still in a state of becoming (Moore and Kosut, 2014). Intraspecies mindfulness is a practice of speculation about nonhuman species that strives to resist anthropomorphic reflections. It is an attempt to get at, and with, another species in order to move outside of our human selves—while also recognizing that both "human" and "other" are cultural constructions. In our practices with bees, we used our own sensory tools of seeing, hearing, touching, tasting, and smelling bees—their bodies, their habitats, and their products. Getting with the bee meant acquiring new modes of embodied attention and awareness. Getting at the bee has also meant that we must confront the reality that the human species is created, materially and semiotically, through interconnectivity to bees.

In this light, our fieldwork and analyses pay particular attention to the everyday lives of the bee, attempting to decenter our human selves in the process—to become more animal in our intra-actions with bees—becoming with them instead of becoming as distinct from them. Our creation of the term and practice of intraspecies mindfulness is predominantly drawn from the work of Karen Barad (2007). Her articulation of intra-action is where worlds come into being through the mutual constitution of entangled entities. This requires that as fieldworkers, we interrupt our tendency to think of bees as the object of study and that we resist thinking of ourselves or the beekeepers as static, bounded, and permanently fixed entities. Instead we need to see all—ourselves, bees, the beekeepers, and other objects—as matter that is in the world and with politically fraught boundaries that are created through entanglements and conflicts.

NOTES

1   Of course, social scientific studies of insects are not unheard of. Indeed, sociobiologist Edward O. Wilson with his colleague Bert Holldobler (1990) has dedicated much of his research to understanding the life of another social insect, the ant. Wilson famously likened ant behavior to a form of socialism where self-sacrifice for the good of the colony is commonly practiced.

2   http://www.eutimes.net/2013/05/russia-warns-obama-global-war-over-bee-apocalypse-coming-soon/ (accessed May 30, 2013).

3   K. Helmetag (2010). Think of them as your new pet. *New York Magazine*. Available at: http://nymag.com/guides/everything/urban-honey/66172/ (accessed August 27, 2012).

4   L. J. Moore and M. Kosut (2013). *Buzz: Urban Beekeeping and the Power of the Bee*. New York: New York University Press.

5   There is much interactional research on animals who are not traditionally defined as pets; see Weider's (1980) analysis of laboratory chimps and the concept of minded-ness/intersubjectivity; Whatmore's (2001) study on elephants and tourism networks; and Jerolmack's (2009) ethnography of pigeons in New York City, among others.

6   Beekeepers conduct hive checks about once a week in spring and summer to make sure the queen is healthy and the bees show signs of laying brood (larva), and also check on honey production. Hive checks were also a way for beekeepers to control swarms due to over-crowding and to check for mites such as *Varrora*. We participated in sugar bees, a less invasive way to ward off such mites by dusting bee frames with powdered sugar, which encourages them to clean themselves off and ideally dislodge any mites in the process.

7   Both authors are longtime Brooklyn residents with no beekeeping experience upon entering the project.

8   Using a variety of plants, like burlap or pine needles, beekeepers calm bees with a smoker so that bees cannot smell each other's alarm pheromones and trigger the entire hive to attack the human interloper/predator.

REFERENCES

Alger, J. and Alger, S. (1997) Beyond Mead: symbolic interaction between humans and felines. *Society and Animals* 5(1): 65–81.

Alger, J. and Alger, S. (2003) *Cat Culture: The Social World of a Cat Shelter*. Philadelphia: Temple University Press.

Arluke, A. (2003) Ethnozoology and the future of sociology. *International Journal of Sociology and Social Policy* 23(3): 26–45.

Arluke, A. and Sanders, C. (2008) *Between the Species: Readings in Human Animal Relations*. Boston: Pearson.

Barad, K. (2003) Posthumanist performativity: toward an understanding of how matter comes to matter. *Signs: Journal of Women in Culture and Society* 28.3: 801–831.

Barad, K. (2007) *Meeting the Universe Halfway: Quantum Physics and the Entanglement of Matter and Meaning*. Durham, NC: Duke University Press.

Bennett, J. (2010) *Vibrant Matter: A Political Ecology of Things*. Durham and London: Duke University Press.

Best, S. (2009) The rise of critical animal studies: putting theory into action for animal liberation into higher education. *Journal for Critical Animal Studies* 7(1): 9–54.

DeMello, M. (2012). *Animals and Society: An Introduction to Human-Animal Studies*. New York: Columbia University Press.

Haraway, D. (2003) *The Companion Species Manifesto: Dogs, People, And Significant Otherness*. Chicago: Prickly Paradigm Press.

Haraway, D. (2008) *When Species Meet*. Minnesota: University of Minnesota Press.

Holldobler, B. and Wilson, E. O. (1990) *The Ants*. Cambridge, MA: Harvard University Press.

Jerolmack, C. (2009) Primary groups and cosmopolitan ties: The rooftop pigeon flyers of New York. *Ethnography* 10(4): 435–457.

Kirksey, S. E. and Helmreich, S. (2010) The emergence of multispecies ethnography. *Cultural Anthropology* 25(4): 545–576.

Moore, Lisa Jean and Mary Kosut. (2014). "Among the colony: Ethnographic fieldwork, urban bees and intraspecies mindfulness." *Ethnography* 15, no. 4: 516-539.

Morton, T. (2010) *The Ecological Thought*. Cambridge, MA: Harvard University Press.

Myers, O. (2003) No longer the lonely species: a post Mead perspective on animals and sociology. *International Journal of Sociology and Social Policy* 23(3): 46–68.

Raffles, H. (2011) *Insectopedia*. New York: Pantheon.

Sanders, C. (1993) Understanding dogs: Caretakers' attributions of mindedness in canine-human relationships. *Journal of Contemporary Ethnography* 22(2): 205–226.

Seeley, T. (2010) *Honeybee Democracy*. Princeton, NJ: Princeton University Press.

Taylor, N. (2007) 'Never an it': intersubjectivity and the creation of animal personhood in animal shelters. *Qualitative Sociological Review* 3(1): 59–73.

Weider, D. L. (1980) Behaviouralistic operationalism and the life-world: Chimpanzees and chimpanzee researchers in face-to-face interaction. *Sociological Inquiry* 50(3/4): 75–103.

Whatmore, S. (2001) *Hybrid Geographies: Natures Cultures Spaces*. New York: Sage.

15

Un/Re-Making Method

*Knowing/Enacting Posthumanist Performative Social
Research Methods through 'Diffractive Genealogies'
and 'Metaphysical Practices'*

NATASHA S. MAUTHNER

I am interested in . . . building diffraction apparatuses in order to study the entangled effects differences make. One of
the main purposes will be to explore the nature of entanglements and also the nature of this task of exploration.
—Barad, *Meeting the Universe Halfway,* 2007, 73–74

I approach Karen Barad's work as a natural-social scientist seeking to
develop a posthumanist performative way of enacting social scientific
world/knowledge-making projects and practices.[1] On my reading, this
demands un/re-making social research methods:[2] undoing their humanist representationalist enactments, configurations, and genealogies; and
assembling posthumanist performative enactments, configurations, and
genealogies. At the same time, the un/re-making of method requires
un/re-making the very practices of un/re-making method. This chapter
is a contribution toward this project (see also Mauthner, 2015, 2016). It
enacts a posthumanist performative approach to knowing/enacting (the
un/re-making of) social research methods through the articulation of
two proposed material-discursive practices for knowing/enacting (the
un/re-making of) social research methods: "diffractive genealogies" and
"metaphysical practices." These practices are posthumanist performative
ways of knowing/enacting social research methods as both objects of
study (that can be un/re-made) and agencies of observation (that can be
un/re-made). They are "diffractive" (Barad 2007; Haraway 1992, 1997) in
that they account for the posthumanist performative metaphysics they

embody and enact. I begin by highlighting aspects of Barad's metaphysical framework that are most relevant to my discussion, with a particular focus on her elaboration of the agential, material, and constitutive nature of world/knowledge-making practices. This is followed by a discussion of diffractive genealogies and metaphysical practices as ways of knowing/enacting (the un/re-making of) social research methods. The final section illustrates my approach through a case study of Lyn Brown and Carol Gilligan's (1992) *Listening Guide* feminist method of narrative analysis, a method I have been engaged with for more than two decades.

Barad's Posthumanist Performative Metaphysics and Diffractive Methodology

The question of the relationship between mind and matter, thought and thing, word and world has been debated at least since the time of the ancient Greeks (Chalmers 1990; Russell 1946). As Bertrand Russell explains in his *History of Western Philosophy* (1946, 10), theologians, philosophers, and scientists have, through the ages, grappled with fundamental metaphysical questions:

> Is the world divided into mind and matter, and, if so, what is mind and what is matter? Is mind subject to matter, or is it possessed of independent powers? Has the universe any unity or purpose? Is it evolving towards some goal? Are there really laws of nature, or do we believe in them only because of our innate love of order? Is man what he seems to the astronomer, a tiny lump of impure carbon and water impotently crawling on a small and unimportant planet? Or is he what he appears to Hamlet? Is he perhaps both at once?

Barad's oeuvre challenges the ontological terms of, and material conditions of possibility for, this long-running theological-philosophical-scientific debate by questioning the assumed ontological given-ness of matter, meaning, and the matter/meaning dualism. Matter and meaning, she suggests, are not ontologically separate and bounded entities that *inter*-act with one another. They are ontologically "entangled" and "*intra*-actively" co-constitute one another out of "ontologically primitive relations" (2007, 333)—what Barad calls "phenomena." Barad's

posthumanist performative metaphysics—"agential realism"—is committed to a relational ontology that refuses to "take separateness to be
an inherent feature of how the world is" (2007, 136). As she explains:
"Posthumanism doesn't presume the separateness of any-'thing', let alone
the alleged spatial, ontological, and epistemological distinction that sets
humans apart" (2007, 136). This relational ontology, however, is not
taken as ontologically given. Relationality and ontology are understood
as dynamically, intra-actively, ongoingly, and agentially performing, un/
doing, and (re)constituting themselves. In this sense—and drawing on
Derrida's (1994) notion of hauntology to describe the indeterminate
relationship between being/non-being, present/absent—Barad's metaphysics is premised on an ontology/hauntology of in/determinacy in
which not only the ontology of the world is taken to be indeterminate
outside of specific constitutive practices, but in/determinacy and ontology themselves are put into question (Barad 2010; see also Shrader 2010).

Barad therefore contests the metaphysics of essences and metaphysics
of presence underpinning the matter/meaning dualism that has framed
philosophical-scientific debates by questioning the assumption that mat-
ter/meaning identities and boundaries, and related binaries, are given
and present at all. The presumption that the ontology of the world—not
only what it is but whether and how it becomes—is already settled has
led philosophical-scientific debates to focus on questions of epistemology: whether and how knowers can understand a world that is assumed
to be already there and already constituted in determinate forms. The
exclusion of ontology—achieved by treating matter either as "a passive
surface awaiting the mark of culture" or as "the end product of cultural
performances" (Barad 2007, 183)—has made possible a representationalist metaphysics by presuming that, as Rouse (1996) explains, meaning
is directly accessible in a way that matter is not. Representationalism
"separates the world into the ontologically disjunct domains of words
and things" (Barad 2007, 137) only to face the challenge of resolving the
ontological gap (of its own making) between representations on the one
hand (meaning) and entities awaiting representation on the other (matter). A representationalist account and enactment of scientific practice
constitutively excludes the material practices through which representations are produced by treating them as passive and neutral techniques
(Barad 2007, 53; Law 2004, 152). Representationalism thus intra-actively

makes possible a humanist metaphysics, and its underpinning human/ nonhuman dualism, by positing the existence of (active/human) knowers who use (passive/nonhuman) instruments to produce knowledge (meaning/representations) about the world (matter/that which is supposedly represented). Representationalism, and its marking/making of assumed binaries—human/nonhuman, active/passive, subject(ivity)/ object(ivity), matter/meaning, material/discursive, theory/practice, metaphysics/method, ontology/epistemology—is inscribed in, and generative of, enduring epistemological questions concerning the possibilities, limits, and uncertainties of human knowledge about a supposedly preexisting natural-social world.

Barad attends to neglected ontological questions by allowing "matter its due as an active participant in the world's becoming" (2007, 136) against the backdrop of a history of Western metaphysics that denies the agency of the world and constitutively excludes matter's "ongoing historicity" (Barad 2003, 821) and own processes of formation and powers of materialization. She redefines matter as itself dynamic and agentive, making possible her reframing of the relationship between matter and meaning as one of mutual entailment and ontological inseparability. Materiality is always already discursive—material phenomena come into being through, and are inseparable from, discursive practices—and discourse is always already material—discursive practices are ongoing materializations of the world and not merely human-based activities. On this approach, matter and meaning only become intelligible—determinate and meaningful—through specific "agential intra-actions."

Endowing matter with agency (where agency is an enactment rather than a fixed property), and its attendant reconceptualization of matter, meaning, and the matter/meaning relation, open the way for taking the material and constitutive nature of scientific practices seriously. Barad's notion of practices as inseparably material-discursive is inspired by Niels Bohr's philosophy-physics. Bohr's interpretation of quantum physics led him to question the assumed inconsequential role of measurement in classical Newtonian physics and to suggest that "quantum physics requires a new logical framework that understands the constitutive role of measurement processes in the construction of knowledge" (2007, 67). Bohr proposed that the world is inherently ontologically indeterminate in the absence of specific measurement practices:

[T]here is something fundamental about the nature of measurement interactions such that, given a particular measuring apparatus, certain properties *become determinate*, while others are explicitly excluded. Which properties become determinate is not governed by the desires or will of the experimenter but rather by the specificity of the experimental apparatus. (Barad 2007, 19)

Bohr understood the experimental or measuring apparatus as a physical-conceptual device that embodies, materializes, and gives meaning to specific concepts to the exclusion of others. On his account, concepts are *specific material arrangements* of experimental apparatuses and not abstract ideations or inherent attributes of independently existing objects. As Barad explains:

[H]e understands these issues—concerning word and world—to be inextricably linked. According to Bohr, our ability to understand the physical world hinges on our recognizing that our knowledge-making practices, including the use and testing of scientific concepts, are material enactments that contribute to, and are a part of, the phenomena we describe. (Barad 2007, 32)

Barad (2007) builds on Bohr's "proto-performative" formulation of the apparatus, and particularly his critical insight about the materiality of concepts. In contrast to Bohr's humanist belief in the existence of individual humans that are separately determinate from physical-conceptual measurement apparatuses, Barad's posthumanist elaboration of the apparatus refuses to take the human/nonhuman binary as given by attending to the production of the human (the discursive), the nonhuman (the material), and the boundary between them. Barad draws on and extends Butler's and Foucault's accounts of the material and constitutive nature of discursive practices—by conceptualizing materiality in terms of its own agentive processes of materialization—to rework Bohr's "physical-conceptual devices" into "material-discursive practices." On this approach, scientific practices are "world-making" (Haraway 1997) practices that bring specific worldly configurations into being through their *material-discursive specificity*. These practices generate an intra-active relation between the apparatus and its object of study: they enact "agential cuts" which produce "agential separability," rather than absolute separations, between the apparatus and its object. They "cut together-apart (one move)" (Barad 2014, 168). Both the apparatus and its object of study are ontologically indeterminate outside of the material-discursive practices that intra-actively enact and co-constitute them. It is in this sense that the apparatus (enacted through material-discursive practices) is understood as an ineliminable and constitutive part of the world it helps to produce. Barad's posthumanist performative conceptualization/enactment of scientific practice, and its focus on the inseparably material-discursive nature of these practices, therefore moves beyond both representationalist formulations and performative accounts that highlight the performative nature of discursive practices without accounting for "*how* discursive practices matter*" (Barad 2007, 136).

In seeking to develop a methodological practice for enacting a posthumanist performative metaphysics—that is, a practice that can attend to and account for its own metaphysical specificity and that of the object of study it intra-actively produces—Barad draws on the physical phenomenon of diffraction. Building on Haraway's (1992, 1997) suggestion of embracing a different optics in science studies—diffraction rather than reflection—and on a longer genealogy of the concept of diffraction threaded through quantum physics and feminist theory (Barad 2014)—Barad proposes that we think of scientific practices in terms of "diffraction apparatuses." In physics, diffraction is "an intra-active phenomenon, and as such does not hold one set of concerns as preexisting or stable or primary over another" (Barad 2011, 449). On this approach, "knowing does not come from standing at a distance and representing but rather from *a direct material engagement with the world*" (Barad 2007, 49). On my reading, this material engagement takes the form of diffractive practices that account for their non-innocent (Haraway 1991, 121) metaphysically specific rationalities, ontologies, genealogies, and performativities.[3] It requires specifying the metaphysical assumptions that are materially discursively embodied and enacted in the intra-active co-constitution of the "agencies of observation" and their "objects of observation." This metaphysical specificity is *how* the material nature of discursive practices helps constitute the world.

Un/Re-making Method: Knowing/Enacting Method through
'Diffractive Genealogies' and 'Metaphysical Practices'

An agential realist approach to world/knowledge-making projects
requires reconfiguring world/knowledge-making practices, including
un/re-making social research methods: undoing their humanist representationalist, and assembling posthumanist performative "figurations"
(Haraway, 1997; Casteñada, 2002).[4] At the same time, this project of un/
re-making method necessitates un/re-making the very practices that are
used to un/re-make method, in order that these practices enact a posthumanist performative metaphysics and diffractive methodology. This
entails reconfiguring the ontological nature of: (1) the practices used
for un/re-making method; (2) method as the object of study of these
practices; and (3) the practice-object relation so that practice—un/re-
making practices—and object—method—are conceptualized/enacted
as ontologically indeterminate outside of the practice-object relation
that intra-actively constitutes them. I propose enacting this ontological reconfiguration through "diffractive genealogies" and "metaphysical
practices." These practices are diffractive in that they account for their
metaphysical specificity (their posthumanist performative rationality,
ontology, genealogy, and performativity). They signal the metaphysical terms on which they engage/with/as-part-of the world. Diffractive
genealogies and metaphysical practices are ways of simultaneously
exploring *and* enacting method—they act as both agencies of observation and objects of investigation. In this configuration, methods come
into being as, and are ways of enacting/knowing the world through, diffractive genealogies and metaphysical practices. They are "practices of
knowing in being" (Barad 2007, 185): onto-epistemological practices that
enact the inseparability of knowing and being, and the entanglement of
agencies of observation and objects of observation.

Diffractive Genealogies

My notion of diffractive genealogies is informed by the work of Barad
(2007, 2010), Butler (1990), Derrida (1995), Foucault (1979, 1984, 1990,
1991), Haraway (1992, 1997), and Somers (2008). By diffractive I mean
a practice that does not take the ontology of the world as already

constituted. By genealogy I mean a practice that can materialize onto-logical processes of formation "at different scales" (Barad 2007, 246), or what Barad (33), drawing on Bohr, calls "phenomena": "the *ontologi-cal* inseparability of agentially intra-acting components." Genealogies are understood here as intra-acting material-discursive relations and practices: dynamic topological reconfigurings, entanglements, relation-alities, (re)articulations, en/foldings of the world (Barad 2007, 141). By diffractive genealogies I mean genealogies that account for the ontologi-cal practices through which these genealogies, and their objects of study, are constituted. Diffractive genealogies, then, do not innocently go back in time and through space searching for origins and tracing a past and a history that really happened. Diffractive genealogies intra-actively and topologically (re)configure the genealogies they produce. They are underpinned by the ontological assumption that neither the genealogi-cal practices that are engaged, nor the genealogies that are generated, nor the "spacetime manifold" (Barad 2007, 246) threaded through and by genealogies, are ontologically given.

Metaphysical Practices

On a posthumanist performative approach, the ontology of method is not taken as given. What a method was/is/becomes is inherently inde-terminate and unspecified outside of the specific material-discursive practices that enact it in specific configurations, in intra-action with wider practices. Methods are dynamic, open-ended, ongoing, and "spe-cific material reconfigurings of the world" (2007, 142) that, through their material-discursive specificity, help materialize their objects of study in specific, determinate, and intelligible forms. The notion of methods as "metaphysical practices" helps to enact this ontological (re)configura-tion of method by taking the material, agential, and constitutive nature of methodological practices seriously. On this approach, these practices are metaphysical because they (necessarily) inscribe and enact specific metaphysical commitments—"forms of rationality" (Foucault, 1991, 79)—to the exclusion of others. Characterizing methods as *metaphysi-cal* practices helps add further specificity to the notion of methods as material-discursive practices. It emphasizes that methods do not merely embody and enact *theoretical* presuppositions—specific concepts of, for example, agency, structure, identity, society, causality, change, development, process, autonomy, relationality, time, and space. Critically, they embody and enact *metaphysical* presuppositions about the ontological/hauntological nature of these objects of study, the methods used to investigate them, and the method-object relationship.

On my account, metaphysical practices are the so-called techniques and technologies that make up the social scientist's methodological toolbox. Examples include: questionnaires; interview schedules; focus group questions; experiments; surveys; research designs (e.g., cross-sectional, longitudinal, experimental, participatory, action research, ethnographic, etc.); sampling strategies; observation schedules; ethnographic observations and fieldnotes; data recording practices and technologies; transcription conventions and protocols; translation practices; psychometric instruments and tests; measurement indexes and scales; econometric models; statistical techniques and software; data analysis code books, coding schemes, templates, and software; data visualization; social network analysis; indicators and classification systems; data archiving standards, systems, architectures, and software; meta-data schemes, standards, architectures, and software; ethical practices (e.g., informed consent, data anonymization, pseudonymization); and so on. These tools are reframed here as metaphysical, rather than merely technical, matters: they are the material-discursive practicalities and constraints of knowing/enacting the world. By taking the agential, material, and constitutive nature of methodological tools, techniques, and technologies seriously, this metaphysical (re)configuration of method makes it possible to overcome the metaphysics/method divide and related dualisms (human/nonhuman, meaning/matter, active/passive, culture/nature, agency/structure, subject(ivity)/object(ivity)) that underpin humanist representationalist figurations of social research methods.

Methods and the Making of Worlds

Knowing/enacting methods through diffractive genealogies and metaphysical practices reconfigures the nature of social science research from knowledge-making to world-making projects. This approach decenters the notion of the historically and culturally located intentional researcher using readymade methods to understand preexisting social worlds and/

or preexisting respondents' accounts of these worlds. It equally displaces the imperative to reflexively account for the *influence* of metaphysical assumptions on how methods are used, a proposition that assumes that metaphysics and method are separate to begin with. Instead, the material-discursive/metaphysical tools, techniques, and technologies though which social science world/knowledge-making projects are enacted take center stage. On this account, these tools come into being as diffractive genealogies and metaphysical practices that are implicated in "worlding" the world (Barad 2007; Haraway 2008) in dynamic, open-ended, and non-arbitrary ways. Specific enactments of specific tools inscribe specific material and conceptual presuppositions, constraints, and exclusions in such a way that enacted realities are "materially specified and determinate for a given practice" (2007, 155). These tools are not arbitrarily constructed and determined by intentional researchers, nor do they act alone of their own free will. They are genealogically constituted in intra-action with "the larger material configuration of the world" (171) of which they are part—humanist representationalist/posthumanist performative enactments of metaphysics, methods, and their objects of study—which provide the material conditions of possibility for the realities that can and cannot be made through world-making projects and practices. As Barad writes, "things don't just come out any way we'd like them to . . . there is a sense in which 'the world kicks back'" (215). Reconfiguring method as diffractive genealogies and metaphysical practices allows for the material agency, historicity, and response-ability of social research tools, and their objects of study, to materialize.

Un/Re-making Social Research Methods

Having specified the notions of diffractive genealogies and metaphysical practices, I now outline my approach to diffractively knowing/enacting (the un/re-making of) social research methods in terms of the following processes:[5] (1) specifying and accounting for the posthumanist performative specificity of the diffractive genealogies and metaphysical practices through which research methods are diffractively known/enacted (un/re-made). This is enacted through diffractive genealogies of agential realism and its constitutive other, humanism representationalism; (2) unmaking humanist representationalist method and its

humanist representationalist object of study by: (2.1) unmaking humanist representationalist methods by taking them as an object of study and
diffracting them through a posthumanist performative framework to
materialize their humanist representationalist rationalities, ontologies,
genealogies, and performativities. This is enacted through diffractive
genealogies of humanist representationalist figurations of research
methods; (2.2) unmaking the humanist representationalist object of
study of humanist representationalist method by diffracting it through
a posthumanist performative framework to materialize its humanist
representationalist rationalities, ontologies, genealogies, and performativities. This is enacted through diffractive genealogies of humanist
representationalist figurations of the object of study of humanist representationalist method; (3) (re)making posthumanist performative
method and its object of study by: (3.1) (re)making posthumanist performative methods to embody and enact posthumanist performative
metaphysical commitments (rationalities, ontologies, genealogies, and
performativities). This is enacted through diffractive genealogies of
posthumanist performative figurations of research methods; (3.2) (re)
making a posthumanist performative object of study of posthumanist
performative method to embody and enact posthumanist performative metaphysical commitments (rationalities, ontologies, genealogies,
and performativities). This is enacted through diffractive genealogies of
posthumanist performative figurations of the object of study of posthumanist performative method. I expand on these processes below.

Accounting for a Posthumanist Performative Framework

Accounting for a posthumanist performative framework entails undertaking diffractive genealogies of metaphysical practices intra-acting at
different scales in the dynamic, ongoing, and open-ended production of
agential realism. This includes diffractive analysis of the bodies of work
and scholars that Barad's agential realism intra-acts with in its constitution: developments in quantum physics, science studies, feminist theory,
the philosophy of science, post-structuralism, deconstruction, and other
critical social theories; and the work of Niels Bohr, Judith Butler, Jacques
Derrida, Donna Haraway, Michel Foucault, and Joseph Rouse, among
others (see, for example, Barad, 1996, 1998, 2010). It also explores further

transdisciplinary and "transversal" (Dolphijn and van der Tuin 2012, 14) (re)makings of agential realism, including intra-actions with, for example, the work of Jane Bennett, Henri Bergson, Rosi Bradotti, Gilles Deleuze and Félix Guattari, Tim Ingold, William James, Bruno Latour, Gertrude Stein, Alfred North Whitehead (see, for example, Blackman 2014; Dolphijn and Van der Tuin 2012; Hicks and Beaudry 2010; Sehgal 2014; Suchman 2007; Van der Tuin 2011. See also the chapters in this volume). Diffractive genealogies of agential realism necessarily enact its constitutive other: diffractive genealogies of humanism representationalism. On this approach, neither agential realism, nor a humanist representationalist metaphysics, nor the boundary between them, is understood as ontologically given. Their relation is one of intra-action and mutual constitution.

Unmaking Humanist Representationalist Method

A humanist representationalist configuration of method assumes that both method and its object of study are already constituted, and that method and object are ontologically separate and separable. A diffractive genealogy materializes the metaphysical practices through which these ontological assumptions and rationalities are embodied and enacted in specific enactments and configurations of method. Unmaking humanist representationalist method entails: (1) diffracting specific figurations of social science tools, techniques, and technologies through agential realism to materialize the embodiment and enactment of these (humanist representationalist) ontological assumptions and rationalities. The following questions can guide this investigation: how do these figurations enact method as already ontologically constituted?; how do these figurations enact method's object of study as already ontologically constituted?; how do these figurations enact the method-object relation in *inter*-active terms? (2) undertaking diffractive genealogies of these figurations to materialize wider practices at different scales through which they are ontologically and intra-actively constituted. Of these wider practices we can ask how they intra-actively constitute the material conditions of possibility for the enactment of humanist representationalist figurations of methods through their ontological assumptions about method, object, and the method-object relation; (3) investigating the performative effects—the ontological and political objects and claims—made possible by humanist representationalist figurations of methods in intra-action with wider practices.

Unmaking humanist representationalist method through diffractive genealogies helps "denaturalize" (Somers 2008, 10) their apparent self-evidence and given-ness (Foucault 1991). It materializes humanist representationalist methods as "contingent historical outcomes [that] simply take on the appearance of being the only possible reality" (Somers 2008, p. 10). In this sense, diffractive genealogies bring into being not only methods' generative powers of materialization—their world-making powers enacted through their metaphysical specificity—but also their materialization of power—enacted through the naturalization of this privileged metaphysical specificity (Derrida 1995). Diffractive genealogies help shake methods' "false self-evidence," demonstrate its precariousness, and make "visible not its arbitrariness, but its complex interconnection with a multiplicity of historical processes" (Foucault 1991, 75). This approach to social research methods replaces a "politics of identity"—which takes the ontology of method as given—with a "politics of ontological/hauntological im/possibilities"—which unsettles, (re)opens, and (re)works method's im/possibilities for being/becoming. This approach makes possible diffractive, open-ended (re)makings of what method, and its objects of study, were/are/might yet be (Barad 2010).

(Re)making Posthumanist Performative Method

A posthumanist performative (re)making of methods entails ontologically reconstituting them so that they are no longer enacted as readymade techniques for discovering preexisting realities but as ethical, response-able and accountable metaphysical practices that help constitute particular worlds in non-arbitrary ways. This entails: (1) (re)making posthumanist performative figurations of method by embedding posthumanist performative ontological assumptions and rationalities in social research tools, techniques, and technologies so that they enact themselves and their object of study as ontologically indeterminate outside of the specific practices through which they are intra-actively co-constituted; (2) (re)making genealogies of posthumanist performative enactments and configurations of research methods; (3) (re)making genealogies of posthumanist performative enactments and configurations of the object of study of posthumanist performative method.

Un/Re-making Brown and Gilligan's *Listening Guide* Feminist Method of Narrative Analysis

I illustrate my approach to un/re-making (the un/re-making of) method through a case study of Brown and Gilligan's (1992) *Listening Guide* feminist method of narrative analysis—a method I "inherited" (not in the sense of a given inheritance) through working with Carol Gilligan during the period 1992–1995, and used, taught, and studied for more than two decades (see Mauthner, 2016). I undertake a diffractive genealogy of the *Listening Guide's* listening practices—as articulated in Brown and Gilligan's book, *Meeting at the Crossroads: Women's Psychology and Girl's Development* (1992)—to materialize: (1) the *Listening Guide's* humanist representationalist enactment of itself, its object of study, and the method-object relation; (2) its humanist representationalist genealogy constituted in intra-action with second-wave feminism and its identity-politics and voice-giving humanist representationalist philosophical, theoretical, methodological, and political project; (3) possibilities for a posthumanist performative (re)making of *Listening Guide* practices.

The Metaphysical Specificity of the Listening Guide Practices: A Humanist Representationalist 'Inheritance'

The *Listening Guide* was constituted in the wake of Carol Gilligan's publication of her influential book, *In A Different Voice* (1982; see also 1977). Gilligan argued that supposedly neutral and objective psychological theories and methods carried gender biases and assumptions that systematically devalued women's psychological development by privileging moral decision-making and reasoning practices that turned out, empirically, to be more common among men than women. Existing research, she suggested, was based mainly on male samples and premised on the assumption that the attainment of autonomy, separation, and independence was a more advanced developmental stage than the formation of relationships, connectedness, and interdependence. In a series of empirical studies on men's and women's experiences of moral conflict and choice, Gilligan heard different—empirically gendered—voices and modes of reasoning about moral issues. She argued that women's sense of agency was tied primarily to their relationships, and that their moral decision-making was based on concrete and context-specific principles and relationships—what Gilligan termed an "ethic of care." Men's identity, she suggested, was associated with separation and independence, and their moral decisions were based on autonomous judgments and an "ethic of justice," which privileged universal, abstract moral and ethical principles. Gilligan argued that "theories formerly considered to be sexually neutral in their scientific objectivity . . . instead . . . reflect a consistent observational and evaluative bias" (1982, 6) leading to "an omission of certain truths about life" (1982, 2). She suggested that better, less biased theories and methods were needed to address this theoretical and methodological flaw. She called for including women's voices, perspectives, and experiences in order to reveal hidden and undistorted truths, and develop more accurate theories, about women's (and men's) lives.

Following publication of *In A Different Voice*, Gilligan and her colleagues established the Harvard Project on Women's Psychology and Girls' Development to conduct further empirical explorations of the "different voice" identified in her earlier work. This included the development of an innovative methodological approach—the *Listening Guide* feminist method of narrative analysis—elaborated over many years (e.g., Brown et al. 1989). The method would lend itself to hearing a broader range of different voices and help generate different empirical and theoretical understandings of identity formation and moral development. The *Listening Guide* was constituted in the context of a broader narrative turn characterized by growing interest in narrative approaches and a perception that, compared to standard interview practice and code-based analytic approaches in the social sciences, narrative methods were better able to capture the full range of human experiences—including subjectivity, meaning-making, and intentionality (e.g., Mischler 1986; Riessman 1990).

The *Listening Guide*, as detailed in *Meeting at the Crossroads*, entails listening to narratives in several stages each time listening for different "voices" (see Brown and Gilligan 1992, 27–30). The first stage focuses on listening for the plot, and on the influence of the listener's identity on how the story is heard. The second stage centers on listening for the self, "for the voice of the 'I' speaking in this relationship" (27) with the interviewer. It attends to "shifts in the sound of the voice and in narrative position: the use of first-, second-, or third-person narration" (ibid.) and how these shifts signal changes in the narrator's perceptions and experiences of herself. The third stage listens for how relationships enable girls and women to "freely express themselves," while the fourth stage listens for "the ways in which institutionalized restraints and cultural norms and values become moral voices that silence voices, [and] constrain the expression of feelings and thoughts" (29).

Approaching these practices through a posthumanist performative framework helps materialize their humanist representationalist configuration through their enactment of ontological assumptions in which the *Listening Guide* practices and their objects of study are taken as ontologically separate and already constituted. The *Listening Guide* conceived itself as a "progressive" method that could overcome the limitations of previous "gender-biased" methods "by taking girls' voices seriously," thereby generating "a better understanding of women's psychology" (Brown and Gilligan 1992, 9). Its progressive features were understood to include a recasting of method as a "relational practice" (22); a way of working that, by creating "resonant relationships between girls and women," could bring girls' and women's "voices more fully into the world" (7). The *Listening Guide* explicitly rejects the notion of a neutral, distanced, and detached researcher. Influenced by Mischler's (1986) work, Brown and Gilligan argue that narratives are "co-constructed" through respondent-researcher relationships. Yet the *Listening Guide* *enacts itself* in representational terms as an improved method (more relational, less biased, more objective and value-free) that is better able to "capture" reality (11). It implicitly takes up a teleological account of science in which the *Listening Guide's* progressive features are understood as means of getting closer to preexisting and undistorted truths about women's (and men's) lives. The *Listening Guide* therefore opens itself up to the same critique that it directs toward "gender-biased" theories and methods in that both approaches *implicitly* claim to represent the world in scientifically and politically neutral and objective ways.

A Diffractive Genealogy of the Listening Guide: Second-Wave Feminism and the Identity-Politics and Voice-Giving Project

The *Listening Guide* can be understood as intimately entangled with second-wave feminism. This humanist representationalist identity-politics project was concerned with giving voice to groups of people whose experiences and perspectives were seen as having been marginalized by theories and methods that claimed neutrality and objectivity but embodied male, white, middle-class, heterosexual, and Western norms and values (see also Chodorow 1978; Miller 1976; Oakley 1981; Smith 1987). Second-wave feminism, along with other large-scale political movements of the second half of the twentieth century (around race, ethnicity, sexuality, disability), were based in claims about the injustices done to particular social groups (e.g., hooks 1984; Lorde 1984; Rich 1979). These movements were underpinned by, and helped generate, a philosophical body of literature that took up questions about the nature, origin, and futures of the identities being defended. The notion of "identity politics," which comes into being at this time, involved political arguments focused on membership of a group that supposedly had shared interests, perspectives, and identities including shared experiences of injustice (Somers 1994). Identity political formations typically aimed to secure political freedom of, and greater self-determination for, these marginalized constituencies (Heyes 2014). The metaphysical assumption underpinning identity politics is that these identities are preexisting, and can be discovered (and therefore given equal rights) if different theories, methods, and politics are used. Gilligan's collaborative program of work—including the *Listening Guide*—can be understood as constituted through, and constitutive of, this movement. It sought to find theories and methods better able to hear, and accurately represent, voices, experiences, and identities that were understood as being inaccessible to patriarchal frameworks.

This representationalist configuration of the *Listening Guide* was made in intra-action with broader representationalist configurations and enactments of philosophical, theoretical, methodological, and political projects. In particular, the notion, and possibility, of accessing "experience" was at the center of Western feminist activism in the 1960s and 1970s, and feminist theorists and empirical researchers of the late 1970s and 1980s followed these early feminist activists by urging scholars to think from, and rely on the authority of, experience (DeVault and Gross 2012). As feminist oral historian Sherna Gluck (1984, 222) noted, "Refusing to be rendered historically voiceless any longer, women are creating a new history—using our own voices and experiences." Significantly, it is this specifically representationalist configuration of theory, method, and politics—and the assumption that it gives unmediated access to "essential" and preexisting truth(s) about women's voices, lives, and experiences—that allows women to be heard, and that makes possible second-wave feminism's identity-politics project and political claims for women's equal rights. On a posthumanist performative approach, the *Listening Guide's* representationalist configuration can be understood as critically and *productively* entangled with second-wave feminism. Diffracted through the metaphysical terms of this methodological, theoretical, and political project, the *Listening Guide* helped women's voices be heard at a time and place when these voices were otherwise marginalized. The posthumanist performative critique, then, is not that the *Listening Guide* enacts a specifically representationalist configuration—for methods necessarily embody and enact specific metaphysical commitments to the exclusion of others. The critique is that this *necessary metaphysical specificity*—and the specific ontological and political identities and boundaries it performs into being—is taken as given rather than accounted for.

Re-making the Listening Guide through Posthumanist Performative Metaphysical Practices

(Re)making posthumanist performative *Listening Guide* practices reconfigures their metaphysical specificity so that they enact themselves and their object of study as intra-actively constituted. This entails (re)making listening into a metaphysical practice that intra-actively produces its objects (narratives, voices, identities, relationships, structural and cultural norms) in intra-action with wider posthumanist performative practices. This is enacted through diffractive genealogies of the metaphysical practices—at different scales—through which listening and its objects are enacted in humanist representationalist/posthumanist performative configurations. This project lies beyond the scope of this chapter. For the purposes of this discussion I attempt to reconfigure the *Listening Guide* 'listening for the 'I'" from a humanist representationalist, to a posthumanist performative, practice.

The *Listening Guide* enacts 'listening for the 'I'" as a neutral and passive practice that puts the listener in touch with a preexisting 'I'. A posthumanist performative reconfiguration entails remaking 'listening for the 'I'" into a metaphysical practice that is intra-actively constituted with the 'I' it produces. This is enacted through diffractive genealogies of what we might call 'I'-practices: metaphysical practices that embody and enact specific metaphysical figurations of the 'I' (in the form of ontological assumptions about presences/absences, in/determinacies), including the *Listening Guide* practices. Diffractive genealogies of 'I'-practices materialize the ontological processes of formation, and generative powers and effects, of specific metaphysical configurations of 'I'-practices (see also Foucault 1980). On this approach listening for the 'I' is (re)configured into a genealogically constituted metaphysically specific 'I'-practice that intra-actively materializes genealogically constituted metaphysically specific 'I's as part of larger genealogically constituted metaphysically specific world-making projects and practices. In particular, this posthumanist performative reconfiguration is intra-actively made possible in part by critiques of the feminist identity-politics and voice-giving project, its substance metaphysics or metaphysics of essences, and its humanist representationalist figurations of identity, the 'I', and 'I'-practices (e.g., Butler 1990; Butler and Scott 1992; Haraway 1991; Lather 1991; Scott 1988, 1991, 1992).

The issue I attend to here is how to reconfigure the metaphysical specificity of 'listening for the 'I'. One way of contesting the ontological given-ness and self-evidence of this practice, and the preexisting 'I' it supposedly represents, is to explore the cultural and historical contingency of 'I' modes of speaking and telling. Whereas in English the use of subject pronouns (such as 'I') is obligatory, in other languages—such as Chinese and Japanese—they can be dropped. In languages with the possibility of "pronoun drop" (Kashima and Kashima 1998, 465), identity is constituted through, for example, verb inflections rather than pronoun use. In other words, there is no 'I'-practice here; but rather what we might call a 'non'I'-practice'. Furthermore, languages vary in the number of first- and second-person singular pronouns. For example, where English has just one first-person singular pronoun—'I'—Japanese has several, such as *watasi, boku,* and *ore* (Kashima and Kashima 1998). Each one of these pronouns enacts and constitutes identity in a specific way, as Kashima and Kashima (468) explain: "Perhaps a man may index himself by *watasi* when he states his opinion as an officer of a company, whereas he may use *ore* when he reveals his feelings as a friend." Kashima and Kashima (1998) note that pronoun usages—or "deictic systems"—help constitute social relationships and power relations as well as identity, and are themselves constituted through culturally specific situated practices. In our terms 'I'/non'I'/multiple'I'-practices—in the form of pronoun use/drop and/or verb inflections and/or multiple pronoun usages—are genealogically constituted metaphysical practices that constitute not only a determinate and specific subject but its existence/non-existence. Indeed, the genealogical formation and metaphysical specificity of 'I'/non'I'/multiple'I'-practices is illustrated, for example, in the constitution of the Japanese literary genre of the 'I-novel' at the beginning of the twentieth century—an autobiographical/confessional narrative style written in either the first- or third person that is presumed to depict events that correspond to the narrator's life and experiences, and that emerged in an intellectual climate that emphasized the value of the self at a time when Japan was (re)opened to the West (Buckley 2009; Fowler 1992). Whereas a humanist representationalist enactment of the *Listening Guide's* 'listening for the 'I'" takes 'listening' (method) and the 'I' (object) as separate and already constituted, a posthumanist performative reconfiguration (re)makes 'listening for the 'I'" into a 'listening for 'Is'/non'Is'/multiple'Is'" practice and makes possible the materialization of genealogically constituted metaphysically specific agential intra-actions of 'I'/non'I'/multiple'I'-practices and 'Is'/non'Is'/multiple'Is'.

Taking the Material Nature of Social Research Methods Seriously

This chapter attempts to enact a posthumanist performative way of engaging in social scientific world/knowledge-making social science projects and practices through a diffractive methodology that is articulated in terms of diffractive genealogies and metaphysical practices. These diffractive practices, I suggest, are posthumanist performative ways of knowing/enacting social research methods. They take the material, agential, and constitutive nature of methods seriously by reconfiguring so-called social science tools, techniques, and technologies into genealogically constituted metaphysical practices that embody and enact specific metaphysical commitments to the exclusion of others. On this account, methods can never be neutral for they *necessarily* enact themselves and the world in specific metaphysical— humanist representationalist/posthumanist performative—figurations. The issue is not avoiding, but accounting for, the material-discursive/ metaphysical specificity of methods, their agential cuts, and their inclusionary/exclusionary effects. This, following Barad, is an ethical, as well as an ontological and epistemological, concern. It is a matter of ethical responsibility and accountability for the real ontological, ethical, and political world-making consequences of enacting metaphysically specific methods. In agential realist terms, responsible and accountable practices produce "objective" science, where objectivity is defined as "*accountability to marks on bodies in their specificity by attending to how different cuts produce differences that matter*" (Barad 2007, 348). On this approach, objective social science requires ethical accountability and responsibility for the diffractive genealogies and metaphysical practices through which methods are produced, and intra-actively produce their objects of study, as part of larger materializations of the world.

A posthumanist performative approach makes possible an ethical and "affirmative" (Van der Tuin 2011) engagement with methods in the form of a diffractive appreciation, and (re)working of, their genealogically constituted humanist representationalist configurations. Engaging with Brown and Gilligan's *Listening Guide* on these terms materializes a method whose rationality, ontology, genealogy, and performativity is not taken as given but as intra-actively constituted through specific but open-ended material-discursive and metaphysical conditions of possibility: a method that comes into being non-innocently as an instrument of, and instrumental to, second-wave feminism's humanist representationalist identity-politics and voice-giving project. At the same time, attending to the *Listening Guide's* material and metaphysical constraints and possibilities opens up a space for reconfiguring the *Listening Guide* on posthumanist performative terms, thereby contributing to the making of posthumanist performative worlds.

NOTES

An earlier version of this chapter was presented at the *Mattering: Feminism, Science & Materialism* conference held at the City University of New York in February 2013. I am grateful to Andrea Doucet for drawing my attention to this conference and for the opportunity it provided to meet and share lunch with Karen Barad. I also thank Victoria Pitts-Taylor, and anonymous reviewers, for comments on a previous draft of this chapter. My engagement with the *Listening Guide* spans more than two decades and I thank Andrea Doucet and Carol Gilligan for sharing parts of this journey with me. My postdoctoral fellowship with Carol Gilligan at Harvard University in 1994–1995 was made possible by scholarships from the Fulbright Foundation, the American Association of University Women Educational Foundation, and the Harold Hyam Wingate Foundation.

1 I use the term "natural-social" to refer not only to my interdisciplinary training in both the natural and the social sciences, but also to denote the ontological inseparability, and intra-active constitution, of the "natural" and the "social."

2 The notion of "social science" and "social research methods" are not taken as ontologically given but as having been constituted through material-discursive practices that enact a separation between the social sciences and the natural sciences, and between research methods and other world/knowledge-making practices (e.g., through the production of textbooks on social research methods).

3 I use the concept of rationality to convey Foucault's notion that "'practices' don't exist without a certain regime of rationality" (1991, 79).

4 Drawing on Haraway's (1997) articulation of the concept, Casteñada conceptualizes "figuration" as material-discursive practices that incorporate a dual process of "constitutive effect and generative circulation" (2002, 3). On this approach, figurations of social research methods are understood as both sedimentations of particular material-semiotic practices and ongoing generative materializations of particular, but contestable, worlds.

5 This is my own approach to a posthumanist performative (re)configuration of social research methods. For examples of other *posthumanist performative* approaches to method, see Davies 2014; Hultman and Lenz Taguchi 2010; Lenz Taguchi 2012; Lenz Taguchi and Palmer 2013; Mazzei 2014; Nordstrom 2015; Palmer 2011; Tamboukou 2014. For examples of other *performative* approaches to method, see Law 2004, 2009; Law, Ruppert, and Savage 2011.

REFERENCES

Barad, Karen. 1996. "Meeting the universe halfway: realism and social constructivism without contradiction," pp. 161–194 in *Feminism, Science, and the Philosophy of Science*, ed. Lynn H. Nelson and Jack Nelson. AA Dordrech: Kluwer Academic Publishers.

Barad, Karen. 1998. Getting real: technoscientific practices and the materialization of reality. *Differences: A Journal of Feminist Cultural Studies* 10 no. 2: 87–128.

Barad, Karen. 2003. Posthumanist performativity: toward an understanding of how matter comes to matter. *Signs* 28 no. 3: 801–831.

Barad, Karen. 2007. *Meeting the Universe Halfway: Quantum Physics and the Entanglement of Matter and Meaning.* Durham and London: Duke University Press.

Barad, Karen. 2010. Quantum entanglements and hauntological relations of inheritance: dis/continuities, spacetime enfoldings, and justice-to-come. *Derrida Today* 3 no. 2: 240–268.

Barad, Karen. 2011. Erasers and erasures: Pinch's unfortunate "uncertainty principle." *Social Studies of Science* 41 no. 3: 443–454.

Barad, Karen. 2014. Diffracting diffraction: cutting together-apart. *Parallax* 20 no. 3: 168–187.

Blackman, Lisa. 2014. Affect and automaticy: Towards an analytics of experimentation. *Subjectivity* 7 no. 4: 362–384.

Brown, Lyn M. and Carol Gilligan. 1992. *Meeting at the Crossroads: Women's Psychology and Girl's Development.* Cambridge, MA: Harvard University Press.

Brown, Lyn. M., Mark B. Tappan, Carol Gilligan, Barbara A. Miller, and Dianne E. Argyris. 1989. "Reading for self and moral voice: a method for interpreting narratives of real-life moral conflict and choice," pp. 141–164 in *Entering the Circle: Hermeneutic Investigation in Psychology*, ed. Martin J. Packer and Richard B. Addison. Albany: SUNY Press.

Buckley, Sandra. 2009. *The Encyclopedia of Contemporary Japanese Culture.* London: Routledge.

Butler, Judith. 1990. *Gender Trouble: Feminism and the Subversion of Identity.* London: Routledge.

Butler, Judith and Scott, Joan W. 1992. Eds. *Feminists Theorize the Political.* New York: Routledge.

Casteñada, Claudia. 2002. *Figurations: Child, Bodies, Worlds.* Durham and London: Duke University Press.

Chalmers, Ian. 1990. *What Is This Thing Called Science?* Buckingham: Open University Press.

Chodorow, Nancy. 1978. *The Reproduction of Mothering.* Berkeley: University of California Press.

Davies, Bronwyn. 2014. Reading anger in early childhood intra-actions: a diffractive analysis. *Qualitative Inquiry* 20 no. 6: 734–741.

Derrida, Jacques. 1994. *Specters of Marx: The State of the Debt, the Work of Mourning, and the New International.* New York: Routledge.

Derrida, Jacques. 1995. *Archive Fever: A Freudian Impression.* Chicago: University of Chicago Press.

DeVault, Marjorie L. and Glenda Gross. 2012. "Feminist qualitative interviewing: Experience, Talk, and Knowledge," pp. 206–236 in *The Handbook of Feminist Research: Theory and Praxis*, ed. Sharlene S. Hesse-Biber. Thousand Oaks, CA: Sage.

Dolphijn, Rick and Iris van der Tuin. 2012. Eds. *New Materialism: Interviews & Cartographies.* Ann Arbor, MI: Open Humanities Press.

Foucault, Michel. 1979. *Discipline and Punish: The Birth of the Prison*. New York: Vintage Books.

Foucault, Michel. 1980. "Confessions of the flesh," pp. 194–228 in *Power/Knowledge: Selected Interviews and Other Writings 1972–1977*, ed. Colin Gordon. Brighton, Sussex: Harvester Press.

Foucault, Michel. 1984. "Nietzsche, genealogy, history," pp. 76–120 in *The Foucault Reader*, ed. Paul Rabinow. New York: Pantheon Books.

Foucault, Michel. 1990. *The History of Sexuality: Volume 1 Introduction.* London: Penguin.

Foucault, Michel. 1991. "Questions of method," pp. 73–86 in *The Foucault Effect: Studies in Governmentality*, ed. Graham Burchell, Colin Gordon, and Peter Miller. London: Harvester Wheatsheaf.

Fowler, Edward. 1992. *The Rhetoric of Confession—Shishosetsu in Early Twentieth-Century Japanese Fiction.* Oakland: University of California Press.

Gilligan, Carol. 1977. In a different voice: Women's conceptions of self and morality. *Harvard Educational Review* 47 no. 4: 481–517.

Gilligan, Carol. 1982. *In A Different Voice: Psychological Theory and Women's Development.* Cambridge, MA: Harvard University Press.

Gluck, Sherna B. 1984. "What's so special about women: Women's oral history," pp. 215–230 in *Oral History: An Interdisciplinary Anthology*, ed. David Dunaway & Willa K. Baum. Nashville, TN: American Association for State and Local History.

Haraway, Donna. 1991. *Simians, Cyborgs, and Women*. New York: Routledge.

Haraway, Donna. 1992. "The promises of monsters: A regenerative politics for inappropriate/d others," pp. 295–337 in *Cultural Studies*, ed. Lawrence Grossberg, Cary Nelson, and Paula A. Treichler. New York: Routledge.

Haraway, Donna. 1997. *Modest_Winess@Second_Millenium.FemaleMan©_Meets_Onco-Mouse™*. New York and London: Routledge.

Haraway, Donna. 2008. *When Species Meet*. Minneapolis: University of Minnesota Press.

Heyes, Cressida. Identity Politics. *The Stanford Encyclopedia of Philosophy* (Winter 2014 edition), Edward N. Zalta (ed.), http://plato.stanford.edu/archives/win2014/entries/identity-politics/. Accessed April 21, 2015.

Hicks, Dan and Mary C. Beaudry. 2010. Eds. *The Oxford Handbook of Material Culture Studies.* New York: Oxford University Press.

hooks, bell. 1984. *Feminist Theory from Margin to Center*. Boston, MA: South End Press.

Hultman, Karin and Hillevi Lenz Taguchi. 2010. Challenging anthropocentric analysis of visual data: a relational materialist methodological approach to educational research. *International Journal of Qualitative Studies in Education.* 23 no. 5: 525–542.

Kashima, Emiko S. and Kashima, Yoshihisa. 1998. Culture and language: The case of cultural dimensions and personal pronoun use. *Journal of Cross-cultural Psychology* 29 no. 3: 461–486.

Lather, Patti. 1991. *Getting Smart: Feminist Research and Pedagogy With/in the Postmodern*. New York: Routledge.

Law, John. 2004. *After Method*. Abingdon: Routledge.

Law, John. 2009. Seeing Like a Survey. *Cultural Sociology* 3 no. 2: 239–256.

Law, John, Evelyn Ruppert, and Mike Savage 2011. *The Double Social Life of Methods*. CRESC. : Goldsmiths Research Online. http://research.gold.ac.uk/7987/. Accessed February 10, 2015.

Lenz Taguchi, Hillevi. 2012. A diffractive and Deleuzian approach to analysing interview data. *Feminist Theory* 13 no 3: 265–281.

Lenz Taguchi, Hillevi and Anna Palmer. 2013. A more 'livable' school? A diffractive analysis of the performative enactments of girls' ill-/well-being with(in) school environments. *Gender and Education* 25 no. 6: 671–687.

Lorde, Audre. 1984. *Sister Outsider: Essays and Speeches*. Trumansburg, NY: Crossing Press.

Mauthner, Natasha. S. 2015. "The past was never simply there to begin with and the future is not simply what will unfold": A posthumanist performative approach to qualitative longitudinal research. *International Journal of Social Research Methodology* 18 no. 3: 321–336.

Mauthner, Natasha. S. 2016. "The Listening Guide feminist method of narrative analysis: Towards a posthumanist performative (re)configuration," in *Feminist Narrative Research: Opportunities and Challenges*, ed. Jo Woodiwiss, Kate Smith, and Kelly Lockwood. London: Palgrave Macmillan.

Mazzei, Lisa. A. 2014. Beyond an easy sense: a diffractive analysis. *Qualitative Inquiry* 20 no. 6: 742–746.

Miller, Jean. B. 1976. *Towards a New Psychology of Women*. Boston: Beacon Press.

Mischler, Elliott. G. 1986. *Research Interviewing: Context and Narrative*. Cambridge, MA: Harvard University Press.

Nordstrom, Susan. N. 2015. Not so innocent anymore: making recording devices matter in qualitative interviews. *Qualitative Inquiry* 21 no. 4: 388–401.

Oakley, Ann. 1981. "Interviewing women: a contradiction in terms," ppm 30–61 in *Doing Feminist Research*, ed. Helen Roberts. London: Routledge & Kegan Paul.

Palmer, Anna. 2011. "How many sums can I do?" Performative strategies and diffractive thinking as methodological tools for rethinking mathematical subjectivity. *Reconceptualizing Educational Research Methodology* 1 no. 1: 3–18.

Rich, Adrienne. 1979. *On Lies, Secrets and Silence: Selected Prose, 1966–1978*. New York: W. W. Norton.

Riessman, Catherine. K. 1990. *Divorce Talk: Women and Men Make Sense of Personal Relationships*. New Brunswick, NJ: Rutgers University Press.

Rouse, Joseph. 1996. *Engaging Science: How to Understand Its Practices Philosophically*. Ithaca and London: Cornell University Press.

Russell, Bertrand. 1946. *The History of Western Philosophy*. London: George Allen and Unwin Ltd.

Scott, Joan W. 1988. *Gender and the Politics of History*. New York: Columbia University Press.

Scott, Joan W. 1991. The evidence of experience. *Critical Inquiry* 17 no. 4: 773–797.

Scott, Joan W. 1992. "Experience," pp. 22–40 in *Feminists Theorize the Political*, ed. Judith Butler and Joan Scott. New York: Routledge.

Sehgal, Melanie. 2014. Diffractive propositions: Reading Alfred North Whitehead with Donna Haraway and Karen Barad. *Parallax* 20 no. 3: 188–201.

Shrader, Astrid. 2010. Responding to *Pfiesteria piscicida* (the Fish Killer): Phantomatic Ontologies, Indeterminacy, and Responsibility in Toxic Microbiology. *Social Studies of Science* 40 no. 2: 275–306.

Smith, Dorothy. 1987. *The Everyday World as Problematic*. Boston: Northeastern University Press.

Somers, Margaret. 1994. The narrative constitution of identity: a relational and network approach. *Theory and Society* 23 no. 5: 605–649.

Somers, Margaret. 2008. *Genealogies of Citizenship*. Cambridge: Cambridge University Press.

Suchman, Lucy. 2007. *Human-Machine Reconfigurations: Plans and Situated Actions*. Cambridge: Cambridge University Press.

Tamboukou, Maria. 2014. Archival research: unravelling space/time/matter entanglements and fragments. *Qualitative Research* 14 no. 5: 617–633.

Van der Tuin, Iris. 2011. "A different starting point, a different metaphysics." Reading Bergson and Barad diffractively. *Hypatia* 26 no. 1: 22–42.

16

Experimental Subjects Kick Back

A Provocation for an Alternative Causality in Biomedical Research and Bioethics

MARSHA ROSENGARTEN

My question is not what each of us shall do in order to go on.
It is rather how to resist—not in the name of the past, but in
calling for a different future.
—Isabelle Stengers (2011: 86)

[R]eality is sedimented out of the process of making the
world intelligible through certain practices and not others.
Therefore, we are not only responsible for the knowledge
that we seek, but, in part, for what exists.
—Karen Barad (1998:8; 2007:390)

Within the health and medical experimental science research fields, it is apparent that a conception of linear causality prevails. As the term suggests, there is the idea that causes achieve an effect or series of effects according to a spatial distance between the cause and effect but also that this takes place chronologically: something happens at one point in time and its effect is experienced elsewhere such that both the entity that gave rise to the effect and the effect exist as if distinct in themselves. In the words of Alfred North Whitehead (1997:194), we have the presumption that the world comprises "individual substances, each existing in its own right apart from any necessary reference to each other." In order to sustain such a view and, indeed, to account for effects as they must arise somewhere, entities—perceived as individual substances such as bodies, drugs, virus, and so forth—are attributed with intrinsic capacities. That is to say, they are reduced to a finite contribution and possibility in the relevance of their existence. In practice, methods are designed in response to this view with the explicit intention to isolate entities of inquiry for the identification of probable causes (Rosengarten and Savransky, 2015). To put this another way, the methods of experimental science maintain a conformation to a conception of causality that has already delimited what can be learned from inquiry. It is alongside this performative of causality that we find bioethics. As a form of ethics derived from moral principles set down to protect research subjects, it accords with and hence legitimizes precisely that which is deemed prior to the inquiry as relevant (Michael and Rosengarten, 2013). Ironically, and no doubt worryingly, it endorses the exclusion of precisely what may come to matter to the researched while purporting to protect them from any untoward interests of scientists.

In this chapter I want to use the contributions of both Isabelle Stengers and Karen Barad to rethink the problematic I have outlined above, notably the conception of causality and the exclusion of what may be of relevance to research subjects. The discussion that follows is part of a broader inquiry that I have been engaged in for some time. It may be summarized as a concern with what a feminist social studies of science perspective might look like when tackling the method of the randomized control trial (RCT), a method that has come to be lauded for enabling evidence-based medicine.

My interest in RCTs comes out of a lengthy study of HIV biomedical innovation, for now settling on the nature of the RCT as a technology and with reference to questions of ethics. Here I pursue this interest by reflecting on one specific finding from a set of trials conducted with the aim of demonstrating the efficacy of an HIV biomedical prevention technology. A trial involving young single women called Fem-PrEP produced "flat results"—no evidence of the efficacy of a pill-a-day HIV pre-exposure prophylaxis (PrEP)—whereas two other preceding trials did find PrEP highly efficacious. "Flat," in reference to Fem-PrEP, means that the same number of women assigned to take the pill (28) and those who were randomized to take a placebo (28) became HIV infected.[1] According to the design of the RCT, where a statistically significant difference is required between product and placebo arms, flat results are indicative of trial failure. Follow-up publications soon translated these results from a problem in the method of the trial, to one arising from the behaviors of a subcategory of women: "young single women." These behaviors comprised a lack of conformity to the trial protocol that required daily adherence to a dosing regimen involving a PrEP or placebo pill and false reporting of adherence. False reporting of adherence has been deduced from diagnostic tests that showed no take-up of the drug in the blood of many of the females on the product arm of Fem-PrEP, despite the latter's claims of good dosing adherence (Corneli et al., 2014). Needless to say, other differences within the trial's findings have not been taken up to complexify this. For example, among some of the follow-up articles by those involved in conducting the trial, there is the suggestion that the behaviors may, in themselves, be due to a number of factors. This is drawn from significant statistical variation in adherence patterns across the three separate Fem-PrEP trial locations (Corneli et al., 2014: 329).

It is also worth noting that all three PrEP RCTs were approved as bioethical in their aims and conduct. Each had demonstrated to public health and/or university ethics committees that the potential benefit from the research outweighed the risks it posed; prevention counseling and condoms were provided; informed consent in relevant languages was obtained from the participants; care was instituted for those who experienced "adverse events" or "intercurrent" infection (HIV infection while enrolled in the trial but not caused in any conventional sense by the product under test). In short, procedures were in place to guide research practice toward a hoped-for predetermined anticipated benefit while minimizing what might be conceived to harm. As is the case with all RCTs, responsibility is seen to reside with the researchers whose interests—similarly conceived within the causal and hence reduced framing of possibilities that I have outlined—have long been recognized as not necessarily aligned with those of the researched.

Although neither Stengers nor Barad write directly on RCTs, the two epigraphs provide a framework for reflecting on the trial findings and the manner by which the research subjects have become responsibilized for this failure. The first epigraph is from a discussion by Isabelle Stengers (2011a) on the importance of recalcitrance, specifically the expression of an objection by those subject to irrelevant or insulting questions by the experimental sciences. For Stengers, such resistance makes way for the cultivation of what may come to matter to the researched, that is, to those for whom science claims to act. The refusal to give what others have decided is required offers something novel to the unilateral modes of thought and inquiry that can be said to characterize much of what are claimed to be the "experimental" sciences.

However, the achievement of recalcitrance is not straightforward when it comes to humans, at least according to Stengers. She is explicit in stating that science does not have the power to produce recalcitrance and, more often than not, it is the case that human research subjects will endeavor to be influenced in their responses by what they understand to be the agenda of science. In other words, what matters to them is likely to be mediated by what they perceive is expected from them. Insofar as recalcitrance cannot be prompted, it may be deduced as all the more precious and requiring of care if it should come to happen. As will become evident, it is this sort of care that may be called for and valued in the undertakings of biomedical research.

My own process in the writing of this chapter could be described as an attempt to stage a dialogue between Stengers and Barad, with interjections from a few notable others such as Bruno Latour and Martin Savransky. The dialogue is mounted in response to a series of questions that serve, in the first instance, as a structuring device for my review of the Fem-PrEP findings. If successful as provocations to think causality and ethics more relationally, I would like to think that the questions or, more aptly, the process of questioning, may function as an alternative causality and ethos in itself. This will be for the reader to judge.

Needless to say, questions are formulations that by their very nature partake in or constitute problems. But their posing need not be assumed to demand an answer that solves the problem. Rather, as Stengers (2011:10) suggests in her reading of Whitehead, a question may serve as an opening to an adventure that involves an attentiveness to a worldliness in process. It is a speculative engagement with a processual world, speculative because it is a world that cannot be fixed for the purpose of resolving (see also Savransky, 2016). Indeed, Stengers says that when the adventure turns out badly—and here we may consider scientific inquiry that delimits what matters to the research—it is important that we ask "what has happened to us?" and that we do so in a manner that will enable other ways of situating us "not as defined by the past, but as able, perhaps, to inherit from it in another way" (2011:13,14). Taking Stengers's claim as my point of departure, the overarching question here is whether the mode of inquiry that delivered the Fem-PrEP trial as a failure can be turned, retrospectively, into an adventure that might furnish different possibilities for the future.

If we look to Barad's work it is apparent that the trial itself is complicit in its said failure. Indeed, if we apply her concepts of "intra-activity" and "agential realism," failure becomes an achievement of a process in contradistinction from that of conventional causality. In her own account, the concepts of intra-activity and agential realism were formulated by drawing on her work as a physicist and notably the influence of Niels Bohr but, also, the provocation of feminist theory. She makes clear in her early piece *Getting real: technoscientific practices and the materialization of reality* and in her book *Meeting the Universe Halfway* that crucial to her project has been extending Judith Butler's (1993) theory of performativity to offer a more satisfactory engagement with materiality, viewing Butler's work as limited to the work of language or discourse.

In some respects, Barad's work might be argued as linking Butler's theory of performativity and what it offers to rethinking ethics with that of a Science and Technology Studies (STS) orientation to process and a relational ontology. Intra-activity, in Barad's key examples, is the entanglement of no less than the discursive and the fleshy nature of bodies and technological software and hardware. It is this entanglement that Barad asks us to attend to by providing the additional concept of agential realism. By pointing to an iterative process—a performative process—that achieves a politico-ethico investiture in the process of materialization, we are alerted to our agency and hence responsibility in how matter matters in the double sense of becoming material and of concern:

> In essence, agential realism theorizes the material dimension of regulatory apparatuses in terms of the materiality of phenomena; it thereby provides an account of their causal (but nondeterministic) materializing effects in the intra-active production of material-discursive bodies. Hence, materialization is not only a matter of how discourse comes to matter but how matter comes to matter. [...] materialization is an iteratively intra-active process whereby material-discursive bodies are sedimented out of the intra-action of multiple discursive apparatuses through which these phenomena (bodies) become intelligible. (Barad 1998:10)

Of the various examples of intra-activity and agential realism in Barad's work, one most frequently cited is the materialization of a fetus through the generative process of ultrasound imaging. This process is not an exchange between entities but an intra-action of the reception and transmission of sound waves, entangled with phenomena that emerge as the distinct entities of fetus, hardware technology, image and so on. What comes to appear as the fetus emerges through the affective becomings of what Barad (2007:179) describes as the "nonarbitrary, nondeterministic causal enactments through which matter-in-the-process-of-becoming is iteratively enfolded into its ongoing differential materialisation." The materialization of the fetus takes place through a process of agential realism whereby the design of technologies affects what materializes. In the case of the fetus, the ultrasound technology intra-actively represents it as if a free-floating entity apart from the maternal body, thus reiterating the expectation of a Cartesian subject: the "individual" available to a rights-based discourse and the troubling questions about "life" that ensue with this. In the United States, this discourse can be seen at work in the recourse to the rights of the fetus in anti-abortion debates (Barad, 1998:15). Thus, the process of materialization comes to be culturally inscribed in a manner that conforms to a prior conception of what "is."

If we apply Barad's analytic to the Fem-PrEP RCT, the failed trial outcomes are no longer confounding but are an achievement of the specific intra-activity of the mode of recruitment, the differentiated complexities of day-to-day life of those recruited, a mode of prevention counseling plus, at the very least, the PrEP or placebo pill. Through its day-to-day requirements and modes of surveillance—intended or, at the very least, hoped to bring benefit—the failed RCT effectively materialized "young single women at risk of HIV" as dubious entities—"less" capable, "less" reliable, "less" trustworthy than the contemporaneous emergence of those in the other "successful" trials, that is, the iPrEX trial with men who have sex with men (MSM) and the Partners PrEP Study with women and men in regular serodiscordant heterosexual relationships. Barad's analytic also enables a reconsideration of the ethical dimensions of the RCT. That is to say, we can attend to the work of "agential realism," whereby the process of discursive-material entanglement involving human and non-human factors has taken place to materialize non-adherent women research subjects.

Elsewhere I have argued that, unlike other fields, such as law or education, there is an immediate and necessary involvement *in* and not just *with* "biological" and technoscientific devices of biomedical reach (Rosengarten, 2004:212). In other words, scientific technologies may partake in the materialization of the world in specific ways whose different effects mark it out from other forms of intervention. When Barad states: "we are not only responsible for the knowledge that we seek but, in part, for what exists" (1998:94), we can assume the "we" refers to the performative work of the discursive entangled in the design of technological apparatuses. But the we is still a slippery concept in the sense that it must also be tied to an emergent and highly situated process, whereby we can presume that the discursive that gives shape to a research agenda is, itself, an outcome of a prior process of intra-activity. What is clear is that we can never be sure "who" can be held responsible for "what" unless we are able to disentangle the process. Hence, although Barad provides us with a more relational account of responsibility through a distributed account of agency and hence poses causes as the achievement of a relational process, the argument has the flavor of a type of causal loop. At what point, we might ask, can we locate differences in the relational process such that an alteration—the novel—becomes a possibility? If everything is an intra-active process of an agential realist entanglement of the material-discursive, it is difficult to imagine where we might determine what matters. As Martin Savransky (forthcoming) argues, we require words that may allow us to affirm, simultaneously, the relational, intra-active processes by which the different creatures of this world come into existence as well as the radical *irreducibility* of the stubborn fact of their "existence."

This is not to dismiss the import of the combined concepts of intraactivity and agential realism. But it is to raise a caution about embracing Barad's emphasis on relationality, if we are interested in speculative possibilities. Despite her efforts to recuperate the concrete nature of existence that has suffered neglect in an over-emphasis on social constructionism (1998), the dynamic co-affective ontology that she proposes leaves us to wonder about how the world "kicks back." In reference to the Fem-PreP RCT, the intra-active process that I have described brings into being a specific gender differential. But only to do so in a manner that returns the situation of this differential to a problematic future. In

contradistinction to its intentions to enable women to protect themselves against HIV, the trial has been successful in reformulating a concern with female vulnerability and especially single female vulnerability
such that, what was understood as arising from gender asymmetries, has
become a problem residing *with* and, by implication, in single women.

Drawing from Barad, I have suggested that the RCT can be viewed as
an actor participating in relations that re-gender the field. However, the
process, as such, calls for something else, something I want to suggest
in my appropriation of the phrase "kicks back." It is here that Stengers's
contribution on recalcitrance becomes especially pertinent. But before
elaborating on what I have proposed as a care for recalcitrance, I need
to say a little more about what the intra-activity process has effected
and especially the contrary manner in which responsibility has morphed
into a charge of causal effect well outside the terrain of conventional
bioethics.

If we pause to consider what has taken place with Fem-PrEP, we see
that the habitual mode of responsibilizing—curiously, a responsibilizing
of research subjects for which there is no accountability in bioethics—
has doubled the very real material effects of vulnerability to HIV.
Although the RCT was premised on and thus recruited the research subjects on the grounds that the latter were vulnerable to HIV, its enactment
of the PrEP pill, the RCT, and the young single women research subjects
as if stable, distinct entities has occluded consideration of the processes
by which the women are still vulnerable to HIV.

In collaboration with Mike Michael, I have argued that the PrEP pill
emerges through heterogeneous relations enacted through the work of
the RCT that, in turn, give form to the RCT (Rosengarten and Michael,
2009). These relations may include, for instance, the local context that
affects access to pills, the experience of pill taking, sexual practices and
risk, intimate relations, attitudes to HIV, possibly body size, metabolics,
genetics, and more. In other words, whatever "PrEP" is, it is an achievement of this heterogeneity. The experimental subjects in their becoming
with the PrEP pill might also be viewed in this way. In place of compar-
ing what is assumed to be like for like—notably, those in the "successful" RCT and those in the "failed" RCT with a pill[2]—what is stake here
is how the research might engage with emergent differences. Each of
the three RCTs I have mentioned was undertaken bearing in mind the

potential for different HIV risk relations to be at work. This is apparent in the choice of MSM and transgender females in the successful iPrEX trial as well as females and males in stable "serodiscordant relationships" in the successful Partners PrEP Study. Hence, with particular reference to the Partner's PrEP study that involved females of different ages— including young women—in an existing relationship with a known and stable HIV-positive male partner (Partners PrEP), it could be counter-argued that these females and the trial emerged through very different material-semiotic risk relations when compared with the single females in the failed trial (Fem-PrEP). I have qualified this claim with "it could be counter argued'" because I also want to resist the tendency to lapse into the stabilizing effects of categorization that may be said of such a claim.

In order to expand a little more on the possibilities of difference or, more precisely, differentiations in the course of the research process as preparation for my return to recalcitrance, I want to draw on Bruno Latour's article *How to Talk About the Body? The Normative Dimension of Science Studies*. Here Latour makes the claim: "to have a body is to learn to be affected" (2004:205), and, in doing so, quickly dispenses with the sort of fixing or conception of stability that can be seen as necessary to the mode of quantification for the purposes of generalization that is the ultimate aim of the RCT. Latour's example is the training of "noses" in the perfume industry, a process that involves a trainer, an odor kit, and a body which, in their association or, we could say, relationality, enable the becoming of a [new or more expansive] nose. The body is open to the enhancement of capacities that extend into and proliferate affect. As Latour himself puts this: "Acquiring a body is thus a progressive enterprise that produces at once a sensory medium *and* a sensitive world" (2004:207). Contrary to the quantitative measures of what is enacted as a stable distinct entity by the RCT model, the odor kit does not generate objects, that is, "noses," to be evaluated for accuracy; it does not achieve uniformity. Indeed, unlike the performative of a category of persons with a shared attribute or set of attributes that, in turn, enable further modes of categorization, differentiations in capacity emerge to resist such modes. As Latour (2004:208) explains, there are emergent differences in the sense of smell that may not be registered by all; and those that may be detected which do not correspond to the chemical structure of the fragrances. Matter may thus be conceived as the achievement of an affective processual relationality, giving rise to the ongoing possibility of more differentiation.

Latour's emphasis on emergent differences might be applied to the RCT, bearing in mind the aim of the RCT is to provide generalizable evidence. For Latour the desire to generalize is not, in itself, bad. But it becomes so when the act serves to "eliminate alternative versions." He goes on to say:

> good ones [generalisations] are those that allow for the connection of widely different phenomena and thus generate even more recognition of unexpected differences by engaging a few entities in the life and fate of many others. (2004:220)

If we leave aside the practical implications for the current RCT method, Latour's work can be seen to nuance the process of intra-activity. The differences that he raises and which could be seen to emerge from a process of intra-activity give scope to that which exceeds the discursive of agential realism. In his study the trainer and the odor kit can be said to bear the work of investiture in their relations with the body, but these relations generate new differences. In this way, the linear causal relation in the habitual question of "who" has caused "what" is replaced not only with an entanglement, but with an account of doings that resist conformity to the pre-determined discursive. Hence, it may be a valuable qualifier to the emphasis on process and where we might begin to consider a more situated conception of responsibility along with causality (Rosengarten and Savransky, 2015). That is to say, it enables us to keep sight of the process by which differences emerge in the processes of knowledge and existence-making raised by Barad in the epigraph.[3]

In order to consider the implications of the above re-rendering of the RCT with an attention now to the question of responsibility to research, I want to ask how a more relational conception of the world can be reconciled—if at all—with the problematic of knowing in advance. I have already flagged that the possibility of a different future requires relinquishing hold of a method that forecloses on ways of knowing that exceed the research framework. And I have suggested that the RCT might orient itself to an ethos that sees value in differences in order to become more relevant to its research. In this next section, I want to consider what this means for trial procedures and outcomes: Can there be a "method" that involves not knowing in advance, as is the very basis of the RCT and its determinations of who, what, and how to test? Can not knowing in advance be reconciled with the intentions of bioethics?

To the first of these challenging questions, I believe it is possible to say, in advance, no. This may seem rather a perverse statement given the position I have been developing, but my reasons are based on the intentions of "methods" as normatively devised to pursue the pre-determined (see Savransky, 2013). This does not mean that RCTs cannot be more cognizant of the relations they generate as suggested above and which I shall come back to in my conclusion. But one further qualification can be offered at this point. My rather blunt "no" can also be understood as a constraint on how a problematic such as knowing in advance might be tackled. It would be absurd to assume that we can proceed without knowing some things in advance. Indeed, it is absurd to think that a neomaterialist scholarship—as proposed in different ways throughout this collection—would involve sweeping dismissals of any of the means that bring us to engage it.

In response to my second and third questions on not knowing and bioethics, it seems that there is call to find some way of achieving their reconcilation, that is, there is a responsibility to what comes to matter. In place of an institutionally grounded ethics and its weighing of good versus bad and benefit versus risk or the cool requirements of adhering to basic cognitive modes of information that rely on and institute a notion of individual responsibility, it seems evident from what I have covered so far that we require a mode of responsibility that enables us to move beyond or at least extend the current frame of what is called bioethics. Here I turn again to Stengers, who succeeds in wrestling responsibility away from linear causality and hence what she suggests is a type of non-thinking notion of responsibility:

> When you are about to act, do not rely on any general principle that would give you the right to act. But do take the time to open your imagination and consider this particular occasion. You are not responsible for what will follow, as you are not responsible for the limitations of your

imagination . . . what you are responsible for is paying attention as best you can, to be as discerning, as discriminating as you can about the particular situation. That is, you need to decide in this particular case and not to obey the power of some more general reason. (2005a:188)

There is a daring in this radical rethinking of responsibility. It asks for a hesitation, a pause in the presence of the supposed safeguard of principles such as those of international bioethics. We are challenged to rely on what may come of thinking, of imagining, of engaging more fully with what motivates our action in contrast to an unthinking conforming to authority. In short, it calls for an attentiveness to what it is that we do think, that is, to what it is to know. To say this with a slightly different inflection, what is called for by Stengers is a mode of attentiveness to what might become, without presuming it can and should be foretold. This returns me to the notion of recalcitrance. If recalcitrance is posed as an objection that emerges in the relations of research, how might we be attentive to its possibilities for a different future?

As I have mentioned in the beginning of the chapter, recalcitrance for Stengers (2011a:84) has the propensity to move us to new knowledge-producing connections. But she sees it as a direct possibility only when working with non-human entities and a provocation in relation to the human subjects of research. To reiterate, non-human entities remain resistant to the research agenda of the scientist, whereas human research subjects do not remain independent of questions asked of them. By giving the answers they believe are expected, human research subjects leave the scientist unknowing about what actually matters to the researched (Stengers, 2011:83). That is to say, the research is without precisely what might be assumed as the rationale for inquiry. In such cases the task for social inquiry becomes, as Sorenson et al. (2001) put this, to cultivate recalcitrance. But this is perhaps unnecessary when we move away from separating verbal responses from actions as relevant forms of recalcitrance. To illustrate how recalcitrance is an emergent phenomenon and departing from problematic conventional conceptions of agency, Savransky (2014) offers the example of the patient leaving in the middle of a therapy session because she experiences a comment or question by the therapist as inappropriate. The departure speaks, but not through a verbal articulation that would in some ways concede to the terms of the comment. Rather it is through physical action that does not by necessity concede to the terms of the comment.

Drawing from Savransky's (2014) exposition on how recalcitrance puts authority at risk, I want to propose that the non-adherence by females in Fem-PrEP came about with the authority of the RCT but also exceeded its terms. That is to say, the intra-activity of the trial constrained only the substance (adherence) of resistance but not the nature of the women's challenge. According to Savransky, recalcitrance is not simply a reaction and hence framed as a response only to the exercise of authority, as he notes we may find in the manner in which Michel Foucault's work has been adapted. Rather, it speaks of what matters because it is not a constitutive effect of authority as such but as an effect of a "multiplicity of relations among entities and forces" (Savransky, 2014:101). We may include authority as a force but not necessarily concede to it what matters.

Although it can be claimed that the authority of the RCT has most certainly provoked a response, the recalcitrance should not be reduced to an objection to its reductive aims, that is, pill taking (as has been anecdotally suggested post-trial). This would reduce or again occlude the complexities of the women's lives and to the differences amongst them. Instead the women research subjects' recalcitrance can be viewed as a question to authority that by its character stalls or, as Stengers would argue, installs a pause that provokes the possibility of a reflection by the authority of the RCT. To put this another way, it is a resistance to a conception of the future already presumed within the authoritative framework.

To recap, in the context of this discussion I have proposed that the RCT relies on excluding the generative processes involved in what it is to become an experimental research subject. But if we accept that recalcitrance is a mode of resistance that came about with the demands of the trial yet is not to be reduced to the terms of the trial, new questions on ethics and new propositions become possible. By drawing on the contribution of concepts of intra-activity and agential realism within an orientation toward new modes of thinking and hence practice, I have sought to supplement the RCT and its conservative companion of bioethics. The type of alternative I have sketched need not involve relinquishing all attachments to notions of causality, responsibility, accountability, generalizability, or even a certain morality. On the contrary, by working through a series of questions taken from the empirical workings of the RCT, I have attempted to show that each of these conceptions is available to be re-imagined. The experimental research subjects of Fem-PrEP have alerted us to the possibility that there is more to be learned from their coming together with an intervention and, perhaps, specific to the PrEP pill. A number of clues or fodder for a further re-imaging the field may lie with the differences already identified by the Fem-PrEP researchers: for instance, spatial and temporal differences in the research subjects adherence levels as well as differences in relations of support for and negotiation of adherence (Koenig et al., 2013:S92). There is, we might say, a responsibility to examine such differences as they have come to emerge with the RCT method but whose presence may not be immediately intelligible.

The idea by Barad that the material world kicks back reminds us that there is more than we can know and, thus, more than what we partake in making our existence. Here I have proposed by drawing on Stengers, and also to some extent on the work of Savransky, that recalcitrance can be considered to contest or supplement the performative of intra-activity. Although the concept of intra-activity enables us to consider the co-affective nature of different forces or entities such as drugs, protocols, blood tests, visits to the trial site within temporality of the RCT, it tells us little of how an objection may emerge. My appropriation of Barad's phrase expressed as *"experimental subjects kick back"* in the title of this chapter may thus be understood to emphasize the contribution of research subjects well beyond or contrary to the usual. As such I hope it also serves as a further rejoinder to the worrisome attributing of a linear causal responsibility.

NOTES

I am indebted to Martin Savransky for many provocative and immensely helpful conversations on the work of Karen Barad and Isabelle Stengers. I also want to acknowledge Mike Michael, with whom I collaborated on the study of PrEP and without whom key sections of my argument would not have been possible. Of course neither should be held responsible for what I have made from the companionship of their thinking.

1 The FEM-PrEP study recruited 1951 HIV-negative women aged 18 to 35 deemed to be at risk of contracting HIV in South Africa, Kenya, and Tanzania. All the

women were randomized to receive daily PrEP (consisting of the drugs tenofovir and FTC called Truvada in one pill) or a placebo. Over a year, 56 new infections were recorded and these were equally distributed between the *Truvada* and placebo groups (28 in each arm). See AIDS MAP http://www.aidsmap.com/The-FEM-PrEP-study/page/1821879/ [accessed 20 June 2013]

2 In various articles now available on the "failed" trial, "side-effects"—such as nausea, vomiting, and intestinal gas—are mentioned as experiences of PrEP. Interestingly, despite their recognition such effects are implied to be minimal in any measures of what has taken place and always distinct from PrEP efficacy. Indeed, the Principal Investigator for the failed trial saw side effects being minimal possibly due to low dosing adherence and therefore seems not to have considered that their onset may have contributed to low adherence. She states: "Although women in the TDF–FTC [PrEP pill] group had higher rates of some known side-effects than those in the placebo group, the prevalence of these events was modest and consistent with the overall low adherence. However, the rate of adverse events might have been higher if the level of adherence had been higher" (see Van Damme, 2012:419).

3 For a comprehensive engagement with Barad's work on relationality and the need to account for the emergence of objects with relations, see Savransky (in press).

REFERENCES

AIDS MAP http://www.aidsmap.com/The-FEM-PrEP-study/page/1821879/ [accessed 20 June 2013].

Barad, K. (1998) "Getting Real: Technoscientific Practices and the Materialization of Reality." *Differences: A Journal of Cultural Studies* 10(2):1–21.

Barad, K. (2007) *Meeting the Universe Halfway: Quantum Physics and the Entanglement of Matter and Meaning.* Durham and London: Duke University Press.

Butler, J. (1993) *Bodies That Matter.* London and New York: Routledge.

Corneli, A. et al. (2014) "Fem-PrEP: Adherence Patterns and Factors Associated with Adherence to a Daily Oral Study Product for Pre-Exposure Prophylaxis." *Journal of Acquired Immune Deficiency Syndrome* 66 (3):324–331.

Kippax, S. and Holt, M. (2009) *The State of Social and Political Science Research Related to HIV: A Report for the International AIDS Society.* Geneva: International AIDS Society.

Koenig, L. J. et al. (2013) "Adherence to Antiretroviral Medications for HIV Pre-Exposure Prophylaxis Lessons Learned from Trials and Treatment Studies." *American Journal of Prevention Medicine* 44(1S2):S91–S98.

Latour, B. (2004) "How to Talk About the Body? The Normative Dimension of Science Studies." *Body and Society* 10(2–3):205–229.

Latour, B. (2005) *Reassembling the Social: An Introduction to Actor-Network-Theory.* Oxford: Oxford University Press.

Michael, M. and Rosengarten, M. (2013) *Innovation and Biomedicine: Ethics, Evidence and Expectation in HIV.* London: Palgrave MacMillan Press.

Mol, A. (2002) *The Body Multiple: Ontology in Medical Practice*. Durham, NC: Duke University Press.

Rosengarten, M. (2004) "The Challenge of HIV for Feminist Theory." *Feminist Theory* 5(2):205–222.

Rosengarten, M. and Michael, M. (2009) "Rethinking the Bioethical Enactment of Drugged Bodies: On the Paradoxes of Using Anti-HIV Drug Therapy as a Technology for Prevention." Special Issue on 'Living Drugs.' *Science as Culture*18 (2):183–199.

Rosengarten, M. and Savransky, M. (2015) "Situating Efficacy: HIV and Ebola RCTs and the Care of Biomedical Abstractions." Paper presented at Situating Efficacy: Biomedicine, Interdisciplinarity, and the Politics of Intervention Symposium, Brocher Foundation, February 16–17, 2015.

Savransky, M. (2013) "Speculative Methods." Paper presented at Goldsmiths Doctoral Seminar, Goldsmiths, University of London.

Savransky, M. (2014) "Of Recalcitrant Subjects." *Culture, Theory & Critique* 55 (1): 96–113.

Savransky, M. (in press) "Modes of Mattering: Barad, Whitehead and Societies." *Rhizomes: Cultural Studies in Emerging Knowledge*. Special Issue: Quantum Possibilities: The Work of Karen Barad. Edited by Karin Sellberg and Peta Hinton.

Savransky, M. (2016) *The Adventure of Relevance: An Ethics of Social Inquiry*. Basingstoke and New York: Palgrave Macmillan.

Sorensen, C. et al. (2001) "Cultivating Recalcitrance in Information Systems Research." In *Realigning Research and Practice in Information Systems Development. IFIP Advances in Information and Communication Technology*, Vol. 6, ed. Nancy L Russo, Brian Fitzgerald, and Janice I. De Gross. Dordrecht, The Netherlands: Kluwer Academic Publishers, 297–316.

Stengers, I. (2000) *The Invention of Modern Science*. Minneapolis: University of Minnesota Press.

Stengers, I. (2005) "Whitehead's Account of the Sixth Day." *Configurations* 13, no. 1: 35–55.

Stengers, I. (2011) *Thinking with Whitehead: A Free and Wild Creation of Concepts*. Cambridge, MA: Harvard University Press. (Translation of original: Penser avec Whitehead, 2002.)

Stengers, I. (2011a) "Sciences Were Never 'Good.'" *Common Knowledge* 17 (1): 82–86.

Stengers, I. (2011b) "Comparison as a Matter of Concern.'" *Common Knowledge* 17 (1): 48–63.

Van Damme, L. et al. (2012) "Preexposure Prophylaxis for HIV Infection among African Women." *New England Journal of Medicine* 367:411–22.

Whitehead, A. N. (1997) *Science and the Modern World*. New York: Free Press.

ABOUT THE CONTRIBUTORS

Josef Barla is a doctoral candidate in the Philosophy of Technology and a lecturer at the University of Vienna. From 2010 to 2013, he was a research fellow at the interdisciplinary doctoral program "Gender, Violence and Agency in the Era of Globalization" at the University of Vienna. He was a visiting scholar at the Science and Justice Research Center at the University of California at Santa Cruz in 2012/2013 and at the Posthumanities Hub and the Seed Box MISTRA-FORMAS Environmental Humanities Collaboratory at Linköping University in 2015. His research is located at the intersection of the philosophy of technology, philosophies of the body and embodiment, and critical race studies.

Kym Bradley is a doctoral candidate in Sociology at Georgia State University with a concentration in sexuality and gender. Bradley received an MA in Sociology at Portland State University and a BA from the University of California, Irvine in Women's Studies and History. Bradley is author of "(Re)presentations of (hetero)sexualized genders in two and a half men: a content analysis," and is developing scholarship that focuses on the co-constitution of race, gender, and sexual identities.

Stephanie Clare is Assistant Professor of Comparative Literature at the University of Buffalo. She works in feminist and queer theory and has published in *GLQ*, *differences*, and *Diacritics*.

Teena Gabrielson is Associate Professor and Department Head of Political Science at the University of Wyoming. Her research interests include environmental political theory, citizenship studies, and American political thought. She is a co-editor of the *Oxford Handbook of Environmental Political Theory* (2015), and her research has appeared in *American Journal of Political Science, Citizenship Studies, Environmental Politics, Political Research Quarterly, Theory & Event*, and elsewhere. She is currently working on a book manuscript on the material-discursive production of the toxic body and its significance for conceptions of autonomy, agency, and inclusion in the polity.

Julian Gill-Peterson is Assistant Professor of English and Children's Literature at the University of Pittsburgh. His current book project investigates the history of the transgender child through the vitality of the child as organic form to the life sciences, medicine, and the biological body since the late nineteenth century. He is also co-editor of "The Child Now," a special issue of GLQ: A Journal of Lesbian and Gay Studies.

Anthony Ryan Hatch is Assistant Professor in the Science and Society program at Wesleyan University. He has held fellowships from the American Sociological Association and the National Institute of Health. He is author of the book Blood Sugar: Racial Pharmacology and Food Justice in Black America.

Anelis Kaiser, PhD, a co-founder of the international research network, NeuroGenderings, is a Marie Heim-Vögtlin Fellow at the University of Bern, Switzerland, where she is empirically working on the classification and registration of sex/gender in fMRI human science. Kaiser has examined sex/gender in the brain as it relates to exploring the existence of paradigmatic, methodological, and statistical defaults that interfere with assessing the presence or absence of sex/gender differences. She studied psychology and received her PhD from the University of Basel, Switzerland. She has published in neuroscientific journals on the topic of language processing, multilingualism, and sex/gender in the brain and in science studies literature on the topic of sex/gender as constructed category.

Mary Kosut is Cultural Sociologist and Associate Professor of Media Society and the Arts and Gender Studies at Purchase College, State University of New York. She is co-author of Buzz: Urban Beekeeping and the Power of the Bee, editor of The Encyclopedia of Gender in Media and co-author of The Body Reader: Essential Social and Cultural Readings. She is co-founder of GCA, an exhibition space in Bushwick, Brooklyn.

Natasha S. Mauthner is a professor at the University of Aberdeen Business School. She holds a PhD in Social and Political Sciences from Cambridge University and is the author of *The Darkest Days of My Life: Stories of Postpartum Depression*. Her research seeks to develop a performative understanding and practice of social science with a focus on three areas: the history, philosophy, and politics of research methods and practices; data-sharing policy, governance, and practice; and the making of technology, work, and family in everyday practices.

Hanna Meißner is postdoctoral assistant at the Center for Women's and Gender Studies (ZIFG) of the Technische Universität Berlin. Her main fields of interest are feminist theory, social theory, science studies, and postcolonial studies.

Lisa Jean Moore is a feminist medical sociologist and professor at Purchase College, SUNY. She studies and writes about human anatomies, body fluids, honeybees, North Atlantic horseshoe crabs, and food. She is the author of several books, including *Sperm Counts: Overcome by Men's Most Precious Fluid*, *Missing Bodies: The Politics of Visibility*, and *The Body Reader: Essential Social and Cultural Readings*. She lives in Crown Heights, Brooklyn.

Susan Oyama is Professor Emeritus at CUNY's John Jay College and Graduate School. She has spoken and written widely on the nature/nurture opposition, concepts of development, evolution, and information, as well as on essentialism and representation. She is best known for her work on Developmental Systems Theory, to which many were introduced by her book, *The Ontogeny of Information*. She also wrote *Evolution's Eye*, and with Paul Griffiths and Russell Gray, edited *Cycles of Contingency*.

Victoria Pitts-Taylor is Professor of Feminist, Gender and Sexuality Studies, Sociology, and Science in Society at Wesleyan University. She is author of three books, *In the Flesh: the Cultural Politics of Body Modification*, *Surgery Junkies: Wellness and Pathology in Cosmetic Culture*, and most recently, *The Brain's Body: Neuroscience and Corporeal Politics*. She is also editor of the two-volume *Cultural Encyclopedia of the Body*, and a past recipient of the American Sociological Association's Advancement of the Discipline Award.

Marsha Rosengarten is Professor of Sociology at Goldsmiths, University of London. She is the author of *HIV Interventions: Biomedicine and the Traffic in Information and Flesh*, and with co-author Mike Michael, *Innovation and Biomedicine: Ethics, Evidence and Expectation in HIV*, as well as many articles and chapters engaging with feminist theory, biomedicine, ethics and, more recently, the speculative philosophy of A. N. Whitehead.

Deboleena Roy is Associate Professor of Women's, Gender, and Sexuality Studies and Neuroscience and Behavioral Biology at Emory University. She received her PhD in reproductive neuroendocrinology and molecular biology from the Institute of Medical Science at the University of Toronto. She has published her work in *Signs, Hypatia, Neuroethics, Australian Feminist Studies, Rhizomes: Cultural Studies of Emerging Knowledge, Endocrinology, Neuroendocrinology*, and the *Journal of Biological Chemistry*. Her research and scholarship attempt to create a shift from feminist critiques of science to the development of feminist practices that contribute to scientific inquiry in the lab.

Sigrid Schmitz was Professor for Gender Studies and Scientific Head of the Gender Research Office until 2015, and is currently Senior Lecturer at the Faculty of Social Sciences at the University of Vienna. She completed her PhD and an habilitation in biology at the University of Marburg, and was university lecturer at the University of Freiburg/Germany, where she initialized and headed the Forum of Competence "Gender Studies in Computer and Natural Sciences" together with Britta Schinzel. She is currently vice chairwoman of the board of the Austrian Association of Gender Studies.

Banu Subramaniam is Associate Professor of Women's Studies at the University of Massachusetts, Amherst. She is author of *Ghost Stories for Darwin: The Science of Variation and the Politics of Diversity*, and co-editor of *Feminist Science Studies: A New Generation* and *Making Threats: Biofears and Environmental Anxieties*. Trained as a plant evolutionary biologist, she seeks to engage the social and cultural studies of science in the practice of science. Spanning the humanities, social sciences, and the biological sciences, her research is located at the intersections of biology, women's studies, ethnic studies, and postcolonial studies.

Sigrid Vertommen is an assistant at the Middle East and North Africa Research Group of the Department of Conflict and Development Studies at the Ghent University in Belgium. She is finalizing her doctoral research on the political economy of assisted reproduction in Palestine/ Israel, in which she focuses on the ways in which assisted reproductive technologies have emerged as a crucial site of settler colonial bio-politics and bio-economics. She has published her work in several books, including *Critical Kinship* and *Assisted Reproduction in Movement Standardization and Renegotiation*, and journals such as *Science as Culture* and *New Genetic and Society*. In addition to teaching and writing, Sigrid has been actively involved in the organization of the Eye on Palestine Film and Arts Festival in Belgium and in the establishment of a Slow Science group at Ghent University.

Lisa H. Weasel is Associate Professor of Women, Gender and Sexuality Studies at Portland State University. She is author of *Food Fray: Inside the Controversy over Genetically Modified Food* and co-editor of *Feminist Science Studies: A New Generation*.

Janet Wirth-Cauchon is Associate Professor of Sociology at Drake University. Her research and teaching are in the areas of feminist theory, science studies, and psychiatry and mental health. She is the author of *Women and Borderline Personality Disorder: Symptoms and Stories*. She has been a research associate at the Five Colleges Women's Studies Research Center in South Hadley, Massachusetts.

INDEX